URBAN RIVERS

HISTORY OF THE URBAN ENVIRONMENT

Martin V. Melosi and Joel A. Tarr, Editors

URBAN RIVERS

Remaking Rivers, Cities, and Space in Europe and North America

Edited by
STÉPHANE CASTONGUAY and
MATTHEW EVENDEN

University of Pittsburgh Press

Published by the University of Pittsburgh Press, Pittsburgh, Pa., 15260

Copyright © 2012, University of Pittsburgh Press

Manufactured in the United States of America

Printed on acid-free paper

10 9 8 7 6 5 4 3 2 1

Library of Congress Cataloging-in-Publication Data

Urban rivers : remaking rivers, cities, and space in Europe and
North America / edited by Stephane Castonguay and Matthew
Evenden.

     p.   cm. — (History of the urban environment)
  Includes bibliographical references and index.
  ISBN 978-0-8229-6185-7 (pbk. : alk. paper)
  1. City planning—Europe. 2. City planning—North
America. 3. Rivers—Economic aspects—Europe. 4. Rivers—
Economic aspects—North America. I. Castonguay, Stéphane.
II. Evenden, Matthew D. (Matthew Dominic), 1971–
  HT169.E85U73 2012
  307.1'216094091216—dc23   2011048869

CONTENTS

ILLUSTRATIONS

ACKNOWLEDGMENTS

This book originates in a conference held in Trois-Rivières, Quebec, in September 2009 in which a group of historians and geographers convened to discuss the industrialization of rivers in the Western world. A selection of papers from this conference forms the backbone of this book, while additional chapters were solicited to extend the spatiotemporal coverage. We would like to thank those participants whose subject focus fell outside of the frame of the final book but who enriched the conference discussion considerably and made this intellectual project possible, including: Marcus Hall, Matthew Hatvany, Eva Jakobsson, Jonathan Peyton, and Eve Vogel. Several colleagues also sharpened the discussion in their role as commentators: Claude Bellavance, Pierre Lanthier, and Jarrett Ruddy. Finally, Viv Nelles and John McNeill offered very helpful concluding remarks that highlighted common themes and questions and prompted us to reimagine the book's scope. The Social Sciences and Humanities Research Council of Canada, the Network in Canadian History and Environment, the Centre interuniversitaire d'études québécoises, the Université du Québec à Trois-Rivières, and the Canada Research Chair in Environmental History provided funding for the conference and the publication. We greatly appreciate the editorial assistance of Jacinthe De Montigny (Université du Québec à Trois-Rivières). We also thank Eric Leinberger (University of British Columbia) who skillfully drew the maps. At the University of Pittsburgh Press, Joel Tarr and Martin Melosi, series editors, Cynthia Miller, director, Deborah Meade, managing editor, and Alex Wolfe, production editor, all provided guidance and professionalism in the production of the book. Rivers flow through lives as well as cities, and we are pleased to dedicate this book to our wives, Kirsty and Nathalie.

INTRODUCTION

STÉPHANE CASTONGUAY AND
MATTHEW EVENDEN

THE 1870 REPORT OF THE Rivers Pollution Commission in Britain contained a facsimile of a letter written not in ink but with the darkened,
polluted waters of the river Irwell, the notorious stream running through
Lancashire and Manchester.[1] Just as Manchester sometimes stands as the paragon of urban-industrial revolution, so too might the Irwell stand as the paragon of the urban-industrial river: a lessening stream, so fouled and mistreated
as to run the color of ink, allowing an aggrieved citizen to dip a pen in it and
write. The holder of that pen, and the author of that letter, sought to make a
powerful point about the loss of beauty, health, and utility. The river Irwell
stood for much more than a river. The growth of industry in Manchester,
and the explosion of the city in the previous decades, had come at a profound
environmental cost that risked undermining the very foundations of urban-
industrial life.

The ink, letter, and commission all point to some of the ways in which the
Irwell was indeed the paragon of the newly urban-industrial river. The river
had not only changed its physical appearance, hydrology, and ecology, but
its place and purpose in society had also been altered and become the focus
of political conflict. The urban and industrial transformations that remade
modern societies in the West from the mid-eighteenth to the mid-twentieth
century meted out similar results elsewhere. Such changes did not follow the
same course as on the Irwell. In some places, new shipping demands straightened channels, plumbing systems more than industrial processes fouled
streams, and hydroelectric dams turned rivers into reservoirs. Often urban
growth more than industrialization stood as the driving force. But whatever
the scope and motor of change, some patterns were widely experienced: riv-

ers were subjected to a new era of modern engineering and rationalization; new modes of transportation and power generation affected river courses; and the water supply and sewage needs of urban centers altered the flow and ecology of urban rivers as well as distant sources.

While facilitating and supporting urban and industrial growth, the river Irwell, and other rivers like it, also affected the course and form of the new urban era. Rivers shaped cities both internally and externally. The river Irwell ran through Manchester, for example, placing an important division in the city's morphology and structure, a dividing line that was repeated in a host of urban circumstances and that produced similar basic demands for infrastructure, such as bridges, levees, and drains. How the river bisected urban space also contributed to the economic geography of the city and the location of industrial wharves, piers, new housing settlements, and parks. While cities polluted rivers, and sought to benefit from their infrastructural potential, they also had to build atop, around, and in conjunction with rivers. Because rivers delivered risk as well as reward, this could sometimes be a perilous process. The river Irwell may have seemed like a thoroughly conquered, denatured river in 1870, but cities and rivers were always caught up in a multidimensional process of cause and effect.

Urban Rivers examines both the role of rivers in the process of urbanization and the impact of urbanization on rivers. We approach the urban-riverine relationship both from the perspective of environmental history and historical geography, which stresses human and environmental changes and spatial processes. We understand space to be an evolving set of relations conditioned by physical circumstances as well as changing human geographies, not a fixed area or region laid down through time. While human geographers have made the point forcefully that space, like nature, is socially produced, we pull back from the full extent of this constructivist vision and ask how environmental circumstances changed space and put limits on human geographies.[2] The environment, in this sense, embodies a dynamic set of natural processes, partly shaped by human actions, partly independent of them, and in many instances, so intertwined as to be inseparable.[3] Throughout the edited volume, we pursue the space of cities and rivers within and beyond the urban area to understand how the internal organization and functions of the city responded to the opportunities and challenges of river environments and to trace the external authority of cities over space in tapping, transforming, and controlling distant waters.

The term "urban rivers" is most often associated today with the goals of ecological restoration. In a range of contexts, environmentalists have called for the reintegration of rivers into urban life through pollution abatement, parks development, and pathway construction.[4] The river that is to be regained in this view is that which was "cut off" from the city by transportation infrastructure such as railroads and highways or "ruined" by smoke-belching factories and industrial facilities. The ideal endpoint is a river with green edges, accessible for recreation, carrying water of fine quality and color. In part an aesthetic vision, the idea of the "urban river" also highlights the particular features of riverine transformation that cities have imposed, including changed patterns of sediment deposition and erosion, hydrology and ecology, owing to heightened pollution levels, paved catchments, and canalized stream channels.[5] While we accept that cities impose particular environmental effects on rivers, we do not imagine that cities and rivers have ever been truly separated. Our use of the term "urban river" is therefore neither normative nor aesthetic but descriptive and analytical. We define urban rivers in a descriptive sense as rivers that flow through cities, and in an analytical sense as those rivers that have been folded into the process of urbanization, whether flowing through urban centers or not.

URBAN RIVERS BUILDS UPON and connects three separate bodies of scholarship dealing with the industrial city and sanitary reform, the city's geographical structure, and the city as an environmental polity. First, any book dealing with the transformations of rivers and cities in the modern period must come to terms with the enormous pressures unleashed by industrialization and urban growth and the countervailing force of sanitary reform. The linked processes of urban and industrial growth produced not only many more and larger cities in the nineteenth century but also reorganized their internal structure, produced increased problems of energy, materials, and food supply, and delivered new waste streams in the air, soil, and water. Although the place of water and waste in the industrializing city has long been a preoccupation of urban environmental historians, rivers do not figure prominently in this literature.[6] Stripped of any ecological dynamic, they often appear as mere appendages to waterworks and sewage systems. Recent work recognizes that socio-technical infrastructure has never been independent of the rivers from which urban populations ultimately drink or into which they pollute.[7] Indeed, the nature of rivers, their flow patterns, ecology, and chemical composition, introduce dynamic feedback processes that have frequently disrupted the engineering logic of modern systems.

In part, the inattention to rivers is the logical outcome of the broader preoccupation with sanitary reform. Sanitary reform in the nineteenth-century city aimed to uplift the moral conditions of society by improving the urban environment and its public health. New disciplines emerged in this process, and with them new cultures of expertise. The new figure of the expert—the scientist, doctor, engineer—saw to the provision of hygienic conditions, at the core of which abundant, potable water figured as a tool for moral rehabilitation and the establishment of a liberal order, where conquering water and conquering society went hand in hand.[8] Just as sanitarians worried more about the health of drinking water than the health of rivers, historians of the sanitary city have kept their vision trained on the city's society and environment but not its rivers.

Second, the urban-riverine relationship underlines the importance of a spatial analysis of urban development both within the city and beyond its formal boundaries. Cities are rarely studied as islands, but few urban histories seek to emphasize the urban-rural links that construct the environmental foundations of urban life. The urban-hinterland tradition, most recently reinvigorated by William Cronon's *Nature's Metropolis*, places the greatest focus on the problem but tends to emphasize the land-based linkages, epitomized by the railroad.[9] Rivers, however, have long acted as navigation routes linking cities and hinterlands, and as cities have grown their demands for fresh water and energy have extended urban influence.[10] Like recent scholarship on the "more-than-human geography" of the city, we seek to explore these porous edges, where rivers flow through, with all their truck and trade.[11] Rather than the "paths out of town," we consider the rivers to and from the city.[12]

The spatial analysis of urban rivers not only draws our attention to the link between city and hinterland, but it also suggests a wider hydrological context. Rivers vary over time. With the passage of seasons they flow, freeze, and flood with a host of consequences for water transport, diversions, and hazards. Over the long term, variations in river basin regimes can subtly alter the "normal" patterns of flow or deliver abrupt shifts through floods or droughts. Rivers also vary across space. They unite a spatially extensive network of hydrological flows, reaching back to a height of land forming the outer limits of a basin, but are also characterized by a hierarchy of streams and tributaries. Some rivers are large and some relatively small. It matters where a city is located along a river, of what size, undergoing what dynamic seasonal and historical changes.[13] A delta location introduces different environmental and spatial possibilities and problems for urban growth than a mid-basin location. Such differences have effects not only on trade patterns and the functions of rivers within urban economies but also in terms of governance systems developed to structure watershed management and basin planning. When corrective flood protection work is undertaken, for example, it affects not only a discrete location but also the river's hydrology downstream, sometimes leading to new sediment flow patterns and greater flood episodes.[14] Although river basins, like urban boundaries, are partly social constructions, they create and limit pathways of possibility.[15]

If the links between city and hinterland and city and river basin highlight the importance of a spatial approach, so too does any examination of the river in the city. Although the history of water infrastructure in cities is often approached as a socio-technical system, bridging social management and the range of technological elements that combined to make a dynamic operation, rarely is that system read in terms of the evolution of its spatial structure or of how that structure corresponds to the geography of rivers. Rivers fundamentally organized urban space, bounding it directly or indirectly with a network of surface or underground channels. The river at the heart of the city delivered energy for industrial districts and became a true market, a meeting place of wharves and warehouses, where seaward trade met urban consumers.[16] Extending outward, river valleys carved land transportation routes, with roads and railways running along the river's edge; as these roads crossed the city, they consolidated and disrupted spatial arrangements that supported defense, housing, and the supply of goods. Thus, whether considered as a water system or a transportation system, rivers were always also a spatial system woven into the geographical fabric of the city. Sometimes, engineers and city planners aided rivers to shape the space of modern cities by straightening riverbanks, digging navigation channels, and seeking to cope with flood hazards. Just as new disciplines and experts rose to prominence in the sanitary city, so too the engineering profession and the modern planning office gained greater purchase on the reconstruction of the urban environment at the river's edge.

Third, and finally, thinking about urban rivers forces a broader analysis of the city as an environmental polity. Scholars have analyzed the city as an environmental polity in at least two senses: as a complex problem of governance in which different mechanisms have been developed (and subverted) to distribute environmental services and to regulate economic actions with environmental consequences, and as a problem of environmental justice in which social and environmental inequalities have coincided in space and produced social movements for reform.[17] While this literature has often turned on singular questions of access to water, flood risk, riverine location, and exposure to pollution, such separate issues can and should be read and analyzed in combination. However one conceives of the environmental politics of the city, the important social and economic roles of water must place rivers at the center.

A focus on the environmental polity also reminds us that cities did not respond to riverine opportunities and challenges as one person; they were rather sites of intense competition, debate, and conflict about how to use, treat, and respond to rivers.[18] Such forces must be examined in the context of demographic, technological, and economic drivers that shaped urban-riverine relationships but also in terms of the evolution of law, of notions of property, and public purpose. As a result, in the chapters that follow, we consider the power dynamics of cities, the conflicts between merchants and municipal governments, and different levels of government from the local to the national. This is the traditional fare of urban historiography, but here we tie it directly to the urban-riverine relationship.

THE CASE STUDIES ANALYZED in *Urban Rivers* fall into two broadly defined regional domains, Western Europe and North America. These rough boundaries recognize the comparability of the cases: all within temperate latitudes undergoing broadly similar processes of industrialization, expansion, and urbanization. They also refer to areas where a long history of riverine improvements and urban-riverine relationships left a deep imprint, in terms of ecological change, technical infrastructures, and institutional arrangements, that framed the future uses of the river. These cases are also linked by the fact that they engaged collectively in the diffusion of water technologies in the nineteenth century. Although our aim has not been to chart these technical flows, their existence suggests the level of connection and coherence among cases widely separated in space. By drawing the boundaries in this fashion, we set out to understand whether there might be some broad connections among cities undergoing similar changes. Did cities seek to adapt rivers to industrialization in similar ways? Were they faced with the same legal and political challenges? How did rivers affect the spatial organization of cities undergoing rapid growth and expansion? These kinds of questions can be best answered when some of the factors shaping the cases run along parallel tracks. We are, however, under no illusions that our chosen cases can stand in for a global history of urban rivers, or that they can be simply isolated in some imagined Atlantic or Western world. A recent essay by Matthew Gandy, for example, elegantly makes the case for reading London's history alongside and in connection to Mumbai's.[19] We do nothing of the kind here, but we hope that our comparative analysis might provide foundations for other transnational readings.

We have also elected to focus on a broad temporal period, from the seventeenth to the mid-twentieth century. To be sure, many elements of urban-riverine interaction have ancient foundations, and the growth of at least the European urban system built on a structure partly worked out in the Middle Ages. As Richard Hoffman among others has shown, the role of rivers in urban settlements in the premodern world demonstrates important continuities with the modern period.[20] We are struck nevertheless by the relative explosion of urban settlements, particularly after 1800, that characterized both northwestern Europe and the emerging urban system of eastern North America. Urbanization proceeded apace not only in classical industrial centers like Manchester but in large and complex cities like London and Paris, which both carried out multiple functions as capitals, commercial centers, ports, and industrial hubs. Smaller European capitals and administrative centers like Vienna, Brussels, Oslo, and Edinburgh also witnessed a rapid climb in population and faced all of the political challenges of growth forced by new transportation systems, trade regimes, and water demands. In North America, places that had been relatively modest centers before the second half of the nineteenth century, including Chicago, Cincinnati, and Montreal, grew as organizing points of territorial expansion, building rapidly on the foundations of fur trading posts, missions, and small market towns. Not only did overall population expand at a rapid pace in northwestern Europe and North America in the modern period, but many more people than in previous centuries lived in cities. For this reason alone, it is well to consider how this surge in city building interacted with the rivers that provided some of the critical environmental context of modern urban-industrial life.

URBAN RIVERS SETS OUT TO DISCUSS these issues by looking at urban-riverine relationships in cities of different sizes and shapes being reconstituted by the very dynamics fostered by such relationships. We have grouped the contributions into three parts, being fully aware of the potential for overlap. In the first part of the book, a series of case studies organized around a narrowly defined territory and spanning a relatively short time period reveals how the advent of a new technical regime and industrial order triggered conflicts over the use of an urban river. In many cases, these conflicts originated in ecological changes occasioned by industrial and domestic effluents that hampered traditional and sometimes innovative uses, at times creating tension between industrialization and urbanization processes or between the expanding urban population and the distant rural community. Apart from the sanitary issues involved, use of the river to produce and deliver energy ignited opposition from promoters of urban development and industrialists accustomed to conveniently discharging their waste into the river.

In chapter 1, Chloé Deligne opens the first part of the book with an exploration of the transition between two hydraulic regimes in the early stages of the industrialization of Brussels between 1790 and 1870 and its consequences on the relationships between the city and its hinterland. In the preindustrial era, a diversity of users of the Senne and its tributaries engaged in several disputes over water access and management. Many preindustrial uses ceased following the onset of industrialization, but these disputes were replaced by others that opposed local faubourg administrations and the City of Brussels, which was expanding and redrawing its urban territory. The ecological changes that manifested themselves in the forms of flooding and aquatic pollution intensified these conflicts and forced the redesign of the water intake and sewage network, eventually leading to the disappearance of rivers that ended up being covered and a severance of the ties linking the urban population to its streams.

Riverine transformation poses formidable challenges for a society that needs to adapt its industrial activities to the deleterious aquatic ecology it has created. This is especially true if these activities are based on the use of the water that it has altered. In chapter 2, Jim Clifford examines the case of a London suburb, West Ham, and focuses on the patchwork landscape of the Lea running through it during the rapid growth of London in the second half of the nineteenth century. Using a detailed geographic information system (GIS) database, he tracks the changing suburban landscape from 1867 to 1915 and the consequence of the degraded industrial river that suburbanization and industrialization created out of the Lea. The river Lea offered many possibilities for industrial and urban growth compared to other sites in the Greater London area. Factories benefited from direct access to a river where coal was transported and refuse dispensed. Their multiplication on the shore of the Lea generated environmental problems that prevented London's second river from further encouraging the growth of its manufacturing suburb because its polluted state threatened the economy and public health of West Ham.

In chapter 3, Eyvind Bagle provides another exploration of the relationships among riverine transformation, industrialization, and urbanization. The establishment of various milling industries along the Akerselva River stimulated the growth of Christiana, which became Oslo, at the same time that the urban market accelerated the industrialization of the river. Initially harnessed for driving wood during the protoindustrial era, the Akerselva ended up being tapped to supply fresh water to a growing urban population in Christiana, being harnessed for hydropower production, and subsequently fouled by manufacturing processes. To ensure an adequate supply of fresh water and to modernize its waterworks, the city sought to exercise greater control over the use of the Akerselva, but it was opposed by industrialists. The latter formed the Manufacturers' Association of Akerselva to fight the city's plan. These conflicts were also framed by the Baron Wedel Jarlsberg, heir of the so-called plank nobility and owner of a large portion of the upstream watershed area of Akerselva, who exercised a stranglehold over the management of the river.

Much as the Lea oriented the establishment of industries along its shore in West Ham and supported a particular land use in the Greater London area, a smaller watercourse in the shadow of the mighty St. Lawrence River fundamentally altered the morphology of Montreal, both the city and the island.

The Rivière des Prairies is located on the north shore of the Island of Montreal and forms an extension of the St. Lawrence River. In chapter 4, Michèle Dagenais explores how the Rivière des Prairies—called the Back River because of its distance from the urban heart of the island—was integrated into the urban space of Montreal through different periods and for different uses. The advent of new users, especially with the territorial expansion of the City of Montreal and its urban population, as well as their attending socio-technical systems such as water intake, sewage disposal, and hydropower generation, generated conflicts and transformed the relationships of the riverine population to its Back River. Flooding events and polluted streams but also the creation of a recreational area following the construction of a dam contributed to the changing perceptions of a river whose transformations illustrated the ever-encroaching urbanization process under way in the first half of the twentieth century.

The chapters of the second part of the book focus on different elements of the urbanization process—demographic expansion, technical infrastructure, land use and territorial annexation, exchange and circulation—and how they impinge on river use over an extended territory and time period. More precisely, they show the central role of population growth in reordering the place of the river in the city, in terms of both its physical location in the urban space and its influence over the arrangement of urban districts, as well as the services that the river furnishes in the economy of urban life. As it grew and expanded, the city organized its activities and intensified them according to the availability of and access to a stream that directed the urban society toward a territory to transform and occupy. At the same time, urban infrastructures had their conception and implementation fashioned by the rhythm and ecology of the river.

In chapter 5, one of the two chapters that examine the case of Paris and the Seine, Sabine Barles explores the role of urban metabolism during the nineteenth and twentieth century to arrive at an understanding of the relationships between urbanization and riverine transformations. The formation of an urban river was tantamount to a series of revolutions: industrial, urban, and hygienic. The spatial expansion of Paris during the period and a series of natural catastrophes and epidemics led engineers and political authorities to redesign the Seine basin to ensure a sufficient supply of potable water. The tension became more acute, pitting the City of Paris against its neighboring municipalities and distant communes, when population growth increased the demand for fresh water, while the capacity of adjacent agricultural soil to absorb effluent with fertilizing sewage diminished. The construction of an upstream reservoir and the extension of urban infrastructures, while ensuring fresh water for Paris, did not prevent the deterioration of the Seine, as urban growth in terms of space, population, and industries encouraged the externalization of the city's metabolism, something best illustrated by the outreach of the municipal and departmental governments beyond their territorial jurisdiction.

The extension of urban space by the transformations of large rivers is further explored in chapter 6 in Gertrud Haidvogl's study of Vienna and the Danube. She compares riverine landscapes in the land use systems of the pre-industrial and industrial capital of the Austro-Hungarian Empire. Examples from the Austrian Danube demonstrate the role of floodplains as land resources during the process of population growth in Vienna, as well as the adaptation of riverine communities to changing environmental conditions. The channelization of the Danube for navigational purposes imposed constraints on the use of the settled floodplains, at the same time in high demand by the City of Vienna, which required land for industrial and housing purposes. The Danube and its floodplains, as well as residential developments, ended up being combined in an urban planning scheme to accommodate the demographic expansion of Vienna.

Floodplains are sites of naturally occurring inundations, but once they become settled because of their obvious locational advantages, population and goods become vulnerable. In many cases, floods are not the direct results of the transformation of the river per se but the unintended consequence of intense occupation of the floodplain. As settlement incorporated increasingly complex buildings and infrastructure and integrated them into the urbanization and industrialization processes, damage increased concurrently. As a result, it was not only the death toll and damages to houses that needed to be taken into account but also the delay in industrial production and the reconstruction of transportation, power, and water infrastructure. Hence, urbanization profoundly modified the relationships between cities and rivers—not only by impacting the aquatic ecology, but also by increasing the frequency and intensity of flooding events. In chapter 7, a study of the Ohio River over a two-hundred-year period, Uwe Lübken discusses the consequences of the transformation of floodplains through settlement and urbanization processes. The Ohio River underwent profound changes in the nineteenth century, as it was transformed into a commercial artery with plenty of large cities, industrial sites, and infrastructures to control the regularity of the river flow. Yet, partly as a result of these changes, inundations occurred and affected the cities and their hinterlands on an ever-increasing scale.

Studies of rivers have insisted on their representation in the process of imagining communities and forging national characters. In chapter 8, Jean-Claude Robert explains how Canadian historians and geographers have used the St. Lawrence River in that regard only to insist on a different perspective that connects the river to the historical geography of the City of Montreal. His chapter offers a revealing example of the inward and outward spatial urban production of the river, looking at the structuring of Montreal's urban morphology and the modulation of its hinterland across North America over a four-hundred-year time span. Using different analytical scales, his chapter illustrates the role of the St. Lawrence in specific periods of economic growth, each spurred by specific commodities and trade routes, with their concomitant impact on an urban space that accommodated these commercial activities. Acting as a hub for intra- and intercontinental exchange, Montreal organized its territory by developing its urban built environment along the river shore, moving up along a northern axis. Technological change (albeit unrelated to the Industrial Revolution in this case but rather to land transportation and merchandise stevedoring) eventually lessened the river's impact on the extension of the urban territory, while tertiarization, deindustrialization, and the transformation of the riverfront into a recreational area ended up redefining the urban relationship to the river.

In chapter 9, T. C Smout analyzes urbanization and industrialization in Edinburgh and the surrounding region in the context of the Firth of Forth, a salt embayment of the North Sea, fed by twenty rivers, including the Forth. Rivers feeding the Firth of Forth were put to many uses, but by the mid-nineteenth century the expansion of urban settlements and industrial processes contributed a growing waste stream. Despite the constant need for larger volumes of fresh water for domestic and industrial use, waste continued to be disposed of into the estuary and its tributaries, where epidemics and declining fish populations indicated the extent of pollution. A major source of the problem was the extension of the pollution across a large territory with divided jurisdictions. Attempts to control pollution and ameliorate some of the effects of decades of abuse emerged in the second half of the twentieth century.

Urban societies not only modify the ecology of the riverine environment, they also redraw the boundaries of fluvial space, materially and culturally, bringing to the fore environmental and political issues. In such circumstances, they attempt to design the appropriate means of managing the water and its territory. Experts are then mobilized to referee conflicts between users, which in many cases amounts to balancing the public good and the private interests of individuals, communities, firms and industries, as well as governmental bodies of different levels. The chapters of the third part study cases that illustrate political problems resulting from the imposition of a social order on the nature of rivers. The chapters emphasize the role of experts in providing templates that regulated the riverine relationships of society.

In chapter 10, Frédéric Graber studies debates related to the construction of the Canal de l'Ourcq to supply the urban population of Ancien Régime

Paris with water in sufficient quantity and of appropriate quality. The construction of the canal reconfigured the drainage basin of Paris, which could no longer rely solely on the Seine for its water supply as its population increased, stimulated by spatial expansion and suburban annexation that also integrated water-intensive industries. Promoted by private entrepreneurs and public engineers, the project led to confrontations between state experts and countryside communities that were to be deprived of their main source of water. The project steered a series of controversies and debates on the superior quality of water from large (the Seine) or small (the Ourcq) rivers and on the actual and future needs of the urban population and therefore the quantity of water to be diverted, as well as on the dispossession of land and water resulting from the construction of such a project and the ensuing compensation to be paid. The construction of the Canal de l'Ourcq exposes the central role of engineers and experts in framing the uncertainties and irregularities that characterize the hydrology and ecology of rivers, and therefore the management of waters.

In chapter 11, Craig Colten compares developments on the Illinois, Potomac, and Chattahoochee Rivers and the upstream-downstream influences of Chicago, Washington, D.C., and Atlanta on their respective river basins. This comparison reveals the importance of the basin perspective in understanding the urban, ecological, and geographical factors responsible for fashioning the relationships between a city and its riparian hinterland. The case studies exemplify the respective role of social priorities and natural processes in the modification of hydrologic regimes and watershed boundaries. They also present the different experts and water management institutions called in to resolve conflicts between users historically constituted along a transformed riverine system whose territory had been reconfigured to meet the needs and desires of the municipal and regional political elite.

Notwithstanding the role of human actors in diverting and inverting rivers, ecological dynamics have also blurred and modified river pathways and forms. In chapter 12, Shannon Stunden Bower demonstrates the complexities surrounding the spatial definition of the watershed, a concept that encompasses the contemporary understanding of the relation between rivers and the lands they traverse. Her chapter focuses on the history of water management in the province of Manitoba, Canada, with events there serving as a case study to observe the rescaling of the watershed by governmental officials and frictions arising from the discrepancies observed between the boundaries of rural municipalities and those drawn to accommodate environmental patterns. Tensions between private property lines and municipal boundaries as well as with ecological processes and governmental efforts to rescale water management did not materialize in disputes between communities or promoters and riverine populations. However, the autonomy and authority of municipal communities were undermined by the emergence of a new administrative entity, the watershed district, which involuntarily expressed at another level the disharmony between humanity and nature.

In the conclusion we situate both the particular and more general forces that shaped the urban-riverine relationship across Western Europe and North America. We ask how urbanization and industrialization fundamentally altered the use of rivers in cities and with what environmental and social consequences, ranging from the siltation of rivers to the elevation of expertise in river management. Finally, we consider how these transformations also reached beyond the city center and the rivers cutting through urban space. One of the outcomes of urban expansion and industrial growth, we argue, was the rescaling of urban-riverine relationships.

PART I.
INDUSTRIALIZATION AND
RIVERINE TRANSFORMATIONS

⤳ 1

BRUSSELS AND ITS RIVERS, 1770-1880

Reshaping an Urban Landscape

CHLOÉ DELIGNE

RUSSELS, THE CENTRAL CITY of the Austrian Low Countries of the eighteenth century, became the official capital of Belgium in 1830. It was a
medium-sized city of northwestern Europe, with some 80,000 inhabitants in
1770 and nearly five times as many a century and a half later (about 385,000
inhabitants around 1880).[1] Not unusual in the European context, this growth
occurred in a particular territorial framework. In fact, unlike other large Belgian cities (Liège, Antwerp, Ghent), Brussels did not merge administratively
with its old faubourgs (suburbs) during the period. The latter retained all
their political autonomy even though they had begun to form an urbanized
unit with the central city. In 1830, despite its status as capital, Brussels was
therefore paradoxically just a commune "like any other." This reality, which
was rooted in the country's and state's complex relationship with the capital
and on some level distanced the city from its faubourgs, was a characteristic
feature of the political-administrative framework that structured Brussels's
growth between 1830 and 1989 and still does even today.

In this context, the radical transformations in water use during the nineteenth century, the transition from an Ancien Régime water regime to an industrial water regime, were particularly significant, participating fully in the
redefinition of relations between the city and its inhabitants and, even more,
between the city and its suburbs. In order to better convey and demonstrate
how this transition occurred and what its consequences were, I use a four-
stage approach. I first underscore the importance of embracing a large scale,
not only from temporal and spatial but also functional perspectives, while
describing the hydrogeographical context of the Brussels region. After briefly
describing the workings and uses of the rivers at the end of the eighteenth

century, I provide a detailed chronology of the transformations of the many uses of water in the region as a whole during the nineteenth century. Finally, I show how and why these transformations affected not only the ecological workings of the region's water system but also the political relations among the actors in the management of the territory in question.

A SYMPTOMATIC DISAPPEARANCE

One of the defining events in the transformation of Brussels's landscape in the nineteenth century is known as the "covering of the Senne." Behind this famous name, familiar well beyond strictly Brussels circles, lies a massive urbanistic operation that "buried" the Senne in underground waterways, connected the sewage network up to it, and erected rectilinear boulevards lined with prestigious buildings above, modeled on Haussmannian Paris.

Carried out between 1867 and 1871 under the direction of urban authorities, this massive undertaking is so closely associated with the disappearance of a now-idealized old city that the mere mention of it still evokes a sense of nostalgia today. Approved in 1865, just before a new cholera epidemic wiped out the working quarters clustered around the river, the covering of the Senne had the stated objective of eliminating an "open-air cesspool," a "well of infection," and erecting in place of this "gaping sewer" new, salubrious quarters that would better serve and be better suited to the capital of the young Belgian state (created in 1830). All in all, as studies devoted to it have shown,[2] the operation merged the hygienist objective of eradicating quarters deemed unhealthy with the bourgeoisie's desire to remodel the urban center in its own image.

However—and the studies fail to adequately put this into perspective—the covering of the Senne was much more than an urbanistic operation: it was also a symptom of a more general transformation of relations between European cities and their water, for which the simple causal relationship with urban growth and water pollution must be substantially qualified or at least fleshed out. It is interesting to note, for instance, that some years before the Senne disappeared from the urban center another stream in the Brussels area (the Maelbeek) was covered in the same way, although it lay outside the urban core in as-yet largely unbuilt areas of the capital's eastern faubourgs, where demographic growth had barely begun.[3] Here, urbanization was clearly not the sole imperative behind the stream's disappearance. We will return to this question later. Thus, from the mid-nineteenth century on, when demographic growth and industrialization were generating new ways of devising and amalgamating the territory,[4] the river and the streams no longer ranked as essential components: they could, and sometimes had better, disappear.

To better understand how streams and rivers could be excluded from the urban landscape as well as the consequences of this exclusion, we must adopt broader temporal and spatial perspectives than those considered by most studies up until now. We must not reduce the transformation of the urban and peri-urban rivers in Brussels to either simply the covering of the Senne or the period from 1865 to 1872, but we need to consider the rivers and their transformations in their entirety, over the longer term.

THE RIVERS OF BRUSSELS

Let us begin by synthesizing some basic contextual information. The Senne basin of northwestern Europe is a very small sub-basin within the Escaut basin, which covers a total surface area of some 1,200 square kilometers (figure 1.1). The distance from the river's sources to its mouth is approximately 60 kilometers.

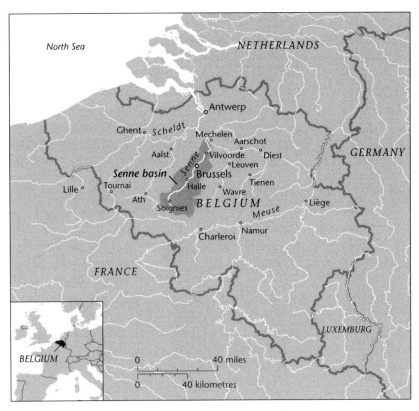

FIGURE 1.1. The Senne, a tributary of the Escaut, in present-day Belgian geography. To the south is the Meuse basin.

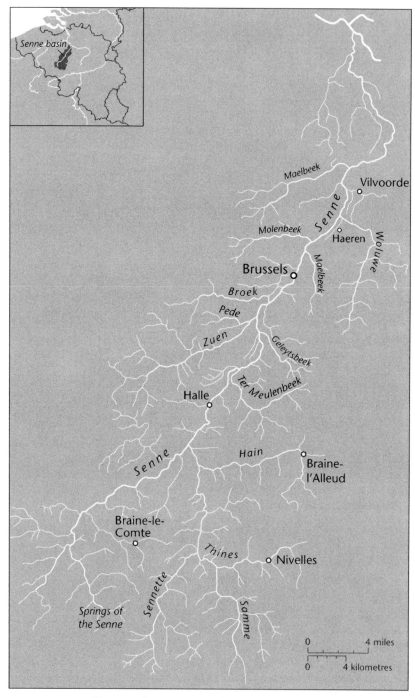

FIGURE I.2. Map of the Senne basin, its main tributaries, and towns and cities.

The water regime of the Senne is considered pluvial as it is directly influenced by precipitation, which also means that it is subject to strong, sudden variations in flow and therefore also to flooding. The flow of the Senne at the entrance to Brussels can still vary considerably today, rising from one to two cubic meters per second (low-water mark) to sixty to one hundred cubic meters per second (during a storm) in the space of a few hours. The average annual flow of the river at this given location is about five cubic meters per second, with broad monthly variations from this average.

The Senne is rightly considered "the" river of Brussels given the economic role it has played in the city's development since the Middle Ages. An important trade route connecting Brussels to the Escaut and, beyond that, to the central North Sea area from the eleventh century on, a power source for many mills beginning in the twelfth century, an indispensable resource for the activities and development of staple economic sectors (textile, brewing, tannery, etc.), it was also a major axis of the social and spatial structure of the urban territory.[5] It is easy to forget, however, that it was far from the only river in Brussels. Seven tributary streams ran, at least in part, through the present-day Brussels area: the Ter Meulenbeek, the Geleytsbeek, the Maelbeek, the Woluwe, the Zuen, the Pede, and the Molenbeek (figure 1.2). Despite their size, which might seem minute in other urban contexts, these streams structured the geography and economy of the city and its suburbs over the centuries.

While unnavigable, they too played a key role in the integration of the territory: beginning in the medieval period, their flows were intensely exploited and developed to operate a large number of mills and an important fish farming industry. These facilities were supported by entrepreneurs whose capital was generated by the urban market and, in return, generated production that was sent back to the city.

THE MEDIEVAL HERITAGE: A WATER "SYSTEM" UNDER STRAIN

At the end of the eighteenth century, the water landscape of the city and its surroundings was still largely heir to a situation that was created in the Middle Ages and had changed little since. The Senne and its feeder streams were a tight series of workings where the mills and fish farm ponds had a fundamental impact on the water circulation process.

Thus, circa 1770, the center of the city alone showed a surprising concentration of mills: about ten factories operated within a perimeter of a few hundred square meters, exploiting the few arms of the river to the utmost.[6] This concentration was not exceptional. It was typical of many neighboring urban centers (Tournai, Liège, Namur, Leuven, etc.), but the demographic importance of Brussels, which was then the main city of the Austrian Low

Countries (roughly corresponding to what would later become Belgium), left
its mark on the system well beyond the city limits: according to the compiled sources, the number of mills located within a twelve-kilometer radius
of the city can be estimated at between 110 and 130, while the basin as a whole
had about 210. These facilities were primarily used to mill grains but also
served other, more clearly industrial functions. The mills were used to grind
the sprouted barley required for beer making (malt), to crush the oleaginous
plants needed to produce oil (primarily for lighting), to extract the bark tan
essential for the leather industry, to pulp the fibers (from rags and used cloth-
ing) required to make paper, to sharpen knives, weapons and tools, and so
on. The crown of mills laid out around Brussels thus reflected not only the
city's demographic importance ("mouths to feed") but also its functions, both
industrial (beer and leather) and administrative (paper mills). Subject to later
research findings, we can assert that it had no equal in the surrounding regions. From that time forward, some peri-urban streams, particularly those
on the east side of the basin (the Maelbeek, Woluwe, Geleytsbeek, and Ter
Meulenbeek), seemed to be veritable "energy chains"; there was generally a
mill every few hundred meters.

Simply put, mill operations are designed to ensure that the right quantity
of water is available at the right time. In other words, the miller must be able
to both store water to be used in times of drought and eliminate overabun-
dant water (due to storms, extended periods of rain, etc.), which could also
hamper the operation of the water wheels. In terms of layout, mill operations
were therefore centered around "reservoirs" (ponds) and a number of water
channels, some to feed the optimal amount of water onto the water wheel (the
races) and others, on the contrary, to drain away undesirable, or surplus, water (the overflow channels). These ponds and channels were themselves outfit-
ted with gates and mechanisms that controlled water entry and exit.

Likewise, the number of ponds (all artificial and dug in medieval times)
that punctuated the course of the peri-urban rivers was equally impressive.
On the Maelbeek, a stream some ten kilometers long, the Ferraris map (circa
1775) shows nearly eighty bodies of water, large and small, fed by the stream
and its diversions, including about twenty with a capacity of several tens of
thousands of cubic meters. The other streams of the urban fringe, particularly on the east side of the Senne valley, had the same type of morphology.
Most of these water bodies were used for fish farming rather than being directly linked to the stream's role as a power source. Carp (primarily) and pike
were farmed intensely for the nearby urban market and ecclesiastical institutions, who were large consumers of fish (proscriptions regarding regular fast-
ing made fish an extremely common meal, sometimes almost two days out

of three).[7] Management of these fish farming ponds, which were generally operated in groups of at least three (each pond hosting a different age of fish specimen), involved several drainages per year (in step with the key dates of the Christian calendar: Lent, All Saints' Day, and Christmas) and indispensable regular dredging. These ponds were also connected to the hydrographic network by a complex system of feeder and drainage canals. Thus worked and tangled, the water network looked more like intertwined branches than a hierarchical or radicular network.

From that time forward, the millers, like the fish farmers, were essential links in the "working" of the waterways: they were the best placed to monitor, control, and maneuver the flow rate and passage of the water required to sustain their activities. An indication of this acquired level of expertise was that some of them held positions at the Chambre des Tonlieux, an institution responsible for administering the sovereign's rights, including those related to his powers of regalian origin over the waterways. Brabant (one of the nine principalities forming the southern Low Countries) had four Chambre des Tonlieux, one in each of its quarters; the one in the Quarter of Brussels controlled the use and maintenance of all water-related facilities (bridges, mills, flow control mechanisms), as well as stream dredging and gauging of the water levels to be maintained in each part of the water network. From then on, it also assumed arbitral jurisdiction in case of disputes between users. Created in the fourteenth century, it remained active up until the end of the Ancien Régime (1795).

The morphology of rivers in the urban fringe at the end of the eighteenth century thus resembled more of a "water system" composed of channels, reservoirs, interconnections, dams, and weirs than a single, continuous flow of water, as it tends to be portrayed. The complexity of this highly artificial, anthropized hydrographic network goes hand in hand with the multiplication of the actors involved in its management. Mill owners, at least as numerous as the mills themselves,[8] fish farmers, and riparian residents fought regularly over water management. The millers were accused of storing the water behind the gates of their mills too long, occasionally causing flooding upstream, and consequently the destruction of fields and loss of fish. By the same token, they were also accused of causing inactivity in the mills downstream. The fish farmers were accused of not dredging their portion of the waterway sufficiently, thus reducing the quantity of water available for the mills or, on the contrary, of releasing the contents of their ponds too suddenly during drainage and dredging and so forth. Thus, waterway management was repeatedly punctuated by incidents that set its practitioners against one another. The installation of gauges, intended to regulate the authorized water level, never achieved the desired result: in practice, the social organization of the network was based on an endless cycle of conflict and negotiation.

In other words, at the end of the eighteenth century, the waterways of Brussels and its surroundings could be considered as heavily occupied and "under strain." However, it was these very conflicts and needs, both contradictory and complementary, that provided a certain balance in the management of the waterways, which as a result were constantly monitored by a large number of interested, concerned actors. These conflicts and tensions, which can be traced at least as far back as the fourteenth century, necessitated the creation of arbitration and control bodies. The above-mentioned Chambre des Tonlieux fulfilled part of this role. The various users also sometimes sealed agreements, sort of river "contracts," to better manage the drainage and maintenance schedule. The situation was nevertheless very far from the Wateringen (water boards) that existed in some parts of the County of Flanders and the Northern Low Countries (later the United Provinces) from medieval times onward, which were responsible for permanently maintaining and controlling the operation of the water system in certain territories on the local level.[9] At the end of the Austrian period (1704–1792), the state, wishing to centralize the administration of the Low Countries as a whole, created the Jointe des Eaux in 1772 as a sort of permanent committee responsible for addressing problems caused by flooding and water flow, but during its short life it essentially grappled with problems in the northern part of the country and paid little heed to Brussels.

Needless to say, Brussels's rivers were not used solely for power and fish farming in those days. As in any city, they were also the receptacle for a wide variety of waste from domestic and artisanal activities. This waste material increased the organic content of the rivers considerably and tended to accumulate in certain areas (particularly at the convex bend of meanders and upstream from dams and obstacles). These deposits increased siltation and obstruction of the waterways, which aggravated flooding when the water was high and caused greater inconvenience and health hazards during periods of low water or drought. This was particularly true for the course of the Senne, which flowed through the city center, precisely where artisanal activities and the population were most concentrated.

All in all, the workings of the rivers of the region on the eve of the Industrial Revolution can be characterized as a water system put under strain by its many uses, and the water system's main problems (flooding and pollution) arose from difficulties in balancing shortage and abundance as defined by the differentiated needs of the users. One could add that the waterways of the region functioned mainly for the benefit of the city: Brussels's hydraulic territory, meaning the zone within which its effects, both attractive (market)

and repulsive (pollution), were felt, extended well beyond its territorial limits. Water defined a sort of *silent territory* with no administrative status.

DISAPPEARING USES

As many studies have shown, innovations brought about by the Industrial
Revolution and scientific progress, like the fundamental changes that took
place in sociopolitical and economic structures in Western Europe between
the late eighteenth century and the late nineteenth century, had radical consequences, both direct and indirect, on the role of rivers and water in the urban
landscape (whether seen from a social, economic, or ecological perspective)
and the modalities of water supply to urban populations.[10] These transformations manifested themselves in different ways, depending on the city, region,
or country, and at different times, but they all contributed to the profound
transformation that marked relationships to water in this area of the world
during that period.

In the case of the Brussels region, this transformation resulted in a particularly intense "invisibilization" (covering over, underground flow, etc.)
and distancing (remote intakes, elimination of public water points, etc.) of the
water resources used by the population. One by one, the activities and needs
(energy, artisanal, fish farming, domestic, and other uses) that had engendered
the necessary coexistence of people and local water up until the end of the
eighteenth century disappeared, until finally the authorities were able to cut
the last links in the name of public hygiene. At a time when aspirations for
more ecological management of cities (shorten and relocate material cycles,
reduce pollution and the ecological footprint, conserve resources, etc.) entail
the reconstruction of relationships between people and their local resources, it
might be useful to take a closer look at what once permitted their coexistence
and how and why it unraveled.[11]

During the first stage, which lasted from approximately 1780 to 1850, it
was not so much technical innovations or urbanization that lay at the root
of early changes to the uses and workings of Brussels's rivers but rather the
transformation of social structures, particularly the secularization of society. The suppression of ecclesiastical institutions in the context of the French
Revolution,[12] laxity in the observance of the Christian fasts, as well as improved transportation methods that made ocean fish easier to ship, spelled a
very rapid end to fish farms and the Brussels-area ponds that housed them.[13]
One study has shown that the area occupied by such ponds fell by nearly 60
percent from 1775 to 1860.[14] The figure reproduced in figure 1.3, comparing
the morphology of the Maelbeek (a hydronym etymologically meaning "the
mill stream") at the two extremes of this time period, provides a striking illustration of this: almost all the ponds, reservoirs, and water bodies virtually

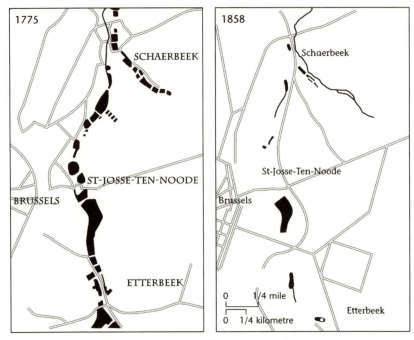

FIGURE 1.3. Comparison of the Maelbeek valley over a period of about eighty-five years. Adapted from maps by Ferraris (1775) and Ph. Vandermaelen (1858).

"evaporated"! Here, one can see very clearly how the disappearance of the surface water, streams, and ponds preceded urbanization, which was still at a very early stage in this area of the suburbs in 1858.

Observation of flooding in the Brussels region would tend to indicate that the dramatic decrease in these "hydraulic annexes," especially on the rivers nearest the city, had repercussions on the hydrographic system's capacity to absorb floodwaters. Indeed, in case of heavy rain, water could not be retained anymore in these ponds and basins and would overflow the beds and channels. According to the increased damage incurred and number of floods, flood severity increased significantly in the first half of the nineteenth century, giving rise to numerous complaints from inhabitants and many inquiry committees set by the authorities.[15]

On the other hand, during the same period, mills that had sometimes been on the streams of the region for centuries stayed where they were. They continued to be essential to the city's supply or found new life as a foothold for emerging industries (most notably papermaking). A number of new mills were even built. The industrialization of the Brussels region was an inescapable reality during this first stage (1770–1850); it occurred early and was fairly massive. In the eastern part of the region, where the terrain was hillier and

urbanization occurred at a faster pace, this involved mostly medium-sized enterprises, while in the western part, which extended into the Senne River
valley (where the Charleroi Canal would soon be built to access the coal basin), it involved larger industrial complexes (metal factories, textile and food
industries, etc.).[16] Indeed, it was here that manufacturers were still able to find
cheap land adjacent to the transportation infrastructure (the canal, opened in
1832, and then the railway, in 1835). Thus, while industry did not abandon
the area of the rivers to the south and east of the city in this first stage, it developed to a much greater degree to the west of the city, in the Senne River
valley. The river no longer played the major role in this positioning, except
perhaps insofar as it had created a socio-spatial structure where the urbanized,
bourgeois eastern side of the valley contrasted with the industrial, working-
class western side.

Growing industrial activity also contributed to the discharge of a greater
amount of organic matter (pollution) into the rivers. A retrospective, quantitative approach has shown that the glue and gelatin factories, breweries, paper
mills, and industrial tanners, the very industries particularly well represented
in the region, were at the top of the list of most-polluting industries of the
nineteenth century.[17]

Waste from papermaking activities, centered around the mills and primarily located east and south of Brussels from the fifteenth century onward,
mainly affected the rivers of the suburbs, giving rise to sporadic conflicts over
water quality.[18] Around 1850, the textile industry, which had an impressive
start in the last third of the eighteenth century and then a pronounced decline
after 1815 (i.e., after the fall of the Napoleonic Empire and the sudden opening up of markets), remained responsible for discharging organic waste estimated at about fifteen tons per day into the hydrographic system from three
faubourgs located immediately south of the city, the equivalent of the domestic organic waste generated by a population of 150,000 inhabitants today.[19]
To this must be added the likely decrease in the flow of the Senne through
the city following the construction of the Charleroi Canal (1832). This canal,
which connected Brussels to the Hainaut coal basin, was exclusively fed by
water drawn from the Senne upstream from the city. Thus depleted, the river
was even less capable of flushing away the sewage.

Accounts of pollution of Brussels's rivers, both within the city and in its
urban fringe, multiplied. They emanated as much from farmers downstream
from the city, who complained of no longer being able to water their livestock without poisoning them, as from manufacturers unable to use the water
from "their" river due to pollution upstream, inhabitants annoyed by odors
and fumes, and even officials concerned about the contamination of lower-
city wells that supplied water to the most vulnerable inhabitants. All these

accounts describe, in the language of the day, bacterial fermentation that generated nauseating fumes and contaminated the pools from which a large part of the population drew its water. This pollution was not completely new, of course—industry had been dumping its waste into the waterways since the Middle Ages—but, in the context described, it grew. This deterioration in the quality of the surface water, coupled with the more dramatic flooding, ushered relations between Brussels and its water into a new stage.

This second stage, which started in the 1850s, was characterized both by the search for "pure" water for the population and a drive to eliminate "dirty" water or wastewater. In 1855, the quest for healthy water led to the creation of the city's first residential water distribution system; entirely organized by the public authorities, meaning the City of Brussels authorities, this was also the first "modern" water distribution system in the country. The system of underground channels was designed to draw water from sources in the valley of the Hain River, a Senne tributary about thirty kilometers south, and feed it by gravitation to a large reservoir built in the upper reaches of the city.[20] From there, the water was distributed to the various quarters, first to the more affluent inhabitants, the only ones who could afford to subscribe to the service. Water, which up until then had been free, thus became a paid service, and residential access to water only spread very slowly as a result.[21] At the beginning of the twentieth century, nearly half a century after the network was commissioned, the city waterworks, the Service des Eaux de la Ville, had extended very modest service to a few neighboring municipalities. By then, a second network organized by the faubourg communes was also in operation (since 1891, see below). Daily consumption for this second network was about seventy-one liters per subscriber, reducible to twenty-five liters if the public use of this water supply (to feed fountains, certain ponds and public buildings, for street and sewer cleaning, and for firefighting) were taken into account. In fact, only 37 percent of the volume distributed was eventually delivered to homes.[22]

At the same time, the authorities undertook to systematize and standardize the wastewater drainage system (sewers) in the city streets. Thus, in 1848, the first pipes were laid in the Brussels subsoil, pipes whose ultimate outlet was none other than the Senne. Far from resolving the water pollution problems in a city whose population density was rising steadily, the systematization of the sewage network added a substantial quantity of domestic organic matter to a river already choked with industrial waste. The hygiene issue was only exacerbated (cholera epidemics) by contamination of the surface and well water used by many inhabitants. As in many industrial European cities of the day, government officials sought solutions. They finally opted for a "solution" as original as it was radical: burying the river in the urban sub-soil, combined with a prestigious, urbanistic operation that would eliminate all the "unhealthy" quarters in the center, meaning the poor, working-class quarters. This operation, as we saw earlier, is better known as the "covering" of the Senne.

In the second half of the nineteenth century, Brussels therefore buried its river; from that point on, it was completely hidden as it made its way through the city. The public water points scattered throughout the public space also disappeared with the gradual spread of residential water distribution. In the urban periphery, where some rivers continued to flow out in the open, only two uses for them remained: for energy and production on one hand and as an outlet for industrial waste on the other. However, the energy role gradually disappeared as industry traded water mills for steam engines and preferred to locate nearer the new communication routes (navigation canals, railways) rather than along the old waterways.

A simple reading of how relations between Brussels and its water evolved in the nineteenth century would be that the Brussels region changed from a socio-hydraulic regime that could be described as "visible" and "strained" by its multiple uses to a regime that was "concealed" and "distended" as its uses disappeared one by one.

THE NEW GEOGRAPHY OF CONFLICT

Tensions between the city and its periphery were evident throughout the transition from one water regime to the other, but they were particularly acute in the second stage described above and transformed the geography of water conflicts. Flooding was the first issue to create tension between the city and the outlying communes, both upstream and downstream from the city. The communes immediately to the south (i.e., upstream), like Ander-lecht, Saint-Gilles, and Forest, for instance, accused Brussels authorities of preventing water from flowing properly during high water periods by refus-ing to drain excess water through the navigation canal, which they jealously sought to preserve from siltation and alluvia. This navigation canal was of vital economic importance to the city, which from then on considered its sur-vival to be of much greater interest than that of a few hundred inhabitants of the suburban "villages." Communes farther away from the city also accused the canal of being a major disturbance for water flow in the wetlands; they complained that its creation in the Senne alluvial plain had amputated a large surface area that had served to absorb floodwaters.[23]

Another line of dissention pitted city authorities against manufacturers on the periphery. When Brussels set off in search of healthy water for its distribution system, it kindled the anxiety of surrounding towns, who were affronted every time a new project was unveiled. When the city studied the project of the engineer Delsaux, for instance, who proposed sourcing water in the Woluwe valley, a few kilometers from the urban center (see figure 1.2), some fifty manufacturers promptly banded together to oppose the project, which would ruin their activities by depriving them of their water.[24] The project of the engineer Delaveleye, who explored the possibilities of intakes on the large southern periphery, sparked similar opposition; no fewer than twenty-six enterprises located along the coveted tributary, the Hain (see figure 1.2), and the Senne considered that they were entitled to compensation if the project went ahead. In the end, a variant of this project was selected, and the manufacturers were left uncompensated. Within a short time, eighteen thousand cubic meters of water were drawn daily from the Hain springs for the inhabitants and services of Brussels,[25] further reducing the flow of the small river still used by a fair number of small industries.

Tensions also ran very high between the city and its more immediate faubourgs over the distribution of the harnessed water. When Brussels established its water conveyance and residential distribution system in 1855, none of the city's faubourgs had the financial resources required to organize a similar distribution network on its territory (still sparsely occupied). Some of them nevertheless had a bourgeois population apt to demand this type of modern, prestigious service. Initially, faubourg authorities allowed the city waterworks of Brussels to deal directly with those of their residents who could afford to pay for home water distribution; the waterworks extended its network into the faubourg quarters that were sufficiently affluent and populated to justify the investment and ensure a return. But in 1870, on the pretext that the deficit between its expenses and revenues (from subscriptions) was being covered by taxes paid by city residents but not by residents of the faubourgs, the city imposed a higher fee on the latter, demonstrating flagrant discrimination that faubourg authorities were unable to tolerate. A veritable "water war" ensued between the City of Brussels and the four wealthiest faubourgs to the east (figure 1.4), involving aborted negotiations, threats, justifications, and, finally, protracted legal proceedings.[26] In 1891, in the aftermath of the proceedings, the four faubourgs joined forces to build and organize their own distribution system, sourcing water more than eighty kilometers south of Brussels in the Meuse drainage basin (see figure 1.1).[27] Requiring true technical prowess due to the distances and terrain involved, this network symbolized victory over nature, as it was tamed by the engineers and ingenious technicians, as well as over the City of Brussels. The faubourg communes did not fail to mark this victory by putting up allegorical statues and

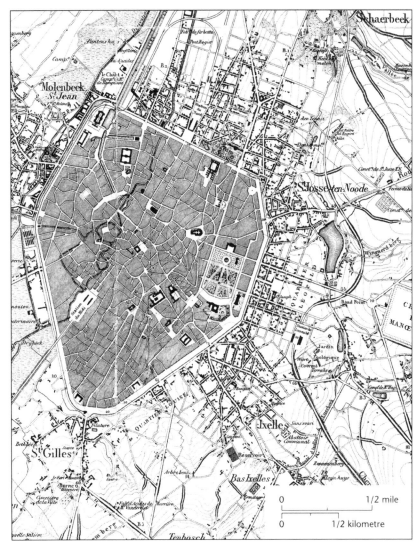

FIGURE 1.4. The City of Brussels (shaded) and its adjacent faubourgs, around 1860. To the east, the faubourgs of Saint-Gilles, Ixelles, Saint-Josse, and Schaerbeek. The Senne can still be seen crossing the city, but the Charleroi canal can also be seen on the left. A few larger industries are also shown. Adapted from a map by Ph. Vandermaelen (1858).

monuments at key sites in the urban space. These two distribution systems coexisted for over forty years, each extending into new communes. It was not until 1933 that they finally merged into a single intercommunal (public) structure, in which the founding communes (Brussels and the four faubourgs) long played a preponderant role.

IN THE END, THIS ACCOUNT gives rise to a number of elements of analysis. First, it is important to highlight that the transformations that rivers in the Brussels region underwent in the nineteenth century cannot be reduced to simply industrialization or the spread of urbanization. Certainly, industry's use of rivers as a source of energy increased slightly in the nineteenth century with the creation of new mills, but the milling infrastructure was for the most part already in place well before the industrial era. From this precise point of view, it was therefore not a question of the massive industrialization of the waterways. On the contrary, the hydrogeography of industrial activity would see major changes with the gradual establishment of large industrial complexes to the west of the city, near the new transportation infrastructure (canal and then railway). The rivers in the city center and the eastern and southern suburbs, where industry was concentrated until the late eighteenth and early nineteenth centuries, generally only continued to support small-scale industry. To some extent, we could therefore say that they underwent relative deindustrialization compared to what took place to the west of the city.

Similarly, the urbanization often invoked as the cause of the disappearance of streams and rivers from the urban space must also be qualified. The extremely rapid disappearance of fish farming practices, whose impact on stream management cannot be understated in the case of Brussels, also supplanted the actors in this activity, the fish farmers. Yet, ponds and fish farmers played a major role in the functioning of the waterways, the first absorbing flood waves and minimizing flooding, and the second acting as essential links in the necessarily concerted waterway management chain. Flooding and the disappearance of the various players were the fundamental causes of the disappearance of the waterways, both from the economy and from the urban ecology, with urbanization and pollution of the waterways later contributing to the process.

The transformations of the connections between society and water described in this chapter were at the heart of the territorial reorganization of Brussels during the nineteenth century; furthermore, they added fuel to new tensions between the city center and its faubourgs. One of the characteristic traits of the political administrative framework that structured the growth of Brussels from the early nineteenth century on indeed lay in the very difficult relations between the city and its outlying faubourgs. In this context, water became one of the subjects, instruments, and stakes in these difficult relations.

Thus, at the end of the eighteenth century, one might say that water conflicts revolved around the waterways, almost tracking the small streams and their arms from their source to where they joined the Senne. From upstream to downstream, the many actors with an interest in stream management (millers, fish farmers, riparian residents, manufacturers, farmers, and so on) collaborated or clashed over the streams. This territory was silent, without any administrative status, but it was nevertheless very real. One might also say that Brussels exercised power over the urban and peri-urban rivers. Its very existence (population, market, entrepreneurs) conditioned the need to make the rivers work. The rapid disappearance of the ponds in the late eighteenth and early nineteenth century and the resulting increase in the severity of flooding, coupled with greater pollution, forced Brussels authorities to seek "solutions." Implemented without any consultation of the neighboring faubourgs and communes, these essentially consisted of the multiplication of increasingly distant intakes and the systematization of the sewage network ultimately connected to the main river, which would soon be buried under the city. By acting this way, Brussels gradually established an "octopus-like" water territory, completely different from the one that had existed for many centuries. Henceforth, not only would the city go underground to draw its "fresh" water from well beyond its strict geographic limits, it would also split the networks into as many water tentacles as there were uses: one for navigation (the canal), one for distribution, and one for sewerage, the other uses for water having by then virtually disappeared. In this new configuration of the water territory, it was not just the inhabitants who were disconnected from the local resources but also the city, which stepped back from its periphery while at the same time imposing its choices on increasingly remote areas. In this new territory, it was no longer users (millers, fish farmers, market gardeners, inhabitants, or hikers) who were pitted against each other in conflicts over water management but rather administrations concerned about the success of their investments (publicly owned companies for water management and distribution, sewage system management, the Port of Brussels, etc.). This led to a complete transformation of the population's relationship to the environment.

2

THE RIVER LEA IN WEST HAM

A River's Role in Shaping Industrialization on the Eastern Edge of Nineteenth-Century London

JIM CLIFFORD

GREATER LONDON GREW FROM a little over one million to about eight million people during the nineteenth century. This massive population growth transformed the city's relationship with the natural environment and placed increasing pressure on the city's hinterlands. One of the most significant examples was the reengineering of local rivers and streams to supply water, facilitate transportation, and carry away wastes. In *The Thames Embankment*, Dale Porter explores the complex history of London's relationship with the Thames, as new bridges transformed the river's flow and sewage degraded the water quality. He examines the huge engineering project of the 1860s that "solved" these problems by embanking the river in central London and diverting sewage to the edge of the metropolis.[1] On a smaller scale, the expanding urban landscape buried numerous tributaries during the eighteenth and nineteenth centuries, including the Fleet, Westbourne, Tyburn, and Effra Rivers and Hackney Brook. In contrast, the river Lea, a larger tributary of the Thames, remained above ground and played an essential role in shaping suburban development on the eastern and northeastern periphery of Greater London.[2] While urban growth helped to transform the Thames of central London into a revered marvel of civil engineering, the Lea remained a working river, peripheral and unpleasant, but essential in shaping Greater London's new industrial heartland on the eastern edge of the metropolis. During the nineteenth century, the Lower Lea River helped to create West Ham, the largest manufacturing suburb in Outer London, as its multiple streams provided a readymade transportation network. By the century's end the conflicting uses of the Lea had diminished the river's capacity to support industrial development. Most importantly, river pollution and sedimentation

had made transportation increasingly difficult. As a result, the river had begun to obstruct and complicate the industrialization it had once facilitated.

During the second half of the nineteenth century Outer London grew
significantly faster than inner London. The core-periphery relationships in
the city changed, as the Metropolitan Board of Works (MBW) absorbed the
older suburbs in 1855 creating inner London, and new communities grew beyond London's redefined borders collectively forming Outer London. In the
east of London, the river Lea formed the jurisdictional limit of the MBW.
The wetlands of the Lea industrialized as factories migrated from the city
center in search of cheaper land, improved transportation, less regulation, and
more space.[3] During the 1880s, West Ham's local board of health incorporated
as a country borough (figure 2.1), independent from the MBW and its successor, the London County Council (LCC).[4] The autonomy of West Ham,
however, remained limited and a person walking from the East End into West
Ham at the turn of the twentieth century would not have noticed an abrupt
transition; the suburb was in many ways a continuation of East London.

Location mattered in the development of Greater London. West Ham was
a "river suburb," bounded by the multiple streams of the Lower Lea in the
west and the Thames in the south. The Lower Lea flowed through alluvial
wetlands and branches into a delta-like collection of nine streams, called the
Stratford Back Rivers, as it entered the Thames Estuary six kilometers east of
the Tower of London.[5] The location of West Ham in relation to London, the
Thames Estuary, and the Lower Lea together created a favorable economic
region with several environmental advantages that drew hundreds of factories and over a quarter million people to the suburb during the nineteenth
century. Many of the same factors that enabled industrialization in this location contributed to the emergence of significant environmental problems.
The flow of the Thames and Lea Rivers along with the expansion of sewage
systems and the prevailing winds placed the suburb at the receiving end of
much of Greater London's growing surge of water and air pollution.[6]

The Lower Lea and the local population shared a long history of transforming the landscape of the marshlands in West Ham Parish. The Lea
flooded and carried silt down to the marshes, where people built tidal mills,
dikes, and drained wetlands, for many centuries before the massive suburban transformation of the river and landscape in the nineteenth century.[7] The
growth of coal-fuelled industry vastly increased the scale of transformation;
a process that accelerated after the first railway arrived in 1839. The river carried the fuel of the industrial economy and supplied water for the boilers. As a
result the banks of the Lower Lea were encased with factories, and its streams
filled with barges, sewage, and other forms of pollution.[8]

The Lea's capacity to fuel the industrial economy with coal and its proxim-

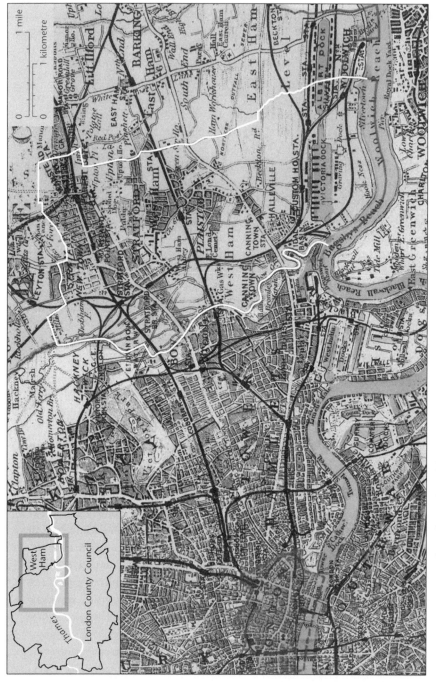

FIGURE 2.1. West Ham and London. Adapted from a map by Edward Stanford, *Outer London* (1901), available at the David Rumsey Historical Map Collection, www.davidrumsey.com.

ity to and distance from central London together contributed to the nineteenth-century industrial development of the Lea's wetlands. Noxious and polluting industries remained close to the London market, but their location on relatively inexpensive marshlands downwind from the better parts of the city, and outside the jurisdiction of the increasingly powerful London government, shielded them from most public health and environmental regulations.[9] During this same period the old manufacturing core of London experienced protracted industrial decline.[10]

The transportation network created in the Lower Lea facilitated the growth of industry at a particularly significant moment in the development of Greater London's industrial economy. The combination of the high cost of transporting coal on land and the relatively small scale of most factories made the waterlogged Stratford Marsh an attractive location for industrial development during the second half of the nineteenth century. The temporal factor was essential, as a few decades later, electricity, cheaper rail costs, larger factories, and the growing importance of roads increasingly freed industries from their reliance on waterways, and the appeal of the Lea's cramped, flood-prone wetlands declined. As a result, the wetlands and riverbanks in West Ham never fully industrialized and some pockets of undeveloped marshes and farmland remained well into the twentieth century.

The Lea and West Ham mutually influenced one another during the nineteenth century to create an industrial river and suburb. The significant suburban growth within the wetlands and on the river created a hybrid suburban landscape where factories were intermixed with marginal housing stock, dust heaps (garbage dumps), pig barns, farms, allotment gardens, and small patches of marshland.[11] This landscape remained in a state of flux well into the twentieth century. Both intentional and accidental human intervention, along with the varied flow of the Lea and the tides, created a high level of instability in the new suburban environment. Prolonged use, abuse, and neglect decreased the utility of the Back Rivers by the end of the nineteenth century, and this contributed to the slowing of development and later to the decline of industry in West Ham.

THIS CHAPTER IS A CASE STUDY of an important economic and environmental region in London's suburban fringe that raises questions about the interaction between urban processes and riverine ecosystems. I am particularly interested in understanding the shifting spatial pattern of industrial transformation at the scale of the suburb. Geographic information systems (GIS) software provides a useful tool for tracking spatial change over time.[12] The GIS database for this project includes a series of maps, some published and others found in archives, dating from the eighteenth to late nineteenth centuries.[13] New spatial data were then created by comparing the series of maps and identifying features, including roads, rivers, drainage ditches, railways, industrial sites, and dockyards. Together these "vector" layers create historical land-use maps for the Lower Lea and its wetlands within West Ham. The lines and polygons that identify the various land uses are linked with other details in database tables such as their names and the years they were built. The data created from these maps have been augmented with information found in mail directories, rate assessments, contemporary reports, and secondary sources.[14]

The GIS database was manipulated to focus attention on industry sites, rather than residential, municipal, or commercial buildings. Factories were identified, and the dates of construction and closing were added when possible (when the exact dates are not known they were replaced with years when these sites appear on maps for the first and last time). Along with these dates, the industries have been delineated into categories such as engineering, building, chemical (including soap factories and animal rendering), food processing, and gasworks. With this information entered, the GIS database was used to create a time series of maps from 1810, the 1850s, 1867, and 1893, showing the industrial and suburban development in stages. The 1867 and 1893 maps also include the complete road network, recorded on the Ordnance Survey maps, to help represent the residential expansion on the Lea's wetlands in the second half of the nineteenth century.

THE LEA'S PROXIMITY TO London brought it into close and intensive contact with humans many centuries ago, and much of the natural river had been transformed into canals, reservoirs, and flumes to ease transport, supply water, and harness the river for power. The first GIS map (figure 2.2) shows the hybrid of natural and engineered streams that made up the Lower Lea in the early years of the nineteenth century.

The dotted lines represent the Lee Navigation, which included the canalled sections of the Lower Lea. The main stream of the Lea, sometimes called the Old Lea, had "improvements" as early as the fifteenth century.[15] These were augmented during the canal building craze of the late eighteenth and early nineteenth centuries with the addition of the Limehouse Cut (1760s), which created a second mouth of the river and provided a direct route to London that avoided the long bend in the Thames around the Isle of Dogs, and the Hackney Cut, which improved navigation up the Lea valley (1770). In the nineteenth century the Hartford Union Canal (1830) linked the Lee Navigation network with Regent's Canal. As these canals enhanced the Lea for transportation, the "improved" western section of the Lower Lea became increasingly divided from the remaining tidal streams.

The solid white lines on the map represent the more "natural" and tidal

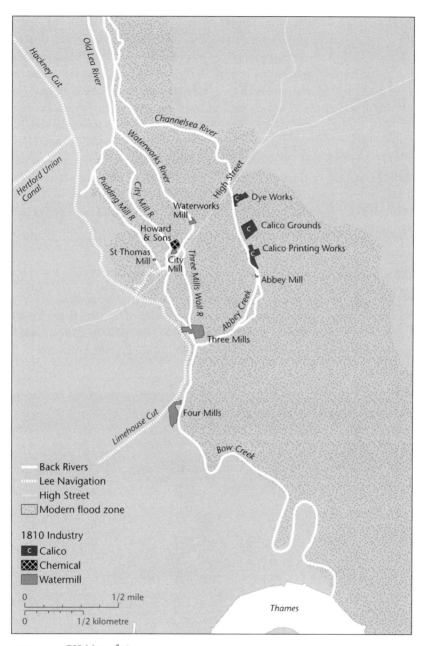

FIGURE 2.2. GIS Map of 1810.

Stratford Back Rivers from Temple Mills to the Thames. However, even these streams likely underwent various forms of human intervention during the thousands of years people inhabited this area. Moreover, in this low-lying topography it is likely that the beds of the Lea meandered over the centuries as siltation and regular floods shifted channels and made new streams.[16] As a result, it is difficult to tell the natural from the artificial riverbeds, but it is likely that the straight-running streams had been manipulated in the past by mill owners.

Watermills began the industrial transformation of the rivers on a small scale by harnessing tidal energy in the early Middle Ages, and a large-scale drainage program transformed the river's wetlands and increased the height of riverbanks centuries before the railroads arrived. The *Domesday Book* recorded five watermills on the Lower Lea at the end of the eleventh century. These mills harnessed the tides in this flat landscape, first to grind grain and later to mill other goods such as oil seeds and gunpowder.[17]

The tidal mills were augmented during the early modern era with a number of windmills, such as the one seen in figure 2.3 from around 1800.[18] The windmills suggest exhaustion of the potential energy of the tides in the Lower Lea by the early modern period and the resulting limits on industrial expansion so long as they were restricted to the locally available renewable energy.[19]

FIGURE 2.3. View of West Ham Mills by the river Lea in West Ham, circa 1800. Reprinted with permission from the City of London, London Metropolitan Archives.

In the sixteenth and seventeenth century Stratford and West Ham attracted a number of silk weavers. Unfortunately, no maps record the exact location or size of these workshops, but some of them seem to have been concentrated around the Bow Bridge, as Stratford-Bow was the location of a riot against the Dutch engine loom in 1675.[20] Calico printers arrived in the late seventeenth century to replace the dying silk trade, and during the eighteenth century they grew to occupy ninety-one acres of marshlands.[21] This began the process of industrial expansion along the banks of the Lower Lea.

Apart from this growing presence of Calico printing, and the continued use of the tides for milling, the landscape and economy in West Ham and the Lower Lea remained largely agricultural through the first decades of the nineteenth century. The population was relatively small, with about six and a half thousand people recorded in the 1801 census.[22] However, when compared with the rest of Essex, West Ham was the second most populous parish after Colchester, suggesting the process of suburban growth was already under way.[23]

Farming and market gardening activities dominated the economy in West Ham at the end of the eighteenth century. Plaistow became a center for growing potatoes, and livestock were assembled and fattened on the reclaimed marshes before delivery to the London market.[24] While traditional rural agriculture might be seen as the antithesis of modern urban industry, the early modern landscape transformations created for farming and gardening in the Lower Lea Valley provided an essential element for later industrial growth: land. The responsibility for flood defense and land drainage in West Ham passed from the Stratford Langthorne Abbey to a Court of Sewers after the dissolution of the monasteries in the sixteenth century. In the centuries that followed the marshlands drained by the court increased from 1,747 acres in 1563 to 2,369 acres by 1850.[25] The 1850s GIS map (figure 2.4) includes an extensive network of drainage ditches and gives a good approximation of the land reclaimed by the onset of major industrial development. The land drainage had far-reaching implications during the nineteenth century, as the ditches created for agriculture provided an early (and inadequate) sewer system for the growing population. Furthermore, the shape of the ditches helped structure the residential spaces, much the same way the rivers influenced industrial spaces, as builders located housing along the ditch banks.[26] These early developments began the process of landscape transformation in West Ham that provided an essential element for later industrial and suburban growth.

The 1810 GIS map (see figure 2.2) shows the location of the mills, calico grounds, and Howard and Jewell's (later Howard and Son), an early and important chemist (drug) factory and laboratory built on the land adjacent to City Mills. There are no good surveys of the built environment from the turn

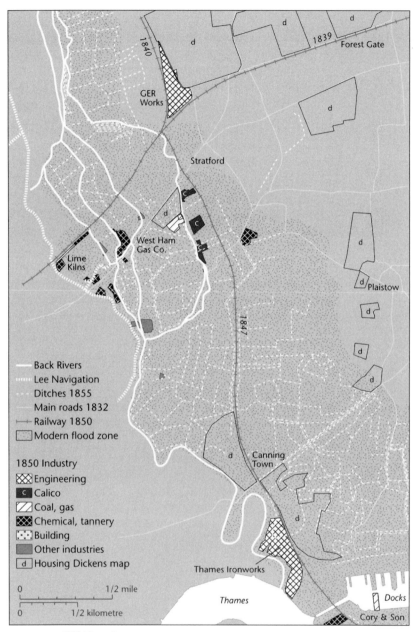

Back Rivers
Lee Navigation
Ditches 1855
Main roads 1832
Railway 1850
Modern flood zone

1850 Industry
Engineering
C Calico
Coal, gas
Chemical, tannery
Building
Other industries
d Housing Dickens map

0   1/2 mile
0   1/2 kilometre

Forest Gate

1839

1840

GER Works

Stratford

d

d

d

d

d

West Ham Gas Co.

C

C

Lime Kilns

d

Plaistow

d

d

d

d

1847

Canning Town

d

d

Thames Ironworks

Thames

Docks

Cory & Son

FIGURE 2.4. GIS Map 1850s.

of the nineteenth century. This map has been created by using other sources, such as later maps, to identify what industrial sites existed by 1810. For this reason some industries are missing, while others appear larger or smaller than they would have been in 1810. The calico grounds were found in the lands of the former abbey, on the banks of the Channelsea River, and they were probably more extensive than this map shows.[27] The map is also missing the lime kilns (identified on the 1850s GIS map, figure 2.4), some of which were probably established by this time to meet the demand created by the calico printers.[28] Despite these omissions, the map still provides a good approximation the small industrial footprint during the first decade of the nineteenth century.

This limited manufacturing presence, which did not change significantly during the first three decades of the nineteenth century, resulted nevertheless in a range of conflicts in the 1820s because of the changing patterns of water use and their consequences for flooding. A series of pamphlets record a prolonged conflict between mill owners and the upstream communities over improved dikes built to trap more of the tide for the large Three Mills and Four Mills.[29] Tensions between the mill owners and the upstream community increased in the early nineteenth century because engineering projects in the Lea valley and higher levees together increased the severity and frequency of flooding. The canal beds of the Lee Navigation increasingly replaced the Old Lea as the river's main channel, and suburban growth and farmers continued to reclaim wetlands, decreasing the watershed's ability to absorb heavy rainfalls.[30] Together these "improvements" increased flooding, as the canals carried the water down to the Lower Lea faster, where mills and bridges slowed the water's final progress toward the Thames. A major flood in 1824 sparked the conflict between the large mill owners and the upstream community.

Three documents remain from the Committee of the Floods of the Lea (1824–1830), and while they are decidedly one-sided in their critique of the millers and the Court of Sewers, they provide useful insight into this early conflict over the industrialization of the river. The reports claim the miller increased the embankments between Bow Creek and the Old Lea above the legal limits:

> A flood more devastating than had occurred for some time, attended by a loss of £10,000 in 1824, aroused the attention of the inhabitants; they investigated the cause of this calamity, and observed it did not extend below the mill dams, and on inquiry into the right of the millers to inflict these cruel injuries, found that this damming and penning up of the Lea was not only in opposition to the laws of the realm, but specifically prohibited by the 39th of Elizabeth, statute of sewers. The process appeared to have been

gradually effected by the owners of these mills becoming Commissioners, and a standing Jury, part of whom were chosen from either the servants of the Commissioners, or employed by them.[31]

The new embankment increased the frequency and severity of flooding, limited the transportation potential of the Lower Lea, and threatened the health and property of their upstream neighbors.[32] The last of the pamphlets suggest the millers won this case, leaving a deep rift in the community between the two large mills and the upstream landowners and industrialists.[33]

The conflict between the millers and the upstream community came at an interesting moment, as after the 1820s the ability to retain larger amounts of tidal water to power mills stopped being a major limiting factor of industrial development. The Lea remained essential to the energy regime of West Ham's industry, but instead of moving the waterwheels, the river facilitated the transportation of coal and filled boilers. Despite the declining importance of mills, this early conflict brought to light environmental problems created by industrial and urban growth. Flooding caused by the development of wetlands and engineering of riverbeds continued throughout the century and the conflict between millers and other users of the river remained problematic. In fact, water pollution combined with flooding as two of the major environmental problems in the Lower Lea at the century's end. The ancient rights held by the millers delayed efforts to address both of these problems until the 1930s.[34]

The expanded transportation infrastructure constructed between the late 1830s and 1855 ushered in the era of major industrial development. The population in West Ham tripled during the first half of the nineteenth century, and a variety of new factories were built along the banks of the streams near High Street or the railway. The coal-fuelled industrial economy began in earnest with the first railroad in 1839. During the 1840s, rail lines crisscrossed the Lower Lea's wetlands and a major rail yard grew along the northern banks of the Channelsea River. During the same decade, the first iron shipyard was established at the mouth of Bow Creek. These two industries, seen in the 1850s GIS map (figure 2.4) became the leading employers during the second half of the nineteenth century. Finally, by 1855 the low-lying marshlands to the south were transformed by the construction of a deepwater dock. Together the transportation infrastructure and the related heavy industries brought about the first stage in the transformation of the Lower Lea into an industrial center.

Some travel narratives from this period record the early awareness of the environmental damage that came with industrial development on the Lower Lea. Charles MacKay's *The Thames and Its Tributaries* (1840) describes a walk along the length of the Lea and ends with disparaging remarks about the final stretch of the river in West Ham: "Bromley-le-Bow . . . is the last of the pleasant villages that ornament the Lea, which is then lost amid the ship-yards, manufactories, and long straggling outskirts of the shipping districts of the metropolis. Divided into several branches, aided by canals, polluted by gasworks, and other useful but unfragrant factories, it loses its character of a retired and rural stream. Its very name is taken from it at the end of its useful career, and it unites itself with the Thames, neglected and unhonoured, under the name of Bow Creek."[35]

Four years later James Thorne reuses this observation in his description of walking along the Lower Lea: "But by this time our river has ceased to be either picturesque or interesting: lime-kilns, calico-printing, and distilleries are the most prominent objects . . . and however useful these may be, they are not agreeable to either nose or eye."[36] With the arrival of the railroads and docks between 1839 and 1855, the renewable but limited energy of the tides was largely replaced by the abundant but polluting energy of seaborne coal. The scale of industrial expansion began to accelerate, and the pleasant rural landscape gave way to a productive but more objectionable landscape shaped by factories, railways, and dockyards, all of which consumed large amounts of coal. Even during the early years of this transformation MacKay and Thorne both underlined this trade-off, noting the unpleasant consequences of industrial development while acknowledging its importance. Their reactions to the Lower Lea reflect the cultural tension discussed by James Winter between enthusiasm for economic and technological development and the growing awareness of the "heaps" of pollution and otherwise blighted landscapes left for the future by industrial innovations.[37]

By the 1850s, two gasworks and the first heavy chemical factories also emerged on the banks of the streams. The calico industry remained a significant presence but was declining as sewage increasingly polluted the once pure water of the Stratford Back Rivers forcing the printers to relocate.[38] This connection between environmental degradation and industrial collapse foreshadowed the later weaknesses of the whole Stratford Back Rivers factory zone. As we will see, the pollution of the rivers eventually degraded their navigability and decreased their geographical advantages. Finally, the bottom right of the 1850s GIS map shows part of the Victoria Docks, completed in 1855, which transformed the landscape in the south of West Ham and became a major employer in the suburb.[39]

The small industrial site visible within Victoria Docks was arguably the most important development during the 1850s. The William Cory and Son coal depot installed hydraulic cranes to transfer coal from oceangoing vessels to river barges, creating the key link in the energy regime of the Lower

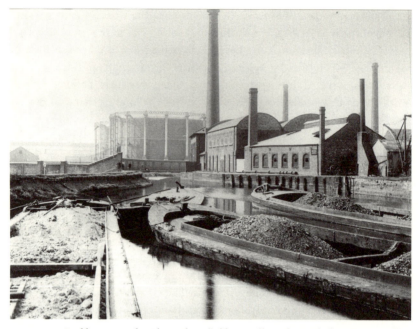

FIGURE 2.5. Coal barges on the Channelsea. "Abbey Mills Ingham Clarke & Co 1902."
Reprinted with permission from the Newham Local Studies Library and Archive,
Newham, Greater London.

Lea, which, according to John Marriott, was the main reason for industrial
growth in West Ham.[40] An early historian of West Ham's industrial development, Archer Philip Crouch, found that Cory and Son's reduced the price of
seaborne coal in the mid-1850s to "7s. 6d. per ton, while the railborne coal
remained at 12s. 6d. per ton."[41] In 1859, Cory and Son commissioned a local shipyard to build a floating river wharf so they could unload oceangoing
ships without paying dock fees, further decreasing the relative cost of coal.[42]
Coal barges, like the ones seen in figure 2.5 from 1902, allowed the Stratford
Back Rivers to supply energy to any factory along the banks of the navigable
portions of the rivers.

   The Lea remained integral in supplying the energy for industrial development as steam engines became the main source of power. The Lower Lea
was a readymade transportation network for coal barges, reducing the cost
of energy and making this eastern suburb more competitive with northern
England than the older industrial landscapes in London proper.[43] The industrial history of Greater London is fairly complex. J. L. Hammond's often
repeated quote that the Industrial Revolution was "like a storm that passed
over London and broke elsewhere" provides the basic argument for the stan-
dard treatment of London's industrial history.[44] In London, small workshops

dominated the manufacturing sector, and this has been used as evidence that the Industrial Revolution never really took root in the city.

Raphael Samuel and Marriott take exception to this line of argument. Samuel argues that much of the Industrial Revolution was indeed driven by small-scale manufacturing, and he suggests that too much focus has been placed on the emergence of large factories.[45] Conversely, Marriott demonstrates that Greater London did have a significant number of large factories. By refocusing attention to the east of Greater London in the Thames estuary, we find a center of heavy industry at the end of the nineteenth century, which was comparable to many of the industrial cities in the north. The large factories in West Ham, Woolwich, Greenwich, and Beckton are often disregarded as exceptions to the rule, but that is only true if we see them in the context of London's economy and geography, instead of comparing this factory zone to other industrial cities. West Ham alone compared favorably in terms of population with many northern cities, but when combined with Poplar, Woolwich, Greenwich, and Beckton, this cluster of heavy industry and transportation infrastructure formed an important industrial region.[46] Marriott's interest in large-scale industry in this region means he focuses on the concentration of large factories in the south of West Ham, those located on the Thames. He points out that only a few of the factories valued over a thousand pounds in the early 1880s were located along the Lea.[47] I believe the smaller river deserves more attention, as it was the crucial incubator for industrial development on the edge of London, and collectively, the many factories along the Lea created an important industrial landscape. The explosion of industry that reshaped the Lower Lea in the second half of the nineteenth century was an important example of how Hammond and others have misrepresented the geographic development of the Industrial Revolution in Britain by downplaying the importance of Greater London.

The infrastructure development and expanded industrial footprint that can be seen when comparing the 1850s GIS map (figure 2.4) and the 1867 GIS map (figure 2.6) provides evidence of the increased scale of industrial and suburban transformations in West Ham. The first detailed surveys of the built environment came in the 1860s with the Stanford's Library Maps (1862) and the first series of the Ordnance Survey (1867).[48] The increasingly crowded maps reflect the start of the industrial boom that would continue through to the end of the century.

The arrival of the railways, docks, and related heavy industry clearly contributed to the beginning of the rapid industrial growth in West Ham, but there is an ongoing debate about the other factors that contributed to this process. Many contemporary commentators, including the Outer London Inquiry Committee, pointed to West Ham's independence from new regu-

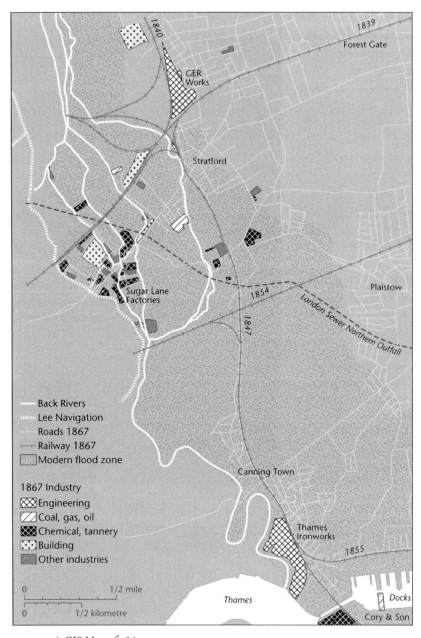

FIGURE 2.6. GIS Map of 1867.

lations against noxious trades in London to explain the remarkable growth after the 1850s.[49] This would be consistent with the growth of polluting industries beyond the boundaries of a number of American cities, including St. Louis, Chicago, and New York.[50] Marriott, on the contrary, argues that the efficient transport of coal was more important than West Ham's independence from London.[51] His perspective is supported by the presence of noxious industries on the London side of the border, which confirms lax enforcement of regulations in the eastern fringe of London.[52] The evidence suggests that both factors contributed to the industrialization of the Lower Lea. The high concentration of noxious trades, the peripheral location, and weak local government undoubtedly contributed to factory owner's choice of West Ham, as did the lower cost of coal. West Ham was also simply the next area to be developed in the surge of urban and suburban growth that flowed out of London during the nineteenth century. Its location downwind and down water from central London, adjacent to East London, and on a wetland unsuitable for a pleasant middle-class suburb, made it a logical space for industrial development.

The 1867 GIS map (see figure 2.6) recorded the early stages of modern industrial development as the chemical industry established itself along the banks of the Back Rivers north and south of High Street, including a growing cluster of factories on Sugar Lane, near Bow Bridge, and on the old calico grounds near Abbey Mill. Along with the chemical factories, the map also includes brick fields, lime kilns, and lumberyards to support the rapid expansion of the built environment in West Ham and East London. However, Powell explains that it is often difficult to distinguish between sites of industry and locations simply used to store building materials.[53] The map also reflects the dramatic collapse of calico printing, all of which left the area by the 1860s due to the declining purity of the Channelsea's water.[54] Another feature on this map is the "Modern flood zone" GIS layer, found in a recent Newham environmental report, which closely approximates the former wetlands once drained by open ditches.[55] Throughout the second half of the nineteenth century these ditches were increasingly replaced with sewers in the built-up area. This layer allows us to keep track of the industrial and residential development built within the reclaimed wetlands of the Lower Lea and Thames estuary.

The 1867 GIS map includes a significantly increased street network on the wetlands of the Lower Lea. The majority of the capillary streets serviced the growth of housing on the reclaimed marshes in the decade after the construction of the Royal Docks. Looking back to the 1850s GIS map, the polygons labeled "d" identify the areas of completed and planned residential growth found by Alfred Dickens during his public health investigation in 1855. As

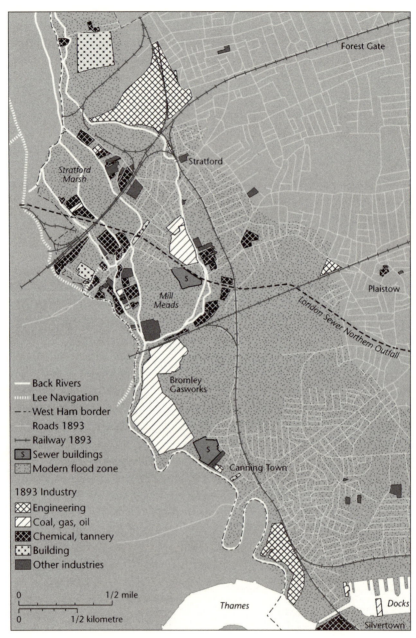

Back Rivers
Lee Navigation
West Ham border
Roads 1893
Railway 1893
Sewer buildings
Modern flood zone

1893 Industry
Engineering
Coal, gas, oil
Chemical, tannery
Building
Other industries

Forest Gate

Stratford Marsh

Stratford

Mill Meads

Plaistow

London Sewer Northern Outfall

Bromley Gasworks

Canning Town

0   1/2 mile
0   1/2 kilometre

Thames

Docks

Silvertown

FIGURE 2.7. GIS Map of 1893.

there are no full surveys of housing or of smaller streets before the 1860s, these development zones provide limited evidence of the residential footprint on the reclaimed wetland after the completion of the docks. The GIS map from 1867 shows how these zones filled in with population in the following decade, with significant growth in Plaistow, Canning Town, Stratford, and Forest Gate. The final GIS map from 1893 (figure 2.7) shows the remarkable growth in population during the last three decades of the nineteenth century, as all of these residential districts expand dramatically.

West Ham and the Lower Lea underwent the most intense period of industrialization and suburbanization during the final three decades of the nineteenth century. The population surpassed 267,000 people by 1901, making the newly independent borough London's largest suburb.[56] The 1893 GIS map, largely based on the Ordnance Survey maps that capture West Ham at the height of the industrial boom, shows a significant increase in factories along all the branches of the Lower Lea. A similar pattern developed along the Thames in the south of West Ham in Silvertown. The Silvertown factories tended to be significantly larger than most of the factories on the Lower Lea (excepting the GER rail yard and the Bromley Gasworks). These large factories, along with the expansion of the docks and the massive Beckton Gasworks east of West Ham, all help to explain the population growth. Marriott's article on industrial development focuses much of its attention on the bigger factories in Silvertown, which he places at the heart of the forgotten Industrial Revolution in the Thames estuary.[57] The Silvertown factories were larger and more valuable, but the Lower Lea factories were far more numerous. For this reason, the continued growth along the Lower Lea is of significant interest as all of these small, medium, and large factories combined to alter, sometimes drastically, the river and landscape of the Lower Lea.

Industrial development on the wetlands of the Lower Lea occurred in conjunction with suburban development on these marshes. Comparing the 1867 and 1893 GIS maps reveals the dramatic increase in residential roads on the reclaimed wetlands. The areas near High Street in western Stratford, and the large concentration of housing built on reclaimed marshlands to make Canning Town, increasingly descended into impoverished residential neighborhoods. Many of these homes were located near or among the factories. At the same time Forest Gate and New Town in the north of Stratford, which were both located on higher ground away from the rivers, emerged as the more prosperous neighborhoods in West Ham and created a clear north-south social division in the borough.[58]

The Lower Lea became a suburban river at the same time as it transformed into an industrial river. The population in the wetlands shared the river with the factories, using it to supply drinking water (via the East London Waterworks Company's pipes) and, until the early twentieth century, to carry away partially treated sewage. The unpleasant environmental conditions, created by building a suburb on former wetlands and the density of both factories and homes, resulted in degraded living conditions.[59] The environmental situation corresponded with social problems, as these homes generally attracted people who could not afford to live in more desirable circumstances. There were some positive elements in the relationship between the local population and the landscape, as former wetlands provided space for recreation, with the establishment of sports fields and allotment gardens.[60] By the century's end, hundreds of thousands of people interacted daily with the Lower Lea by working, walking, living, and playing in the reclaimed marshlands.

The 1893 GIS map (see figure 2.7) shows the continued reliance on the Lower Lea for transportation: there were very few factories constructed any distance away from the rivers. The many small islands created by the branching rivers filled with small and medium-sized factories, and the former Abbey and calico grounds became the locations for many chemical factories. The industrialist Edward Cook, in an interview with an author of a travel narrative exploring London's industrial landscapes, described the relative importance of the Lea to his East London soap factory for transportation: "'That is our highway,' he remarked, following my gaze 'that and the railway that runs into our own siding, though we find sufficient road-work to justify us in keeping fifty horses and vans in constant use.' Steam cranes hoist the material on to the wharf, and a system of rails serves to bear it to any part of the works. The tallow and fats used in soap-making, however, find their way by a steam lift to the top of the main factory, where they are started on their evolutionary journey."[61] Cook's soap factory, Cook and Company Soap Factory, was situated on the Lee Navigation canal at Bow Bridge, so Mr. Cook had the advantage of a well-maintained water "highway" to supply his factory. Most of the factories instead had to rely on the Back Rivers, and their declining quality limited industrial development on the Lower Lea. The largest addition to the map since 1867, the Bromley Gasworks, was the last major industrial site constructed along the Lower Lea rivers, and it was the first major failure.

The Imperial Gas Company's Bromley Gasworks failed in its competition with the larger Beckton Gasworks a few miles east of West Ham on the banks of the Thames. The Bromley Gasworks utilized inferior technology compared to the world-class Beckton Gasworks. To make matters worse, Beckton could unload coal directly from oceangoing vessels, whereas the Bromley location necessitated the transfer of coal to smaller river barges, increasing the cost of fuel.[62] In 1876, a few years after the construction of the Bromley Gasworks, the owners of the Beckton, Gas Light and Coke Company bought the

Bromley Gaswork's parent company, Imperial Gas Company.[63] The Bromley site remained secondary in the large network of gasworks owned by Gas Light and Coke Company because they were unable to solve the coal supply problems. After investigating the cost of a direct rail link between Beckton and Bromley and failing to find oceangoing ships that could pass up Bow Creek, the company resigned itself to filling barges at their Beckton pier, which reduced the economy of making gas at the Bromley site.[64] As a result, the map exaggerates the size of this gasworks, as the site was never fully developed, and large open spaces on the Bromley site remained in use for market gardening, growing osiers, and later allotment gardening.[65] Of course, such open spaces did not diminish the size of this industrial site; the gasometers remain a large artifact of the industrial heritage of the Lower Lea to this day.

The Bromley Gasworks example reflected a wider trend in the economic development of West Ham. The Lea's natural transportation network created an economic advantage for smaller factories, but as the scale of industrial production continued to expand in the late nineteenth century, locations with access to the Thames held a significant advantage over those on the Lea. This pattern began in the mid-nineteenth century with the growth of large factories in Silvertown and continued to the 1930s with the construction of a massive five-hundred-acre Ford factory on the Dagenham marshes.[66] The scale of industrial development and its demand for larger amounts of energy outgrew the geography of the Lower Lea and West Ham.

During the height of the industrial development, problems began to arise with the condition of the Lower Lea's Back Rivers. The 1893 GIS map (see figure 2.7) shows the incomplete transformation of the Lower Lea, despite the remarkable economic activity in the immediate vicinity during the late nineteenth century. Much of Stratford Marsh and Mill Meads remained undeveloped during the height of industrial development. The build-up of pollution and sediment in the Stratford Back Rivers and the conflicting demands on the whole of the river Lea decreased the utility of this water network as the century continued. Photographs, including figure 2.8 of Abbey Creek (on the right) and the Channelsea River (on the left), provide some indication of the poor condition of the rivers at the turn of the twentieth century. The open landscape of Mill Meads can be seen in the right of figure 2.8, directly across from the chemical factories on the banks of the Channelsea River.

A wide range of causes led to a decline in the water quality of the Lower Lea: Layton and Walthamstow dumped sewage into the Channelsea River; overflow pipes discharged into the Old Lea and Abbey Creek; garbage from dust heaps (dumps) spilled into the northern portion of the streams; and the Lea carried silt from up the valley through straight and deep canals to the streams in the Lower Lea.[67] During dry summers the waterworks companies

FIGURE 2.8. Channelsea River, south of Abbey Mills, 1900. Reprinted with permission from the Newham Local Studies Library and Archive, Newham, Greater London.

diverted the vast majority of the Lea's water and little other than sewage effluent trickled down to meet the tide in the Stratford Back Rivers. The upper reaches of the back rivers, as a result, became increasingly polluted and congested.[68] Presumably the factories also dumped waste into the rivers or onto land adjacent to the rivers. West Ham's sewers dumped partially treated effluent into Bow Creek, and this sewage probably also carried industrial waste. A local newspaper, the *West Ham Guardian*, reported in January 1899 that West Ham finally prosecuted a large Silvertown firm, Burt, Boulton & Haywood, for dumping waste into the municipal sewers. The paper suggests the borough had turned a blind eye to this practice in the past and argued for a new policy of enforcement. While Burt, Boulton & Haywood's waste would have flowed to the Silvertown treatment plant and then into the Thames, other firms likely dumped waste into the main sewer network that ended up in Bow Creek.[69] The Public Health Committee minute books also contain regular references to problems with river pollution. In 1899, for example, the committee received complaints about the polluted condition of the Channelsea, Waterworks, City Mill, and Thames Rivers.[70] Moreover, present-day environmental monitoring shows that the Waterworks River and sections of Bow Creek are among the worst rivers in Greater London, and the Lea remains one of the most polluted rivers in England—some of this toxic pollution likely traces back to the heyday of industrial development along these streams in the late nineteenth century.[71] Together this evidence suggests the Back Rivers experienced a precipitous environmental decline during the period of rapid industrial growth in the Lower Lea Valley.

The Lee Conservancy Board (LCB) and the Corporation of West Ham shared jurisdiction over the Back Rivers, but neither wanted the responsibility of upkeep, as the streams were toll free and both bodies were limited in what they could do by the millers' long-standing rights to use the flow of the tides for power.[72] From the 1880s onward the LCB's engineer, Joseph Child, began planning for the eventual canalization of the Back Rivers, and in 1892 he attempted to work with affected interests to develop a plan. The complexity of the competing groups in the Lower Lea led the engineer to drop his plans.[73] The condition of the rivers continued to deteriorate during the last years of the century as sewage in the Channelsea threatened public health and the Back Rivers became increasingly difficult to navigate.[74] In 1908, the issue came to a head once again when J. G. Morley, West Ham's engineer, approached Charles Tween, the new LCB's engineer, complaining that the rivers were in terrible shape after another decade of neglect. According to the lengthy correspondence between the two engineers all of the rivers had problems with excessive silting, causing significant delay in traffic in the Bow Back River and an almost complete reduction in flow down the Pudding Mill River, even during floods.[75] The condition of the rivers threatened the West Ham economy, as the rivers became difficult to navigate, and the congested streams increased the frequency of floods.[76] Together these factors provide a partial explanation for why large sections of marshland remained undeveloped in 1893.[77] The poor condition of the rivers, along with a range of factors identified by Marriott, including the growing scale of industry, increased use of electricity, and improved overland transportation, all combined to end the industrial boom in the Lower Lea valley in the early years of the twentieth century. As William Ritchie & Son's jute factory closed in 1904, and Thames Ironworks fell on bad times and eventually closed in 1912, West Ham transitioned from a vibrant economic center to the heart of the unemployment crisis of 1904–1905.[78] The absence of adequate environmental regulation and management contributed to this economic decline.

Despite the small scale of the Lea, its long history of human intervention along with the intensity of its suburban transformation, and the centrality of West Ham to the out-migration of industry in Greater London, make this waterway an important example of an industrial river. This detailed history of a small area that underwent large-scale modifications provides a useful comparison to those studying much larger rivers in Europe or North America. The small area allowed for the use of a detailed series of maps that track the industrial development of the Lower Lea in West Ham through the nineteenth century to explore how the river facilitated, and then limited, the growth of an industrial landscape.

The river Lea played an important role in the development of the industrial and working-class suburbs on the eastern edge of London. Humans and the river had long shared the labor of transforming this section of London's hinterland. As the metropolis grew, West Ham took on a growing importance, first as a location of intensive agriculture and later as a site of industrial and residential expansion. The abundance of tidal back rivers, along with jurisdictional independence from London's regulations, facilitated the development of the industrial economy on the marshlands of the Lower Lea. The vast majority of the factories relied on the rivers to carry cheap coal and other raw materials, so the wandering streams determined the layout of the industrial district. Like the factories, much of the residential growth took place on the former wetlands of the Lea. The steady growth of suburbs upstream from West Ham augmented the tensions between the industrial and suburban landscape and the river that flowed through it. The long history of dumping human and industrial waste into the river at the same time that the water company diverted much of the river's summer flow resulted in foul streams trickling down to the tidal Back Rivers in West Ham.

The history of industrial growth in West Ham demonstrates the importance of paying close attention to both temporal and spatial factors. Hundreds of factories transformed the alluvial wetlands of the Lower Lea into a manufacturing suburb during a particular point in the development of Greater London's industrial energy regime. The rivers provided an efficient means to supply fuel for industrial growth and gave the Lower Lea a competitive edge over other industrial zones in Greater London. By the early twentieth century the decreasing utility of the streams, the limited size of the remaining industrial sites, and the growth of electricity as an alterative to coal for powering industry combined to decrease this economic advantage and led to West Ham's slow decline in the twentieth century. As a result, the river Lea played an essential role in shaping both the rise and decline of the industrial economy in West Ham.

⌁ 3

AN URBAN INDUSTRIAL RIVER

The Multiple Uses of the Akerselva River, 1850–1900

EYVIND BAGLE

RICHLY ENDOWED WITH hydropower resources, especially in the country's western and central alpine regions, Norway based much of its economic development on electrochemical and other power-consuming industries in the twentieth century. Yet it was along the banks of a small river, partly running through the southeastern capital city of Christiania (renamed Oslo in 1925), that an initial industrialization process took place from the 1840s onward. The Akerselva (or the Aker River) is less than ten kilometers long and divided into twenty falls that cascade downward 150 meters from the river's principal outlet to the Oslo Fjord basin. Frequently reduced to a mere trickle, the river nevertheless was the power source for mechanized textile and grain mills and various other enterprises serving Christiania's urban markets. The industrialization of the Akerselva contributed significantly to a tremendous growth rate of a former provincial town of the Danish realm.

This chapter discusses the Akerselva waterpower system as a formative factor in the industrialization process, with an emphasis on the technologies prior to hydroelectricity. It will trace how the power potential was developed and outline the river's crucial role in urbanization, both causing and being affected by the establishment of industry.[1] The industrialization of the river entailed challenges to public and private uses, both contributing to and contesting the modernization of the city's waterworks infrastructure. The ensuing conflicts will be analyzed with an emphasis on the activities of industrial capitalists.

A "HUNDRED WHEELS IN MOTION"

The city of Christiania emerged in the first half of the nineteenth century as the capital of a new nation-state, although one not yet politically independent.[2] Preindustrial Christiania was, despite piecemeal expansions, recognizable as the town founded by the Danish King Christian IV in 1624. Laid out in renaissance fashion, with quadratic sections of cobbled streets and predominantly stone houses, its population was by the time of independence from Denmark in 1814 about 11,000, making it a miniature capital by Scandinavian standards.[3] The majority even lived outside the city proper, in the less expensive wooden house settlements of the Aker municipality, the boundaries of which encompassed Christiania.

Situated at the end of a fjord with access to the North Sea, Christiania's economic position in the seventeenth and eighteenth centuries rested on its role as a privileged trading town and principal port for the eastern forestry districts of Norway.[4] The staple products shipped abroad, in particular to Britain and the Netherlands, were timber and boards. For the latter, water-powered frame saws had been erected since the mid 1500s in several rivers in the southeastern parts of the country, and the Akerselva emerged as the busiest among these. The development of sawmilling entailed changes in riverine hydrology; dams increased the number of waterfalls from five to twenty. The coarse and broad iron blades of the saws produced a considerable amount of sawdust that entered the river as waste.

Sawmills were complemented by grain and a few other categories of proto-industrial mills, and the Akerselva had "more than a hundred wheels in motion" by 1804.[5] The timber exports were from the late 1600s regulated by grants of royal privilege. The trade gave rise to a rich class of entrepreneurs labeled retrospectively as the plank nobility, whose members formed a core of the administrative and economic elite of late colonial Norway. The owner of most of the upstream watershed area of the Akerselva, Baron Harald Wedel Jarlsberg (1811–1897), descended from this class of patricians.

In addition to providing power for the processing of timber, the Akerselva supplied fresh water to the city. The waterworks was established for fire protection and for convenient access for the inhabitants. This was a system built around a main wood conduit from a downstream position at Vøien (figure 3.1) down to the Akershus Fortress adjacent to the city center. Established at the time of the city's founding in the 1620s, the waterworks enabled a network of continually running hydrants on street corners and squares. Wealthy citizens paid for extensions into their yards. One of the costliest extensions occurred with the new waterworks known as the Mellomverket in the 1720s, following two serious fires and the destruction wrought by a besieging Swed-

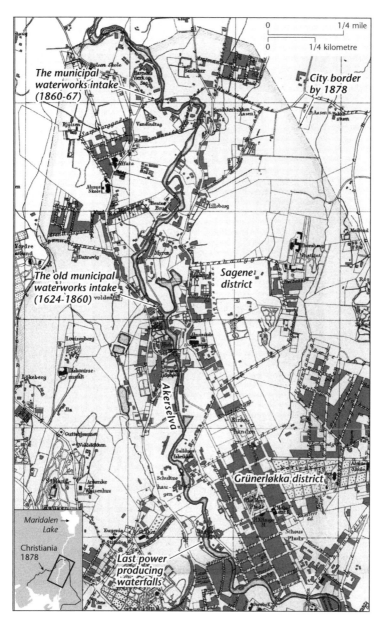

FIGURE 3.1. The Akerselva running through the Sagene and Grünerløkka districts, the river's "busiest stretch." The waterworks intake was moved upriver first in 1860 and then finally all the way up to the outlet at the Maridalen Lake in 1867. The map contrasts the haphazard settlement pattern of the Sagene dictrict with the much more planned newcomer Grünerløkka. The placement of some of the prominent industrial establishments may be discerned, such as Seildugsfabrikken (Christiania Seildugsfabrik), Hjula (Weavery), and Myren (Engineering Workshop). Excerpt adapted from a map of Christiania appended to a municipal account on the city's development in 1887, *Femtiaars-Beretning om Christiania Kommune for Aarene 1837–1886*. Map used courtesy of the Oslo City Archives.

ish army in 1716.[6] Two further extensions occurred in 1833 and again in 1847. All extensions relied on the established water intake in the Akerselva.

From the 1840s onward, a radical transformation of the Akerselva began as old sawmills gave way to mechanized textile production and new engineering industry. In 1855, there were forty-six factories along the river. Nearly half of these, nineteen to be exact, were established in the ten-year period after 1845.[7] Table 3.1 lists the ten largest enterprises, with an indication of waterpower and labor force developments in the second half of the nineteenth century.

The origins of early Norwegian industrialization may only be briefly outlined here. A rapid growth of population paved the way for new markets, both for consumption and for labor. The dominant branch within the new in-

TABLE 3.1. The largest industrial enterprises in Akerselva

| | | | Nominal head and horsepower | | | | |
| | | | 1869 | | 1922 | | Workforce |
Name	Founded	Type	Head[1]	HP	Head	HP	1909
Nydalens Compagnie Upper	1855	Spinning, weaving, dyes	14.7	154	19.1	765	1053[2]
Nydalens Compagnie Lower	1845	Spinning, weaving, dyes	5.6	118	10.5	422	—
Christiania Spigerverk	1853	Nail/rolling mill	6.3	65	15.1	305	417
Bjølsen Valsemølle[3]	1884	All-roller grain mill	5	105	16.5	659	—
Bentse Brug[4]	1835	Paper mill	5	108	5.9	236	—
Myrens Engineering Works	1854	Mechanical works	3.8	32	8,3	370	393[5]
Hjula Weavery	1855	Spinning, weaving, dyes	6.9	48	7.3	292	543
K. Graah[6]	1845	Spinning mill	13.1	112	15.8	630	348
Christiania Seildugsfabrik	1856	Sailcloth	9.4	164	9.4	376	863
Nedre Foss Mill[7]	1842	Grain mill	8.8	133	9.7	388	—

Notes: [1] Converted from Norwegian foot measure to meters.
[2] Total for Nydalens Compagnie (Upper + Lower).
[3] Figures from 1869 pertain to old grain mill.
[4] Paper mill closed down in 1899. After that various industries occupied the site. Owned by Myrens Engineering Works since late 1890s.
[5] Number includes affiliate at Fredrikstad Engineering Works. Sources come from Hans Bull, *Akerselvens Brukseierforening 1867–1917* (Kristiania, 1918), s. 82; "Utbygget vannkraft i Norge: En foreløpig oversikt utgitt av NVE 1922" (Kristiania, 1923), 8–13; *Norges Oficielle Statistik: Industristatistik* (1909), 21–22.
[6] Includes the Vaaghalsen works.
[7] Old mill site, modernized after a fire in 1842.

dustries, the textile mills, relied on rising consumption of cotton in Norway from the 1830s onward. Britain's repeal in 1842 of the Machine Acts, which prohibited the export of industrial technology, also proved crucial. Technology transfer took place as Norwegian entrepreneurs acquired "packages" of British processing machinery, which to some extent included personnel.[8]

There were considerable demographic movements from the countryside into the urban centers and especially to Christiania. Between 1815 and 1845 the population of Christiania more than doubled. Most of the arriving citizens lacked formal trade or craft skills. Women found work within the new textile industries, many ending up with a lifetime of servitude at looms and spinning machines. A confident new breed of industrial entrepreneurs employed them. Keeping a keen eye on developments in the leading economies of Europe, the new industrialists were usually of established family origins with access to capital through personal networks.[9]

The primary goal of any ambitious entrepreneur was of course to return capital on his individual enterprise. Integral to this was the recruiting, and by extension the lodging, of labor close to the factories. Thus the new factories along the Akerselva were complemented by living quarters under industrial ownership. The industrial architecture arising along the Akerselva was modeled on German and British antecedents, thanks to professionals like the German-trained engineer and architect Oluf Nicolai Roll (1818–1906).[10] An active fashioner of the new industrial environment, Roll's versatility reflected the generalized character of many technologists at the time. His many capacities included direct ownership of mills and acting as technical consultant and architect for other enterprises. He designed industrial buildings, machinery arrangements, and developed turbines and hydropower technologies.

Why did the Akerselva become the hotbed for the new industries? The simple answer is that it supplied accessible energy within the vicinity of the urban center and port of Christiania. The alternatives would have been less river-bound locations facilitated by steam power. Steam technology was not unknown to contemporary industrialists. The country's first railway was opened northbound from Christiania in 1854. However, at about the same time stationary steam power was calculated to cost about six times as much as waterpower from the Akerselva.[11] Even a burgeoning conflict between the city and industry over control of the flow, which began to develop with increased utilization already in the 1840s, could not disturb this picture. The development of the river conducted in previous generations, both by business and municipal waterworks, laid the basis for path dependency.

The new class of capitalists that Roll represented bought into parts of the river as individual riparians, under the same legal regime that existed in the preindustrial era. However, the new textile and mechanical mills incorporated capital that needed continual operation to return profits. Quickly, the whole river and its remote upper watershed commanded interest. The river's economic geography comprised roughly four separate sections, and we will take a look at these in turn, from north to south.

NORDMARKA AND THE WATERSHED

The Akerselva's main catchment area has always comprised a large forested area northwest of Oslo, since 1760 called Nordmarka. The watercourse begins its runoff at a little more than 700 meters above sea level. From the first lake of Ølja (528 meters above sea level), the water finds its way through lakes and streams down through Perhusvann (499 meters above sea level), Katnosa (464 meters above sea level), the two Sandungen lakes (391 meters above sea level), Hakloa (373 meters above sea level), and the Bjørnsjøen (337 meters above sea level), before it reaches the reservoir of Maridalen Lake (149 meters above sea level).[12] The distance from the Ølja to the Maridalen is about forty kilometers.

To contemporary Christiania citizens, Nordmarka was very remote.[13] However, the area was economically important to forestry and the timber trade. The main proprietor in the mid-nineteenth century was Baron Harald Wedel Jarlsberg, who had inherited the Nordmarka estate, along with several others, from his maternal grandfather Peder Anker (1749–1824). Peder Anker personified the plank nobility, serving as Norway's first prime minister in Stockholm. Anker developed Nordmarka with roads; he established ironworks and technologically advanced timber transport routes.

After 1815 the economic base of the plank nobility collapsed, in part due to British tariffs favoring Canadian timber.[14] Log harvesting and transportation in Nordmarka nevertheless continued under Wedel Jarlsberg, supplying construction ventures in Christiania among other things. Each spring floats of lumber passed through the rivers and lakes in Nordmarka over a six- to ten-week period from the end of May onward. The lumber was floated stage by stage, and in between several dams were closed to amass water. This reduced the downstream flow, which in turn created problems for both factories and the municipal waterworks. The problems were no less difficult when the water was released, as it often caused flooding all the way down to the fjord.

THE FIRST RIVER SECTION DOWN TO NYDALEN

The uppermost section of the Akerselva is the approximately three-kilometer stretch from the outlet at Maridalen Lake down to, and including, the Nydalen area. This section consisted of two locations with ample waterfalls. Here Wedel Jarlsberg's Brekke Sawmill processed timber from the upstream forestry described above. After that there was a peaceful stretch before the river reached the Nydalen area.

The pond at Brekke Sawmill precipitated an early literary environmental eulogy by the folklorist and forester Peder Asbjørnsen (1812–1885). He claims in "Kvernsagn" ("Mill Tale"), published in the early 1840s, that sawdust was forming a lid on the surface of the pond and had depleted the stock of trout even at this upstream location.[15] His conversational partner in the tale relates that the situation has deteriorated over the course of thirty years. Fish were an important nutritional and economic supplement to the poorer segments of the Christiania population. However it is hard to gauge how badly the urban fish markets were affected. The inner part of the city's fjord supplied a plentiful food basket of cod, flounder, eel, and herring.[16] Nevertheless, Asbjørnsen's complaint is one of several reminders that the river had suffered adverse environmental effects prior to the industrialization of the 1840s and 1850s.

The largest industrial enterprises settling in this section of the Akerselva were the Nydalens Compagnie from 1845 (figure 3.2), originally a cotton spinning factory, and the metalworking Christiania Spigerverk in the 1850s. The factories with their workers' barracks, schools, and hospitals formed conspicuous industrial communities within the larger frame of agricultural production. In fact the Nydalen stretch remained a decidedly rural section of the

FIGURE 3.2. The mills in Nydalen, painting by Johan F. Eckersberg, 1851. The painting is a pastoral portrayal of modern industry. It illustrates well the rural situation of the upriver Nydalens Compagnie, some six years after it commenced operations. Photo: Rune Aakvik/Oslo Museum.

river well into the twentieth century, industrialization notwithstanding. The area did not become city territory until the Aker municipality was annexed by Oslo in 1948.

Prior to that Christiania's expansion into Aker was executed in two main rounds, first in 1859 and then in 1878. The prospering industrial areas along the Akerselva, that is, Sagene and Nydalen, were coveted by Christiania. This was in contrast to a string of mushrooming "suburbs" in the eastern part of Aker. There the ratio of poor inhabitants (which would have constituted a municipal responsibility) to taxpayers (i.e., business, craftsmen, and industrial workers employed all year round) was much less favorable. Whereas most of the Sagene District was included in the city in the first major border adjustment of 1859, the area of Nydalen stayed outside the city even in the 1878 enlargement.[17]

Nydalens Compagnie exerted a major influence on the river. The mill developed the largest dams in the river, used the most hydropower, and for long periods became the region's largest employer. In the late 1860s the mill expanded with dye works. Textile dying contributed severely to industrial pollution of the Akerselva, made worse when dying mills shifted to synthetic processes in the 1870s and 1880s.[18]

SAGENE AND GRÜNERLØKKA

After Nydalen and a quiet part of the river, the Akerselva ran into its busiest stretch. From the northern Bjølsen falls down through the Nedre Foss lay fourteen of its twenty once power-producing falls. The district of Sagene (from the definite plural of "sag," Norwegian for "saw") was the proto-industrial center of the Christiania region. Despite its location too far north of the city to count as an "organic suburb," connection between Sagene and the city was well established by the 1850s. The sawmills and the other proto-industries (tanneries, oil mills, soap distilleries, breweries, paper mills, and more) were owned by Christiania merchants. The district was central to the larger labor market of the area. Even before becoming a part of the city in 1859, Sagene had institutions of an urban character, including several schools, a police station, and an orphanage.[19]

The industries developing in this area after 1840 were first and foremost textile mills, spearheaded by Hjula Weavery, Knud Graah's Nedre Vøien Spinderi, and Christiania Seildugsfabrik. Furthermore, some old grain mills were modernized, the still extant Bjølsen Valsemølle emerging as the major player. In addition to this, a thriving metalworking engineering industry took hold, with the workshop at Myren the most prominent. Myren produced most of the turbines installed in the Akerselva's waterfalls before 1900. In addition, some brickyards, instrument makers, and a woodworking industry flourished, constituting a diverse industrial structure that opened a variety of work opportunities.

The Myren company itself utilized waterpower from the river, and the tempo of its development illustrates the commodification of the river. Myren initially shared the flow of water with three other ventures. On the west bank a grain mill and a brickyard had the rights to 7/12 of the flow. On the opposite side another grain mill and Myren divided the remaining 5/12.[20] In 1896, Myren bought out the other shareholders, except for 1/12 that was still used in the summer season by the brickyard.[21] In much the same manner as other industries bought and expanded waterfalls as their operations required more power, the individual development of waterfalls stretched over decades.

It is along the river section running through the present-day boroughs of Sagene and Grünerløkka that mid-nineteenth-century industrialization made its most lasting contribution to Oslo's city architecture. The still extant buildings of mills like Hjula Weavery and Christiania Seildugsfabrik hovered on the riverbanks. Their exteriors were "determined by the desire that the production facilities be a manifestation of social prestige," that is, that of the rising industrial bourgeoisie.[22] Much more functional at all times were houses erected for workers, exemplified by the Nedre Vøien Spinderi three-story log houses with twelve apartments. The owners of industry entered into construction, as the mills at Sagene lay too far from town for daily commuting.[23]

The development of the Grünerløkka area, just south of Sagene, partly closed the gap. Grünerløkka was from the outset a planned environment, with broad streets and rectangular blocks. Purchased by the merchant and philanthropist Thorvald Meyer (1818–1909) in 1861, it included several squares and parks. Here a less direct link existed between factory and lodging quarters than at Sagene. Still, housing for the working classes remained a driver for development apartments filling up with families, unmarried women and men, widowers, and students. Subletting was usual, often entailing strangers residing in the family den. Heavily developed in the decades after 1870, the Grünerløkka five- to six-story apartment buildings ("barracks") were modeled on the German style, one of the reasons that Christiania came to be known in the late nineteenth century by the nickname "Little Berlin."[24]

VATERLAND

The Nedre Foss falls constituted the Akerselva's last set of waterfalls. From there on it meandered through the Fjerdingen and Vaterland Districts, a partly urbanized area before industrialization. Vaterland was in the early 1800s a prosperous suburban district with thriving small businesses, which declined in the second half of the century.[25] This area came to be the recipi-

FIGURE 3.3. The Vaterland Bridge seen from the south, photograph by Ole Tobias Olsen from 1865. See the newly erected tenements on the eastern bank (right). Residents used boats to get out on the fjord, in a gradually more polluted environment. The first public sewer in Christiania was let into the river by this bridge in 1846. Photo: Ole T. Olsen/ Oslo Museum.

ent of much of the river pollution. Nevertheless, this was the only navigable section of the river with access to the Christiania fjord. Tenants enjoyed the privilege of using boats (figure 3.3), a feature visible in pictures well into the 1960s, when most of the Vaterland stretch was enclosed in concrete.

At the estuary where the Akerselva enters the Oslo Fjord lay the Bjørvika harbor, a space that provided storage for boards and timber and teemed with tall ships. An isthmus later called Nyland ("New Land") was created by efflu- ents from sawmills over the course of the seventeenth and eighteenth centu- ries. The area was also industrialized in the 1850s, when the Nyland shipyard commenced business. A steam-powered yard from the outset, its proprietors did not participate in the manufacturers' collective activities to gain control of flow. The east- and northbound railway nexus further contributed to the milieu of steel and steam; from 1854 the Eastern Railway Station was located west of the river from Vaterland.

A CROWDING RIVER ENVIRONMENT

In the decades after the initial wave of industrialization, Christiania's growth took off: from the 1850s to the 1880s the number of citizens approximately tripled, and then it doubled to reach 227,000 by 1900.[26] The population increase in the Sagene District, the core area of river-bound industrialization, showed many of the same characteristics until the 1870s.[27] The expansion affected the Akerselva in various ways.

Factory emissions sparked questions about the river's water quality, and the 1850s registered public uneasiness about the river supplying fresh water. An 1854 chemical analysis however found no cause for alarm, conditioning its own conclusion by stating that factory effluents had not been monitored. To contemporaries, trusting their eyes and noses in the evaluation of water quality, pollution produced changes in their interaction with the river. Time-honored domestic functions, especially cooking, laundering, and bathing, were affected to an increasing degree. At Sagene, women were known to fetch cooking water in the river apparently until the 1880s.[28] No wonder then that residents in this area made the most vociferous complaints, like this one from 1861: "All day and night a lot of poisonous bleaches and dyes are released . . . making the river odorous, stale, and worthless for human uses." [29]

Neither analyses nor protest hindered further pollution of the Akerselva. Wastes from production processes increased in scale and scope, as noted previously with synthetic dying. The sheer numbers of inhabitants living in proximity to the river also had an impact. The outhouse lavatories of tenements, makeshift systems for disposal of human wastes, led to excrement emptying or seeping inexorably into the stream. The first public effort at handling sewage in the city came about in 1846, when a pipe from the Nytorvet Square was placed directly into the river at Vaterland Bridge (see figure 3.2), starting a practice of unfiltered disposal that lasted until the 1930s. Around 1900, forty-seven pipes or creeks served as open sewers with direct outlets into the river.[30]

Ominously, the crowding environment created favorable conditions for the spread of waterborne diseases.[31] Christiania was struck by six severe outbreaks of cholera from 1833 to 1866. The death toll of the 1853 outbreak was particularly steep, as close to one thousand six hundred people—about five percent of the city's population—perished from June to November. Through the 1800s the city was also frequently hit by typhoid fever, a potentially mortal gastric illness. Fighting these scourges became high priority for the city's health board. The city's medical establishment mainly ascribed to the miasmatic theory of contagion, holding that epidemics spread via foul odors and gases ("miasmas") from decaying offal, trash, and matter piled up around tenements in the poor areas. The course of the 1853 cholera epidemic puzzled physicians and authorities, as it moved into affluent sections of the city. In retrospect the water pipe of the Mellomverket has been singled out as main carrier of contamination. The direct linkage offered by open sewers spilling into wooden water pipes eluded even doctors influenced by the work of the British epidemiology pioneers John Snow and William Budd.

MODERNIZING THE WATERWORKS

After an extension of the old waterworks in 1847 that proved to be of very limited success, supplying water to the expanding city became an urgent issue for the municipality. An indicator of the increasing complexity of urban utilities, both motivations and ambitions for the new works were multifaceted. By now the technological framework of the old system was admitted by all to be inadequate.

The increasing pollution of the Akerselva ushered in discussions of its source. Some, most vocally the new waterworks director Johannes B. Klingenberg (1817–1882), maintained that the harmful effects of industrial pollution were exaggerated and that opposition to downstream water withdrawal in the river was built on "false pretences."[32] The commission for the new waterworks plan was not as optimistic. Pollution thus was a major motivator for relocating the water intake. The specter of cholera and other epidemics, though very present in the city's social life, was missing in these discussions. The budget for the new waterworks plan, which aimed at tripling the water supply to the city, was quickly approved after a disastrous downtown fire in 1858. The rescue effort made evident the shortcomings of the wood pipes, as they by no means mustered the pressure for the necessary water.

The waterworks plan signaled several innovations. First, there was the question of raising the height of the water intake to engage more pressure in the entire system. Parts of the new territory included in the 1859 enlargement were situated at higher altitudes than the existing water intake. This issue also revolved around the question of the source, since the city knew that moving the intake upriver would increase tensions with industry. Alternative water sources were dismissed as too costly or technically unfeasible. Second, there was the question of replacing the centuries-old wooden pipes with cast iron to contain and distribute the pressure better, expanding the grid with redistribution pools at several downstream positions. This technological shift had the unforeseen, but highly beneficial, long-term effect of lowering casualties from waterborne diseases. The iron pipes admitted fewer spills.

A further ambition of the new works was to start supplying water directly into houses and apartments, starting a development with great differences in standards between the rich and poor of the city. Nevertheless, this was a technological shift that set the stage for construction of higher tenement buildings in the city, like the "barracks" at Grünerkløkka mentioned above.

After two years of construction, the new waterworks started up in 1860 with the new intake placed upstream of four more power-consuming enterprises, including the Myren Engineering Workshop. The new location was at the Treschow Bridge, just below the city's north border. Extensions of the new iron-pipe grid continued, and soon it was evident that the altitude rise of about twenty meters would not suffice. Pollution continued to be a cause for concern. An old culprit was especially singled out for attention, sawdust from upstream mills, such as Wedel Jarlsberg's Brekke Sawmill, that managed to clog the new iron pipes. Despite attempts at filtering, the 1860 conduit was kept only for seven years.

The municipality then decided to move the intake all the way up to the outlet at Maridalen Lake. Furthermore the city installed a backup pipe at the Nydalen Dam.[33] The urge to move the water intake even further upstream has in hindsight been ascribed to the increasing awareness of water supply as a transmitter of cholera. The historian Tor Are Johansen has found no evidence that cholera was an issue in the 1867 move.[34] Again, moving the water intake upward was followed by fortuitous but unforeseen effects on public health.

While the move was beneficial to city health, it set off a legal battle between the Nydalens Compagnie and the municipal authorities. The company claimed the outtake entailed considerable losses. Downstream manufacturers regarded increasing withdrawals from the municipal waterworks intake in the Akerselva as a threat to the level of flow needed to run their machinery. The shift of the intake in 1867 now affected *all* the water-consuming factories and mills in the river, a fact that proved decisive in making the manufacturers formally associate in the Akerselvens Brugseierforening (Manufacturers' Association of the Akerselva, ABF). In December 1866, twenty-two proprietors met to discuss the situation. They agreed to appoint a committee to suggest measures to ensure the factories a more even, and if possible a larger, flow of water in the Akerselva than what was then attained. The preamble to the laws of the association, approved in January 1867, spelled out their aims: "The proprietors at Akerselva form an association, the purpose of which is to attend to the factories' interests in the Akerselva water supply and any item therewith connected."[35] The elected management consisted of representatives from three of the largest textile mills on the river, reflecting this industry's domination.

All the manufacturers supported the Nydalens Compagnie legal case against the city, which became the arena for the struggle for control over the water supply. The struggle went through many phases in the 1870s. From both the city's and the manufacturers' point of view the relationship to the Nordmarka estate was essential. In 1871, Wedel Jarlsberg invited the municipality to purchase all his possessions, including sawmills and more. The city showed only reluctant interest in obtaining the Nordmarka reservoirs, and nothing came of it. The ABF was also actively working on the baron. From the outset the proprietors tried to include him in their cause by offering him membership in the association. They went as far as to reassure him that he was entitled to maintain any private interest—even if this contradicted the preamble of the ABF. [36] The baron nevertheless turned down the invitation.

Parallel to these discussions, negotiations were carried out over minor dam projects in Nordmarka. In 1869, Wedel Jarlsberg allowed the discharge at Hakloa Dam to be lowered to increase the reservoir capacity of Maridalen Lake. This was the ABF's first development project in Nordmarka, and a first step on the industrialists' way to an extensive disposition of the water resources. The legal breakthrough came in 1876; Wedel Jarlsberg and the ABF closed a contract in which the baron transferred the rights of management—not ownership—of his dams in Nordmarka to the ABF. In return, the ABF paid the baron four hundred thousand kroner. The association also obliged itself to organize the lumber floats in the watercourse, which in time proved to be a costly affair. This was the price the ABF was willing to pay to put the association in a considerably more powerful position vis-à-vis the Christiania municipality.

By 1877 the city had lost the case against the Nydalens Compagnie twice, leaving an appeal to the Supreme Court as the last legal option. The city finally also applied to the central government for rights to expropriate a portion of the flow of water. This legal avenue had been available since the early 1850s, but the liberal conservative government of the city displayed considerable reluctance to wield it.[37] By Royal resolution, permit was granted in 1879 to take out 375 liters per second from the Akerselva. When the municipality had obtained this right the tables were turned, and it became more interesting for the manufacturers to seek a settlement. There was still the matter of compensation to work out.

The settlement was made in 1885, when the municipality bought the right to take out 310 liters per second from the outlet at Maridalen Lake for the sum of 1,050,000 kroner. To critics the settlement constituted theft from the public purse. The municipality was, however, largely content to let the dam at the Maridalen outlet be transferred to the ABF free of charge in exchange for the manufacturers relinquishing all claims raised in the case against the municipality. The waterworks was furthermore allowed to construct conduits according to its own specifications from Maridalen Lake to the city. The settlement was under pressure from its very inception. In the same year the agreement was signed, the city proposed to increase the outtake from 310 to 500 liters per second. The still rapid population growth bore down on the ABF. One could only expect rising demand on water as infrastructure increasingly allowed for domestic utilities such as bathtubs, water heaters, and eventually toilets.

Another technological shift influenced developments: the advent of electric power. Several manufacturers had used their waterfalls to generate electric lighting from the late 1870s, well in advance of this becoming a public utility.[38] In the early 1890s the municipal monopoly for provision of electricity was established, using first steam power aggregates. They could not, however, provide sufficient power for the operation of the electric tramways system, which expanded its reach from the mid 1890s. Hydropower options were obviously neither available nor sufficient in the Akerselva, but the city acquired the Hammeren falls upstream of Maridalen Lake. The plant was onstream in 1901.

In response to these developments the ABF proposed a plan, worked out by the association's secretary and inspector, Lorentz Eger. It stipulated a comprehensive increase of the flow to Maridalen Lake and the Akerselva by transferring parts of the neighboring Hakadalen watercourse through tunnels into the Nordmarka catchment basins. This was to be a joint project, where the city would be responsible for the required legal expropriations. The ABF budgeted three million kroner to carry out the project, initially planned to take place over a seventeen-year period. The city would gain the right to withdraw 1,235 liters per second by the new arrangement, and Eger boasted that the settlement would guarantee a water supply for eight hundred thousand people (a size that the city of Oslo has yet to reach). After a heated political debate, the city approved the plan with some adjustments in 1899. The work was then executed much faster than presupposed in the original plans.

The 1899 agreement implied the resolution of the main conflict over water supply between the city and the manufacturers. The city had obtained water supplies that were deemed to be sufficient in the long haul. The relative importance of the waterpower supplied to manufacturers was at this time also in decline. By 1902 steam accounted for 70 percent of Christiania's industrial power; hydropower made up a further 26 percent, and gas and thermal electricity just 4 percent.[39]

INDUSTRIAL CONTROL OVER FLOW?

The ABF was established with a clear aim to influence the conditions in the watercourse to the benefit of the manufacturers. Did they succeed? To what degree was the Akerselva with all its components, in particular the upstream watershed area, harnessed in the sense of making the river a part of a technological system?[40]

At the general assembly in November 1869 the management of the ABF announced that it had obtained the Baron Harald Wedel Jarlsberg's permission to lower the dams of Hakloa and Helgeren Lakes. Due to problems with fundraising, the lowering at Hakloa was the only one to be completed. The work was executed in the winter of 1870. Investigations and plans were carried out by two of the manufacturers, the proprietor of Myrens Engineering

Works, Jens Jensen (1817–1890), and the manager at Christiania Seidugsfabrik, the engineer Henry Heyerdahl (1825–1903).[41] The goal was to increase the storage capacity of Maridalen Lake.[42]

Only minor construction followed the work at Hakloa until the contract on the right of management for the dams was closed in 1876. In dry spells negotiations were carried out with the baron to facilitate discharges down to Maridalen Lake to supply the manufacturers with running water. In July 1874 the flow of water in the Akerselva was limited to the extent that "the factories are on the brink of having to close down operations all together."[43] The ABF's chairman Jørgen Meinich (1820–1911) then asked Wedel Jarlsberg to release water down to Maridalen Lake. The baron acquiesced on the condition that he be compensated for any lumber lost due to the prolonged storage in water.

The ABF sought to obtain an overview of precipitation, catchment, runoff, and temperature conditions in Nordmarka. This would permit an estimate in economic terms of the value of the stream flow. The purchase of the right of management in 1876 was based on comprehensive studies of the hydrological features of the watercourse. Hired as consultant to the manufacturers' association, the engineer Jens Vogt (1830–1892) submitted his report in November 1874. The report concluded that by further damming lakes such as Bjørnsjøen, Helgeren, and Maridalen, the manufacturers stood to increase the regular flow of water by 35 percent.[44] This estimation formed the basis for the contract of 1876.

A gain of that size was, however, long in coming. In the first years after 1876 the association had to be content to execute relatively minor projects to rationalize the consumption of water during the lumber floats. In each case permission still had to be obtained from Baron Wedel Jarlsberg. In most cases it was granted, with certain adjustments on the size of the projects.[45] Essential tasks were the clearing of races, reparations of older dams, and lowering of the dams' natural water levels.

Financial constraints limited the degree of the works the ABF could initiate. A comprehensive damming project at Bjørnsjøen, according to plans made by Jens Jensen of Myrens Engineering Works, had to be abandoned in 1882 due to lack of funds.[46] The turning point came with the settlement between city and industry in 1885. The compensation paid to the ABF put the manufacturers in a much better position to finance their projects.[47]

The main development projects were indeed started in the years after 1885, with a specifically active period until 1891. The erection of a granite dam at Bjørnsjøen and the development of the section known as the Olja-Pershus watercourse were the most conspicuous efforts. Measures were also taken to improve the coordination of the regulatory means in the watercourse. New technologies were quickly implemented: In 1881 the ABF installed a private telephone net between Hakloa, Bjørnsjøen, Skjærsjøen, the outlet at Maridalen Lake, and Christiania. In 1891 the association introduced automatic measurement of the water level in Maridalen Lake.

The main result of the different projects was a substantial increase in the Akerselva's flow. According to Hans Bull, an engineer and chronicler of the ABF, the mean flow in the river between 1850 and 1860 was 2.47 cubic meters per second. This increased to 2.95 cubic meters per second from 1872 to 1884. In 1889 normal flow of water was reported to be 3.7 cubic meters per second.[48] From 1891 the discharge of water in times of ample precipitation was increased to 5 cubic meters per second and more. The nominal increase resulting from the several projects was thus close to 70 percent. The municipal tapping was but a fraction of this flow.[49]

New investments in turbine technology accompanied the flow increase. Looking at the late nineteenth century as a whole, it is evident that after 1885 a sharp rise in power generation occurred.[50] The individual investment decisions with their bias in production conditions notwithstanding, the pattern certifies that the collective action taken up by the manufacturers' association had a direct link to each individual company's increased exploitation of waterpower.

The projects entailed that the regulation of the watercourse to a large extent was under the control of the manufacturers' association. The ABF was successful in taking over the regulation of discharge from Maridalen Lake in 1883, and after that time the water was discharged subject to weekly decisions by the management of the ABF. The regulation was carried out by setting the mass of water to be released over a specified number of hours during the week. These amounts were decided by majority rule of the three-member management. Until the passing of the first Factory Act in 1894, the maximum discharge period was 156 hours a week. After that water was no longer to be released into the river during daytime on Sundays and holidays, thus reducing the average maximum discharge span to 143 hours a week.[51]

Having largely affirmed that the ABF gained central control over flow, it must be emphasized that the control attained often resulted in controversy. The ABF's regulatory power over discharge was subject to conflicts between long-term interests in keeping the reservoirs as full as possible and more short-term and acute needs for power supply in individual factories. In periods with little rainfall and runoff the discharge periods were often limited, leaving the level of discharged water mass as regular as possible.[52]

IN THE SECOND HALF of the nineteenth century, the Akerselva was a linchpin in two vital urban technological systems in the rapidly growing capital city of Christiania. To a newly established class of industrial capitalists, the flow provided multiple services as power producer and convenient disposal site. To the municipality, the river and its watershed remained the main source of water supply and, to a less organized degree, an instrument for sewage disposal. To both industrial and municipal systems, created through path dependency from previous practices, the perceived and experienced shortage of water supply presented what the historian Thomas Hughes has labeled a "critical problem."[53] Resolution of the problems emerged through a variety of political, legal, and technological avenues. Technological resolution was only brought about when the other factors were in alignment, as was the case with the major compromise of 1899, which brought about a major increase in supply.

The systems were mutually dependant on the other functioning, regardless of this chapter's highlighting of conflicts and legal battles over water supply. The city had a stake in industrial enterprises flourishing, as shutdowns would entail unemployment and increased poor relief. The industrialists also had a stake in clean and healthy water being supplied to the population from which it recruited labor. The city was plagued by cholera epidemics in the years between 1833 and 1866, and the modernization of the waterworks—including the upstream movement of the water intake that aggravated industry—was a major contributor to reducing the impact of the epidemics. As a consequence of the contemporary understanding of contamination, these were largely unpredicted results.

Although the industrial capitalists were responsible for changes of the riverine environment, they were not omnipotent in their dealings with it. They certainly effected changes of an adverse nature, sparking protest from residents close by. Many of these same residents were nonetheless dependant for their livelihood on the industries flourishing. The protests were heard and contributed to the upward movement of the municipal water intake in two rounds, which again renewed antagonisms.

This chapter has also attempted to illuminate the multilayered relations between the industrial enterprises on the Akerselva. They rallied to support the upstream Nydalens Compagnie when it anticipated economic loss from municipal extraction. When it came to dealing with the uneven power procurement in the river itself, downstream mills had scarcely any other means than appeals and suggestions for technological relief. Throughout, the furthermost upstream riparian of them all, Baron Wedel Jarlsberg, wielded the most power over developments. His interest was the keeping of an old system of production. This remained intact well after the period under scrutiny and cost its owner less to operate as a result of the new industrialists' development of the waterpower system.

〜4

THE RIVIÈRE DES PRAIRIES

More than Montreal's Backyard?

MICHÈLE DAGENAIS

A new horizon is opening up to the east and to the west, on each side of the obstacle of Mount Royal. . . . Like two armed columns advancing, these two shoots are drawing closer and closer together to the north of the green oasis of Mount Royal and closing the circle. . . . Development is not over . . . particularly between the mountain and the Rivière des Prairies, and then in the small neighboring municipalities. Thus, Montreal can still expand considerably without leaving its island.

—Pierre Dagenais, "Le milieu physique"

THE MILITARY METAPHOR in this excerpt is an apt description of the drive to conquer territory and nature in the first half of the twentieth century. The spread of urbanization seemed inexorable, as did the progress that it heralded. Like other commentators of his era, the geographer Pierre Dagenais observed the setting from what he considered to be the front of the city, facing the St. Lawrence River. From this viewpoint, the Island of Montreal's north side appeared as merely a backyard, an appendage to industrious Montreal awaiting imminent urbanization. Yet, even as the geographer penned these lines, the "back" of the city and the Rivière des Prairies, a waterway sometimes referred to as the Back River, were in the throes of transformation. They were much more connected to Montreal, through a set of infrastructure facilities, particularly those related to water, than he seemed to assume.

Although it is only a secondary arm of the Ottawa River some thirty miles long, the Rivière des Prairies is generally considered a waterway in its own right. It rises in the Lake of Two Mountains to the west of Montreal and flows along the north shore of the island into the St. Lawrence at the northeastern tip of the island (figure 4.1). From the end of the nineteenth century, the Rivière des Prairies, particularly its central section between Cartierville and Montreal North, was pressured from many sides as the City of Montreal spilled over its borders and spread to the crest of the island. While the already

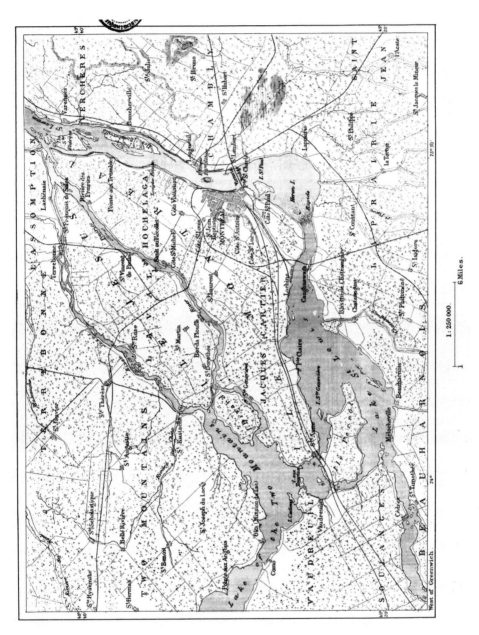

1 : 250 000.

1   6 Miles.

FIGURE 4.1. Montreal and its environs, 1900. Bibliothèque et Archives nationales du Québec.

urbanized districts on the south side disposed of their sewage by dumping it into the St. Lawrence, the new areas on the north side discharged theirs into the Rivière des Prairies, as did the small communities that developed along its shores. Contrary to the bucolic image of the Rivière des Prairies that prevailed at the time,[1] this was a watercourse on its way to being integrated into the urban space, with various uses that did not fail to provoke debate and conflict.

The construction of a hydroelectric dam in the 1920s at the Sault-au-Récollet rapids, located next to the town of the same name, represented a major turning point that accelerated the river's transformation. The plan to dam the river provoked strong fears and objections, not because of the opposition of preindustrial users of the waterway but more due to a clash between two developing sociotechnical systems.[2] While the first such system centered on the use of flow differentials to generate electricity, the second, on the contrary, rested on the essential role played by the diluting power of the rapids in the drainage plan for the north side of the Island of Montreal.

This chapter examines the genesis of these two systems, whose consequences would redefine both the river's configuration and Montrealers' relationship to the river itself. Each system initially raised the issue of access to running water and the modalities surrounding its exploitation. By escalating the river's utilization, they called into question the preexisting arrangements that had allowed relatively compatible uses of the Rivière des Prairies to coexist. The two systems led to the adoption of a new definition of the waterway and its status as a public good, which became necessary in order to effect changes to it. Up until the beginning of the twentieth century, it was the navigability of a waterway that determined its status as a public good.[3] However, this changed with the proposal to use flow to generate electricity. As elsewhere in Canada in the wake of the discovery of electricity, hydraulic power acquired the status of a natural resource. In the case of the Rivière des Prairies this dimension prevailed over other considerations and other uses from that time forward. It became the primary yardstick against which the right of use and protection of the public interest were measured.

The legitimacy and role of the Rivière des Prairies as a waste depot were already well established when the dam project appeared on the horizon.[4] What was at play, then, was no longer protecting the river's natural beauty but rather adapting the infrastructure that it had become to the new context created by the presence of the dam, with the aim of controlling the degree of contamination. At that time recreational use of the river was on the increase. In a context where the St. Lawrence next to Montreal had been largely transformed into a harbor facility, the Rivière des Prairies seemed like an oasis, all the more appreciated as its shores were easily accessible by urban transit. The dam did not appear to be a problem in this case. On the contrary, there were indications that the resulting changes in flow would be positive for aquatic recreation. It was rather the deterioration in water quality that threatened the use of the river by certain categories of citizens. These, then, were the factors that led to the river's urbanization and its new links to the expanding city.

A POPULAR RIVER

While relatively shallow (six to twenty feet deep), the Rivière des Prairies had many sets of rapids. There were four between Île de la Visitation and the Lake of Two Mountains, including the Île-de-la-Visitation and Sault-au-Récollet rapids next to Montreal, precisely where the power dam was to be erected.[5] It was in fact here that the Sulpician religious order built a dam to power saw-mills and flour mills in the eighteenth century.[6] Over the decades the site had attracted small manufacturers whose facilities and mills were bought by the Back River Company at the beginning of the twentieth century. That company went on to specialize in the production of brown paper for construction.

Since the fur trade era the river had also been used by the voyageurs to bring their hunting spoils from the backcountry into the city. During most of the nineteenth century, it was also used for log drives. The drives ended when entrepreneurs opted for the railway at the end of the century, even though it seemed more economical to transport the logs by water than by train at the time.[7]

With the creation of a railway network connecting the Island of Montreal to the north shore in the second half of the nineteenth century, some members of the Montreal elite built secondary residences on the shores of the Rivière des Prairies. As of the 1890s, when tramway and bus service were introduced on the wide avenues connecting the Rivière des Prairies to the St. Lawrence, it became possible to travel across the island daily from home to the workplace. With this development, urban nodes formed, particularly at the heads of the bridges connecting the Island of Montreal to Île Jésus. One by one, these small municipalities established water intakes in the river and dumped their sewage back into it. During the same period, the Rivière des Prairies was being increasingly used as a depot for sewage from the central districts of Montreal, on the crest of the island. In other words, by the time the hydroelectric dam projects were formulated, the river was already being heavily solicited. In the early 1920s it received wastewater from seven collector mains in Montreal and at least three on the Île Jésus side.

The initial requests sent to the Quebec Ministry of Lands and Forests asking for the right to "exploit the hydraulic force" of the Rivière des Prairies were formulated in the 1910s.[8] They proposed the construction of a dam and power station on the rapids located at the foot of Île de la Visitation. River-side municipalities got wind of these plans and rose up to voice their fear of the "disappearance of the river." They felt that the artificial rise in water level resulting from the building of a dam would inundate the Sault-au-Récollet rapids, which ensured that municipal sewage discharged at that location was carried offshore. Founded just a few years earlier, the young municipality of Montreal North even foresaw that "the entire section of the river by the territory of the old town of Sault-au-Récollet . . . and the territory of Montreal North will be drained dry or nearly dry." These riverside territories "would suffer enormously from the disappearance of the river," it continued, "which is not only useful to us, but enhances the beauty of the site." It therefore demanded the creation of facilities to "receive our sewage at the outlet and maintain some level of water in this part of the river, where the flow is to be diverted."[9]

The City of Montreal was even more strident in expressing its reservations, in keeping with its use of the river. In its brief to the minister it underscored that there were a good dozen collectors with outlets downstream from the proposed dam and two more upstream. This was the case because the city's drainage system was built on the basis of the "existing and natural conditions" and was well adapted to the topography: "The City of Montreal is forced, given the configuration of the ground, to drain the part of its territory that lies in the Rivière des Prairies basin into that river. . . . The construction of this dam will have the direct effect of destroying the City's sewers."[10] While greatly concerned about the imperilment of its network that was so well adapted to local conditions, the municipality paid little heed to the problems caused by its use of the river.[11]

Island of Montreal municipalities essentially shared the fear that the river flow would change and with it the existing arrangements for their drainage systems. On the north shore of the Rivière des Prairies, Saint-Vincent de Paul, the only municipality to assert its opinion, tried instead to profit from the situation. The mayor drew up a list of demands and implied that he would agree to the project if the citizens' rights were protected. In addition to compensation for riparian landowners whose properties would be flooded, he demanded the right to use the water stored in the reservoir upstream from the future power station. He hoped to obtain the assurance that landowners would be allowed to draw water, fish, and circulate freely on the reservoir in summer and winter. Finally, he asked to be allowed to eventually build an aqueduct to draw water from the reservoir for his population.[12] While interested in the dam projects, the provincial government was influenced by the arguments of the municipalities. For this and other reasons, it did not back the initial proposals.

THE HYDROELECTRIC DAM

THE CONCESSION OF THE RIVERBED AND HYDROPOWER

The third dam proposal, submitted by the Montreal Island Power Company, was the project that finally got the green light from the Quebec government in the early 1920s.[13] The decisive factor in the proposal's success was the company's grasp of the dam's potential repercussions on the local water regime. The plan presented by the Montreal Island Power Company was based on a number of technical reports containing much more elaborate calculations and forecasts.[14] In particular, the company used river flow data compiled by the federal government since 1871. It was thus able to present a very precise picture, not only of the "performance of the river" but also of its own ability to exploit it.

The "concession of hydropower" to the aspiring company did not mean that the power existed as such, ready to use. It still had to be produced. As the gradient of the Rivière des Prairies is gentle, the flow rate would first have to be increased. This entailed blocking the Sault-au-Récollet rapids using a dam to hold back the water and create a reservoir above the future power station. The level of the Rivière des Prairies would thus be artificially raised to a maximum agreed level of fifty-five feet above sea level. The creation of artificial flooding upstream from the dam would inundate the rapids and small islands, along with a third of Île de la Visitation. While one of the earlier proposals anticipated a flooded area extending about ten miles, meaning up to the Cheval-Blanc rapids at Île Bizard, the third proposal reduced this to a distance of four miles, up to the Bordeaux bridge (figure 4.2).[15]

This flooding was in no way dramatic, assured the engineers mandated to present the project to the Ministry of Lands and Forests. On the south shore, the Montreal side, "there will be practically no land of any value flooded." Most of the land to be flooded was on the north shore, and only "a few small residences" would be affected. They underscored that these inconveniences would be more than compensated for by the fact that the flooding of the rapids would transform this part of the river into a huge basin. Thus, from the dam to the Bordeaux bridge, the river would become a "still pool," "a safe and easily navigable stretch of water for boating and pleasure purposes during the summer months."[16]

While these explanations and forecasts satisfied ministerial officials, they failed to address the hygiene issue. Indeed, the higher water level and loss of flow velocity resulting from the erection of the dam would necessarily hinder sewer drainage and flow, and there was every indication that it would worsen it. The debate on the dam project demonstrates how "natural" it had become

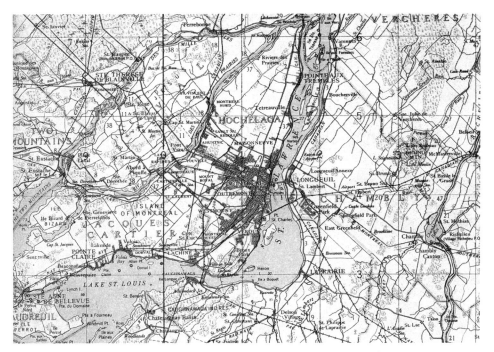

FIGURE 4.2. Map of Montreal, 1940. Canada Department of National Defence, Bibliothèque et Archives nationales du Québec.

to think of waterway functions in these terms. The provincial hygiene bureau, the Conseil supérieur d'hygiène de la province de Québec, was in fact primarily concerned with the maintenance of the sewage dilution capacity of the Rivière des Prairies and every other waterway.[17] The issue was therefore not the river itself but its function as a collector main and the sewage systems of riverine communities. The map displayed as figure 4.3, produced in 1922, clearly shows the infrastructure that the central section of the river had become. Later negotiations surrounding the building of the dam were conducted in reference to this second function of the river.

But the situation was complicated by the fact that the City of Montreal had been slow to implement the solution that had already been discussed for several years, namely the installation of an interceptor to concentrate the sewer effluent at a single site, downstream from the inhabited areas along the river at the northeast end of the island. In this context the hygiene bureau found it difficult to force neighboring municipalities to treat their sewage.[18] For the time being, as a quick solution had to be found to the impending new conditions to be caused by the presence of the dam, the authorities in question

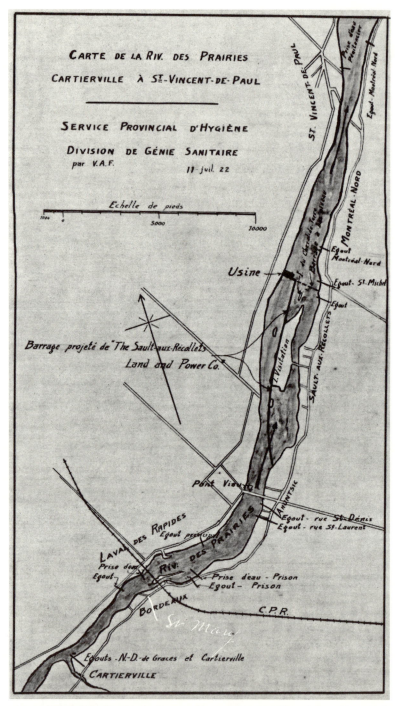

FIGURE 4.3. Map of the Rivière des Prairies between Cartierville and Saint-Vincent-de-Paul, Provincial Hygiene Service, 1922. Archives nationales du Québec, Direction du Centre d'Archives de Québec.

agreed on a drainage plan tailored to the new context. Modalities were established for the effluent, according to whether it was rainwater or sewage and was discharged upstream or downstream from the dam.[19]

"THE COMPANY IS TAKING OVER THE RIVER"[20]

Judging that the project "is of public interest and will bring considerable industrial development to the north side of Mount Royal," the government finally signed a lease with the Montreal Island Power Company in late February 1923. This lease set the conditions under which "the required sites on the Rivière des Prairies for the construction of factories, dams, and piers" would be leased and granted "the right to submerge the banks, islands, and flats as needed for such development."[21] The facilities would include a run-of-river power station on Île Jésus, as well as two dams. The first, five hundred feet long, would connect the head of Île de la Visitation to Montreal and divert water toward the main dam.[22] The second, larger dam would be built beside the station and extend seven hundred feet from the north shore to the middle of the river. It would contain a spillway equipped with thirteen gates to allow water to be released during high-water periods. It was also designed to allow fish to swim freely around either end, and a gate was to be built to allow for log floats and "the safeguarding of the public rights generally."[23] Government authorities deemed that they were respecting the principle of collective interest by including these provisions, when in fact they were granting the company usage rights that would considerably limit the river's other vocations. In this era of rapid hydropower industry growth, practices that allowed maximum utility of the river current were considered the most conducive to economic development.[24] Flow thus became a commodity from which political authorities expected to receive revenues to fill the public coffers. The contract signed to this end was an emphyteutic lease that set out the leasing conditions for the area. The lease was for a sixty-year term and provided for an annual rent of $6,000 per year, as well as a royalty payable to the government based on the quantity of horsepower produced.

The contract's existence was not reported in the newspapers until after it was signed in June 1923.[25] While the news did not cause an uproar, this approach did induce a certain malaise. The handful of letters sent to the Ministry of Lands and Forests in the ensuing years attest to the state of ignorance in which the public found itself, particularly in municipalities on Île Jésus. A resident of Pont-Viau gave a good description of the sense of disarray: "I am writing to you for information . . . on the dam. . . . We have been hearing about this project for a few years . . . without knowing the facts."[26] However, the start of construction was delayed for several years, which appears to have temporarily subdued signs of discontent.[27]

FIGURE 4.4. Hydro-power plant on the Rivière des Prairies, n.d. Hydro-Québec.

The fears reemerged when work resumed in 1928. In the interim, Montreal Island Power Company, obliged to revise its calculations, was given permission to flood a larger area than initially planned. Like on the south side of the river, the company was authorized to "submerge the banks of the North side between the same limits as in the first lease."[28] As a farmer from Pont-Viau asked: "Are you going to grant the company the right to flood our land before said company has even acquired it?"[29] When questioned, Mr. Amos, an engineer, explained that hydroelectric companies did indeed have that right at that time: "We understand that the company is in discussions with landowners to reach an agreement to buy the portions of riverside lots that might be affected. In the event that agreement cannot be reached, the company will have to resort to expropriation."[30] The Rivière des Prairies power station was commissioned in 1929 while construction was still underway, and was finally completed in January 1930 (figure 4.4).

A NEW RIVER, A NEW HABITAT

LEARNING TO LIVE WITH THE FLOODING

At the time that the power station and dam were built, the population density on the north side of the island, from Cartierville to the eastern tip, was still relatively low. The old towns and villages of Cartierville, Bordeaux, Ahun-tsic, and Sault-au-Récollet had all been annexed by Montreal in its drive to expand its territory in the 1910s. From then on, they formed the municipal district of Ahuntsic, with a population of several tens of thousands.[31] Other-wise, the independent municipalities of Saint-Michel, Montreal North, and Saint-Léonard-de-Port-Maurice, adjacent to the municipality of Rivière-des-Prairies, remained largely agricultural until the 1940s (see figure 4.2). Île Jésus, on the north shore, was also a largely agricultural territory, with a few village cores along its shores. During the depression of the 1930s, several hun-dred citizens unable to pay their municipal taxes began moving here, living in small, makeshift cabins along the river.[32]

How did the power station and dam transform the river and the life of the riverside population? The main measure of this is the legal proceedings taken by riparian residents against Montreal Island Power. Once the dam was built and the station was in operation, flooding began, and with it, legal actions. The water in the reservoir created upstream from the dam did not behave as expected, not to mention that the flooded area exceeded the limits agreed to in the contract granting the company the river's hydropower.

Complaints poured in from the moment the station was commissioned in 1930. Residents decried the damage that occurred in winter to their proper-ties in the western section of Laval-des-Rapides, a full mile from the western edge of the floodable area. This municipality saw its filtration plant damaged by March floods.[33] When questioned, Montreal Island Power Company re-torted that all the complaints being made were in relation to "properties above Bordeaux Bridge, that is to say, above the point in the river where the effect of our dam runs out."[34] This response was a clear sign that the company refused to acknowledge that the dam might be causing damage outside the area that it had been allowed to flood. A few months later, however, it reversed its posi-tion after the provincial government firmly denied any responsibility for the situation, having "neither leased any portion of the banks upstream from the bridge nor allowed the Company to push the water back to there."[35]

In the late fall of 1932, the government received new complaints, this time concerning properties located ever farther upstream, in the area of Abord-à-Plouffe: "My land is often flooded and it is undeniably due to the Montreal Island Power dam. . . . I understand that river levels are currently high af-ter the heavy rain, but I have noticed that even in the summer . . . the level of the river was much higher than previous years, before the dam was built. I ask myself what right this Company has to prevent us from fully enjoy-ing the properties that we have acquired with our own money."[36] The prob-lem reached new heights in December 1932, when particularly large ice jams formed. Newspapers reported that on December 12 the river level rose by ten feet in the space of five hours. The flooding was caused by the breakup of an "ice bridge on the Lake of Two Mountains. Once broken apart, huge blocks of ice were carried by the current into the Rivière des Prairies and finally piled up. . . . The dam soon froze solid due to intense cold, and the water trapped downstream from the Montreal Island Power Company power station did not take long to spill over the two banks."[37] The investigation held soon after by the Quebec streams commission (Commission des eaux courantes du Québec) on the situation in the Lake of Two Mountains confirmed that the ice jams on the Rivière des Prairies had been caused in particular by exceptional rains in the fall. This did not prevent the water service from assessing the damage along the Rivière des Prairies, in preparation for "legal actions [that] are to come before the courts around the beginning of February."[38] It noted that the jams had reached unsurpassed heights, and that "the thickness of the ice . . . in places where there was packing [is] extraordinary, being from 20 to 25 feet."

The water service's report noted that jams were not a new phenomenon on the Rivière des Prairies, but that they now formed upstream from the dam where previously they had tended to occur further downstream. Regardless of the cause, the issue was to find a way to prevent them. Yet the solution was anything but simple, as reported by the chief engineer for Montreal Light, Heat, and Power: "It would not be very wise . . . to lower the water level in the plant . . . because doing so would threaten to cause the jam to pack and provoke even greater flooding. . . . As for dynamiting . . . the results are completely insignificant compared to the danger involved."[39] The public apparently felt that Montreal Island Power Company should lower the water level by opening the floodgates wider when climatic conditions required.

A QUESTION OF ENVIRONMENTAL JUSTICE

Thus, each party had a different experience and understanding of the problems that arose along the Rivière des Prairies. For local populations, the floods primarily resulted in the property deterioration and loss of value. Flooding was experienced in an immediate, concrete way, through the stress and damage endured. The sense of loss also related to more intangible aspects, such as familiarity of the place and attachment to a certain way of life and its related activities. For the government, engineers, and company officers, it was another matter. As their daily lives were not affected, they found themselves in a relationship of disconnection from the local transformations. Furthermore, they had a more global vision of the river, a sort of bird's-eye view, developed from the various technical reports with which they worked and the documents produced for the legal proceedings.[40]

Consequently, the way in which the conflicts and their methods of resolution were understood also diverged. While riverine residents, when they had the financial means, could claim reparation for damages sustained on an individual level, it was also for them a question of social justice, and they demanded a political solution. Thus, property owners continued to send letters to the minister, as the letter from the secretary-treasurer of Abord-à-Plouffe demonstrates: "The Company laughs at our claims, and if we are to have justice . . . we will have to get it from the courts, which many cannot do for lack of money. . . . Our population's legitimate rights are being aggrieved . . . the Government should take charge of the matter . . . and assert its maxim of Liberalism . . . , and afford us the comfort of its strong and valuable assistance."[41] For their part, representatives of the state viewed the flooding issue primarily in terms of enjoyment of property. In their letters to the plaintiffs, they imply that the resolution of litigation in this regard fell under private law. In their eyes, flooding constituted an unintended consequence of a river exploitation system put in place for the public good and therefore did not threaten the public interest. This did not prevent the government, or rather its civil servants, from acting as a sympathetic intermediary between local residents and the Montreal Island Power Company.

As for the company, it appeared to maneuver its way through the 1930s. In some instances, it acknowledged or was forced to acknowledge that the power station's operation caused unforeseen effects and that corrective action was required. At other times, it initially appeared to want to secure its reputation and prove its technical capabilities and mastery of the situation. As Arthur Amos reported in reference to Montreal Island Power Company's chief engineer: "He disliked these murky situations and preferred that we decide immediately that if there was damage, it should be paid for; all these complaints were unlikely to create a favorable impression of the company in the eyes of the public."[42] During these years, the company nevertheless settled "a hundred or so claims from riparian landowners on the north shore of the Rivière des Prairies."[43] In return, it was given the green light to raise the water level to sixty-four feet above sea level from mid-November to mid-May, while the original contract stipulated that it should not exceed fifty-five feet.[44]

If the situation was complex in legal and political terms, it was equally complex on the environmental front, as the landscape changed and situations evolved. Each new dispute meant once again going through the process of establishing the merit of the complaints, determining the precise cause of the floods, and trying to settle the dispute. The dam's effect on the flow and water level of a changing river had to be determined as precisely as possible so as to limit amounts claimed in damages by the plaintiffs. Yet, it was not only the presence of the dam that continued to transform the river but likely also development upstream on the Rivière des Prairies, the Lake of Two Mountains, and even the Ottawa River.[45] Thus, despite work done to manage the river's current in a rational, controlled manner by integrating it into a system related to power generation, the rhythms of the river gave rise to instability. They upset plans and rendered various adjustments necessary, at least in the early decades following the commissioning of the dam.

"NO SWIMMING!": A RECREATIONAL AREA ON THE SHORES OF A POLLUTED RIVER

Once the power station started up, contamination of the river became more acute. In the 1920s, the amount of sewage discharged into the river increased, with wastewater from riparian communities on the north shore being added to the domestic waste from Montreal households. In this context, it became even more crucial to "stop the disposal of solid 'sewage' material into the still water upstream from the dam."[46] While the question continued to be framed in terms of hygiene, there were new concerns related to the recreational use of the water. All these debates indicated the extent of the changes occurring in the river, as well as in the way it was viewed and used.

Since the 1910s, petitions relating to the steady deterioration of the water in the Rivière des Prairies had been accumulating. The petitioners appropriated hygienist arguments to alert the authorities to the fact that "nauseating, pestilential odors" were emanating from the river and constituted an imminent threat to the health of local residents. Landowners, temporary residents, and tenants were among the two hundred signatories of one of the main petitions: "Some come to spend the summer and others for a bit of clean air, but they find it poisoned."[47] The situation also worried the promoters of the future Belmont amusement park, who were hesitant to acquire a desirable piece of land at the edge of the river in Cartierville after seeing that "the city sewer makes the water in the bay oily, stagnant, foul, and unsuitable for canoeing or any other use."[48] In these and many other texts, we also see signs of the desire for a pleasant environment, suitable for the vacation and recreational activities that were fast developing.

In 1928, the director of the provincial hygiene service (the Service provincial d'hygiène, which succeeded the Conseil supérieur d'hygiène) asked municipalities that dumped their sewage into the Rivière des Prairies to remedy a situation that was deemed to be increasingly acute.[49] As soon as the power station started up, an order from the public service commission (Commission des services publics) enjoined Montreal to build an interceptor "that will receive water from the various collector mains and carry it downstream from the dam [and] should provide for the drainage of a large territory, for a good number of years to come."[50] The public service commission also demanded that a treatment plant be built at the interceptor outlet. Domestic sewage

FIGURE 4.5. Regatta on the Rivière des Prairies, 1937. Conrad Poirier, Bibliothèque et Archives nationales du Québec

would be treated there before being discharged, while surface water would be carried directly to the river by storm sewers.

The order arrived smack in the middle of the Depression. The difficulties into which the municipalities were plunged relegated drainage projects for the north shore of the island to the bottom of the heap. The public service commission nevertheless tried again in 1933, reiterating the urgency of treating sewage before it was discharged into the river.[51] It mentioned how important swimming had become in the Rivière des Prairies, especially downstream from the dam, an area where "the water . . . is very dirty." "This part of the river," fretted the sanitary engineer Lafrenière, "is used more and more each year for recreational purposes, and in season, a large number of City of Montreal residents swim there."[52] The swimmers undoubtedly enjoyed the shoals that had formed at this spot after the dam was built. The upstream section was also sometimes mentioned. At Île de la Visitation, the river split into two arms, the more southerly forming a small channel sheltered from the current, likely also a good swimming spot.

The popularity of swimming on the Rivière des Prairies side as well as along the other shores of Montreal was such that the municipal bureau of hygiene (Bureau d'hygiène municipal) felt obliged to adopt a regulation controlling it as far as possible. This limited the practice to "areas for which the municipal hygiene service and the police department had issued a permit."[53] Beginning in 1937, the municipal service adopted even more restrictive provisions, prohibiting any swimming in "the waters of the St. Lawrence and especially the waters of the Rivière des Prairies that wash around the city territory [and] do not provide the assurance of cleanliness that permits swimming without any drawbacks."[54] Swimming "near the sewer outlets" was thus prohibited, as well as in areas where the current was fast, "like the Rivière des Prairies."

The river, full of "charm with its narrowings and widenings, its meanderings and rapids," also attracted vacationers: the more affluent settled in the area upstream, toward the village of Sainte-Geneviève, "in an agreeable, more private setting," while the less fortunate tended to gather on the downstream side, in "the less privileged area." According to the geographer Raoul Blanchard, the parish of Rivière-des-Prairies was "invaded by 3,000 people, 95 percent of them French, in the summer season. . . . As there are not nearly enough lodgings available, 75 new houses and 600 to 700 small cabins have been built recently."[55] All these cabins, a good number of which were makeshift, also contributed to water contamination,[56] not to mention the dance halls, restaurants, and small hotels that set up along the shores and used the water from the river.

The situation was deemed sufficiently critical to incite nearly two thousand "citizens and voters from the Ahuntsic district of the City of Montreal and the municipalities of Montreal North and Rivière-des-Prairies" to sign a petition addressed to municipal, provincial, and federal authorities in 1937. They demanded "that a radical, definitive remedy be applied to the odious, persistent public nuisance caused by the pollution of the waters of the River." It is interesting to note that the petitioners mainly blamed the City of Montreal, which had neglected to build the treatment plant as required by the provincial government.[57] A second request also raised the issue of the injustice done to the local population. It was unclear why they remained prey to an "intolerable situation," while during the same period, public works programs had resulted in "the beautification of Île Sainte-Hélène (in the St. Lawrence across from Montreal) and the construction of an artificial lake on Mount Royal."[58]

ALL THINGS CONSIDERED, the military metaphor used in the excerpt at the beginning of this chapter is not entirely misleading. In the twentieth century, urbanization on the Island of Montreal indeed advanced undeterred, and its fallout disrupted the Rivière des Prairies area, which lay in line with the central part of the city. While some sections of shore had been developed since the eighteenth century, the changes that took place two centuries later marked a major turning point. They led first to the integration of a large section of the river into Montreal's sewage system, and then, at the end of the

1920s, the building of a hydroelectric dam transformed the riverine environment to an even greater extent.

These developments upset old arrangements and disrupted the living conditions of the riverside population to varying degrees. The river and its banks, which lay outside the City of Montreal limits and were only loosely connected to its territory up until the end of the nineteenth century, seemed to be overwhelmed by advancing urbanization a few decades later. The mere presence of the dam is clear evidence of this. From 1930 on, it cut the river in two and dominated the landscape. The development of the dam to generate electricity in large measure determined all other uses. Moreover, the dam aggravated the water pollution problem in this area; it changed the river flow, thereby causing the increasingly abundant sewage being discharged to gather along the shoreline.

The dam had consequences on another level. By lessening the intensity of the rapids, it changed the flow of the Rivière des Prairies, which created new conditions that were favorable for swimming. The already popular area became even more attractive. In summer, hundreds of Montrealers flocked to enjoy it. And even though with time the river's contamination was increasingly condemned, the discourse of hygiene authorities and the warnings published in the newspapers and posted on the banks had little impact.

Riverside residents felt the fouling of their river, which deteriorated before their eyes, to be an injustice. With petition after petition, they attempted to check the transformation of their surroundings. Perhaps their loud protests also express their fear and resentment in the face of the invasion from the city, which translated not only into the effluent from Montreal sewers but also the presence of hoards of urban tourists who enjoyed the river without having to live with the daily disadvantages, as they returned to their quarters at the end of the summer.

It remains difficult to determine precisely the impact of transformations in the riverine environment over the period studied. This is all the more true because the situation can only really be reconstructed through the criticisms of the changes that occurred. It is clear that the dam caused flooding whose effects were very real, as was the growing pollution of the river from sewage disposal. Yet, even as both hygiene authorities and riparian residents voiced criticism of what had become of the Rivière des Prairies, Montrealers flocked to its shores to relax.

It is therefore clear that the process of urbanization of watercourses is not simply synonymous with the deterioration of riverine environments. It sometimes leads to perceived improvements in living conditions, as the case of the Rivière des Prairies shows. One must look beyond the discourses condemning such changes to consider the range of situations. This is all the more appropriate as the shores of the Island of Montreal underwent an even greater wave of urbanization after the Second World War. At the time, with the growing appeal of riverine environments, hundreds of suburban homes were built along the Rivière des Prairies. They contributed to the continued colonization of the shores through deforestation and the installation of retaining walls and docks, transforming the riparian environment to a still greater degree. In this way, even harnessed and imprisoned by infrastructure, the river helped reconfigure Montreal's territory.

PART II.
URBANIZATION AND THE FUNCTIONS OF RIVERS

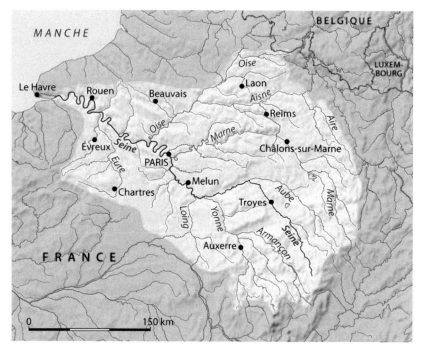

FIGURE 5.1. The Seine watershed, 78,650 square kilometers. Map by Sylvain Théry.

⌒ 5

THE SEINE AND PARISIAN METABOLISM

Growth of Capital Dependencies in the Nineteenth and Twentieth Centuries

SABINE BARLES

THE LINKS BETWEEN PARIS and the Seine are as old as the city itself, whose history can hardly be imagined without that of its river.[1] The Seine and its tributaries (figure 5.1) assured Paris's supply of commodities of (nearly) every kind and provided the energy essential to the skilled crafts, the preparation of flour, and therefore of Parisians' bread. Their metabolic role is therefore very old, and they channeled many flows of matter and energy toward the capital. On one hand, this role was mechanical: transport and energy production were driven by float, slope, and flow. Paris's role as a capital city also led early on to the urbanization of the hydrographic system, in the sense that the rivers, even far from Paris, were organized according to Parisian requirements and controlled by Parisian public officials.

From the end of the eighteenth century, the industrial and urban revolutions nevertheless led to a transformation of relations between Paris and the Seine. While the latter remained an important supply route, this role declined, initially for power and then for all but the heaviest commodities, with the arrival of rail and then roads and later the globalization of trade. But the river *gained* two capital functions in every sense of the term: as a water supply—not that it did not provide this before but very little—and, later, as a receptacle of Parisian excreta. Finally, and from the point of view of urban metabolism and support of inward flows, the river became both an inflow itself and an outlet for outflows. The urbanization of the Seine and its tributaries therefore changed in both nature and form and resulted in the creation of upstream and downstream urban dependencies.

INDUSTRIALIZATION, URBANIZATION, HYGIENISM:
THE NEW ROLE OF WATER, 1800–1890

The urbanization of the Seine and part of its basin preceded the Industrial Revolution by several centuries. The role of the river grew from the seventeenth century, with the development of rafting for fuelwood, which extended Paris' energy supply area.[2] The need for lumber rafting also gave the Parisian administration a fundamental role in the management of the hydrographic system far upstream from the capital. In the nineteenth century, however, fuelwood rafting receded to make way for navigation and rail transport, as well as alternative energy sources. Nevertheless, the Seine and its basin did not lose their Parisian functions, due to the emergence of a new need: cleaning. Water became a universal cleaning agent that guaranteed public, urban, and corporeal hygiene.[3]

This transformation was reflected in the growth in the capital's control over the resource. At the end of the eighteenth century, water distribution relied primarily on the Seine, supported by a few springs (Belleville, Pré-Saint-Gervais, Arcueil). Water carriers provided a portion of the service, and Parisians drew on wells and sometimes rainwater for the balance. Prior to the revolution, doctors, architects, and engineers fought for broader water distribution, which was finally implemented under Napoleon with the construction of the Canal de l'Ourcq (a tributary of the Marne), which served both as an aqueduct and a navigation channel (figure 5.2).[4] The decision was taken in 1802, and work began under the supervision of the civil engineer Pierre-Simon Girard; the Bassin de la Villette, Paris' first major water reservoir of the modern era, was completed in 1808. Production capacity increased twelvefold between 1807 and 1852, while unit consumption quintupled. This network was primarily used for street cleaning,[5] and it was not intended to serve individuals; it was therefore doubly public: first, because it was planned, built, and managed by the public sector, and second, because it was destined for public spaces. It was designed in contrast to the doubly private London system, which, according to French engineers, had led to a degradation of hygiene conditions in the English capital.[6] The inconvenience of the Parisian solution was that it relied on public funds to finance the infrastructure, which is why, from the 1830s, the city began to seek ways to develop private subscriptions, albeit tentatively at first.[7]

Urban growth strengthened in the Second Empire—Paris abruptly gained four hundred thousand inhabitants with the 1860 annexation of the outer communes; the demand for comfort asserted itself among the middle class; the emphasis was on the need to clean private spaces and the importance of corporeal hygiene; the incessant coming and going of domestic water and

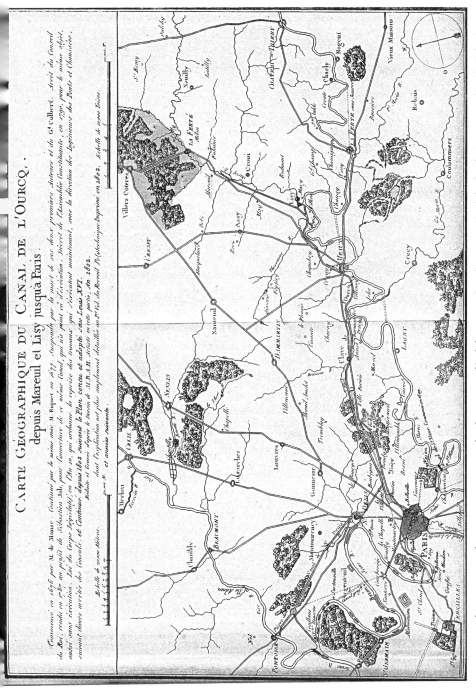

FIGURE 5.2. The Ourcq canal project, 1802. From *Plan de Paris avec détails historiques* (...) *accompagnés: 1) du plan de Saint-Denis* (...), *2) du plan ou carte générale du canal de l'Ourcq* (Paris: Debray, 1803).

bath carriers was increasingly viewed as an inconvenience; and the political context became increasingly favorable to the entrance of the private sector into services. In 1861, the Compagnie Générale des Eaux thus became responsible for the commercialization of water distribution (with Parisian technical services retaining production, distribution, and infrastructure), and domestic supply developed rapidly thereafter. On the eve of the First World War, much of the current waterworks network was in place, and urban consumption stood at 300 to 350 liters per person per day.

This was only made possible by an increase in production capacity. Eugène Belgrand, the civil engineer in charge of Paris's water distribution and sewage works, sought "pure, clear, fresh water,"[8] which led him to opt for spring water.[9] Among the many possibilities offered by the Seine basin, he identified those of the Somme-Soude, a tributary of the Marne in the Champagne Pouilleuse district, which was channeled for use through a 214-kilometer diversion.[10] However, the project met with "blind resistance [on the part of the] population of the Marne,"[11] and later gaugings were much less favorable than Belgrand would have supposed. In the end, the solution was a double one: intakes in both the Seine and Marne and the diversion of a number of nearby springs, marking a new broadening of Paris's hold over water resources. Thus, the 131-kilometer-long Dhuis aqueduct was built in 1865, the 173-kilometer Vanne aqueduct in 1875, and the 106-kilometer Avre aqueduct was built in 1893[12] while other springs were diverted early in the twentieth century—Loing and Lunain in 1900 and Voulzie in 1926.

The sewerage system was also profoundly transformed.[13] As in most European cities, urine and feces were collected in cesspools, as it was strictly forbidden to dispose of them in sewers. During the first half of the nineteenth century, when animal manure was in short supply, sewage became highly valued for its fertilizing qualities. Urban growth led to the search for new dump sites for sewage transformation, which since the eighteenth century had taken place at Montfaucon, on the doorstep of Paris. In 1818, a new dump was opened at Bondy, beside the Canal de l'Ourcq, some ten kilometers from Paris. This new dependency of the capital remained in service until 1900. Until 1848 (when Montfaucon closed), sewage was transported there by the canal in containers loaded at the La Villette sewage depot. With the proliferation of filtering *tinettes*, which separated the liquid matter from the solids, a pipeline was built along the canal to drain the liquid directly from the depot to the dump. The solid matter continued to be transported by boat.

After the 1832 cholera epidemic, the City of Paris also began building a sewer system that only collected street water—from rain and street cleaning—and was in fact composed of subnetworks, each with its own outlet into the Seine in Paris. These certainly contributed to a change in water quality, but it was limited by the absence of human excrement: one could therefore conclude that the value assigned to excrement, associated with the initial decision not to distribute water to households, delayed the urban contamination of the Seine but did not prevent its industrial contamination by the 1840s. The situation began to deteriorate in the 1860s. In 1852, hookup for gray water (household water other than water from privies) became mandatory, and, under certain conditions, liquid from cesspools could be drained into the sewer. At the same time, traffic intensified, and the Parisian cavalry grew. Despite the high value accorded to manure, its collection, along with that of street sludge (in the absence of garbage boxes), was not always efficient. With the spread of macadamized roadways, large quantities of sand were washed into the sewers from road wear. Consequently, levels of both materials in suspension and organic matter in the sewer water rose. With Belgrand having undertaken the unification of the sewage network, the effect was moved downstream from Paris, starting in Clichy, where all the sewer water was discharged as of 1858 (sheltering Paris and the rich first loop of the Seine from contamination). The sanitary conditions of adjacent communes deteriorated, while silt deposits in the river, evidence of "the pollution of the Seine,"[14] hampered navigation. At the same time, the wisdom of "all in the sewer" was questioned, and sewage reform was proposed: beginning in the 1860s, private depots for the fabricating of fertilizers of human origin multiplied, befouling Paris and its adjacent suburbs; the coming and going of the contractors who emptied the cesspools was condemned as cumbersome, unsanitary, and obsolete.

The engineers, agronomists, and hygienists based their plans on a fundamental principle: "sanitation and agricultural science lean . . . toward the same goal."[15] The pipeline to the sea thus permitted the irrigation and fertilization of the surrounding fields; the separating system comprised a fertilizer plant at the end of the network used for human excreta; the steady flow of effluent (with continued collection of solids from the cesspools) and the sewage system were not proposed in isolation but rather in association with agricultural irrigation. The Seine department capital began contemplating this solution in the 1860s. The civil engineers Adolphe Auguste Mille and Alfred Durand-Claye—ardent proponents of irrigation, as "one ton of sewage is worth 0.10 French francs, given that to manufacture it, one would need to buy 0.10 francs worth of raw material"[16]—conducted experiments in Clichy and obtained amazing results: some yields were three to six times larger than those in neighboring gardens. With land in Clichy becoming cramped, the capital entered into an agreement with the commune of Gennevilliers in 1869 to pursue its experiments, first on 6 hectares, then 127 hectares in 1875, and 450 hectares in 1880.[17] About fifty thousand cubic meters per hectare of sewer effluent was sent there each year, and according to Dr. Hippolythe Marié-

Davy, the results were compelling but controversial.[18] The only thing that remained was to implement the sewage system.[19]

There is no need to revisit the ensuing battle,[20] which ended late in the nineteenth century with the victory of sewage system proponents. The important thing is that sectarians of this process only entertained the concept because it simultaneously provided both agricultural valorization—transforming solid waste into a liquid asset—and sanitation. However, it required large surface areas for irrigation, in response to the agronomist Pierre-Paul Dehérain's injunction: "we must . . . push further into the Seine valley, which is wide enough and long enough to fully absorb the foul river that is now disgorged at Asnières."[21] The sewage farms thus stretched progressively westward, to Achères in 1889 and to Méry-Pierrelaye and Carrières-Triel in 1899, with the spreading surface area culminating at 5,300 hectares in 1905—despite considerable local opposition.[22] The results, in terms of the hoped for effect, did not disappoint. Parisian mortality steadily declined in the ninetenth century (for a number of reasons, only one of which was hygiene), and the sewage farms allowed a large proportion of the organic material discharged by Parisians to be removed from the river, while generating good agricultural yields. In 1906, barely a quarter of the total nitrogen transported in the Parisian outfalls was discharged directly into the Seine.[23] The remainder was sent to the sewage farms, where 40 percent was retained. One third of the nitrogen received drained out of the fields, but the ammonia in it was nitrified, limiting the impact of this effluent on oxygen levels in the water—oxygen depletion being one of the main effects seen at the end of the nineteenth century. More generally, the recycling rate for nitrogen from food rose from 20 percent in 1817 to 24 percent in 1869 and 40 percent in 1913 (for all types of valorization).[24]

The net results for the century would therefore appear very positive from the perspective of the City of Paris. For the price of the creation of dependencies upstream—intake and diversion of springs, intakes in the Seine and the Marne—and downstream—sewage farms[25]—the capital was able to meet the growing need for water, limit its contribution to the fouling of the Seine, and improve intra-urban sanitation.

THE CRISIS OF 1890–1920

The situation was in fact much grimmer. The annexation of the outer communes in 1860 had in some sense "erased" a large part of the suburbs: in the 1856 census, 68 percent of the population of the Department of the Seine (or 1,174,000 inhabitants) lived in the capital; by 1866, this figure stood at 85 percent (or 1,825,000 inhabitants). From then on, the proportion of Parisian residents in the department's population steadily shrank, to 79 percent in 1886,

74 percent in 1901, and 66 percent in 1921, when the population of Paris peaked at 2,906,000 inhabitants and the rest of the department accounted for 1,505,000 residents. The population of the capital then stagnated and even declined, while the suburban population continued to grow. After the First World War, this was supplemented by unprecedented spatial growth, consisting primarily of "faulty allotments"[26] with grossly inadequate viability. Jean-Pierre Lecoin has shown that urbanization occurred at a rate of 236 hectares per year between 1870 and 1906 and 1,850 hectares per year between 1920 and 1935. In 1870, 20,800 hectares were urbanized, 29,300 hectares in 1906, and 57,000 hectares in 1935.[27]

This process raised as yet unheard of problems in terms of sanitation in general and water in particular. First, the City of Paris, using the same principle that it applied to all public utilities, implemented its projects unilaterally. An initial department-wide sanitation project elaborated between 1881 and 1885 advocated the conveyance of downstream water to Achères and upstream water to Créteil, where the department had sewage farms. These plans were "rapidly abandoned . . . ; in fact, the city was content to discharge the wastewater into the Seine and the Marne,"[28] leading Dr. Adrien Gastinel to write, in 1894, that "over 600,000 inhabitants (of the suburbs) only have access to the contaminated water of the Seine and the Marne."[29] In the summer of 1900, "very loud complaints [were] made about the persistent fouling of the river."[30] In August and September 1900, 450,000 cubic meters of effluent per day were indeed discharged between Créteil and Conflans-Sainte-Honorine,[31] which was added to the effluent from the capital and completely untreated with the average flow over the year in the Parisian mains running at 730,000 cubic meters of effluent per day. The question was studied in detail by the agronomist Paul Vincey in 1905: the inventory of direct (that is, untreated) wastewater discharges showed that these were even higher in the suburbs than in Paris.[32]

The crisis was precipitated by two climatic events. The exceptional (one-hundred-year) flood of 1910, which resulted from the simultaneous overflow of the Yonne, Loing, and Grand Morin rivers on one hand and the Marne and Haute-Seine on the other, produced an estimated eighty-four million francs (F1950) in damages, with twenty-four thousand Paris homes flooded, fifty-five thousand people hospitalized, and the temporary shutdown of multiple services and navigation for three months.[33] The duration and amplitude of the event had a profound effect on public morale and quickly led to the establishment of a commission, headed by the science academician Alfred Picard, specifically for the purpose of defining prevention methods.[34]

The commission formulated certain improvements to the flow of water in Paris and downstream, which constituted relatively inexpensive, marginal measures. It also outlined weightier measures aimed at fully safeguarding the Parisian built-up area, including both the urbanized area and suburbs, from flooding. It first dismissed solutions like afforestation and turfing—too costly, unprofitable, and requiring excessively large surface areas—or injection wells, "a seductive principle" that did not stand up to "serious study,"[35] then the commission discussed three possibilities already envisaged in the nineteenth century. The construction of reservoir dams upstream from the basin could complete the thirteen existing reservoirs, used for navigation, whose storage capacity was too small: eighty million cubic meters, while two hundred more were needed. However, the commission "deemed additional studies useless and firmly rejected the system. However powerful the interests of Paris and its suburbs, those of the upstream valleys will not be sacrificed to them. To aggravate the situation of these valleys would be an act of violence that would go against justice, and against which public conscience would rise up."[36] What remained were the diversion canals, which would allow part of the flow to be diverted either to the south for the Seine, or to the north for the Marne, and the dredging of the Seine from Paris to Poses to support the "Paris a seaport" project.[37] The south canal was rejected as too expensive: the diversion of the Marne from Annet to Épinay, achieved by dredging the bed of the Seine from Suresnes to Bougival, seemed much more useful, as it would also allow steam navigation. In the end, the commission remained fairly prudent, and its findings were never acted upon.

The following year was marked by pronounced drought that revealed the limits of the Parisian system: the Seine was sluggish, and its water polluted.[38] The general council of the Department of the Seine insisted on the need for a cleanup program for the suburbs.[39] However, the war delayed any decision making, and conditions continued to deteriorate. The resource was being depleted: twenty-eight cubic meters of water per second was being drawn by the built-up area in the 1920s (not counting thermal power plants), whereas the low-water flow rate in the Seine was barely thirty-five cubic meters of water per second,[40] to the extent that the state was forced to refuse the City of Paris (which then consumed a total of fifteen cubic meters of water per second on average, two-thirds of which was drawn locally) an increase in quantities drawn; the capital could no longer ignore the problem and dismiss it as a mere "suburban issue." Furthermore, water quality was deteriorating: increased consumption meant a corresponding increase in wastewater, both urban and industrial, that the river's sluggish flow rate could not dilute, while the effluent from the power stations was causing an alarming rise in temperature.[41] In order to carry weight with the capital, the suburban communes created the Syndicat des Communes de la Banlieue de Paris pour les Eaux (SCBE) in 1922, which grouped together most of the communes in the department (sixty-eight of eighty in 1942, plus seventy-one adjacent communes; the Syndicat de la presqu'île de Genn-evilliers covered another nine Department of the Seine communess, with the three remaining communes using independent networks).[42]

The quantitative and qualitative degradation of the local resource gave rise to a number of projects, all based on a similar principle of tapping water from other watersheds, all formulated before the crisis and all reactivated by it. The first and longest lived of these was to draw a portion of the water of the Loire valley[43]—an idea that was implemented on a small scale in the seventeenth century for timber rafting needs.[44] The two others were much more ambitious (figure 5.3). In 1888, Guillaume Ritter, a Swiss civil engineer, proposed the diversion of some of the water from Lake Neuchâtel in the Swiss Jura mountains, which would supply up to 2.5 million cubic meters of water per day to the Parisian built-up area through a 36.8-kilometer trans-Jurassic tunnel and a 470-kilometer aqueduct.[45] Neuchâtel would benefit from the de-watering of the Seeland marshes and an influx of tourism—"the other Swiss regions had their glaciers; Neuchâtel would have one of the modern marvels of technical art to show tourists."[46] Swiss neutrality would guarantee supply. However, the longest-lasting project involved the diversion of some of the water from Lake Léman. One version of this concept was drafted in 1890 by Paul Duvillard, head of hydraulic works department for Creusot, who dem-onstrated the advantages of Lake Léman over Lake Neuchâtel, which "is located entirely in a foreign country, and its water flows into the Rhine, a German river,"[47] while Lake Léman is "fed to a large degree by the national water of the Savoie, which finally flow into the Rhône, on French soil."[48] This plan called for the construction of a 507-kilometer aqueduct. The Loire valley and Lake Léman projects were contemplated seriously during the in-terwar years.

In parallel, the engineer Henri Chabal took up the reservoir dam concept rejected by the flood commission of 1910, and, in 1920, he proposed an ar-rangement aimed primarily at controlling summertime shortages, based on the creation of twenty-three reservoirs classified according to three levels of decreasing urgency, the third simply being to safeguard Paris from a flood like the one in 1910.[49] These plans were challenged on the supply front by proponents of the Loire valley waterworks and on the flood control front by proponents of the Marne diversion.[50]

The sewage farms were also showing their limits. The quantities trans-ported by Parisian outflows alone—which grew alongside water consump-tion, sewer hookups (32 percent of Paris households in 1900, 68 percent in 1914, and 86 percent in 1930) and, to a lesser extent, the sealing of surfaces—became too great for the available land surface, as the legal irrigation dose was set at 40,000 cubic meters of effluent per hectare per year. By the beginning

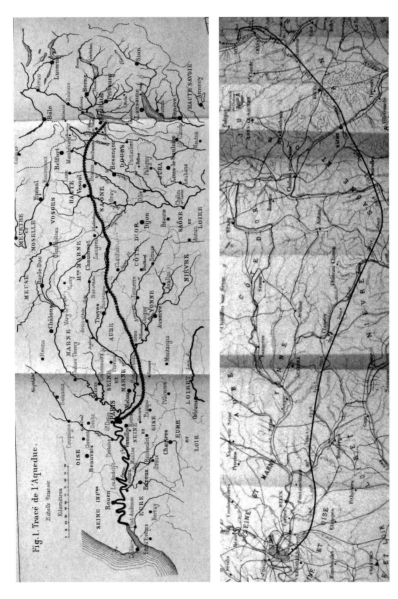

FIGURE 5.3. Projects for the diversion of water from Lake Neuchâtel (*top*) and Lake Léman (*bottom*) at the end of the nineteenth century. Top image from Guillaume Ritter, *Alimentation de la ville de Paris en eau, force et lumière électrique au moyen d'une dérivation des eaux des lacs du Jura suisse* (Paris: Chaix, 1888); bottom from Edmond Badois and Paul Duvillard, *Les eaux françaises du lac Léman à Paris et dans la banlieue* (Paris: Société d'études pour l'adduction des eaux françaises du lac Léman à Paris et dans sa banlieue, 1898).

of the twentieth century, their filtering capacity was exceeded: on the eve of the First World War, 7,500 hectares would have been needed to absorb all the sewage from Paris, and by the 1920s, it was nearly 10,000 hectares.[51] Such land surfaces became even more difficult to find as the built-up area expanded. Furthermore, sewage irrigation was being increasingly called into question internationally: the immensity of the surface areas required, the continuous nature of sewage water flow versus the seasonal demand for fertilizer and irrigation, hygiene risks associated with the crops and their cultivation, and the extent to which operating costs exceeded the proceeds from produce sales.

Parisian technical services nevertheless remained very attached to this solution, which, for them, still presented the dual advantage of valorization and protection of the Seine. The alternatives—mechanical, chemical, biological, or electrical treatment—only addressed the latter concern and generated cumbersome sewage sludge. In 1899, Georges Bechmann, the civil engineer in charge of the Paris waterworks, while acknowledging its many limitations, wrote: "When agricultural irrigation with sewage water is carried out with the meticulous care that it entails . . . , it always produces remarkable results in terms of yield. The quantity of produce is always considerable, and sometimes prodigious. The same land easily yields two harvests, the same field four or five hay crops in our climates."[52] Eight years later, Vincey once again strove to demonstrate the superiority of "sewage farming, more capable than any other means of wastewater purification of bringing about the effective cleanup of the rivers."[53] Again in 1923, the chemist Guiselin evoked "these prolific market garden fields that were once uncultivated, desolate plains a few kilometers from Paris, which sensible irrigation with sewage from the capital have rendered luxuriant and green."[54] Thus, in the 1920s, technical services decided to irrigate the dry Champagne region, devastated by trenches, to "re-stimulate agriculture on grounds ill-suited for farming, because the soil is too chalky, and thus too dry in summer due to cracking."[55] Two versions of the project were studied, both based on building a 140-kilometer-long aqueduct, one to the north of Reims, where 38,000 hectares of land lay, and the other to the south of the Marne, where 28,000 hectares could be found.[56] The sewage removal and processing problem would finally be solved, once again to the benefit of agriculture.

ANOTHER STEP TOWARD URBANIZATION, THE LATE 1920s–1970s

Despite the scale of the crisis that everyone agreed was deplorable, little action was taken until the end of the 1920s. This immobility was partly explained by the war, coordination difficulties between the City of Paris and the Department of the Seine, and the opposition of the municipalities affected by the Parisian projects. In addition, this period saw the honing of water treatment methods, most notably using ozone as of 1913 and chlorine as of 1927,[57] and the issue of the quality of the resource became less crucial as a result.

But Paris sewage never irrigated the Champagne region: in the 1930s, the technical discourse changed radically, and the agronomic virtues of sewage were dismissed. As the civil engineer Pierre Koch noted in 1935, when he was head of the Seine department's sewerage system, the respective proportions of nitrogen, phosphorus, and potassium of such water did not correspond to the needs of the soil, and the legal dose (forty thousand cubic meters per hectare per year) was but "a compromise between farming and purification interests,"[58] which at one time were thought to be the same. Competition from the new industrial fertilizers took care of the rest. Koch concluded: "Whatever means were used depending on the country, the times and the local circumstances, the community has systematically faced the same pitfalls: economic, for those interested in at least partial coverage of their costs; and technical, in terms of the quantity of sewage processed per hectare and its seasonal distribution, given the requirements of the hygienists."[59] And he added: "It is above all the insufficiency of the available surfaces, particularly in the suburbs of large cities with 'extensive' development, that has oriented efforts, since the beginning of the century, toward artificial biological facilities."[60]

Artificial biological purification was indeed aimed at "the setting to work of the same microbial agents as those that accomplish natural purification, but in such a way as to produce the maximum amount of disintegration of organic matter within the smallest possible space and in the shortest lapse of time."[61] Experiments had been conducted on bacterial beds in England as of the end of the nineteenth century and on activated sludge a bit later. In the 1930s in France, artificial biological purification became the means of treating sewage. It was adopted in the Paris built-up area, and the departmental sewerage system plan finally became a reality. In the 1910s, the responsibility for network organization and wastewater purification was transferred from the communes to the Department of the Seine; in 1928, the department sewage service became part of the Paris municipal department of public works, which allowed the project to be combined and gave Paris a dominant role. The many memoranda prepared by the Commission départementale des eaux, de l'assainissement, des ordures ménagères et des fumées (particularly in 1922, 1925, 1926, and 1928) finally led to a general sewerage system scheme presented in 1929,[62] which was approved by the general council that same year. The general sewerage system was declared a public utility in 1935, and the project was designed to meet needs up until 1970.[63]

Based on a network of main sewers laid out in fan array with the branches converging at Achères, it used the same principle as the Parisian network but on quite another scale and with the support of two wastewater plants. The

FIGURE 5.4. Wastewater plant, Achères, 1960. Base mémoire de l'assainissement, Syndicat interdépartemental d'assainissement de l'agglomération parisienne.

first had existed since 1908 in Créteil (Mont-Mesly station), where various experiments had been conducted by the Department of the Seine, which was already seeking an alternative to sewage irrigation "due to the impossibility of finding sufficient land surfaces for this purpose."[64] Of a lower capacity (20,000 cubic meters of sewage per day in 1931),[65] it was maintained on a provisional basis until the 1970s pending the completion of the 1929 scheme and connection of the communes in the southeastern suburb of Achères.[66] The second plant was much larger: Achères I, commissioned in 1942 despite "the fierce opposition campaign . . . led by local residents of the region,"[67] had a purification capacity of 200,000 cubic meters of sewage per day. Due to subsequent extensions, it long held the record as the largest wastewater plant in the world (figure 5.4) after that of Chicago. Sewage farming continued to be practiced, particularly for sewage sludge, but surface areas decreased over the years, to 4,500 hectares in 1949,[68] 4,040 hectares in 1966,[69] and 2,000 hectares in 1983.[70] Parisian technical services witnessed this decline with regret, however. In the 1950s and 1960s, they again spoke of "large yields," with "often two market garden crops a year," adding that sewage irrigation "contributes, to a considerable extent, to supplying the Parisian market and [that] it plays the role of a price regulator," drawing attention to its "particularly precious contribution" during the war.[71]

However, there was a clear discrepancy between hygiene-related intentions and actual practice. Indeed, Koch emphasized the dual need to protect both inhabitants and the natural environment when he titled the second volume of his course on sewerage of cities "The protection of natural environments and the treatment of urban effluents,"[72] and when he wrote: "as for the purification of residual waters, we need only look at the state of large or medium-sized rivers downstream, or even in their crossing of built-up areas that do not take sufficient care of them, to be persuaded of its usefulness."[73] But investment did not keep up. The period of 1930–1980 was thus marked by constantly lagging purification facilities, whose capacity fell persistently short of requirements and was often under-utilized.[74] The department communes (aside from Paris) were affected by a similar lag: in 1955, nearly half had rates of under 50 percent for building hookups to the sewer network.[75] Having lost all its economic and agricultural value, human excrement was no longer of sufficient importance to justify a proactive policy.

At the same time, a solution to the problem of the summer shortages of water in the Seine was adopted. The reservoir dam projects were reactivated by the 1924 flood, which caused damages estimated at twenty-one billion francs (F1950),[76] and in 1925 there was an appointment of a new commission headed by inspector Dusuzeau, who abandoned the Marne diversion project as too costly and approved the reservoir principle: "These basins, destined to collect winter water to be released in summer, had, consequently, a dual goal: to combat flooding and improve low-water flow, in addition to generating hydro power."[77] Every possible virtue was attributed to them: in addition to their advantages in times of flooding or low water levels, they provided a quantitative solution to a problem that was both quantitative (flow and excessively high or low water levels) and qualitative (dilution of pollution), their cost was reasonable, and they improved navigation, increased agricultural yields, generated power, and developed regional tourism (an argument put forward to facilitate local acceptance).[78]

A new project, adapted from the Chabal project, was adopted by the Ministry of Public Works in 1926 after being presented to the general council of the Department of the Seine.[79] In 1928, the reservoir dam section of the port of Paris technical services department was created for the Department of the Seine.[80] The building of the most urgent dams was approved, and the first three dams were built: Crescent and Chaumençon in the Morvan region and Champaubert-aux-Bois in the Marne. The fourth dam, Pannesière-Chaumard (renamed Pannecière), was declared of public interest in 1929, but construction only started in 1938 due to difficult negotiations with local residents and landowners (seventy-four houses flooded, and 540 hectares had to be purchased),[81] and it was completed in 1950 after a long interruption due to the war. These projects were supervised by technical services of the Department of the Seine, cofinanced by the department and the state.

These four dams allowed for an average supply of twelve cubic meters of water per second throughout the four low-water months. While "it considerably improves the flow of the Seine . . . , this one cubic meter per day inflow is still insufficient to ensure proper dilution of the water whose sources of pollution multiply as the population grows and industry develops,"[82] the Economic Council noted in 1955, adding that reservoir capacity remained insufficient in terms of safeguarding against flooding and did not restore to the Seine "the river status that it loses during the summer months, when it is transformed into a sewer main, which is a great pity for nearby residents and . . . the fish."[83] They in fact only stored 120 to 140 million cubic meters of water (table 5.1), while the Chabal project had provided for ten times more. After new flooding in 1944, 1945, and 1955 (the last followed by severe summer drought), the issue was revived, with the overall goal of raising the storage capacity to a billion cubic meters of water using a second generation of works much larger than the earlier ones (see table 5.1). For Parisian technical services, the main goal was still to "strengthen the river's low-water flow rate," with the battle against flooding being a "secondary goal."[84]

Four sites were studied on the Aube, the Marne, the Seine, and the Serein (a tributary of the Yonne in the Morvan region). The last, which Parisian technical services began to plan in 1945, provoked "very loud protests" throughout the Department of the Yonne, causing an "outcry,"[85] and the creation of the Comité de défense de la basse vallée du Serein, so much so that the studies were put on hold. The Marne reservoir was approved by the general council of the Department of the Seine in 1951 with a project that entailed the submersion of three villages, which did not prevent the Ministry of Public Works from retaining it in principle in 1953 but did lead to "strong agitation"[86] in the Department of the Marne and a comparative study of sev-

TABLE 5.1. Reservoir Dams Built in the Seine Basin, 1931–1989.

FIRST GENERATION: LOW-WATER SUPPORT				
Name	River	Capacity ($10^6 m^3$)	Surface area (ha)	Year commissioned
Crescent	La Cure	15	115	1931
Chaumençon	La Chaleux	20	145	1934
Champaubert-aux-Bois (part of Der-Chantecoq)	La Croye and La Blaise	23	558	1938
Pannecière	Yonne	82	520	1950
SECOND GENERATION: LOW-WATER SUPPORT AND FLOOD PROTECTION				
Name	River	Capacity ($10^6 m^3$)	Surface area (ha)	Year commissioned
Orient	Seine	205	2,400	1966
Der-Chantecoq	Marne and Blaise	350	4,800	1974
Amance and Temple	Aube	170	2,500	1989

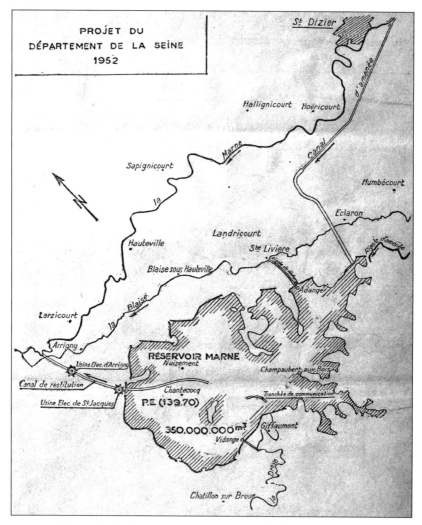

FIGURE 5.5. Project for the Marne reservoir, 1952. From "Problème de la prévention des inondations dans le bassin de la Seine," *Journal officiel de la République française: Avis et rapports du Conseil économique* 1 (1956): 26.

eral alternatives. The Seine reservoir (upstream from Troyes) was approved by the general council of the Department of the Seine in 1954 and declared a public utility in 1959.[87] Renamed Lac Orient, it was the first reservoir to be built, perhaps because it was the least contested given the small number of buildings to be expropriated and families to be resettled—some transactions nevertheless dragged on for some time.[88] The Marne reservoir (figure 5.5), re-named Der-Chantecoq, which absorbed Lac Champaubert-aux-Bois, posed many more challenges and attracted the attention of the Economic Council in 1955, which studied the matter and concluded that while it was "impossible to eliminate the social consequences of creating this reservoir," it was essential to "reduce the painful consequences for the public as much as possible," and proposed the resettlement of farming operations through acquisition or through their creation or relocation "in available farmland in various regions of France, particularly the Southwest."[89] In any event, by the end of the 1970s, the average potential summer inflow was sixty-five cubic meters of water per second over a four-month period.[90]

From the 1930s to the 1970s, the Seine thus experienced its worst moments in terms of the deterioration of water quality due to inadequate treatment facilities and growing water intake, which was never questioned. On the contrary, "the very large volume of water that should be available in a few years will help dilute the sewage to a greater extent and will only require rough purification, which will simplify the issue and considerably reduce the cost."[91] The first reservoir dams likely contributed to a very slight improvement in the situation, sufficient to render water treatment possible but not to preserve the receiving environment, of which there was, incidentally, virtually no mention in the regulations.[92] At the end of the 1960s, in the summer, the Seine was anoxic from Clichy to Andrésy—a stretch of some fifty kilometers—and showed oxygen levels of below two milligrams per liter over the next hundred kilometers.[93] This was despite the five reservoir dams in service at the time, a figure that can be compared to the French water classification in use at that time, considering that under three milligrams per liter, the water quality was mediocre, and that under one milligram per liter, water was unfit for any usage (medium quality needs an oxygen content of three to five milligrams per liter, good quality five to seven milligrams per liter, and top quality more than seven milligrams per liter).

THE SEINE, AN URBAN RIVER

The case of Paris is certainly not unique, but the situation there was likely exacerbated. While the Seine and its tributaries can be characterized as urban rivers and, at least from the sixteenth century on, even as Parisian rivers, it must be said that the urbanization process changed considerably with the Industrial Revolution, the hygiene revolution, and two centuries of urban growth. The basin was in fact put under a heavy strain to supply the Parisian built-up area with water, as well as to absorb the stream of pollutants and other waste matter from the city. This pressure on the resource, matched by pressure on the environment, resulted in profound changes, not only to the aquatic landscape, from the creation of infrastructure (aqueducts, canals) or isolated features (sewage farms, reservoir dams, wastewater plants) sometimes located at great distances from the capital—up to three hundred kilometers along the riverbed in the case of the reservoir dams—but also the ecosystems—anthropogenic creation in the case of the lakes, anthropization in the case of the rivers, and even complete deterioration in summertime. The City of Paris and the Parisian built-up area thus externalized part of their metabolism by creating remote urban dependencies: spaces whose only reason for being was the city and the policies to which it was subject.

What is more, these dependencies were entirely programmed by and under the control of City of Paris and Department of the Seine institutions, even when outside their jurisdiction—to the point that when the Economic Council requested the Ministry of Agriculture's opinion on the reservoir project in 1955, it responded that it was totally uninformed as to the intentions of the Department of the Seine.[94] There may have been land acquisitions or property transfers in some cases but not always; in any event, the springs were managed by the City of Paris and the reservoir dams by the Department of the Seine.[95] Although people living near the planned facilities and even the inhabitants of the sites in question fought back against Paris's power, they had little say in the matter until the 1970s and had to resign themselves to either living with the facilities or moving away.

These spaces also reflected the evolution of agricultural concerns, as the other revolution, the fertilizer revolution, robbed sewage of its value. The consequences of its devaluation were dramatic for the river;[96] and the need for a potable water supply motivated a policy of protecting the resource—and thus the citizens—but not the environment. The solutions contemplated reflect, however, the preponderant role of public engineers in the Parisian and Sequanese administration and their reticular and hydraulic view of environmental and urban issues. The increase in water consumption was never questioned, even at the height of the crisis: the solution was to go and find water elsewhere. Faced with a quality issue—the damage caused to the resource by urban and industrial waste—the engineers responded with a quantitative solution: support for the low-water level. The characteristic faith in self-purification of the first half of the twentieth century did the rest: dilution was sufficient to render the pollution inoffensive.

6

THE CHANNELIZATION OF THE DANUBE AND URBAN SPATIAL DEVELOPMENT IN VIENNA IN THE NINETEENTH AND EARLY TWENTIETH CENTURIES

GERTRUD HAIDVOGL

THIS CHAPTER DISCUSSES the changing relation between the city of Vienna and the Danube River during the nineteenth century and the beginning of the twentieth century.[1] It focuses in particular on the Danube floodplains and their altered role during the processes of urban growth and industrialization. In 1875, the long-debated Danube channelization was accomplished. The river engineering measures had three main aims: to improve the Danube as a navigation route, build stable bridges, and improve flood protection for the expanding city and suburbs. Vienna was an important European center, since 1558 the capital of the Holy Roman Empire, and later of the Austrian and the Austrian-Hungarian monarchy, with industrial and commercial roles in addition to its administrative functions. Its industrialization, as in other European cities, also produced considerable population growth. As a result, the provision of land resources for industrial, commercial, and residential buildings was a basic challenge for the municipal authorities that in the second half of the nineteenth century targeted the vast Danube floodplains for urban development. In contrast to other river sections, the floodplains were used only extensively in the preindustrial town; they became increasingly integrated with the city from the middle of the nineteenth century onward, particularly after river channelization.

This chapter explores how, from the middle of the nineteenth century, the transformation of the river for transportation and flood protection measures was connected to the spatial development of the city. It will discuss why the Danube floodplains became an important land resource in the course of industrialization, and then it will present different channelization and urban planning projects as well as their connection to urban and riverine changes. Finally, this chapter highlights how the Danube structured the spatial organization of the city after the channelization. What becomes clear is that the development of the floodplains occurred progressively over time but depended upon the deliberate channelization of the river and the planning of the urban government to be fully integrated into the urban environment.

RIVERINE CHARACTERISTICS OF THE AUSTRIAN DANUBE AND THEIR CONSEQUENCES ON SETTLEMENT

The Danube is the second largest river in Europe after the Volga in terms of length and discharge. On its 2,850-kilometer long course from the Schwarzwald (Black Forest) in southern Germany to the Black Sea it crosses ten different countries.

The Austrian Danube belongs to the upper river section. It is characterized by a strong alpine influence resulting in a high sediment load that enters through tributaries and the main stem. Two main morphological types can be distinguished: in basin sections the river and its floodplains covered vast areas before channelization; in breakthrough sections geological formations limited the lateral movement of the river. In the broad basins sediments were disposed on the river banks and in shallow zones of the riverbed that led to the typical patterns of a braided river system with a main arm, several side arms, and floodplain water bodies connected to the main channel during higher discharges (figure 6.1).[2] These different habitats were highly variable and intertwined. Floods initiated regular dislocations of river arms. Aquatic and terrestrial parts shifted regularly in both space and time: water was transformed into land due to sedimentation processes and land into water as a result of erosion during floods.

In Vienna the Danube crosses the tectonic basin between the foothills of the Eastern Alps in the west and the Carpathian Mountains in the east (creating the Viennese basin). At this point, the river and its adjacent floodplains formed a vast fluvial landscape of several kilometers in width. The preindustrial town was situated on the southern bank outside of the immediate floodplains. The systematic channelization of the Danube in the nineteenth century limited the river width to approximately three hundred meters. It also disconnected most of the floodplains from the river, initiating fundamental hydromorphological and ecological changes. The mean annual discharge amounts today to 1,890 cubic meters per second. Based on hydrological models and analysis of historical records, the one-thousand-year flood discharge is assumed to be 14,000 cubic meters per second.[3] Until the channelization, hydrological and morphological dynamics created an unstable environment that posed particular challenges for the settlement of the floodplains. Seasonal

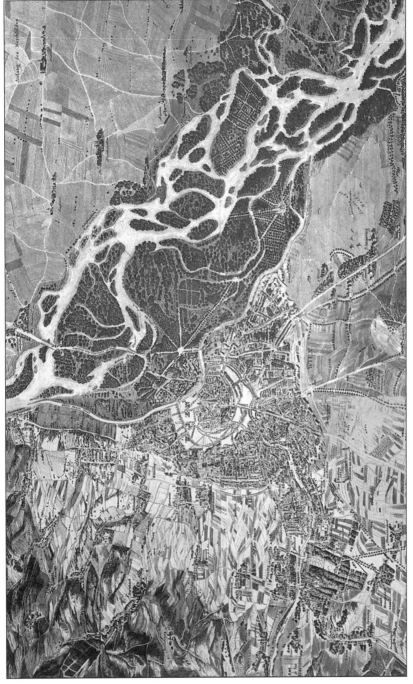

FIGURE 6.1. The braided Viennese Danube system in a map from the 1830s. From Schweickhardt v. Sickingen, *Perspectiv-Karte des Erzherzogtums Österreich unter der Enns 1830–1846.*

floods were often disastrous events for people living along the river. While in the nineteenth century warning systems for river-wide floods enabled riparian settlers to prepare at least for a short period before the flood arrived, wintertime ice jams appeared mostly with little warning,[4] as in 1830 when an ice jam caused one of the most catastrophic floods in Vienna.

Despite the risk of erosion and floods, the city of Vienna and many neighboring municipalities were built on the river, most of them during the High and late Middle Ages. Their exposure to floods and the fluvial dynamic differed depending on their location and elevation. When the old city center was reestablished in the early Middle Ages on a pleistocene terrace at the place of a former Roman fortress it was saved from floods and erosion. However, recent analyses of sediment cores confirm that a Danube flood partly destroyed the Roman settlement.[5] The survival of the medieval city center appears to have occurred because the river's main arm gradually moved northeast.[6] The former main arm, the "Viennese arm," which is nowadays called the Danube channel, shrunk continuously to a small side arm of the river system (figure 6.2). While the security from floods and erosion due to the increasing distance from the river had positive effects, there were economic costs. Vienna lost the direct connection to the main channel of the Danube. Engineering efforts such as dredging of disposed fine sediments and stabilization of the riverbed at the inlet were necessary to enable ships to enter their landing place close to the city center.

The Danube was for Vienna the most important trading route for bulky goods such as wood or stones as construction material. Also, food came at least partly to the city via the river. Apart from its role in urban transportation, the Danube also offered fisheries and drove mills in the emerging urban center. Maps show the large and increasing number of these facilities up to the late nineteenth century. Their locations moved several times due to changes of the riverbed. The community of Kaisermühlen (meaning "emperor mills") was established around such ship mills in 1674. Later fishermen and rafters settled at the same site.[7] The Danube and its floodplain water bodies were also an important source for local fish that were sold at the Viennese fish markets. Nevertheless, already in the sixteenth century fish were delivered from other rivers or fish farms from Bohemia, Moravia, or Hungary either due to limited availability in and around the Viennese Danube (e.g., beluga sturgeon or carp) or due to demand for marine fish (e.g., stockfish or herring).[8] Whenever possible the imported fish were transported on the Danube. However, the important fish farms in Bohemia were not connected via a river or artificial channel, and fish had thus to be transported on roads. All of these economic functions of the river still existed in the nineteenth century, but navigation was the most prominent one for the city as well as for the imperial administration due

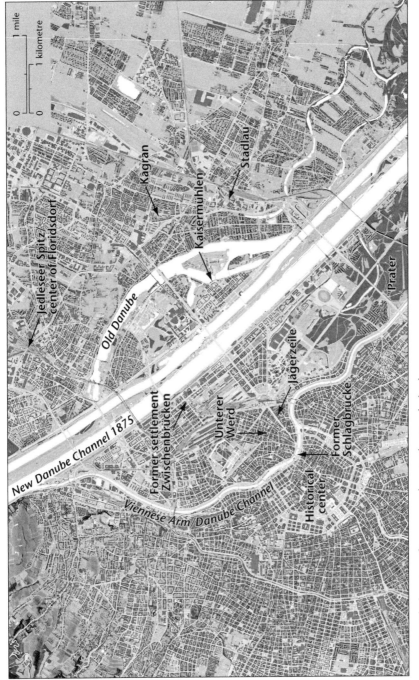

FIGURE 6.2. The location of important places in the Danube landscape.

Jedleseer Spitz
center of Floridsdorf

Kagran

Kaisermühlen

Stadlau

Old Danube

Prater

New Danube Channel 1875

Former settlement
Zwischenbrücken

Jägerzeile

Unterer
Werd

Former
Schlagbrücke

Historical
center

Viennese Arm / Danube Channel

1 mile

1 kilometre

0
0

to the supraregional scale of the Danube. This is clearly reflected in publications of governmental and administrative institutions such as the Ministry of Commerce, the Imperial Construction Council (Hofbaurat) or the Imperial Navigation Council (Navigationsdirektion).[9]

Floods regularly affected land between the various Danube arms and along the north bank of the river. Before the late eighteenth century no large infrastructure stabilized the riverbanks, and small local measures were subject to the local municipal authorities and land owners and tenants who did not spend the necessary financial resources for larger measures.[10] The riverine dynamics clearly constrained Vienna's spatial development throughout the Middle Ages and early modern times. A comparison of historical maps demonstrates that the expansion of the city occurred in this period, with one exception, in suburban areas located around the north, west, and south of the city center at a safe distance from the river (figure 6.3). Indeed, communities along the north bank, which are now contained within the city proper, benefited from the proximity to the urban food market, although they did not experience urban economic growth and remained rural even into the twentieth century.

There was one exception to the general avoidance of the Danube floodplains for permanent settlement. This was the area of Leopoldstadt or—to be more precise—the historical center of this Viennese district called the Unterer Werd. It was situated on the large island next to the city center. Detailed historical records for the earliest periods of settlement are missing, but fishermen and raftsmen settled here around 1300 and built small wooden houses.[11] By about 1450, approximately one hundred buildings had been erected.[12] A bridge (Schlagbrücke) connecting the Untere Werd and the city is mentioned in a ducal decree for butchers from 1364.[13] Until 1782 this was the only bridge crossing the Viennese arm, and it was an anchor for the later development of Leopoldstadt.[14] Street and place names suggest many riverine activities of the settlers. They refer for example to the landing places for ships and rafts and to the storage yards for wood rafted on the Danube. During the sixteenth century imperial hunters founded a second village close to the Untere Werd, the Jägerzeile. It was situated in the vicinity of a large imperial hunting ground (Prater). The Jewish ghetto was established in the eastern part of the Untere Werd in 1624. In the early eighteenth century the village, and in particular the surrounding floodplains, became a favorite place for aristocratic parks and small summer houses of wealthy Viennese citizens. In the 1780s about 250 such private gardens existed.[15] The largest was the Augarten (which means "floodplain garden"), established at the beginning of the seventeenth century. This park still exists but most of the others disappeared by the late eighteenth

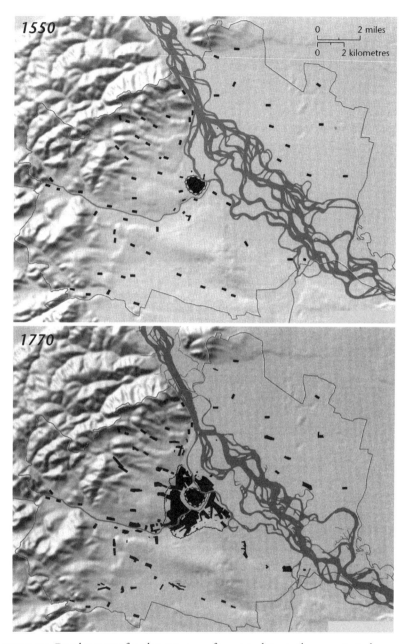

FIGURE 6.3. Development of settlement areas of municipalities in the present city borders, 1550 (*top*) and 1770 (*bottom*). Adapted from from Peter Eigner and Petra Schneider, "Verdichtung und Expansion: Das Wachstum von Wien" in *Umwelt Stadt: Geschichte des Natur- und Lebensraumes Wien,* ed. Karl Brunner and Petra Schneider (Wien, Köln, Weimar: Böhlau, 2005), 22–53.

century, as they were crowded out by an increasing number of residential and especially commercial buildings. The large Danube island next to the Viennese arm also attracted in the eighteenth century ordinary Viennese citizens for leisure activities and enjoyment. Emperor Joseph II (1741–1790; emperor 1765–1790) opened the Prater in 1766 for the public and the Augarten in 1775. Nevertheless it has to be concluded that apart from the few developed areas established for particular reasons most of the island was covered by floodplain forests until the end of the eighteenth century. The situation was similar for all the other Viennese Danube floodplains. Even agricultural uses were limited to very small areas. This is in contrast to the floodplains in other Danube sections that riparian communities integrated into their agricultural systems.[16]

During the nineteenth century industrialization altered the role of the Danube and its floodplains fundamentally, which particularly affected Vienna because the river was the main transportation route for the urban supply of food and economic goods. As a result of industrialization a considerable expansion of developed area can be observed. With the steam revolution, the river's role as a navigation route intensified, and with it calls for channelization. Steam boats—operating on the Danube since the 1830s—were more sensitive to damage in shallow river reaches. In addition ships grew in size requiring a higher draft and flat bends. Railroad expansion also impacted the river. After 1837 the first railway route established in Vienna, the Nordbahn (northern railway), connected the city to coal mines in Moravia. The main railway station was located on the Danube island in the district of Leopold-

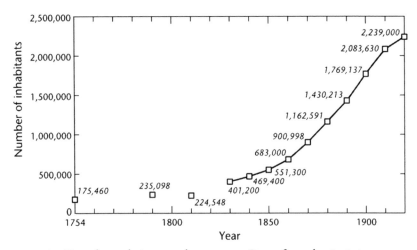

FIGURE 6.4. Vienna's population growth, 1754–1920. Data refer to the city in its present boundaries. For the period between 1754 and 1830 only irregular population data were available. Data are therefore shown as points only.

stadt. In the 1860s plans for a railway line to the northwest also sited the main station on the Danube island, in the vicinity of the northern railway line. Both rail lines depended on stable bridges, as free from flood threats as possible, adding an additional transportation factor to flood control planning.

While the river's position in the emerging transportation system called for fundamental interventions, urban growth made its most profound mark on the river because of the indirect factor of population growth. Like many western European cities, Vienna experienced major population increase from the mid-eighteenth century forward (figure 6.4). From about 175,000 inhabitants in 1754 the city grew to a population of approximately 235,000 by 1790. In the following forty years the population increased to 400,000 by 1830. Although notable in and of itself, compared to later periods, this expansion amounted to a moderate increase. Between 1860 and 1890 the number of inhabitants doubled. The Danube floodplains provided the major opportunity to meet the land requirements of population increase and industrialization.

LAND USE IN THE DANUBE FLOODPLAINS

Considerable changes and extensive uses had affected the Danube floodplains already by the nineteenth century. Forestry and hunting, rather than agriculture, were the dominant land uses, as well as settlements in exceptional places described above. Many of these riparian settlers were fishermen or people involved in navigation or in other commercial activities requiring access to the river. In and around these early settlements, and already in the eighteenth century, land use intensified.

Cartographic evidence from the nineteenth century provides us with a more precise understanding of land use in the floodplains than in earlier periods. In 1816 and 1817 the engineer Christophorus Lorenzo surveyed and mapped the Danube in Lower Austria.[17] His map shows the center of Leopoldstadt densely covered by buildings. Outside of this central built-up area houses appear scattered. Few existed around the toll station Tabor; some were erected by forestry men and hunters. In the still existing entertainment area Prater, a circus, a fireworks establishment, and some further small buildings are indicated. Along the Danube channel storage yards for wood, coal, and stones were established to manage the supply from hinterland areas west of Vienna. Around and after the 1830s new industrial and commercial buildings were erected in Leopoldstadt. A register from 1832 indicates, for instance, a sugar refinery, six textile companies, and one machine factory.[18] Some years later a first steam mill, a railcar company, and a new machine factory were built. Between 1832 and 1857 the number of buildings increased in Leopoldstadt from 691 to 1,061. This number rivaled that of the city center (1,077 buildings).[19] Until 1869—one year before the Danube channelization com-

menced—another 558 houses were added, making the Leopoldstadt the fast-
est growing Viennese quarter of that period.[20]

In the district of Brigittenau only a few buildings existed around 1815
north of the Augarten park and along the Danube channel. Lorenzo's map
suggests among other things the presence of a bleaching trade that required
river access. In the following decades Brigittenau was one of the most affected
floodplain areas for land use intensification. The Kollosseum, built in 1835,
was an entertainment facility with café houses, restaurants, and ballrooms.
On the site of the later northwest railway station, the Universum was created
as a second location for festivals and entertainment. After 1848 a new quarter
was built. The land owner, the monastery of Klosterneuburg, leased it to the
real estate agent Samuel Eckstein who divided the land into small parcels and
rented them out. Renters started to build houses, mostly wooden, haphaz-
ardly, eventually leading the city of Vienna to purchase the area to plan its
development.[21] A slight growth of developed areas can be registered also in
the same period for the municipality of Kaisermühlen. A steamboat station
opened there in 1830 and promoted the importance of the village. In 1850 the
community became part of the new second district of Vienna (Leopoldstadt).

Two further zones in the floodplains developed because of their relationship to the emerging transportation geography. One was established along
the road and the bridge traversing the Danube floodplains. The only existing
connection between both riverbanks actually consisted of three parts. The
first, the Schlagbrücke, connected the city center to Leopoldstadt. The main
road continued to the so-called inner Tabor where a toll station was located.
Here a double bridge crossed the two Danube arms of the Kaiserwasser leading to the island of Zwischenbrücken. On the other end of this island there
was the outer Tabor, another toll station directly before the third Danube
bridge traversing the most northerly Danube channel, which was the main
arm of the river at the beginning of the nineteenth century. On the north
bank the two roads to Prague and Brno split at the Jedleseer Spitz. Here the
historical center of the later community of Floridsdorf emerged. According
to Lorenzo's map, several buildings existed in 1816. Most of them were constructed only a few decades before because earlier maps from 1788 and 1789
showed few houses.[22] Prior to that, meadows covered the area. The built-up
area at the Jedleseer Spitz grew quickly in the first half of the nineteenth century, especially after the Danube Steam Navigation Company built a shipyard there.

Shortly before the Danube channelization, in 1869, the Danube Regulation Commission (DRC) mapped land use in the Danube floodplains. The
DRC based its map on existing cadastral maps and integrated the future Danube channel as an overlay.[23] Compared to Lorenzo's map it shows in particu-

lar the expansion of developed areas in the contemporary twentieth district Brigittenau and the growth around Floridsdorf in the north. It also identified new buildings on the island of Zwischenbrücken along the road connecting the three different Danube bridges. The overlay of the planned Danube channelization clearly indicates that the new channel crossed the outer Tabor. Most houses of Zwischenbrücke would thus have to be abandoned after the Danube channelization, and this was also the case in the Leopoldstadt and Brigittenau built-up areas and cultivated land that covered the complete area north of the Prater. The latter still existed as recreation and leisure area in the vicinity to the city center. The villages on the north banks were still outside of the city borders and grew only modestly in the nineteenth century with the exception of Floridsdorf, which had become an industrial and commercial center.

URBAN DEVELOPMENT AND THE CHANNELIZATION OF THE DANUBE

Ever since the Danube's shift to a northeastern direction was first observed in the thirteenth century, measures to keep the Viennese arm navigable were taken, such as the regular dredging of sediments or the use of stones and wooden structures to fix the inlet. By the end of the eighteenth century, the aims of the Danube channelization started to become more complex. Besides the necessity to provide open access for ships to the city center, flood protection and the improvement of the Danube as a supraregional navigation route had to be considered as well. In the beginning of the nineteenth century another topic gained attraction in the official discussions and projects: the construction of a permanent and stable Danube bridge.[24] Until the Danube channelization only one bridge crossed all Danube arms and the floodplains. Floods regularly destroyed that bridge, at which times ferries had to be used.

Despite various improvement measures, the problems of navigation, traffic, and flood protection were far from solved by the beginning of the nineteenth century. Starting in 1803, a multitude of projects developed in this period aimed at digging one main Danube channel.[25] Seven years later in 1810, Josef Schemerl, the imperial construction director, elaborated another project that had good prospects of being accepted by the federal and municipal authorities. However, in 1815 the newly installed imperial water engineering director, J. Osterlam, blocked the plan because of the technical challenge. Osterlam instead suggested retaining and channelizing the existing main arm of the Danube. The locations for the future riverbed varied among the diverse proposals, but in principle two major strategies can be identified. There could be either a straight cutoff through the existing islands or an enlargement and regulation of the existing main channel, which flowed at that time in the northeast of the present city border—far away from the center and the Viennese arm. River engineers preferred a particular location and course of the new Danube bed mainly because of hydraulic considerations. Discussions about the best solution continued among officials in the following decades, but they failed to develop any comprehensive solution, even with the pressures raised by a devastating flood in 1830 that took many lives and caused considerable financial damages.[26]

In 1850 Emperor Franz Josef I (1830–1916; emperor 1848–1916) established the DRC. The water engineering experts of this committee evaluated the existing projects. They concluded that even if proposals to maintain and regulate the existing channel would cost less, they would provide only a short-term solution; a new channel would ultimately be required.[27] The DRC, however, failed to implement any project. After a major flood in 1862 the government formed a second DRC. In its final report, that second commission considered explicitly the link between river channelization and urban spatial development. It argued that Vienna's expansion had to concentrate on locations in the south and southwest far away from the main transport routes because the risk-prone Danube floodplains and flood-protected banks were unavailable for industry and commercial enterprises.[28]

The majority of the panel of the DRC voted for digging a new artificial riverbed crossing the Danube islands. International experts invited to assess the different proposals supported this position.[29] A minority group nevertheless tried to promote their preferred solution in the official protocols of the DRC and in various articles emphasizing the advantages of maintaining the existing main channel. Both groups had their specific arguments in terms of urban development. The majority group stressed that the connection of the new Danube riverbed to the urban area was a clear advantage from an economic point of view and for urban development. The direct traffic connections to the town via existing and planned railways would be an advantage for the newly built harbors, storage yards, and market places.[30] The minority group argued that their preferred channel would connect a larger spatial zone to the city without the "obstacle" of a river to cross.

None of these projects considered the spatial development of the city explicitly in the various plans and maps, nor did they address the possibility of gaining new land. Johann Mihalik, a river engineer, finally took up these matters when he published in 1865 on his own initiative a "Proposal for Regulation of the Danube in Three Stages."[31] He suggested in the first stage an expansion of the built-up area in Leopoldstadt, in parts of Brigittenau, and in the villages of the future north bank. In a second stage he proposed to backfill the former main Danube channel and to install parks as well as bathing and fishing ponds. In the third stage the floodplains in the north would be available for industry and commerce depending on the access to the Danube as a navigation route.

By the time Mihalik put forward his proposal, the link between the Danube channelization and urban planning had already become a major subject for the Viennese government and urban planners. In 1850, Vienna, which comprised only the old city, had annexed nine suburbs that surrounded the center. The Danube islands, including the large one that was settled centuries before, were now part of the city (Leopoldstadt). A law enacted by the municipal government in 1861 required the establishments of urban plans for the new districts—numbered two to ten—to organize the growth of developed areas and traffic routes. Ludwig Förster, an architect employed by the municipal government, established the plan for the Brigittenau quarter north of the Danube island next to the city center. The main goal was to limit the unregulated growth of houses that started in the middle of the nineteenth century—independent from any Danube channelization.

Two maps developed in 1874 during the Danube channelization considered all the future new land resources in the Danube floodplains. The City of Vienna, which had to contribute a third of the Danube channelization costs and hoped to recover these expenses by selling the newly gained land, published one map.[32] The engineer and urban planner Heinrich Grave published the second map independently.[33] Both maps focused on an increase of residential and industrial areas on the former island next to the city. Grave also envisioned zones for urban growth around Kaisermühlen due to the existence of a steamboat station there.

In 1893 an urban zoning plan conducted by order of the Viennese government fixed the main zones for rental buildings with different heights as well as industrial and commercial zones.[34] It designated the area west of the railway tracks, in the present twentieth district Brigittenau, for rental buildings of the most dense category with a height of four floors. It also assigned in Leopoldstadt a small area to this category. It classified the regions immediately along the south bank of the Danube and between the new and the old main Danube channel as industrial zones and large areas of the former Danube floodplains as recreational lands. A subsequent urban zoning plan in 1908 sought to cope with the challenges produced by the annexation of new districts on the north bank.[35] It proposed an intensification of residential buildings in the former floodplains on the south bank of the new Danube channel. In the newly integrated districts on the north bank, industrial and residential areas were suggested mainly in the fast-growing community of Floridsdorf due to well-established transport connections. A further industrial zone was foreseen in the south around the community of Stadlau, which was connected to the east via a railway line. An extension was planned also for the municipality of Kagran.

As mentioned above the second DRC opted in its final report in 1868 for a new main Danube channel crossing the island of Zwischenbrücke and the second district. The width of the new river channel was 280 meters. The DRC envisioned on the north bank a large, 450-meter-wide inundation zone for flood discharges exceeding the capacity of the dykes. The former main channel was kept as the Old Danube, which was later transformed into a recreation area. Several planners concluded already by the end of the nineteenth century that the channelization project disconnected the north bank villages from urban growth.[36]

After channelization, 260 hectares of new land were gained along the new main Danube channel and most of the floodplains were supposed to be free from floods in the future. The DRC owned large parts of the newly established area and planned a completely new urban quarter along both Danube banks. However, the expectations of the Viennese government and the DRC were only partially fulfilled. One reason for the delayed implementation of these plans was the world economic crisis of 1873 and its aftermath. Nevertheless, by 1885 new built-up zones were established especially along the south bank of the new main Danube channel. Industrial companies benefited also from an easier access to processing water, because the groundwater table was in the former floodplains higher than in other areas of the town.[37]

Kaisermühlen fundamentally changed its character due to the Danube channelization. The ship mills, previously on the main arm of the unregulated Danube, were now on the stagnant Old Danube and had to be demolished. The steamboat station was moved to the city side of the new Danube channel. Most of the income sources of the villagers disappeared, and the area became a place for cheap rental buildings and industry.[38]

In 1904–1905 the villages on the north side of the new Danube channel became part of the city of Vienna. A first attempt to incorporate them in 1892 had failed. In the beginning of the twentieth century new projects on the river changed the context. The projected construction of a Danube-Oder channel and a Danube-Moldau-Elbe channel envisioned the harbors on the north Danube bank and thus outside of the contemporary Viennese border. Moreover, the Viennese government was concerned that industrial companies would migrate to Floridsdorf because of the lower prices for land as well as for food.[39] The integrated communities not only covered industrial ones such as Floridsdorf, Kagran, and Stadlau but also some dominated by agriculture.

By 1910, thirty-five years after the Danube channelization, Leopoldstadt and Brigittenau, as well as Floridsdorf and partly Kaisermühlen, observed a considerable growth in their developed areas. Other small villages on the north riverbank by then part of Vienna increased comparatively moderately (figure 6.5). However, the picture appears differently when considering the

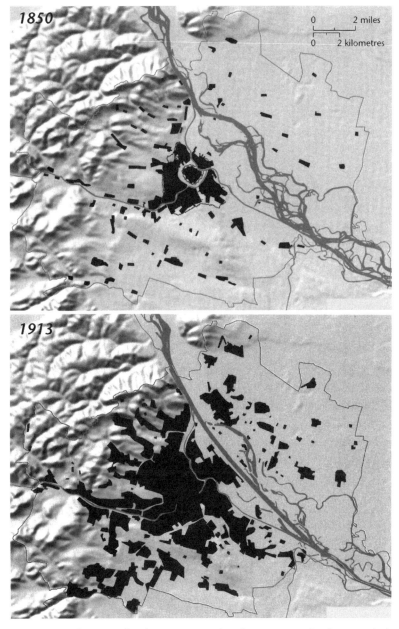

FIGURE 6.5. Development of settlement areas within the present city borders, 1850 (*top*) and 1913 (*bottom*). Adapted from Peter Eigner and Petra Schneider, "Verdichtung und Expansion."

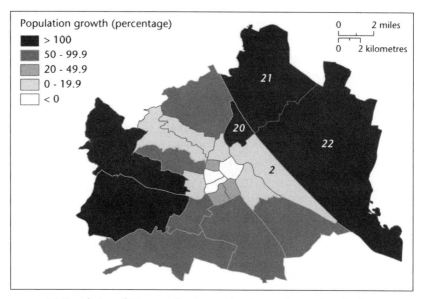

FIGURE 6.6. Population of Viennese districts, 1888 and 1918; the numbers for districts in
the former Danube floodplains are indicated (Second, Twentieth, and Twenty-second
districts).

number of inhabitants and their growth rates in the districts situated in the
former Danube floodplains (districts two, twenty, twenty-one, and twenty-
two). In 1888 the second district, Leopoldstadt, had the highest number of
inhabitants of all Viennese districts (more than 115,000). Most others had a
considerably smaller population especially when considering the large areas of the twenty-first and twenty-second district. By 1918 Leopldstadt still
ranked among the most populous districts, Brigittenau (the twentieth district)
was eighth, and the twenty-second district of Donaustadt was the least populated of all. However, between 1888 and 1918, when the Austo-Hungarian
monarchy collapsed, the districts in the former Danube floodplains had the
highest growth rates. On top was Donaustadt, Brigittenau was ranked third,
and Floridsdorf was fifth. Leopoldstadt had a modest growth rate by comparison because most of the area had already been densely populated; the remaining green space had been dedicated for recreation (see figure 6.6).

IN THE NINETEENTH CENTURY the relation between the Danube and the city
of Vienna changed fundamentally. In the beginning of this period the river
was still a braided system of several kilometers in width. Aquatic and terrestrial areas changed regularly due to hydrological and morphological dynamics. The Danube served mainly as a transport route and local energy supplier,

while the floodplains were a clear limit to urban expansion north and north-east of the present city borders. Their use was mostly dominated by forestry and hunting. Industrialization of the city as well as technological changes required new strategies in the nineteenth century. Various planning projects demonstrate that in the first decades the improvement of transport and flood protection for the villages in the floodplains and on the north bank were in the foreground of river engineers' thinking. Around and after 1850 the enormous population growth of the industrializing town linked river engineering plans closely with urban spatial planning. The Danube floodplains had by then become an important land resource to satisfy the demand for new residential and industrial areas. By the middle of the century land use in the floodplains had already intensified, particularly in areas close to the urban center and along the main roads toward the north and northeast. There were, however, no overarching principles and plans for the establishment of settlements. Only when the Danube floodplains were incorporated formally into the present city borders in 1850 did urban planners initiate projects to organize the location and expansion of developed urban and residental areas and traffic routes. From the completion of the systematic Danube channelization in 1875 the new urban districts in the former Danube floodplains were characterized by high population growth rates and expansion of urban areas. The riverine landscape was now clearly integrated into the urban space, and urban expansion concentrated to a large extent on the former floodplains and on the north banks of the river. The Danube channelization of the nineteenth century was nevertheless only a first step in Viennese flood protection and land reclamation. A flood in 1892 proved that the assumptions for the capacity of the Danube dykes were wrong and the flood profile was too small.[40] Hence in the beginning of the twentieth century the Viennese government continued the debates about the Danube channelization. Some familiar issues came up for discussion, including the provision of additional land and the potential effects on urban space. However, the question of channelization had changed from earlier periods because hydropower entered the debate and marked a new set of considerations.[41]

⤳ 7

RIVERS AND RISK IN THE CITY

The Urban Floodplain as a Contested Space

UWE LÜBKEN

"Trouble is," said an old Cincinnati water-front man, "lots of this land where houses are really always has belonged to the river. . . . People just keep encroaching on the river, with mills and warehouses and wharves, making it narrower and narrower. Then, when it gets high and must spread, there's no place for it to spread except up into somebody's second-story windows."

—Anonymous, quoted in Frederick Simpich, "Men Against the Rivers"

CITIES CONCENTRATE NOT ONLY people, economic wealth, cultural activities, and political institutions but also environmental risk. This holds especially true for river cities where the incorporation of nature into the fabric of urban life often is the most important reason for their existence. The river represents both golden opportunities and manifold hazards. Accordingly, cities benefit in various ways from proximity to water and are threatened by the prospect of flooding. While the interplay of hazard and opportunity can be said to have characterized almost every river town from ancient times to the present,[1] the fundamental processes of industrialization, urbanization, rapid population growth, and technical innovation in the nineteenth and twentieth centuries have significantly altered the patterns of vulnerability.[2] Such shifts come into view most clearly on the urban floodplain, a space that focuses the contest between rivers and cities.

From a hydrological perspective the floodplain is a natural part of the river, a space that "is not covered by the stream at low flow or average flow, but which has been flooded in the past or may be flooded in the future." Floodplains can be broad or narrow and they might be flooded rarely or quite frequently.[3] Because of these unique characteristics, the floodplain constitutes an ecological transition zone, separating two different ecosystems—the aquatic and the terrestrial.[4] While the floodplain thus creates a boundary, it also forms an ecosystem in its own right with a diversified fauna the composition of which mostly depends on such factors as amplitude, predictability, and frequency of water level fluctuations.[5]

Modern societies, however, tend to think of rivers as canals rather than meandering and dynamic streams; they think of them "as having a fixed length but no prescribed breadth, with the result that the floodplain is often used for farms and settlements as if it were not part of the river's system."[6] This separation of the river from the floodplain—both conceptual and practical—was of great importance for the economic success of the Euro-American settler societies in temperate North America along major river systems like the Hudson, St. Lawrence, and Ohio. The urban history of the Ohio Valley in particular can hardly be written without acknowledging the importance of the "floodplain invasions" in the nineteenth and twentieth centuries.

This success, however, came at a cost. Unlike many North American indigenous societies, which also used the floodplains intensively but were much more mobile than their successors and could often simply move out of harm's way with all their belongings, Euro-American settlements and facilities along the river were there to stay. The more or less permanent utilization of the river and its floodplain was crucial for the transformation of the Ohio Valley from a premodern, mostly agricultural area into a predominantly industrial and urban landscape.

Flooding thus became a constant threat even though (or rather because) damaging events happened irregularly and unpredictably. Yet this permanent character of natural hazards in general and the hazard of flooding in particular has so far hardly been addressed by historical research on natural disasters. Although historians have increasingly tackled the problem of studying natural disasters and natural hazards in a systematic way over the last ten to fifteen years,[7] current historical research on these topics suffers, somewhat ironically, from its focus on single events and the emphasis on the destructive aspects of disaster. This limited view can be overcome, however, by looking at such events and hazards from a perspective of risk.

Traditional interpretations define risk as the product of the expected loss of a harmful event and its probability of occurrence. While this view is still prevalent in every cost-benefit analysis of the Army Corps of Engineers, risk is more than just a rational operation. It includes cultural aspects such as memory and identity as well as social factors (which we acknowledge with the phrase, people "put at risk"). Furthermore, most risky situations cannot be entirely transformed into order and certainty but leave behind an often surprisingly large amount of uncertainty.[8] As different as these perspectives may be, they all combine experiences of the past with expectations of the future and hence allow for the writing of a longue durée history of natural catastrophes.

Such a risk-based approach to the history of natural hazards changes the way we look at floods and flood control. The latter can no longer be characterized as a "momentary defense," as "holding an umbrella over your head when it rains."[9] Rather, it has to be seen as a constant process of balancing the immense costs involved in creating and maintaining levees, floodwalls, reservoirs, and nonstructural measures of flood control, with the expected economic, social, and cultural benefits of a river. From this perspective, floods are anything but acts of god; rather they represent the moments when the "vast industrial-agricultural-urban-tourist nexus" located on the riverbanks discloses its vulnerability, when nature reclaims the floodplain as the river's territory.[10]

LOCATION, LOCATION, LOCATION: EARLY SETTLEMENTS AND THE EXPERIENCE OF "HIGH WATER"

Home to several indigenous societies for centuries, the Ohio Country—a loosely defined space west of the Alleghenies and north and south of the Ohio River—had become one of the most contested regions in the world by the middle of the eighteenth century. It was "Center of the Earth" to the recently immigrant Shawnee,[11] it was a prime, if late target of both British and French imperial ambitions, and it soon became the object of desire for thousands of Euro-American immigrants.[12] By the time of the American Revolution, about fifty thousand settlers had already crossed the Appalachians and millions more were to come. According to the British General Thomas Gage, these migrants were "too Numerous, too Lawless and Licentious ever to be restrained."[13] Native American resistance to the land hunger of Euro-Americans de facto ended after the battle of Fallen Timbers in 1794 and the Treaty of Paris one year later.[14]

With an efficient overland transportation system lacking in the hilly and heavily wooded Ohio Country, rivers were by far the best and often the only means of communication. The best time to navigate the Ohio River system was during "high water" in the spring and early summer when melting snow from the mountains and ample precipitation provided for sufficient depth. "Throughout America these swellings of the rivers are called 'the freshes' and are of great importance to the more distant inhabitants," noted Johann David Schoepf, the son of a German merchant who had come to America with the troops of George III in 1777.[15] Christian Schultz, an investor from the East Coast who wanted to sound the economic potential of the Ohio Valley, also noticed the positive effects of high water levels. Traveling down the French Creek and the Allegheny to Pittsburgh, Schultz wrote from a tiny village close to the French Fort Le Boeuf after a very rainy night: "on Monday morning the whole little village was in confusion with the preparations made

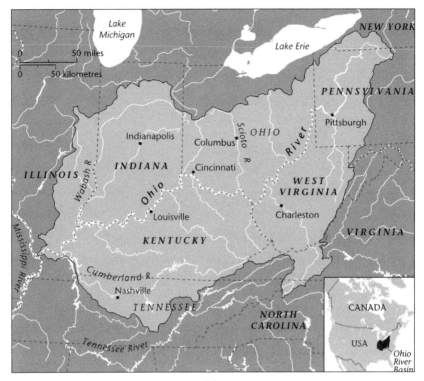

FIGURE 7.1. The Ohio River basin. Adapted from envirocast.net.

the preceding day for starting off with the first of the flood."[16] Thus, "to catch the rise" was, until way into the nineteenth century, the motto for all prospective travelers.[17]

With the first settlements along the Ohio and its tributaries growing in size, Euro-Americans quickly found out, however, that the river bottoms offered not only fertile soil and convenient access to water supplies and transportation routes but also entailed hazards, most importantly the danger of flooding. Almost every new settlement along the Ohio or one of its tributaries painfully experienced the variability of the rivers and hence the risks of locating along them.

Fort Pitt, the former French Fort Duquesne that was soon to become the city of Pittsburgh, witnessed devastating floods in its earliest stages. Located at the tip of land where the confluence of the Allegheny and the Monongahela Rivers forms the Ohio, the site had many obvious advantages for the founding of a military outpost or a city. Here, it seemed, access to the Ohio Country could be easily controlled and the vast markets in the West and, via the Mississippi in the South, promised a bright future for its inhabitants. "No place in the West seemed more certain to be the site of a great city," historian Richard C. Wade noted, and "Nature itself had made the suggestion unmistakably."[18] As early as January 1762, however, the waters at the forks of the Ohio climbed so rapidly that the walls of the fortress were swept into the river. Only one year later, the river rose even higher and surpassed the old record by one and a half feet. A local merchant described the scene: "[the settlers] began to muster off, but ye dead Faith of Several prompt'd 'em to delay carrying away their Goods until ye Water was got so high that they had to break in ye Roofs or Gable Ends of ye Houses to get them away in Battoes."[19]

Further down the river, in Marietta, located at "the Point between the Ohio and Muskingum Rivers, flooding became an almost constant threat and a severe impediment to the city's growth. The first settlement in the Northwest territory or, as historian Reuben Gold Thwaites later described it, the "Plymouth Rock of the West,"[20] experienced flooding in less than a year after it had been founded. On February 18, 1790, Thomas Wallcut, a former officer in George Washington's revolutionary army who had moved to Marietta, wrote in his *Journal* about the rise of the Muskingum River: "We soon had the tea-kettle on, and got our coffee boiled; and before we could get our breakfast done, the water came in so fast that the floor was afloat, and we stood in water to our buckles to drink the last dish."[21] All inhabitants of the Point had to abandon their houses. Only three buildings in the settlement were located so high that the water could not reach them.[22]

Floods continued to be a huge burden for the city. Every year in late spring, portions of Marietta were underwater for one or two weeks.[23] "It is not uncommon for a fresh to swell the river . . . to such a degree as to inundate the town of Marietta with two feet of water," Christian Schultz noted in 1807.[24] Nine years later, Andrew Backus, a citizen of Marietta, remarked: "Marietta is situated on a very high bluff, notwithstanding which it is almost annually overflown, to the depth of eight or ten feet, especially the lower part of town."[25]

As bad as these floods were, however, Marietta was, in its first twenty-five years, only affected by "normal" floods and was spared the big disastrous event. Despite the frequent inundations, the site seemed to fulfill the expectations of the settlers, the result being, as one contemporary witness remarked, that "homes were planted near the river with no apprehension that they would be invaded by the floods."[26] In 1813, however, the city noticed for the first time how hazardous its location actually was. On January 24, it rained so heavily that the Ohio required only twenty-four hours to leave its banks,[27] as Ephraim Cutler noted: "The rise was . . . so sudden as to prevent us from getting our stock off to a place of safety. We drove the cattle to the hill early in the morning, but had to carry our sheep off in a boat about noon, and ferried the horses over in Mr. Cole's flat that evening. We got the hogs into the house, in the course of the night, except eight or ten that were drowned. We also lost two sheep and two calves; one was drowned, and the others perished in consequence of the cold and snow."[28]

If floods reminded the local population of their city's precarious location, periods without catastrophic events tended to erase the memory of disaster. "The long period during which the Ohio had scarcely passed the measure of 'full bank,'" remarked one local historian, "had caused people to well nigh forget that it was liable at any time to make a phenomenal rise and send its broad surging tide up around their houses and into their doors."[29] William Greene, however, a lawyer from Rhode Island who was seeking new opportunities in the West, was not deceived by the temporary tranquility of the river. Because of Marietta's record of inundations, he settled down in Cincinnati instead, reasoning about the former city: "What would induce me to take up my domicile in such a place?"[30]

Cincinnati's location, however, was hardly less dangerous than Marietta's. Two distinct areas characterized the site's topography: the Bottoms, a strip of land running parallel to the river only seven feet above the normal highwater mark; and the Hill, a mile-wide plateau located fifty feet above the Bottoms.[31] Losantiville, as Cincinnati was originally named, was one of the first three settlements within the territory of Symmes's Purchase between the Big and the Little Miami River north of the Ohio. Cincinnati's two early rivals in this area—Northbend and Columbia—however, suffered from Ohio River floods right after their creation, so that many inhabitants fled these settlements and moved to Cincinnati.[32] Thus, "one of the most flood-afflicted spots in the valley" profited from its neighbors' disasters.[33] Historian David Stradling has pointed out that "Losantiville's flood resistance was clearly important to its early success against its local rivals."[34]

TWO TALES OF TWO RIVERS: THE INDUSTRIALIZATION OF THE OHIO

In the early years of Euro-American settlement in the Ohio Valley, proximity to the river was essential. The level and fertile bottomlands were easy to clear and they provided quick access to the river.[35] These early settlements suffered from floods, to be sure, but for two reasons the consequences of inundations did not outweigh the various positive effects of life close to the river's edge. First, the Ohio during this period did not climb nearly as high as it did in the late nineteenth and early twentieth centuries, thus hiding its disastrous potential. Second, the damage potential in the floodplain was still comparatively small.

However, the settlers' preference for the bottomlands created path dependencies, the negative consequences of which cities like Pittsburgh, Cincinnati, or Louisville only experienced after they had tremendously increased the damage potential in their floodplains. The number of "flood refugees" in Cincinnati, for example, rose from about five hundred in 1832, to twenty-four thousand in 1884, and seventy thousand in 1937—a clear indication of the growth of residential buildings in the floodplain.[36]

In 1832, the famous ornithologist John J. Audubon wrote about a journey he had made twenty years before with his wife, two children, and two hired African American rowers. Returning from Pennsylvania to their abode in Kentucky, the Audubons found it expedient, "the waters being unusually low," to purchase a skiff, "a large, commodious, and light boat of that denomination," and sail down the Ohio River all the way from Shippingport, Pennsylvania, to Henderson, Kentucky.[37] "We glided down the river, meeting no other ripple of the water than that formed by the propulsion of our boat," Audubon remembered. "Leisurely we moved along, gazing all day on the grandeur and beauty of the wild scenery around us," yet, he also claimed to have noticed threatening developments: "We foresaw, with great concern, the alterations that cultivation would soon produce along these delightful banks."[38] Isolated cabins of squatters and flatboats loaded either with produce of the headwaters or with migrants looking for a new home all heralded "commencing civilization." Audubon noted the following two decades after the trip:

> When I think of these times, and call back to my mind the grandeur and beauty of those almost uninhabited shores; when I picture to myself the dense and lofty summits of the forests that every where spread along the hills, and overhung the margins of the stream, unmolested by the axe of the settler; . . . when I see that no longer any aborigines are to be found there, and that the vast herds of elks, deer, and buffaloes, which once pastured on these hills and on these valleys, making themselves great roads to the several salt springs, have ceased to exist; when I reflect that all of this grand portion of our Union, instead of being in a state of nature, is now more or less covered with villages, farms, and towns, where the din of hammers and machinery is constantly heard; that the woods are fast disappearing under the axe by the day, and the fire by night; that hundreds of steamboats are gliding to and fro, over the whole length of the majestic river, forcing commerce to take root and to prosper at every spot; when I see the surplus population of Europe coming to assist in the destruction of the forest, and transplanting civilization into its darkest recesses; when I remember that these extraordinary changes have all taken place in the

short period of twenty years, I pause, wonder, and, although I know all to be fact, can scarcely believe its reality.[39]

While Audubon's travelogue certainly romanticized the natural history of the Ohio Valley, it also represented the common notion of a "paradise lost," reflecting the vast transformation of the region and especially the floodplains during the early decades of the nineteenth century.

What Audubon could at best envision, another traveler witnessed firsthand almost a century later. In 1894, Reuben Gold Thwaites, noted historian and director of the State Historical Society of Wisconsin, embarked on a similar but also profoundly different journey. Like Audubon, Thwaites traveled down the river in a fifteen-foot rowboat, accompanied by members of his family, that is, his wife Jessie, their ten-year-old son Frederik, and Jessie's brother, William Daniel Turvill. The Thwaites' journey was even longer than the Audubons' since they departed in Brownsville, Pennsylvania, on the Monongahela, above Shippingport, and disembarked only at the mouth of the Ohio River in Cairo, Illinois, where their boat was loaded into a boxcar and sent home.[40]

At the end of the nineteenth century, floating or rowing down a river was an outdated way of traveling, of course. The historian and his fellow travelers could have covered the nearly 1,100 miles much faster had they boarded a steamboat, not to speak of a railroad. But the Thwaites deliberately chose to travel in the same way Native Americans, early settlers, and the throngs of visitors to the West had traveled for decades in the past, by boat. At the same time, the nostalgic character of the voyage—coming close to a reenactment of those "Early Western Travels" Thwaites had spent so much time and effort on as a professional historian—highlighted the fundamental changes of the river and the floodplains over the course of the nineteenth century.[41]

At the beginning of their journey, still on the Monongahela, the Thwaites party saw coal tipples, "begrimed scaffolds of wood and iron, arranged for dumping the product of the mines into both barges and railway cars." Between Braddock and Pittsburgh, they witnessed "an almost constant succession of iron and steel-making towns." Further down the river at Mingo Junction, Ohio, three miles below Steubenville, the Thwaites visited the local steel plant and were especially impressed by the "weird spectacle presented at night, with the furnaces fiercely gleaming, the fresh ingots smoking hot, the Bessemer converter 'blowing off,' the great cranes moving about like things of life, bearing giant kettles of molten steel; and amidst it all, human life held so cheaply." At Witten's Bottom, on the Ohio side of the river, they were greeted by the "ugly, towering derricks of oil and natural gas wells." In Cincinnati, river traffic was so intense that they had to dodge ferries and towboats until they could float under "great railway bridges which cobweb the sky," while in Louisville, they heard the noise from the great iron bridge far above their heads, "a busy combination thoroughfare for steam and electric railways, for pedestrians and for vehicles."[42]

As is evident in both Audubon's anticipation and Thwaites's description of the Ohio, industrialization, urbanization, rapid population growth, technological innovations, and steadily increasing commerce had a profound impact on the river and its floodplains. The once natural waterway had acquired many new functions. Not only did it have to guarantee the steady flow of increased navigation, but it also had to supply drinking water, dispose of wastes, and serve as an important source of energy. This was true not only for the Ohio, of course, but for many other waterways in industrializing countries. As a result, many rivers were straightened, reduced in length, bordered with levees, and harnessed into narrow channels. Hydraulic engineers sometimes openly enjoyed "pushing rivers around."[43] The primary objective of these measures was the creation of a uniform and regular flow to satisfy steadily increasing industrial, commercial, and agricultural needs, "a happy mean between low water and flood," as the New York Times pointed out in 1895.[44]

In the floodplains along the Ohio River, the concentration of industries, infrastructures, and people continued with tremendous speed. The floods of 1883, 1884, 1913, 1936, and, most importantly, 1937, dramatically disclosed the new patterns of vulnerability that had been created by the changes in floodplain utilization. These developments modified not only the rivers and the floodplains but also the character of floods themselves. "Floods like these have happened before," the New York Times wrote about the Ohio River flood of 1884 (not quite correctly since this extreme event had set new records in many cities along the river): "They have happened, to some extent, when the country was almost untouched by the hand of man. But, unquestionably, the great disasters of recent years are the result of the condition of the earth's surface as modified by human action."[45]

The Ohio River flood of 1937 was, at that time, the most devastating river flood in U.S. history (in terms of economic damage), even worse than the much more famous Mississippi flood of 1927.[46] Altogether, 196 counties in twelve states were affected, from West Virginia down to Louisiana (almost every big flood of the lower Ohio River is automatically transformed into a Mississippi River flood). Approximately 1.5 million people were directly affected by the flood.[47] Between 500,000 and 1 million people were driven from their homes and 137 people died, many due to illness and exhaustion.[48] According to the official report of the United States Red Cross, more than seventy thousand houses and other structures were destroyed or damaged. Livestock losses were estimated to include 1,968 work animals, 3,354 cattle,

31,516 hogs, 243,282 chicken, and 11,425 other animals. Estimates of the total cost of the disaster varied between 300 and 500 million dollars.[49]

Along a stretch of only eight miles of the Kiskimintas River—a "great industrial valley" and a tributary of the Allegheny River—the United Engineering and Foundry Company, the American Sheet and Tin Plate Company, the Appollo Steel Company, the Allegheny Steel Company, and several mines were all damaged, "not to speak of the hundreds of thousands of dollars lost in pay rolls and in dollars and cents to employees of these factories, which were thrown out of work, due to the flood."[50] The industrial utilization of the floodplain was also evident in the damage reports of the Boston-based fire insurance company Factory Mutual. In 1937, more than one hundred of its clients were affected by the devastating flood of the Ohio River, forty-eight in Cincinnati alone. In Louisville, Kentucky, only one of the insured companies was not located in the floodplain, whereas thirty industrial facilities were severely damaged by the flood.[51]

The steadily growing level of flood damage over the last two centuries was caused not only by immense devastation in urban residential areas and at industrial facilities but also by the substantial impairment and destruction of large infrastructural systems. Street and railway tracks often followed the course of natural and regulated waterways, while many modern utilities such as waterworks or power plants depended on the existence of regulated rivers or were an integral part of them.[52] In addition, new infrastructural systems were created along the lines of the old, for example, when telegraph and telephone lines were erected next to railroad tracks. These close connections between rivers and infrastructure, however, made the latter also vulnerable to floods.

The first infrastructure to be affected by floods was often the river itself. Even moderate flood levels could bring river navigation to a standstill.[53] More vulnerable, however, was the riparian infrastructure. Railroads, for example, were often built behind or even on top of levees,[54] and they were thus affected by scour, washouts, or complete destruction during a flood. A single flooded or destroyed section could suffice to cut off the supply of entire cities with essential goods. Traffic and transportation within cities was affected by the flooding and destruction of tracks as well. From January 27 until February 5, 1937, for example, not a single bus or streetcar operated in the city of Evansville, Indiana.[55]

Ironic as it may seem, water supply systems are also critical infrastructure in times of flooding, most of all in urban areas. Especially vulnerable to inundations were traditional wells. But even modern waterworks were overburdened when they had to process too much "raw" water. During the Ohio River flood of 1937, the water supply of almost all big cities along the course

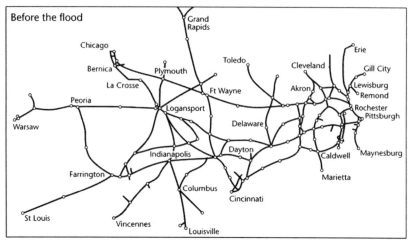

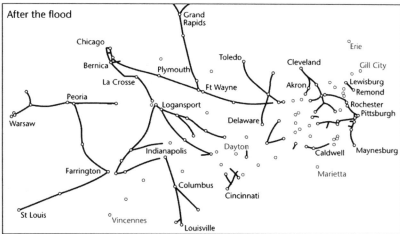

FIGURE 7.2. Pennsylvania Lines west of Pittsburgh before and after the flood of 1913.
Adapted from Lewis S. Bigham, *The 1913 Flood and How It Was Met by a Railroad*
(Pittsburgh: Pennsylvania Lines, 1913), 4–5.

of the river was severely impaired or came to a standstill. In Parkersburg,
West Virginia, flood waters "went over the tops of the deep wells and got into
them." In order to prevent the contaminated water from entering the mains,
the pumps were shut down. At Huntington, breaks in undermined mains
emptied the reservoir and made it impossible to maintain pumping pressure.
In Evansville, Indiana, the boiler house, filtration plant, and pumping station
of the waterworks were located close to the Ohio but on fairly high ground.
Still, the extreme natural event of 1937 affected even this seemingly safe spot.
When the river water threatened to destroy pumps, facilities, and electrical
equipment, the waterworks were shut down completely. Fortunately, the res-

ervoir, which was above the flood line, still contained twenty million gallons
so that water could be distributed to the citizens of Evansville for one hour
each day during the emergency.[56]

Urban gasworks were suffering from similar problems. Here, it was also
water entering pipes and mains that resulted in a collapse of the whole system.
In Evansville, Indiana, during the record flood of 1937, Ohio River water en-
croached upon broken gas pipes of houses and factories and from there found
its way into the mains of the Southern Indiana Gas and Electric Company.
The water sunk and gathered in the lowest parts of the system, sealing off
the pipes and cutting whole neighborhoods off from gas service.[57] In all these
cases, a water level way above the "happy mean" caused contaminations and
infrastructural conflicts.

Finally, it should not be forgotten that rivers and riverbanks also represented what might be called an aesthetic infrastructure. With the advent of
mass tourism, riverine landscapes were amply consumed by the modern traveler. Public houses and hotels in particular benefited from proximity to the
river and an unimpaired view of the water, a proximity that made them also
vulnerable to flooding. Sometimes, not even a seemingly safe distance from
the river helped. The Irving S. Cobb Hotel in Paducah, Kentucky, which at
normal river levels lay about half a mile from the river, in 1937 found itself all
of a sudden three miles from the nearest shore.[58] In 1966, the Lafayette Motor
Hotel ("on the Banks of the Ohio River") in Marietta issued a brochure for its
customers that contained historic flood records of the Ohio River. This kind

FIGURE 7.3. Lafayette Motor Hotel in Marietta, Ohio, during the flood of 1964. Marietta
College, Local History Archives, Folder "Floods (1)."

FIGURE 7.4. Putnam Street Bridge across the Muskingum in Marietta, Ohio, after the flood of 1913. Marietta College, Local History Archives, Folder "Floods (1)."

of information might have been quite useful for the hotel guests since the building had been flooded several feet deep two years before.

Floods also posed problems for bridges. While these structures are, in a metaphorical sense, very often used to describe the ties and connections between peoples, states, and cultures, their infrastructural function is exactly the opposite. Only by separating the various streams can contaminations be averted and collisions avoided.[59] When the water level rises, however, bridges, like many other structures and buildings in the floodplain, dangerously obstruct the flow of the water and often worsen the flood by backing up the river.[60] Also, piers and abutments are highly vulnerable to damage by scour, which can threaten the stability of the whole structure, and to damage by driftwood and floating debris hitting these parts of the bridge.[61]

Another reason why bridges became weak points within infrastructural networks in the case of disasters was due to the fact that during large-scale floods not just one but most often many of these structures were affected.[62] The Ohio River flood of 1913, for example, destroyed four hundred bridges in Ohio and Illinois alone.[63] The Pennsylvania Railroad had to cope with twenty-four completely destroyed and fifty partially damaged bridges.[64] On a stretch of about four hundred miles, the Ohio could be crossed by foot at only five points. At three of these five still functioning bridges, service was severely impaired. The Madison Highway Bridge, for instance, could only be crossed after a ferry had brought the passengers to the approach. The same was true for the Louisville and Nashville Railroad Bridge in Cincinnati, which was also closed for train service. The Covington-Cincinnati Highway Bridge could only be used after a new approach had been constructed.[65] In the mid-1970s, the average annual damage to bridges by flooding in the United States amounted to forty million dollars. In 1965 alone, the Bureau of Public Roads spent seventy-six million dollars to repair this kind of damage.[66]

VULNERABILITY, RESILIENCE, AND RISK

The process of floodplain invasion was, of course, witnessed not only in the Ohio River valley but also in other regions. Gilbert F. White pointed out in 1945 that "economically important encroachments have been made upon flood plains in all sections of the United States. For the nation as a whole, the mean annual property loss resulting from floods certainly is more than $75,000,000 and probably exceeds $95,000,000. The toll in human life is approximately 83 deaths annually. For the heavy damages to health and to productive activity no measuring units are available."[67] In 1940, fifteen out of fifty-nine cities in the United States with 150,000 or more inhabitants were affected by floods on a regular basis. Within this group, eight cities struggled again and again with "serious" floods in "highly important sections" (Springfield, Hartford, Pittsburgh, Cincinnati, Louisville, Kansas City, Denver, and Los Angeles), and "in addition, two cities—Dayton [Ohio] and New Orleans—occupy land which has been fully protected from flood." Cities in the Ohio Valley obviously loom large in this picture.[68]

The increasing human occupation of the Ohio River's floodplains had created new patterns of vulnerability. These patterns were clearly exposed when the river climbed to record heights in 1884, 1913, 1936, and 1937. The distribution of environmental risk did not affect all segments of society in the same way, though. In many cities, low-rent neighborhoods were located in the bottomlands, so that poor people and African Americans suffered much more from floods than those who could afford to live on higher ground. At the same time, flooded cities and regions displayed a remarkable degree of resilience.[69] Often, innovative measures helped overcome problems. For example, during the flood of 1883 in Cincinnati:

> Gasworks were so far submerged that primitive methods of producing artificial light were forced upon the community, and the public lamps on the street corners were dark. . . . The lantern, long disused, was brought from the cellar and the attic by its fortunate owner, while those not so fortunate felt, rather than saw, their way from place to place. A suggestion that merchants and others keep lamps or candles burning in their windows at night for the benefit of the public while the city was without gas,

was not generally adopted until more than a week had expired, on account of the scarcity of the articles named.[70]

Creative solutions were also found where problems of water supply arose. In Louisville, Kentucky, the pumping station of the waterworks had to be shut down because the boilers had been submerged by the rising flood in 1937. The next day, however, engineers "secured a river towboat, moored it next to the river pumping station, and rigged a flexible steam line from the boat's boilers to one of the large, vertical, triple-expansion pumps."[71] For the citizens of Cincinnati, who had to wait 216 hours for the water supply system to be restored, help came from an unexpected source when the Burger Brewing Company used their own wells not to brew beer but to provide drinking water. Each day one million gallons of water was fed into the system.[72] Other emergency water connections were provided by a distillery, a soap works, a dairy, and several industrial plants all of which had deep wells that gave safe water.[73]

More important than such impromptu solutions, however, was the creation and maintenance of a huge system of coping capacities—including physical flood control measures like levees and floodwalls as well as the activities of relief organizations such as the American Red Cross and the allocation of financial aid. The latter was, of course, to a large extent dependent on the economic strength of a certain city, region, or state. Thus, vulnerability to natural catastrophes also became a function of a society's ability and willingness to maintain and eventually expand such coping capacities.

Finally, there is one important area in which these coping capacities seem to have reached their limits. It is true that, as the more recent literature on disasters emphasizes, historical developments of patterns of vulnerability rather than nature itself are to be held responsible for the catastrophic element in natural processes such as earthquakes, storms, or floods. It should not be forgotten, however, that even for societies that are aware of this vulnerability, both the date and the extent of the impact remain unknown. Since the "rhythm" of these natural disturbances runs contrary to the rational demands of commercial, industrial, and urban planning, uncertainty has become a problem in its own right. "A standing fear is a destruction of the value of the real property, and a strain which business and credit cannot endure," an article remarked in the *Washington Post* on February 17, 1883.[74] Thus, the question of how states, regions, and cities should deal with a threat that appears infrequently, on an irregular basis, and with an unpredictable intensity yet with ever-growing damages, became a constantly growing challenge over the course of the last two centuries. Nature, in this respect, was and still is incalculable.

8

THE ST. LAWRENCE AND MONTREAL'S
SPATIAL DEVELOPMENT IN THE SEVENTEENTH
THROUGH THE TWENTIETH CENTURY

JEAN-CLAUDE ROBERT

SINCE THE SIXTEENTH CENTURY, when Jacques Cartier first described the "great river of Canada," voyageurs, cosmographers, and, later, historians and geographers have all drawn attention to its characteristics and features. I do not propose to reiterate them all here. It is, however, worth noting that throughout these writings various authors have presented comprehensive interpretations of the St. Lawrence's role in Canadian history; I would like to focus on certain interpretations that have influenced the work of historians.

Two works that profoundly marked the interpretation of the role of the St. Lawrence took shape in the 1930s: one by the historian Donald Creighton and the other by the geographer Raoul Blanchard. Starting from two different perspectives, their works long structured the historiography and geographical understanding of Canada. In 1936, Donald Creighton published his *Commercial Empire of the St. Lawrence*, regularly republished since,[1] and in 1929 Raoul Blanchard began his major study of Quebec that culminated in a brilliant, five-volume study of French Canada titled *Le Canada français: Province de Québec*, published between 1935 and 1954 due to delays caused by the Second World War.[2]

The historian Creighton wished to show the influence of the St. Lawrence–Great Lakes axis on the construction of a Canadian society clearly distinct from the United States, a Canadian society whose existence depended on the river. Creighton posited the axis as a corridor underpinning the construction of a commercial social economy that aimed to utilize the river to capture trade between Europe and North America. In later work done in the 1950s, Creighton refined his thinking by turning toward a form of geographic determinism: the St. Lawrence–Great Lakes axis, strengthened and extended by the transcontinental railway, created key East-West elements that succeeded in counteracting the continent's strong North-South orientation, thus providing a geographical basis for the existence of a Canadian national entity.[3] It is useful to bear in mind that Creighton wrote at a time when many Canadians bemoaned the loosening of ties with Great Britain, which accelerated after the end of the First World War, and the rise of a continentalism that drew Canada's economy, society, and culture increasingly into the orbit of the United States.

The geographer Raoul Blanchard was induced to discover America by Harvard University, which invited him to conduct regional studies.[4] He chose Quebec and crisscrossed the province, making contacts, creating enduring friendships, and penning a hefty work while trying to establish geography programs at the universities of Laval and Montreal. Blanchard marveled at the network of rivers polarized by the St. Lawrence,[5] and he proclaimed the river's important role in the development of French Canada.

In 1980, the geographer Jean-Claude Lasserre published *Le Saint-Laurent: Grande porte de l'Amérique*, a remarkable overview of the waterway in which he contrasts the river's two primary functions: population and rootedness on one hand and transit on the other. Also worthy of note is the publication in 1996 and 2005 of the two volumes of geographer Pierre Camu's study, *Le Saint-Laurent et les Grands Lacs au temps de la voile, 1608–1850* and *Le Saint-Laurent et les Grands Lacs au temps de la vapeur, 1850–1950*. In addition, between 1986 and 2000, I myself conducted a research program with two colleagues, Serge Courville and Normand Séguin, devoted to the study of the internal dynamics of Quebec's social economy polarized by the St. Lawrence between 1815 and 1871. A report on the work appeared in 1995 as volume one of *Atlas historique du Québec: Le pays laurentien au XIXe siècle; Les morphologies de base*.

I wish to examine the evolution of the role of the St. Lawrence on two scales, first in terms of the history of North America and then in terms of the structuring of the space of the City of Montreal and its immediate surroundings. I propose to review four moments in time: from the beginning to the seventeenth century, the fur-trading era of the eighteenth century, the creation of the port facilities in the nineteenth century, and the revisions of the twentieth century.[6]

FROM THE BEGINNING TO THE SEVENTEENTH CENTURY

The Laurentian landscape is inseparable from the Quaternary glaciations. Compressed and laminated by the glaciers, the St. Lawrence Lowlands were invaded by the waters of the Atlantic some twelve thousand years ago, when the Champlain Sea replaced the ice. This marine episode, which lasted about two thousand years, left behind a flat landscape through which the St. Lawrence carves a diagonal channel from southwest to northeast. Drainage took several millennia, and the first inhabitants gradually drifted in, very likely from the south, to settle in the plain. They were initially hunters and gatherers, but a segment of these groups underwent two changes: first discovering pottery about 1000 BCE, and then experiencing a true agricultural revolution with the advent of growing corn around 1000 CE. This mix of Amerindian hunters and gatherers on one hand and farmers on the other led to the establishment of trade channels, of which many vestiges have been uncovered in the past thirty years by archeological digs.

Central to these channels were the waterways, chief among them the St. Lawrence, carrying the waters of the Great Lakes out to the Atlantic. Moreover, thanks to their central position at the junction of the continent's major watersheds, the Great Lakes acted as the true hub of Amerindian travel. It must be recalled that there is not a very large difference in elevation between the Great Lakes and the head of the Mississippi basin. Furthermore, one of the features of the St. Lawrence is that it is difficult to navigate between the Island of Montreal and the entrance to the Great Lakes. While the spectacular Niagara escarpment and its hundred-meter drop are well known, the St. Lawrence falls another sixty meters between the outlet of the lakes and Montreal. In contrast, the difference in elevation from Montreal to the ocean is a mere seven meters.[7] Aside from the Niagara escarpment, the most important break in flow occurs at the Lachine Rapids, alongside the Island of Montreal, where the river abruptly drops by some fifteen meters (figure 8.1).

Right from the earliest contacts, at least those that we know of, the size of the networks can be inferred: when Jacques Cartier tried to get information from the Iroquoian Chief Donnaconna, his reticence and the tales he told pointed to the intricacy of intertribal trade and the central role of the St. Lawrence.[8] Samuel de Champlain (c.1570–1635) was quick to grasp the implications of this network and dragged France into a venture that lasted from 1608 until 1763.

In fact, one might say that the St. Lawrence imposed continental geopolitics on the French from the outset. Indeed, the participation of the colonial French in a vast Amerindian network hinged on their alliance with the Algonquin (Anishinabeg) and the Montagnais (Innus), hunting and gathering peoples, and also the Huron, a hunting and farming people, who lived around the Great Lakes and were indispensable intermediaries in the fur trade. French alliances fluctuated throughout the seventeenth century and were threatened after 1650 by the Iroquois victory over the Huron, but at the turn of the century, and more precisely at the time of the Great Peace of Montreal in 1701, France achieved a master stroke by obtaining the alliance of all the tribes of

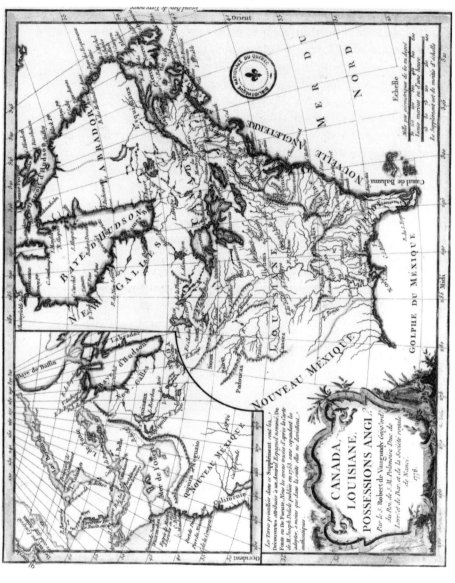

FIGURE 8.1. Robert de Vaugondy, *Canada, Louisiane, possessions angl.*, 1778. This map shows the central position of the Great Lakes in the river systems of North America, particularly the articulation of the Mississippi and St. Lawrence rivers. Bibliothèque et archives nationales du Québec.

the interior, as well as Iroquois neutrality in the event of war with the English colonies.[9]

In this context, Montreal quickly became the gateway to the interior. The island sat at the crossroads of several waterways, lying as it does at the confluence of the St. Lawrence and the Ottawa River, a large tributary from the north, and bordered by the St. Lawrence to the south and the Rivière des Prairies (an arm of the Ottawa) to the north. A few kilometers downstream, the Richelieu River, also known as the Iroquois River, flows into the St. Lawrence and provides a route southward. The small fort was founded in 1642 at the instigation of the deeply religious Jérôme Le Royer de la Dauversière of Anjou, but his utopian plan to recreate a new City of God peopled by devout Frenchmen and converted Amerindians did not resist the call of the continental interior and the Amerindians' lack of interest for long.

The river had an impact on the agricultural landscape. Conceded as a seigneury and acquired by the Sulpicians in 1663, the island was slow to develop. At first, the seigneurs created subfiefs granted to soldiers to establish a network of small forts on the island's perimeter that would act as frontline protection against Iroquois attack. These stockades, particularly those located upstream toward the western tip of the island and well placed to intercept flotillas of canoes, were very soon endowed with stores and used for fur trading. Many such stockades later became parish nodes, structuring the island's rural landscape.[10] The seigneurs then began to divide their land into censives. They kept a few domains for themselves, including two strategically placed on the waterway, and grouped the censives by côte, a set of fields aligned either with the St. Lawrence shoreline or with Mount Royal, the hill near the center of the island. The layout of the fields on the island was therefore more patchwork than the fairly parallel pattern seen elsewhere in New France.[11]

Initially very confined, the urban territory bore the mark of the river. The fortified city was built on a low elongated crest about three hundred meters wide lying parallel to the St. Lawrence, with its two main arteries serving separate functions. Merchants and the military were concentrated along St. Paul Street, an old trail along the river, while Notre Dame Street, built along the top of the crest, became the street of the religious institutions, housing the parish church, the St. Sulpice seminary, Hôtel Dieu, and the convent of the Sisters of the Congregation.[12]

Thus, as early as the seventeenth century, the St. Lawrence imposed an orientation not only on the city, but on the entire colony as well. Furthermore, flowing out of the Great Lakes, it constituted an enduring invitation to exploration and alliances with the Amerindians of the interior.

THE EIGHTEENTH CENTURY: THE FUR TRADE

The century was split by the British Conquest; however, both before and after 1763, the city's economy was structured around the fur trade and the gradual development of a hinterland.

The 1701 Peace of Montreal consolidated France's position and stimulated the colonization process while sparking the expansion of the western posts, a network of palisade forts that marked the presence of the king's troops and Montreal merchants in the heart of the continent. Though bolstered by strong natural growth, the population of New France would never resemble that of the British colonies, as immigration from France remained very low. However, population growth in the St. Lawrence Valley gradually led to the creation of Montreal's first agricultural hinterland. The center of the Montreal plain was slowly settled and new land was opened up.

The territory continued to be marked by the river. More intense exploration and the servicing of the western forts stimulated the development of the village of Lachine, which became Montreal's upstream outport. In fact, the barrier of the Lachine Rapids demanded a transfer of goods, and Montreal being the supply point for the western forts, all supplies had to be conveyed from Montreal to Lachine along a shoddy road. Somewhat farther upstream, at the tip of the island, the fort of St. Anne de Bellevue was the last stop for voyageurs to the Upper St. Lawrence and the point at which traffic forked off in one of two directions. Canoes heading toward the lower Great Lakes continued along the St. Lawrence, while those travelling to the upper Great Lakes turned off to the north and travelled along the Ottawa River to access Lake Huron via a series of portages.

Heightened fur trading and military-diplomatic activities reinforced the specialization of the urban space. Walls were built around the city, starting with a wood palisade in 1685, which was then rebuilt in stone and augmented between 1717 and 1744. The fortified city and its early suburbs stretched out along the edge of the river.

St. Paul Street was still polarized around business, leading to the construction of workshops and "vaults" for storing goods, while the military used a section of the shore to install the "King's Canoery," which provided the required logistical support to Montreal, the *"pays d'en haut,"* or upcountry, and the King's stores. It must be recalled that the alliance between France and the tribes of the interior was to a large extent based on annual exchanges of gifts of goods, as well as the supply of powder and maintenance of the Amerindian allied weaponry.

The British conquest of 1763 completely changed the continental geopolitics, as well as the role of the St. Lawrence in the colonial system. It introduced a rupture in the relationship among the St. Lawrence, Montreal, and the colony. The river lost its role as a continental inroad and instead became a colonial border. In fact, the Royal Proclamation of 1763 divided the territory of old New France by creating an Amerindian zone between the Great Lakes and Appalachian Mountains, created a "Province of Quebec" consisting only of the St. Lawrence Valley between the Ottawa River and Anticosti Island, and redistributed other land to the British colonies in the Gulf (the North Shore of the St. Lawrence, Labrador, and the islands). The St. Lawrence became simply a route to the interior serving the inhabited portion of former New France, which lay between the area immediately upstream from Montreal and Tadoussac. This state of affairs did not last long, however, as Great Britain soon realized that it had failed to achieve the objectives of the royal proclamation.[13]

The proclamation was aimed at keeping Amerindians neutral by banning white colonization beyond the Appalachian Mountains and strictly controlling interior land dealings. It aimed to thus create a true Amerindian protectorate in the West while redirecting the migration of the overflow of settlers from the thirteen American colonies northward to help assimilate the new conquest. But inhabitants of the thirteen colonies did not like being deprived of one of their goals of war—expansion into the interior. Amerindians, in turn, accustomed to a French alliance that treated them as equals, did not wish to be confined to the interior and rebelled in 1763–1764 under the leadership of Chief Pontiac. Great Britain reversed its position and in 1774, faced with agitation in its old colonies, decided to reshape the so-called Province of Quebec by annexing the Amerindian lands to it through the Quebec Act, hoping to thus recreate an entity capable of acting as a counterweight to the thirteen restive colonies. However, this act had very little impact on the role of the St. Lawrence. The American War of Independence ended in 1783 with the partition of the North American interior by a completely arbitrary line that split the traditional aboriginal territory in two. This put an end to the central role of the St. Lawrence in the development of the continental interior. The Amerindians were not deceived, as Pontiac's rebellion showed. However, deprived of their traditional French ally and their Canadian base, the Amerindians were powerless to resist. This sequence of events (1763–1783) marked a profound reorganization of power between European settlers and Amerindians that inaugurated a new phase in the subjugation of indigenous peoples in the continental interior.[14]

Change was slow to come, however. Because Great Britain refused to withdraw from the western forts before the end of the century, the British were able to lead the Amerindians to believe that they would be protected from the United States, while, on the economic front, Montreal continued to use the St. Lawrence as a route into the interior. The Jay Treaty of 1794 ended the imbroglio by giving the British two years to vacate the forts. By then, the city's fortifications no longer served any purpose and had in fact no longer been maintained since the 1760s.

THE NINETEENTH CENTURY: ERECTION OF THE PORT FACILITIES

In the nineteenth century, the city of Montreal underwent dramatic changes. A variety of activities had supplanted the fur trade as the economic base of the city. Between 1800 and 1830, the city became the metropolis of the British American colonies, outranking Quebec City, although the latter remained the capital. The growth process was sparked by the opening up of the West to agricultural colonization. Up until then, Montreal had ruled over a relatively small hinterland consisting of the Montreal plain. With the rapid development of Upper Canada, which became Ontario in 1867, the city acquired access to an extended, populated backcountry. From that time forward, its position as a break-bulk point at the head of navigation on the Lower St. Lawrence and its mouth into the sea generated substantial economic gains for the city, until the middle of the next century.

Such development was made possible by a profound change in the pace of immigration after the defeat of Napoleon, when Great Britain removed the ban on emigration. Beginning in 1815, a virtual flood of humanity swept into America. While most of the emigrants ended up in the United States, the influx was sufficient to stimulate the growth of the Canadian population. This was, in fact, the first wave of population diversification for central Canada. Montreal, for instance, evolved into a primarily British city between 1832 and 1867.

At the same time, the St. Lawrence played the new role of border with the United States. The War of 1812 abruptly revealed the frailty of the British colonial system. The battles took place in the Great Lakes region, and Great Britain discovered the vulnerability of its communication and supply lines. The bottleneck between Montreal and Kingston, at the entrance to the first of the Great Lakes, posed a series of problems, such as slow, costly transport, immediate proximity to the United States, and the need to station a large number of troops there. Great Britain therefore decided to promote the construction of a series of canals to secure supply lines to Kingston and bypass the Lachine Rapids. The main canals were the Rideau (1826–1832) on the Ottawa River, between Ottawa and Kingston, and the Lachine, on the Island of Montreal. Opened to navigation in 1825, the latter quickly became the key to, and symbol of, urban economic growth. Advances in transportation, shipyards, import-export activities, and manufacturing activities ensued, and, thanks to the widening of the canal in 1848 that gave it sufficient hydraulic

FIGURE 8.2. The port from the northeast. Photo by William Notman, circa 1885. This area is now known as the Old Port. In the middle background is the entrance to Lachine Canal. Railroad tracks line the wharf and the piers are not quite developed yet. Note the importance of sailing vessels. On the right-hand side are the Bonsecours Chapel and Market. The rest of the street is lined mostly with warehouses and a few offices. Library and Archives Canada (C-4898).

power, Montreal became the cradle of Canadian industrialization. Clusters of factories grew up on both sides of the canal. At the same time, the Port of Montreal began to develop in the 1830s and by the end of the century had reached a fair size.[15] The onset of railway construction in 1850 also reinforced the river axis (figure 8.2).

These developments had a direct effect on the urban space. The old fortification walls were essentially demolished between 1804 and 1810 to make way for major thoroughfares, particularly along the river. Montreal's territory was reorganized and polarized along a rapidly growing port and industrial axis, and, as a result, the St. Lawrence largely determined land use between 1830 and 1950, including the emergence of a downtown core, growth of industrial and working-class districts, and the development of middle-class districts.[16] It also determined the shape of the city: the urban built environment initially developed as an inverted "T," with the river shore as the horizontal bar and St. Lawrence Boulevard as the axis. The holes filled in over time, but the density and maturity of the fabric remained most apparent along these axes. Outside the city, agricultural land between Montreal and Lachine re-

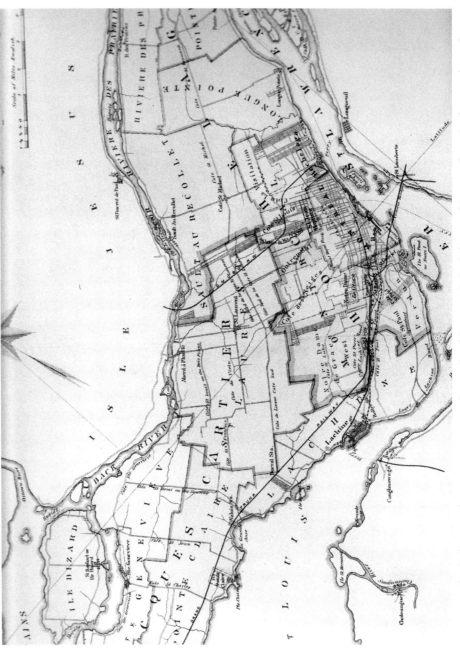

FIGURE 8.3: Island of Montreal. From Henry H. Hopkins, *Atlas of the City and Island of Montreal* (Montreal, 1879). This map shows the location of Lachine Rapids and the Lachine Canal. By 1879, the built area had spilled over the old Montreal, creating an inverted "T" shape. Railway lines are shown, some running alongside the river. Library and Archives Canada (C-12140).

treated to make way for factories and warehouses. The traditional activities of riverside villages were disrupted and polarized by transportation and the needs of the urban market (figure 8.3).

The St. Lawrence became the border but also the link among the British colonies. This link was formalized in 1867 by confederation, which united two-thirds of the remaining British North American colonies, greatly to the advantage of central Canadian cities like Montreal and Toronto.

THE TWENTIETH CENTURY: REVISIONS

Relations between Montreal and the St. Lawrence remained fairly stable until the middle of the century. During the initial years, the Port of Montreal was Canada's largest harbor in terms of handling, benefiting from the influx of western wheat that travelled east by train and was stored in the immense grain elevators so admired by the city's bourgeoisie and architects like Le Corbusier before being shipped to foreign markets. In 1928, it was even the world's largest grain port. The city polarized every transportation axis. The railroads were run out of their head offices in Montreal, and, after the Second World War, Montreal's airport reigned for a quarter century as the sole point of entry to Canada on the Atlantic coast (figure 8.4).

However, around 1950, things began to change radically. Since the 1920s, the economic environments of the Great Lakes region, in both Canada and the United States, had been looking to break free from the domination of the Montreal and New York harbors, which they perceived as an unnecessary hindrance. Between 1954 and 1959, a new generation of canal was therefore built, of sufficient gauge to allow deep-sea vessels to travel upstream. This spelled the end of Montreal's cargo transfer monopoly. Furthermore, ironically enough, the entrance to the new canal was on the south shore of the river across from the city, which meant that ships did not even have to stop there.

Along with the transformation of port operations, the 1950s marked the permanent ascendance of truck transport over rail. However, while the railway tracks had always essentially replicated and bolstered the river and shore axes, roads and highways tended to break loose from them. For Montreal, this entailed a loss of interest in the traditional space-structuring axes like the Lachine Canal, the riverfront, and the railway tracks. Furthermore, beginning in the late nineteenth century and accelerating around the time of the First World War, the old historic center, heir to earlier constraints associated with the river and the fortifications, began to spill beyond its setting, pushing the development axes toward the residential city. Big retailers, for instance, moved from Notre Dame and St. James streets further up the hill, transforming St. Catherine Street, a purely residential artery, into the primary com-

FIGURE 8.4. Montreal Harbor and Lachine Canal around 1950. In the foreground are the Point St. Charles railway yards and shops, leading to Victoria Bridge, inaugurated in 1860. The first shops date from 1854. In the lower middle is the Lachine Canal, with its basins and entrance in the harbor with the first double locks. The central portion of the port is lined with the main piers and, after the Jacques-Cartier Bridge, is stretching to the northeast with the east-end jetties appearing on the upper right. The central downtown area has already progressed well away from the river. The Bonsecours Chapel and Market are barely visible, hidden behind a grain elevator (upper middle right). Canadian National Railways Archives, (CN 53723-4).

mercial axis. Offices and industry followed, and today the downtown core occupies the entire area between Sherbrooke Street and the St. Lawrence, which in fact corresponds to the urbanized area of the whole city in 1870.[17]

Nevertheless, even today, the Port of Montreal remains one of the great Canadian harbors, having become the main transit point for containers. This technological evolution was accompanied by a spatial migration, as the harbor facilities, long concentrated near downtown, are now centered further downstream, in the northeast part of the city. Thus, anyone content to visit Montreal's Old Port cannot form any concept of the vitality of the port activities, as this old heart of the harbor has been stripped of almost all its facilities and redeveloped for recreational purposes. Only the presence of a few old buildings and, in winter, a few boats tied up alongside its quays are a reminder of the importance of commercial navigation.

These changes entailed both the redefinition of the city and river relationship and the adjustment of Montrealers' perceptions. Ecological, tourist, and recreational dimensions are gradually displacing the economic imperatives that once ruled.

In fact, after 1950, the immediacy of the St. Lawrence's impact on the urban territory lessened as development became marked by other factors, including tertiarization of the economy, the automobile, and urban sprawl, which began to accelerate in the 1960s. The edges of the urban agglomeration extend very far from the Island of Montreal and have come to occupy much of the heart of the plain. Today, we can almost say that Montrealers perceive the impact of the river on the city to be mostly limited to traffic jams caused by rush hour congestion on road bridges.

Ironically, Montrealers appear to have rediscovered the St. Lawrence at a time when its role on the city's development is on the decline. The World's Fair of 1967 played a central part in this evolution. Often associated solely with the infamous phrase "Vive le Québec libre" uttered by France's General De Gaulle, Expo '67 in fact marked a new urban awareness for Montrealers, particularly the French-speaking population. Linked to the breakup of the parish structure, which had long informed and guided French Canadians' perception of urbanity, this rediscovery of the city was accompanied by a search for new elements of sociability.[18] In this context, the identification of new meeting places became central. Thus, Expo '67 proposed the transformation of an urban park, Saint Helen's Island in front of Montreal, into a vast mixed space, with green space but also with an urbanized, landscaped area that provided a new outlook on the river and the city. This substitution of a recreational function for the river has since underlain many of the urban development projects, sometimes leading to controversy over the use of the rare Old Port quays still used for shipping purposes, an indication of the speed with which a segment of the population is willing to set aside this aspect of reality.

Tourism has grown since the 1970s. In the Canadian and North American context, Montreal is a city with considerable history. It also has certain features: a downtown with fairly unique Victorian architecture and a strikingly coherent, extensive waterfront.[19] The redefinition of traditional urban functions can be found throughout the city, in its old railway beds transformed into bicycle paths or green belts, old industrial buildings transformed into lofts, and old office buildings converted into luxury apartments.

Such transformations are, of course, not unique to Montreal. They have occurred in many Western cities as the urban economy changed, particularly with the decline of industrial activities and the rise of tertiarization.

THE ST. LAWRENCE THEREFORE played a central role, not only in the city's foundation and development but in the history of Canada and of America.

Once a trade axis marked and traveled by indigenous populations for thousands of years, it served as the backbone of French penetration and organization of the continent. In the eighteenth century, it enabled the creation of a space for contact and acculturation between Europeans and Amerindians, a "Middle Ground" where miscegenation was the norm.[20] With the decisive triumph of the British in 1763, the river's role changed, transforming into that of border zone. The independence of the United States in 1783 only reinforced this change in function. The St. Lawrence's importance as a penetration route was reduced to just a few aspects, like its role as a port of entry for many immigrants. But this was a passive role, as this immigration route was wholly dependent on manpower requirements in the United States, which closed the route promptly whenever this served its interests. However, from about 1835 on, Great Britain sought to strengthen its colonial system in the face of the territorial insatiability of the United States. And, in this context, London promoted the union of its colonies, leading to confederation in 1867; the St. Lawrence played a key role in this, both economic and symbolic. The fact that the very first political meeting on the new constitution was held on an island in the estuary was no coincidence: the steamboat carrying Canadian delegates to the Charlottetown Conference left from Quebec City, and for Upper and Lower Canadians the river was perceived as the element linking the various colonies together.

For Montreal, the St. Lawrence very quickly determined the city's functions and oriented its layout. One can readily assert that the waterway is largely responsible for the failure of the mystical dream of 1642: the city's religious function would never prevail over its commercial function. It was inevitable that the call of the West, of the "pays d'en haut," would prove irresistible. Furthermore, the river was in large part responsible for the city's development and use of the space over time.

The city in fact grew up from the shore beginning in the seventeenth century; its buildings were designed to serve the functions of transport, reception, and distribution of goods. In the eighteenth century, the layout of its streets and fortification walls were linked to the waterway. In the nineteenth century, marked by the city's accelerated growth—from nine thousand inhabitants in 1800 to over two hundred and fifty thousand in 1900—the impact of the functions associated with the river greatly increased as economic development axes were created with the harbor, railways, and industry. Working-class and middle-class districts formed, and the old center began to specialize around 1850. In the twentieth century, the remarkable expansion of the harbor in the downriver direction continued to orient land use. From then on, nearly the entire southern part of the island was polarized around activities related to the St. Lawrence. Beginning in the 1950s, there was a slowdown in traditional economic functions that relied on the waterway, and activities associated with Montreal's role as a cargo transfer port in particular receded to make way for new functions. The economic diversification that Montreal underwent after 1970 made the urban economy less vulnerable to river traffic issues, albeit at the cost of a severe economic slowdown.

Today, the city may appear to have ended its dependence on the river, but, despite the many new economic developments and global and transnational phenomena, the St. Lawrence still remains an essential pole of activity for the city and constitutes a core element of both its urban identity and its landscapes.

9

URBANIZATION, INDUSTRIALIZATION, AND THE FIRTH OF FORTH

T. C. SMOUT

The water environment considered in this chapter is different from the others discussed in this book. The Firth of Forth is a saline embayment of the North Sea that receives the freshwater input of some twenty rivers, most of them small. It divides into two parts at the narrows at Queensferry, now crossed by the Forth bridges (figure 9.1). Above that point it is the estuary of the Forth, with predominantly muddy shores and bottom, naturally fairly shallow except near Queensferry, receiving most of the freshwater input. The estuary is tidal to Stirling and of relatively low salinity due to the difficulty of flushing it completely. Below that point is the outer Firth of Forth, with mainly rocky or sandy shores and bottom, with greater salinity and relatively vigorous scouring. Nevertheless, the ecology of the westerly part of the outer Firth is still locally influenced by fresh water and does not entirely have the same marine biodiversity as the easterly part. This is particularly evident in the distribution of seaweeds.[1]

Edinburgh (with its port of Leith) sits on the Firth of Forth just east of the Queensferry narrows. For at least three centuries from the sixteenth century it was the largest Scottish town, reaching a population of 40,000 inhabitants in the seventeenth century and 90,000 in 1801. It was eventually overtaken by Glasgow in the nineteenth century, but also at that point it embarked on a period of massive expansion that raised the population living within the present bounds to 413,000 in 1901. It is usually assumed that Edinburgh was largely a service center, but in fact in 1901 it was then also Scotland's second industrial city in terms of employment.[2] Growth slowed within the city, though not necessarily in the surrounding area, and in 2001 Edinburgh's population was 448,000 inhabitants.

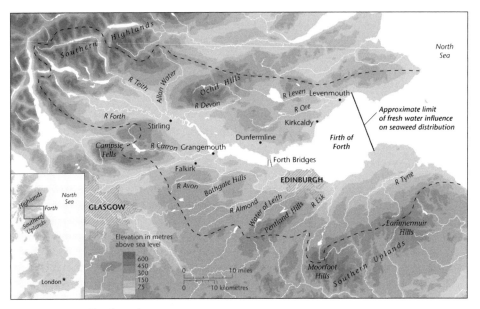

FIGURE 9.1. Forth catchment.

The influence of Edinburgh on industry in the surrounding area has also been considerable (figure 9.2). From the sixteenth century, the coal fields around the Firth, in Lothian around Edinburgh and in Fife on the opposite shore, began to expand. It would indeed have been difficult for the city to grow to the size that it did early on without coal, as peat was in limited supply locally and wood fuel was unobtainable. Edinburgh became "Auld Reekie" from the late seventeenth century and until the mid-twentieth century was famous for its blackened buildings and the pall of smoke that hung over it on calm days: the lichen flora of surrounding woods is still impoverished downwind of the ancient plume. As the capital of the law and the Kirk (also until 1707 of Parliament), and as the home of the printing and publishing concerns that followed the Scottish Enlightenment, it had great need of the paper mills on the Water of Leith and along the river Esk to the east. The need to clothe the citizens encouraged textile mills along the river Devon and river Leven on the opposite side of the Forth. Breweries and distilleries developed within the city and upriver toward Alloa and in Fife.

Nor was Edinburgh the only town or sole source of industrial stimulus. There were early sites of royal palaces at Linlithgow, Stirling, and Dunfermline that became abiding regional market and retail centers, and in Dunfermline's case a manufacturing center for linen. Though as late as 1841 urbanization was still very limited, with only five towns other than Edinburgh and Leith with more than five thousand inhabitants. There were late

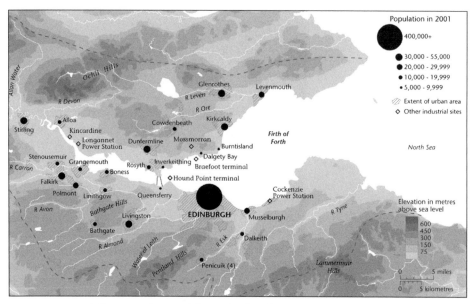

FIGURE 9.2. Urban growth around the Firth of Forth.

nineteenth-century industrial growth points at Kirkcaldy, based on linen and then linoleum, and at Falkirk (with associated Polmont and Stenhousemuir), based on metal and extractive trades. There was also then a huge expansion in the coal industry based on the possibility of movement by rail and steamship, but with its concomitant demise in the twentieth century. At the same time the shale oil industry of West Lothian and Stirlingshire arose dramatically, creating the first mineral oil processing works in the world at Bathgate, but that was even shorter lived. Both these extractive industries left a plethora of mining towns, like Cowdenbeath, later looking for an economic purpose, but they persisted as small urban settlements. Bo'ness was a coal-shipping town with a significant dry dock from 1881; the harbor closed in 1959. Rosyth was a Royal Navy base from 1903 to 1994 and still houses seven decommissioned nuclear submarines. Inverkeithing became a ship-breaking center from 1848 and Burntisland next door a shipbuilding center and later (until 2002) an import point for bauxite for the aluminum industry. The twentieth century saw Grangemouth expand as a harbor and pipeline terminal and the principal oil refining and chemical manufacturing center in Scotland, and Livingston and Glenrothes were created after the Second World War as overspill under the new towns program. While greenbelt policy held Edinburgh itself in check after 1945, there was significant expansion in other outlying towns, like Musselburgh and Dalkeith, and new commuter communities like Dalgety Bay.

Despite an element of deindustrialization in the later twentieth century, large coal-fired power stations were built at Longannet, Kincardine, and Cockenzie, oil shipment points at Hound Point, and a gas cracking plant with associated shipping facilities at Mossmorran and Braefoot Point. Oil rigs were built and maintained at Levenmouth. The urbanization of the area was wide and deep. By 1981 the tidal waters of the Firth of Forth received the drainage from a catchment area in which 1.3 million people lived, 35 percent of them in Edinburgh. This was about a quarter of the population of Scotland.

Water and shoreline were crucial to all this activity. Transport was one issue. When the partners of Carron Iron Company established what is often considered the first modern industrial concern in Scotland in 1759, to make coke-fired iron and cast it into cannon and domestic articles like firebacks and railings, their choice of site on the river Carron close to Falkirk was determined by its navigable position and abundance of fresh water.[3] This was followed by the construction of a canal, 1768–1790, from the river Clyde close to Glasgow, to the river Carron and thus to the Forth estuary near Grangemouth, linking by water the east and west coasts of Scotland, and then in 1822 by the Union Canal, effectively an extension of the Forth-Clyde Canal to Edinburgh.

On the shore itself, transport needs for docks and warehousing, especially at Grangemouth, Leith, Granton, Rosyth, and Bo'ness, demanded land reclamation, a process that had already been going on for centuries for agricultural purposes in the higher parts of the estuary. About half the original intertidal mud flats had been lost to land claim by the late twentieth century. A channel in the estuary was also deepened to accommodate ships for Bo'ness and Grangemouth, with gravel and other spoil dumped over the mud, altering the sea floor.

Power was another purpose for water, and the many unnavigable small rivers that ran into the Firth of Forth became seams of industrial activity. The first cotton mill in Scotland was built at Penicuik in 1773, and the Esk, Water of Leith, parts of the Almond, the Devon, the Carron, and the Leven all became lined with mills to make paper from rags or esparto grass, to grind, slit, or crush various materials, and to turn machines. Where there was no head of water, it might be necessary to build a reservoir: the earliest was Gartmorn Dam near Alloa, built at the opening of the eighteenth century by the Earl of Mar to power pumps for his coal mines.

In the nineteenth century, one of the most important uses of riverine water became extraction or impoundment for drinking, flushing toilets, or for use in industry. The situation in the Forth catchment was complicated by the fact that Glasgow tapped the headwaters of the principal river before any of the towns of the Forth (figure 9.3). That river was the Teith, which rose in the high wet country of the Trossachs east of Loch Lomond before joining the

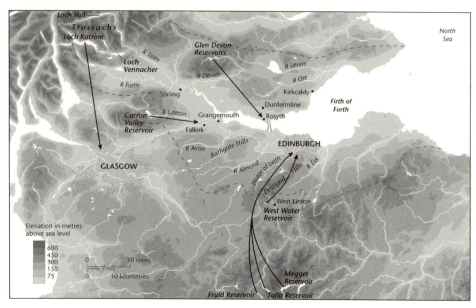

FIGURE 9.3. Main reservoirs.

river Forth, and it actually had a greater volume of water flow than the river that gave its name to the Firth. In 1855 an act was passed authorizing Glasgow to take water from Loch Katrine, which fed the Teith, and transport it thirty-four miles into the city by lead pipe and brick tunnel. The undertaking was completed in 1859, an astonishing act of Victorian engineering panache. John La Trobe Bateman, the contractor, called it, with no false modesty, "a truly Roman work . . . a work which surpasses the greatest of the nine famous aqueducts which fed the city of Rome."[4]

There had been objections from the east of Scotland, including from Stirling, where the town fishing rentals were a major source of municipal income, and from the Admiralty, which feared the diversion of water would ruin the Forth for navigation by depriving it of its scouring ability. Glasgow paid a modest annual sum to Stirling as recompense, and the engineers tried to meet the objections by providing a compensation reservoir at Loch Vennacher downstream from Loch Katrine, complete with fish ladder for the salmon, but the latter did not work very well and the absence of winter floods after the scheme was introduced made the river more sluggish and muddy, less able to flush out pollution. The scheme initially provided about 50 million gallons a day, but capacity was doubled in 1885 and modified again in 1909 to capture additional water destined by nature to feed Loch Lomond. By the time of the First World War, 122 million gallons a day could be sent to Glasgow from these works. The annual value of the fishings at Stirling dropped from £1300 around 1860 to £200 by 1910, though most of the diminution was probably due to increased pollution on the other tributaries of the Forth, as we shall see.[5]

In 1913 the City of Glasgow sponsored a further bill, which would have allowed them to dam Loch Voil, also in the Trossachs but on another tributary to the north, abstracting forty million gallons but sending only twenty-nine million back by way of compensation. This was opposed by the Scottish Fisheries Board, due to the threat to salmon, and it failed to become law through defeat in the House of Lords. Had it passed, it would have removed the biggest remaining source of winter flooding that could flush some of the pollution out of the system.[6]

Edinburgh itself also increasingly needed large volumes of water as it grew in size and industry. Initially it supplemented wells within the city by tapping springs in the Pentland hills to the south and brought them by conduit to standpipes where they were collected and carried to the houses. By 1880 there were 250 such springs, but they provided (even with some help from small reservoirs) only a modest flow, though Edinburgh was now using much more water with flushing toilets in the home. Even this extraction affected the Water of Leith, and the mill owners there received compensation water from a series of small reservoirs in the hills. In a similar way, the flow on the Esk was maintained for the paper mill proprietors. Some of the compensation reservoirs were also in due course used to provide drinking water to the city, but water shortage remained acute in comparison to Glasgow's lavish supplies. The city fathers realized it could no longer be supplied locally, so they began to construct a new reservoir at Talla in the Tweed catchment beyond the Pentlands, opened around 1900 with an aqueduct thirty-five miles long and providing an additional twenty-five million gallons. In the 1960s this was supplemented by Fruid reservoir nearby, and in 1982 by Megget Water reservoir, also on the Tweed catchment, which, along with a further new reservoir at West Water in the Pentlands, now became the main sources of water for the city.[7] The last became a famous roost for up to fifty-five thousand pink-footed geese in winter, and the deep, cold waters of Talla have been used to reintroduce the native Arctic char. Big reservoirs have their biodiversity benefits.

Towns in Fife on the northern shore, on the other hand, initially drew water from a plethora of medium to tiny local reservoirs, their size often reflecting the inability of neighboring towns to cooperate: as late as 1968, Fife and Kinross were served by eighteen different authorities before they were all swept into one regional water board.[8] Here, it was military need that first grappled with the problem of adequate supply, and in the First World War a substantial reservoir was built by German prisoners of war in Glen Devon in the Ochils to bring water to the naval dockyard at Rosyth and to Dunfermline, followed in 1955 by a second reservoir in the same area to supply other towns in west Fife. On the upper stretches of the river Carron a large new reservoir was built in 1939 to provide for the domestic and industrial needs of the growing conurbation around Falkirk and Grangemouth. Carron water obliterated a remarkable area of bog-hay meadows with considerable biodiversity and cultural value, but became itself by the end of the century home to the largest flock of bean geese in Britain.

Thus, from the middle of the nineteenth century onward, engineers commanded the waters in ways unthinkable before. Water flows often bore little relation to river flows and original catchments; Glasgow on the Clyde used the Forth, Edinburgh on the Forth used the Tweed, the towns of Fife and Stirlingshire did use the Forth catchment but often carried the water fifteen miles or more from the impoundment. New lakes appeared, and the level of old lakes rose and fell at the whim of urban demand.

However, the main use of rivers and streams for Edinburgh and throughout the Forth catchment was as a dump, the ultimate waste absorber that would bear away the troubles of industrialization and lose them in the sea. Very little waste existed before the second half of the nineteenth century. Materials were recycled more often, and human dung mixed with the detritus of the home was left in the street for the farmers to collect. This was a practice well organized in Edinburgh since the late seventeenth century, but one that rendered the city, with its high narrow wynds and refuse flung from the windows to the cry of "gardyloo," notoriously smelly. Nevertheless, the farmers of the surrounding parishes found it a rich resource that enabled them to keep their fields under crops with little need for fallow, often with a monoculture of wheat sold to the town baxters who baked it into bread and in turn sold to the citizens so that the whole recycling could begin again. The price of the waste was often a matter of contention between the city fathers and the agricultural interest, the farmers forming cartels to maintain a low price. In 1787 when the turnpike authorities tried to charge for the carts, the farmers refused to move the ordure from the streets until that decision was rescinded.[9]

By the 1840s, however, the sustainable cycle of sewage-to-food-to-sewage was beginning to change under the pressure of urban growth on the one hand and convenient fertilizers on the other. In 1841 the conurbation of Edinburgh was three times the size it had been in 1750; in 1901 it was three times as big as in 1841. Meanwhile, farmers from the 1840s began to find phosphorus and nitrogen cheaply and cleanly available in bags of imported Peruvian guano and manufactured bone meal. As the supply of human waste increased and the demand declined, more of it accumulated for longer and found its way through cesspits into wells. The city was struck by a series of epidemics of a traumatic severity unknown since the days of bubonic plague in the seventeenth century. Cholera struck in 1832, 1848, and 1853 (and mildly in 1866), typhus especially in 1847, and typhoid more constantly. Edwin Chadwick's *Sanitary Report* of 1842 concluded that the Scottish cities were the worst afflicted by "fever" of any in Britain. His solution here and elsewhere was to recommend the closure of urban wells, a supply of pure piped water to homes, and then sewers to bear human and industrial waste away.[10]

Edinburgh resented the expense but could not ignore the logic of death. In 1848 an Edinburgh Police Act gave the local authority extensive sanitary powers and soon a water company was supplying houses throughout Edinburgh and its satellite burghs of Leith and Portobello. Provision per head per day went up from 12 gallons in 1844 to 42 gallons in 1886, although insufficiency of supply long remained a matter for complaint. Cesspools were closed, water closet toilets built, and sewers constructed over the course of thirty years to convey the waste away, though initially only as far as the nearest river or stream. Other household refuse such as ashes remained the responsibility of the council and were separately consigned to landfill, and what could be burned was eventually put into incinerators, with the first destructor, at Powderhall, being built in 1893. In some rural areas, however, the sale of refuse did continue—in 1872 it was reported that the sewage of the workforce mixed with rag dust and ashes was still directly sold to local farmers by the factory owners of Markinch in Fife.[11]

The sewers on the west side of Edinburgh mostly discharged into the Water of Leith at Dalry and quickly became the target of complaint, as they fouled to an intolerable degree the mills that lined the banks and particularly the harbor at its mouth. New legislation was passed in 1854, 1864, and 1889 to improve the problem, and early on an interceptor sewer was built (and eventually extended to capture raw sewage from as far up as Balerno twenty miles upstream) to take the waste directly to a marine outfall beyond the harbor. Elsewhere in Edinburgh, the sewers flowed into small open streams and thence to "irrigation meadows" where the nitrogen from the waste produced lavish crops of grass, enough, Chadwick said, to support four thousand cows. The largest of the streams was the aptly named Foul Burn, which by 1872 was conveying sewage from one hundred thousand people to 250 acres of meadow on the Earl of Moray's land at Lochend and Craigentinny. A smaller stream at Lochrin watered 60–70 acres, part of which is now Murrayfield international rugby ground. However, the Figgate Burn (also known as the Pow Burn or Braid Burn) ran straight into the sea at Portobello, without any intervening meadows, taking the sewage of about a sixth of the city, that of the south side. It was revolting, and litigation between Portobello and Edinburgh eventually, in 1882, compelled the city to construct a covered sewer to carry it straight to the sea.[12]

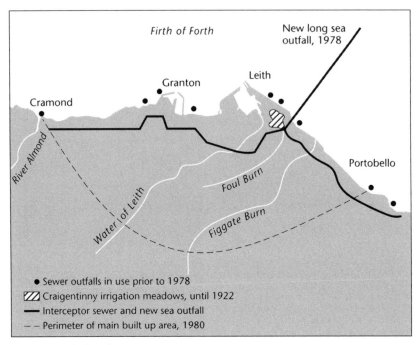

FIGURE 9.4. Edinburgh sewage.

This system of irrigation meadows dated from around 1760 on a small scale, and in 1842 Queen Victoria had chosen to stay with the Duke of Buccleuch at Dalkeith apparently to avoid the smell near Hollyrood. Nevertheless, the utilitarian mind of Edwin Chadwick had been impressed by the value added to sandy wastes by the addition of sewage. From the 1840s the system was extended, and for the next three decades Craigentinny was internationally cited as an example of how the new liquid waste disposal regimes could be made to pay through recycling. The meadows produced grass worth £24–£30 an acre per year around 1870, and the medical officers of health carried out checks that showed the milk as safe as any other. The farmer who lived in the middle with six children declared, "I have never felt the smell or effluvia doing myself or my family any harm."[13] No doubt Craigentinny was also a wonderful site for breeding and migrant birds, as sewage farms were elsewhere in Britain, but no Scottish ornithologist seems to have been hardy enough to find out.

The downside, of course, was the disgusting smell that pervaded the vicinity of the burns and the meadows, and due to the fact that the filtering effect was apparently very slight, the sewage flowing out of the meadows and into the sea was almost as nasty as when it flowed in. In 1922, in the face of falling values for the grass and rising value for the land, Craigentinny meadows were closed, becoming housing and a public golf course. The Foul Burn was covered over, and the entire sewage of Edinburgh from then until 1978 went into the sea with minimal filtration, through eight major outfalls along the shore (figure 9.4).

Sewage was not the only problem, nor Edinburgh the only location for problems. The Royal Commission on River Pollution in 1872 considered the neighborhood excellent for study "because of the curiously specific character of the foulness which the streams and running waters of Mid Lothian severally experience." While the streams draining the site of the capital carry the "personal waste of the large population of that city" and "may be said to represent almost strictly the nuisance due simply to town sewage," the North Esk and the Water of Leith (the latter having been mainly freed of sewage by then) "exhibit almost exclusively the effect of paper manufacture on otherwise unpolluted streams." The Almond, running in from West Lothian, showed in different parts the effects of flax steeping for linen manufacture, of drainage from whisky distilleries, and of "the distillation of oil-bearing shales."[14]

The paper mills on the Esk had been a cause of complaint for decades, and in 1841 the Duke of Buccleuch and two of his neighbors raised a legal process against the manufacturers for nuisance, "stimulated by the horrible stench of a river which flows through their parks and under the very windows of their houses." It took twenty-five years of legal wrangling, until 1866, to obtain a verdict in their favor, cost the Duke £6000, "and the other parties, very much more." Thereafter the nuisance was reported as much reduced, but it still left the Esk nearly as foul as the Irwell below Manchester, regarded as about the most polluted river in England. The Water of Leith suffered in the same way and smelt worse as it had a weaker flow of water to carry the pollution away. The main cause was considered to be the discharge into the rivers of the liquor of the esparto grass used to make paper, an irony as the main harbor for importing esparto, at Granton west of Leith, belonged to the Duke of Buccleuch.[15]

Pollution caused by the paraffin works was even more dramatic. In 1872, witnesses from Linlithgow and Broxburn told of setting fire to streams polluted with oil: "for curiosity I threw in a lighted piece of paper when it blazed up about twenty feet high." The Almond, "previously a charm" and at Cramond Brig "sweet and clean and much used for making tea," had become there "a very dirty turbid river, smelling strongly of paraffin oil . . . useless for all purposes, constituting in summer a horribly offensive nuisance." Even the cattle would not drink from it.[16] Gross pollution by paraffin waste diminished over the following decade when manufacturers found they could profitably recycle some before it entered the rivers, yet the oil-refining industry as a whole remained one of the most serious sources of water pollution in the Forth until well into the 1970s.

When the commission moved outside the immediate Edinburgh region they did not find things better. At the head of the estuary, where the Forth ran in from Stirling, there was terrible pollution, from town sewage and effluent from textile mills, distilleries, and oil works. The river Devon below Dollar was a tributary of the Forth and particularly bad, stinking and rainbow-colored, in summer a "seething mass of polluted and disgusting corruption, deadly in its effects on the life of both man and fish."[17] The river Leven in Fife was much the same, with pollution from untreated sewage, distillery waste, chlorine from paper mills, and bleaches from spinning mills, as well as water extraction from a brick factory and a foundry and potential pollution from a cyanide factory, a creosote works, saltworks, linseed oil mills, and industrial laundries. It was later made particularly bad with the addition of a mass of coal dust from the washings of Fife Coal Company, established in 1877, and other local mines.[18]

Indignation about the state of the rivers ran high among many witnesses before the commission. Colonel Sir J. E. Alexander, a salmon proprietor on the Devon, expressed astonishment that "in a professedly moral and religious community" mill owners and distillers did not of their own accord take every means to keep the rivers clean. He assumed that "hastening to be rich overcomes all scruples" and reported that offenders, when challenged, blamed their neighbors: "It is not my stuff that hurts the fish, it's the chloride of lime from the paper mill, or the essential oil from the distillery, or the petroleum from the secret works."[19]

Manufacturers naturally had a different perspective. The papermakers were concerned lest "blind interdicts" should hamper their competitive position, "considering the paramount importance of manufactures in this country in regard to expense," and the owner of a paraffin works observed that "if manufacturers are hindered for the sake of the streams, it is a mistaken policy." It was easy to imply that it was a class matter, of fish versus jobs, of proprietors versus the people, or of local selfishness versus national interest.[20]

In the event, Parliament largely sidestepped the Royal Commission on River Pollution's report and attended to the manufacturers' anxieties by let-out clauses in legislation. Manufacturers and others were supposed to show they had taken "the best practicable and reasonably available means" to avoid polluting a river. In acts applying to Scotland of 1867, 1876, and 1897, it was left to local authorities to take action, but they were themselves part of the problem and also dominated by the vested interests of local industrialists. Alternatively, a private action for nuisance could be pursued, but this was expensive and protracted, with the likelihood of success uncertain against wealthy industrial interests, unless the complainant had matching aristocratic wealth.

The 1876 act appointed an Inspector of Rivers for Scotland, with powers to issue certificates to manufacturers testifying that they had taken the "best practicable means" to avoid pollution, but by 1885 he had never issued a single certificate as the requirement was "too absolute." However no action followed against polluters. Questions were asked in Parliament as to why a salary of £50 a year was paid to an official who could not carry out his duties, but he was spared the axe.[21] In 1898 the powerless inspector observed that the main offenders along the Devon were three local authorities who poured untreated sewage into the rivers and twenty-nine manufacturers. The river was still as turbid, discolored, and polluted as in Colonel Alexander's day, receiving tributaries "rich in soapy water and the usual constituents of sewage," and on the main river "bells of gas were to be seen breaking on the surface."[22]

In 1902 the Commissioners on the Salmon Fisheries described what had made the river Forth and its tributaries increasingly polluted over the last forty years: the increase of sewage from settlements of all kinds; untreated organic effluents from breweries, distilleries, paper works and tanneries (which deprived the water of oxygen); and toxic wastes such as chlorine from bleaching and paper works, acids from steel and tin plate works, alkalis from wool washing, and gas lime, cyanides, and carbolic acids from gasworks. The only river where sewage was treated in any way before discharge was the Teith (presumably because the main pressures on local authorities in this very rural area were the landed salmon proprietors). On the Devon the local authority of Clackmannanshire always deferred to the problems of the manufacturers. The Forth District Salmon Fisheries Board, though set up under legislation from as far back as 1862 and 1868, remained powerless and unable to afford the litigation necessary to challenge the councils or industry.[23]

Elsewhere in Britain, in the interwar years, improvements in calibrating official standards and in voluntary compliance sometimes helped to mitigate existing problems of waste disposal.[24] In the Forth region, however, these were ineffectual or at least entirely counterbalanced by new industrial and housing developments, with Grangemouth in particular proving a new source of serious pollution from the expanding oil-refining and chemical industries from around 1924. Although a Forth Conservancy Board had been established, by provisional order in 1919 and by Act of Parliament in 1921, with a remit for the "improvement, control, protection, maintenance and conservancy" of the river and Firth of Forth, between Stirling Bridge to a point a little beyond the Forth Bridge, its interests were in reclamation and navigation.[25] Despite a responsibility for the "supply of water" it totally neglected water quality. The reports of the Scottish Fisheries Board throughout the 1920s show the problems of pollution getting steadily worse. The establishment of a Scottish Advisory Committee on River Pollution in 1930, and their detailed reports issued over the next decade, underlined the atrocious conditions and did spade work that proved useful eventually, but the actual problems were not tackled until after the Second World War.

What were the biological impacts of all this? The first indications of their seriousness came from the plight of riverine fish in the smaller rivers. The Leven in Fife with its tributary the river Ore, for example, were considered the most polluted rivers in Scotland. It was reported in 1930 that salmon had not been seen for "very many years," sea trout had disappeared around the 1880s, and brown trout had died out "recently." The entire river, apart from a short distance below Loch Leven, was now "completely devoid of all fish life." Similar reports followed in 1932 concerning the Esk and the Almond, still as lifeless as the Royal Commission had reported them in 1872, and other reports later covered the Avon and the Carron with similar results. Salmon continued to run up the river Forth and some of its tributaries, particularly the Teith, though in much reduced numbers: the drop in the value of the Stirling fisheries by over 80 percent between 1860 and 1910 we have already referred to. Mass kills of fish repeatedly occurred in the river Forth and increasingly in the tidal estuary above Alloa. The Scottish Fisheries Board in 1923 called the death of numbers of salmon and sea trout in the Forth "an annual occurrence" and in 1926 spoke of the large numbers of fish that died on the spring run "in their attempt to penetrate the turbid waters of the estuary," with a similar problem for smolts on their return. In 1937, the board warned of a disaster to salmon and sea trout fishing unless steps were taken to reduce pollution.[26]

One fish, the sparling, or smelt (*Osmerus eperlanus*), did succumb, at least for a time. It was a small, mainly marine species, highly regarded by the Victorian palate, tasting somewhat like cucumber. It was caught in bag nets by the fishermen of Alloa and Kincardine at the head of the estuary and in 1838 it was said that "numbers are sent to the Edinburgh market where it receives a ready sale." It came up the Forth to breed as far as the saltwater reached and at that time was described as so abundant in the river below Stirling that "every stone, plank and post appears to be covered with their yellowish ova." It became steadily rarer. By 1914 only 550 hundredweight were caught in the Forth, though they reached a unit price eight times that for similarly sized sprats in a year when the price for the latter was unusually high. By 1932 the catch was down to 214 hundredweight, and the last mention of a commercial catch was in 1938. A few individuals were recorded as present as late as 1963, but none were then recorded until 1991, when they began to reappear in small numbers as the oxygen content of the water improved.[27]

The first scientific investigations into the biological and chemical plight of the estuary and the wider Firth came in the late 1950s. River Purification Boards had been set up in 1951 by the Rivers Purification (Scotland) Act, the most important legislation since 1876, but until 1960 they had no jurisdiction over the sea: at that point the Lothians Board was given responsibilities for waters in the southern Firth to the edge of West Lothian and the Forth Board for the remainder, including the head of the estuary. They came at a parlous time. There was a period in the middle 1950s when the salmon and sea trout fishery was "in some danger of being wiped out" by extensive mortalities of smolts and of adult fish in the estuary itself.[28] The threat came from heavy biological pollution removing dissolved oxygen from the water, creating "oxygen sag," which was usually at its worst in summer when flow was low. The scientists found a moving barrier of impassable water that floated from about eight kilometers above Alloa at high tide to four kilometers below at low tide, measured as in place for eighteen days out of twenty-five sampled in 1961, with migrating fish lurking below it waiting for a chance to get through. The average levels of oxygen in the river improved after that and by 1976 the estuary was impassable on only three days sampled out of twenty-one. By the end of the century the average levels of dissolved oxygen were twice what they had been in the early 1960s and fully met official standards.[29]

Studying how the life of the mud flats was affected by pollution also began in these decades, notably with an investigation of the situation off Grangemouth, where Imperial Chemical Industries and BP dumped their waste. The immediate vicinities of the outfalls were abiotic, lifeless, but an area just beyond enjoyed very high biomass but limited biodiversity, that is, large numbers of few species, like the dense beds of filamentous blue-green algae near the effluent channels, and fauna "dominated by opportunistic worms," especially annelids and oligochaetes. Great abundance of the latter was also associated with heavy sewage loadings in the estuary up toward Alloa and Stirling and, indeed, wherever else there were outfalls carrying organic waste. Improvements in the discharges in the 1970s and 1980s were beneficial but could not tackle the "large residue of historical contaminants" in the sediments of the estuary or completely remedy the impoverishment of the biodiversity. Nevertheless, the estuary remained rich enough to support big populations of intertidal animals, and therefore of birds and certain fish that fed on them. The macro-invertebrate benthic fauna, attached to the bottom below low-water mark, followed a similar pattern, with only two species in 1987 close to the pollution at Grangemouth but eighty-two in the area close to the bridges and furthest from the outfalls.[30]

Beyond the bridges, the Firth of Forth was a much more marine habitat, with powerful currents helping to sweep away the pollution, which above the bridges had been so confined, out to the open sea. Only in relatively few places along that coast were there serious problems: by far the most pressing of these was caused on the Lothian shore by the sheer volume of trade and sewage effluents from Edinburgh and its immediate surroundings. A report to the Royal Society of Edinburgh in 1972 showed that the situation was not merely bad but in some respects had continued to deteriorate since a comprehensive survey in 1958, despite pressure from the Lothian Rivers Purification Board. The latter had already had some success in tackling purely riverine problems, such as the state of the Almond, which they found an "open sewer" as late as 1955, and the Esk, where miles of riverbed were still covered with esparto detritus, though the technology for dealing with this had been known since the 1870s.[31]

The problem in the open Firth took several forms, some of them familiar from the estuary. There was significant oxygen sag in the vicinity of the main outfalls caused by a mixture of sewage with industrial waste—paper-mill effluent at Musselburgh, spent gas liquor at Granton, gypsum silting from Scottish Agricultural Industries works at Leith, as well as large quantities of spent grain and other waste entering the trunk sewers from the brewers and distillers of Edinburgh. There were characteristic sterile areas at some of the outfalls surrounded by areas dominated by marine worms of large biomass but small biodiversity. There were also large beds of polluted horse mussels and common mussels unfit for human consumption, very grossly polluted beaches, and, worst of all, heavy counts of E-coli bacteria in the sewage slicks, which, under certain circumstances of wind and tide could come ashore and present a risk to public health.[32]

Remedial action was at last forthcoming. The postwar growth in legislation, the River Prevention of Pollution (Scotland) Acts of 1951 and 1965, developed by Tidal Waters Orders obtained by the Lothian Rivers Purification Board, provided a statutory basis for scientific investigations and unremitting pressure from the Board upon Edinburgh City Council and its successor, Lothian Regional Council. The upshot was the construction of the Seafield treatment works near Leith, with a long interceptor trunk sewer necessary to bring the sewage to this single point for treatment, and subsequent discharge down a single outfall 2.8 kilometers long into relatively deeper water. The treatment plant and outfall were commissioned in 1978. The residual sludge was taken away in a boat (aptly named the *Gardyloo*) and discharged to offshore locations outside the Firth of Forth. This method became replaced by total onshore processing and secondary treatment before the end of the century, as European Union regulations forbade dumping at sea.

All this was a tremendous improvement. By the time of the next Royal

Society of Edinburgh report in 1987, it was clear that the Firth was a rapidly recovering ecosystem, and the process has continued ever since. But it did not benefit everything. For one group of ducks that had adapted to feeding on the marine worms and organic residues from the distilleries and breweries, the recovery in water quality was an unmitigated disaster. The greater scaup is a marine duck that breeds in Iceland and Scandinavia and winters in the Baltic, the North Sea, and Atlantic coasts of Britain. The common goldeneye has a rather similar distribution, though is not present in Iceland. The common pochard is much less marine and has a more southern distribution. All three had taken to feeding in large numbers on the outfalls off Edinburgh and similar places, the pochard resting by day on lochs within the city and feeding on the sea at night, the others spending all day at sea. It is clear that the scaup had been rare in the Forth until the early twentieth century, when flocks a mile or more long began to be reported off Leith and fishermen would go out to catch them in nets. In the 1960s the scaup increased still more, and thirty to forty thousand were estimated off Leith in the winter of 1968. Up to four thousand goldeneye were similarly present at this period, and five to eight thousand pochard were counted in the 1960s on Duddingston Loch within the city. For all three species, Edinburgh was the prime British site, and bird watchers came to see the spectacle. As soon as water quality began to improve their numbers began to fall, and by 2010 fewer than one hundred scaup were left in the Firth of Forth. The decline in the other species was scarcely less remarkable, and the disappearance of the pochard flock from Duddingston may have reduced the number wintering in Britain by a third.[33]

The very last of the black spots to be cleaned up was in Fife. The sewage and trade effluents discharged into the river Leven and its tributary the river Ore were intercepted by a trunk sewer constructed by Fife County Council between 1949 and 1965, greatly to the benefit of riverine water, but discharged just offshore into the sea at Levenmouth after only preliminary treatment. As late as 1999, the discoloration of the water made the sewage "easily visible from the esplanade," and detritus was scattered down miles of beaches. The rich inshore discharge also had the effect of increasing the numbers of sea duck, as at Edinburgh though on a more minor scale, and when in 2000 it was at last modernized and improved to European standards, the duck disappeared from here as well.[34]

So the story has a good ending, unless you are a scaup or an opportunistic worm. It tells of an environmental problem largely overcome. It has not of course been completely overcome; relict sediments remain from old industrial processes that can still be released as new pollution, and there are new concerns today, like "diffuse pollution" by soil runoff from agriculture containing nutrients, pesticides, and hormones and by organic compounds even in treated sewage.[35] Nevertheless, the scene is transformed.

How did this come about? It is relatively easy to list the effective steps. The first was the act of 1951 establishing River Purification Boards with powers to license new discharges, followed in 1965 by extension of those powers to license all existing ones (no matter how long standing), and in 1974 by a comprehensive new Control of Pollution Act. The reorganization of local government the following year gave the task of sewage treatment to the new regional councils and also amalgamated the two local River Purification Boards that retained their supervisory and licensing roles. The bigger regional councils were more effective at laying sewers and installing better sewage treatment, but due to financial stringencies the water pollution clauses of the 1974 act were only implemented in stages during the next decade, with some regional councils still struggling to finance larger schemes like the Leven outfall in Fife. The next big step forward was the Environment Act of 1995 that created the Scottish Environment Protection Agency as a supervisory and enforcement body, amalgamating all the River Purification Boards in Scotland, while at the same time actual sewage treatment in the area was taken over from local authorities by a new East of Scotland Water Board and separately funded. In 2002 it was amalgamated with two other Scottish water boards into Scottish Water.

Not least in importance was Britain joining the European Economic Community in 1973, which involved the need to meet a steadily increasing number of demanding environmental directives by the end of the century and beyond. Britain for more than a decade largely evaded and resisted (until threatened with fines) the Bathing Water Directive of 1976, which sought to impose standards of cleanliness that the government considered irrelevant to public health, at least on British coasts. No bathing waters were designated in Scotland until 1986. On the other hand Britain collaborated with the Urban Waste Water Treatment Directive of 1991 that halted dumping at sea, even though British scientists considered the way it was done off the Firth of Forth and elsewhere to be environmentally harmless.[36]

What is much more difficult to explain is why these steps to solve a long-standing environmental problem were taken by society at this particular time. What had been grumbled about but tolerated, even allowed to deteriorate, between 1840 and 1960 (or 1970 in some cases), was suddenly found to be intolerable. Why was heavy investment made at this point and solutions found within a generation?

Part of the explanation may lie in Oliver MacDonagh's celebrated thesis about government growth. This stipulates the concern of the legislature aroused by an abuse, moved to create an inspectorate to tackle it, that, ineffectual at first, builds up over time a professional interest and expertise, and by a feedback mechanism exercises pressure on its creator to act again more effectively.[37] The weakness of the thesis partly lies in its inability to account for variations in the timing of reform, which in the case of water pollution seems singularly long in coming to fruition. Yet the slow growth of expertise, the organization of water and sewerage engineers into an international profession with journals, their growing alliance with science to identify problems and solve them, must have been important. So must the growth of knowledge of appropriate technology, fed by willingness on the part of authority to spend money on the problem and, by its effectiveness in turn (a virtuous circle), lowering cost and further feeding that willingness to spend.[38]

Officials of the river purification boards in Scotland were more anxious for progress than government, protesting against unhelpful official medical orthodoxies about the relative harmlessness of beach pollution and in 1979 planning to identify a series of clean bathing beaches under the European directive but prevented from doing so by the Scottish Office.[39]

Partly the delay was due to the slowly developing character of the problem itself. Before modern sewerage, urban pollution may have been intense but it was not of large bulk, so that even in the 1850s the volume of sewage-bearing water was slight compared to what it rapidly became. Chadwick himself assumed that private irrigation meadows would substantially cope with the problem in Edinburgh. It took time for the shortcomings of the market in this kind of situation to be appreciated and the need for much greater public intervention to be seen.[40]

Solutions in fact came with the growing scale of governance. Victorian local government was far too local to tackle pollution that flowed through many jurisdictions, so the problem grew willy-nilly, whatever Parliament might decree. But when after 1951 the state imposed a supervisory authority as big as a river, then as a catchment, then as Scotland, polluters could not so easily escape, and now that the European Union threatens even sovereign governments with sanctions, there is no escape for anyone. At the same time, the treatment authorities also progressively grew in scale to create and afford appropriate solutions. Big government was needed for such big problems.[41]

Underlying all this was a profound social and economic change in Western countries, which took the form of declining manufacture and a growing service sector. This was especially pronounced in the Edinburgh area, where, for example, in the nineteenth century there had been twenty paper mills on the Esk and the Water of Leith, but by 2000 only one was left and that was on the brink of collapse. In this case the 1970s were a crucial decade, the col-

lapse of the paper industry occurring after Britain joined the European Free
Trade Organization, exposing it to Scandinavian competition. In other instances the causes were less specific, as in the long-term decline of the textile
and metal trades (Carron Company went out of business in 1982). In the case
of the coal industry in Lothian and Fife gradual exhaustion and decline over
most of the twentieth century culminated in general pit closures following
the failed miners' strike in 1986.

As deindustrialization takes place, fewer vested interests survive to pollute the river, fewer jobs depend on them. The average citizen in Scotland
now works in computing programming, for a bank, an insurance firm, in a
shop, for government, in the health sector, or for the tourist industry. Citizens of advanced countries have more money to spend and more time to relate
to "post-material values" such as appreciation of the environment.[42] The defenders of the rivers and the beaches are now no longer the landed gentry but
the working class and the middle class, concerned about their health and their
recreation. The consumer goods that they buy are manufactured cheaply
abroad in China and India, where the same arguments are made that pollution
is essential to keep down costs as were made here a century ago—but it is not
a pollution they need to see or suffer. Rising standards of living in the 1960s
and early 1970s and again at the end of the century led not only to greater
expectations but also to a larger tax base for local or central government to
afford expensive new processing plants and outfalls and the accompanying
bureaucracies of environmental management.

All these things, it may be argued, were beginning to come to a critical
threshold in the 1960s and 1970s, when at the same time events internationally were creating something like a "green consciousness." It focused around
Rachael Carson and pesticide misuse in the United States and Britain, around
the rise of green political parties in Germany and elsewhere in Europe, and
manifested itself by successful campaigns as various as those to restore the
Rhine in Germany, to save old growth forest in America, to prevent another
oil pollution disaster like the wreck of the Torrey Canyon in England in 1967,
and in many European countries to stop new nuclear power stations. People could feel part of an international trend, and the cleansing of the Firth of
Forth belongs very broadly in this context, though not at the forefront, and
late in the 1970s rather than early in the 1960s, as befits a cautious national
temperament.

It is important, however, to stress that the situation in Edinburgh was not
marked by any local protest or organised environmental campaign against the
scandal of gross sewage disposal. The Scottish branch of Friends of the Earth
was founded in 1970: its first relevant publication (a one-page pamphlet on

Sand, Sea and Sewage) arrived twenty-one years later. Even the British charity, the Coastal Anti-Pollution League, founded in 1958, maintained at this time that "there was really no need for expensive treatment works" unless the discharge was "in an estuary or on the shores of a confined stretch of water." Official British medical opinion from 1959 until the late 1980s held that there was no danger from sewage in the sea unless the sea was visually so revolting that you would not want to swim in it anyway.[43]

Of course there were letters to the press in the 1960s and 1970s declaring the situation intolerable and a disgrace to the city, but then there had been such since the nineteenth century. Public pressure was of a more distant and general nature: feeling after the Torrey Canyon incident and pesticide scares, particularly in England, persuaded the Prime Minister Edward Heath in 1970 that it would be politically astute to amalgamate three existing departments into a new Department of the Environment at Westminster (even though for years it had little interest in the environment), and the Scottish Office was obliged to follow its lead. In Germany, France, and the Netherlands, burgeoning green parties in the 1970s had more weight than in Britain, and the Continental system of proportional representation in regional and Parliamentary elections leant them an importance to larger parties trying to form stable coalitions quite lacking in Britain. This translated into pressure on the European Commission to frame effective regulations. Thus public opinion and political bargaining in London and Berlin could count for more than opinion in Scotland.

Over two centuries the urban and industrial river has undergone several transformations. It is no longer in the least a source of power. First the steam engine and then the electric and diesel motors have supplanted the force of water, and Scottish lowland rivers do not lend themselves to hydroschemes in the way that Highland rivers do. The rivers are not thereby necessarily made more "natural," as beavers anciently built dams that had some of the ecological effects of the mills' weirs, dams, and lades. The headwaters of rivers impounded into reservoirs have from 1850 onward replaced wells and burns as sources of drinking water for city and town. And, most importantly of all, the rivers and the Firth of Forth itself went through a long phase that lasted for nearly a century and a half of being dumps for sewage and industrial waste, and the end of this misuse, beginning after 1950, marks a milestone victory for environmental responsibility.

These developments and transformations were brought about by people, yet they had important impacts on biodiversity. The removal of the mills made the river flow differently, to the detriment of dragonflies and frogs but to the benefit of other aquatic life. The construction of the reservoirs created new habitats, especially for wintering geese. The fouling of the rivers and the Firth of Forth destroyed one ecosystem and (in the case of the Firth) created another: the cleansing destroyed that recent system and largely restored the first. Environmental history is never our history alone: it is always, in addition, the history of the organisms at our mercy.

PART III.
TERRITORIALITIES OF WATER MANAGEMENT

10

DIVERTING RIVERS FOR PARIS, 1760–1820

Needs, Quality, Resistance

FRÉDÉRIC GRABER

THIS CHAPTER IS AN INVESTIGATION into the harnessing of rivers to supply cities with drinking water and the sort of issues raised by such ventures. The selected field of study is that of river diversion projects to supply Paris in the late eighteenth and early nineteenth centuries, mainly involving the Yvette and Bièvre Rivers to the south of Paris and the Beuvronne and Ourcq Rivers to the north. By proposing to displace water from the countryside to the city, these projects would not only profoundly reconfigure the land, they would above all pose new questions about the city's relationship with water and with those from whom it decided to take it. These new questions included: Is this the best river to divert? Who is being deprived of water? Should the entire river be diverted? How much is needed? Is the quality of the water compatible with the planned usage, in this case, the consumption of drinking water? These are the types of questions that we wish to consider—what quantity, what quality, who loses—questions that arose for all these projects, with variations specific to each context but largely structured by the first great scheme of this sort, Deparcieux's proposal to divert the Yvette. After presenting some of the features of water distribution in Paris in the eighteenth century, we see how water needs grew to be the focus of diversion projects; we then investigate how these projects raised the issue of water quality in a new way; and finally, we consider in somewhat greater detail the opposition movements against such diversion projects, mainly in the case of the Canal de la Bièvre by De Fer de la Nouerre in the twilight years of the Old Regime.

WATER IN PARIS

The act of diverting water to supply a city is a very old one. References to the Romans, to the splendors and glories of ancient Rome, to a certain model of infrastructure and public administration, is recurrent in the diversion debates[1]—particularly during the Napoleonic regime, when the issue of knowing whether there was more or less water in Paris than there had been in Rome became an important political question.[2] This reference to Rome in the diversion projects oriented the choice of water distribution infrastructure in the city very strongly toward public fountains (the option finally adopted under the French Empire for the distribution of water from the Ourcq), in contrast to the London model of water distribution to homes (the model that the Perier brothers sought to introduce in Paris in 1770–1780, which ended in semifailure).[3]

While the act of diversion is ancient, it remained relatively rare, particularly for the supply of city drinking water. There were some fairly spectacular workings, like the Arcueil aqueduct in Paris in the seventeenth century, the waterworks for the port of Lorient, and the aqueducts of Montpellier and Carcassonne in the eighteenth century. Often, such workings were not initially intended for public use but rather to supply parks, gardens, and palaces and to deliver water to a few public fountains.[4] The prominence of *jets d'eau* in classical gardens motivated many of the diversion endeavors: the Palace of Versailles and its gardens in particular inspired very large waterworks.

Diversion as a means of water supply was virtually nonexistent in Paris in the eighteenth century. More generally, one could say that the water consumed in Paris was only marginally supplied by fountains, of which there were about sixty at the beginning of the century and a scant one hundred by the end of the century, and was mainly drawn from the river and wells.[5] There were a great number of wells—many tens of thousands. River water was primarily distributed by water carriers, who generally used yokes and carried two ten- to fifteen-liter buckets each. They drew the water either directly from the river or from the fountains (fed by hydraulic machines installed on the bridges), which, incidentally, they also sought to control. There were also water carriers who drew water from the river and transported it in barrels on carts to the more distant quarters. The number of these water carriers, who supplied almost all of Paris, is difficult to assess, but it was likely in the thousands.

This was the context that, beginning in the 1730s, gave rise to innumerable projects by engineers, entrepreneurs, and scientists to increase the availability of water in Paris or improve its distribution. This movement was supported by the authorities (municipal and royal), who encouraged private enterprise in the area of water, although usually without financing it.[6] All these actors contributed to the emergence of a discourse on the shortage of water in Paris, particularly in the second half of the century. This shortage must be put into perspective, given both the inhabitants' low consumption (between five and twenty liters per person per day) and the presence of the water carriers, who were, in reality, the distribution system. The Parisian situation at the end of the eighteenth century was indisputably one of scarce, expensive water, but, strictly speaking, the scarcity was first and foremost created by the entrepreneurs, who trumpeted the advantages of cheap, abundant water, and hoped (more or less explicitly) to bypass the water carriers and distribute water via a greater number of fountains or simply directly to the homes.[7]

Two types of projects would face off here, with two very different visions of relations between the city and the water that it drank. First, there were a very large number of projects to pump water from the Seine using various processes, which would then feed a few fountains on the riverbanks and occasionally in a more distant quarter. Most of these projects were of limited scope, generally on the neighborhood scale. The other type of project was river diversion. The idea was not new; there had been several such proposals in the seventeenth century, but none had survived. The Yvette canal is notable here: although it, too, would largely stall at the planning stage, it would radically transform the water debate in Paris in the late eighteenth and early nineteenth century and structure the opposition between the water of the Seine (which flowed through the city) and outside water (which certain people wished to bring into the city).

THE YVETTE AS A MODEL: NEEDS AND VOLUME TO DIVERT

The Yvette diversion project was first proposed in 1762 by Antoine Deparcieux, a member of the Paris Académie des Sciences.[8] Deparcieux was a mechanical and hydraulics engineer but also worked on statistics and demography.[9] This is a point of some importance, as one of Deparcieux's main innovations was to view diversion as a global solution to a water problem that affected the entire city. While Deparcieux revived the now-classic theme of water scarcity, he reformulated it in his own unique way: he evaluated quantitatively the difference between the water available in Paris (which he reduced to the flow of the fountains, 3,600 cubic meters per day at best) and the water needed by its inhabitants, which he assessed at about nineteen liters per person per day. Given a Paris population of eight hundred thousand inhabitants, this led him to estimate a need of about 16,000 cubic meters per day. The fact that Deparcieux had also worked on mortality and tontines, and that he applied his reasoning to populations, suggests why he was the first to envision a global water need for the whole city.

This was a new way of seeing the city, at the crossroads of the development of statistics as a scientific and administrative tool and the emergence of an urbanism that conceives of the city as a whole.[10] By reducing the city to a population whose needs could be quantified, Deparcieux contributed to the birth of an *organicist vision of the city*, made up of global inflows and outflows of food and waste—even if the real focus here was just on water supply for this large body. This also created an *isotropic urban space*. In Deparcieux's calculations, only the average consumption of each inhabitant counted, thus eliminating the local dimension of the water issue: such things as distance to the river (an important parameter for water carrier distribution), the existence of a fountain nearby, or altitude (an essential parameter for pipeline distribution) were no longer important. This abstraction of the city space, henceforth only considered as a whole, went hand in hand with a stated objective of distributing water *throughout* the city. Like most river diversion projects, Deparcieux's proposal was mainly concerned with how the water would be brought to Paris, to a reservoir, and deferred the issue of distribution within the city to a later project, thus allowing this rhetoric of *throughout* to be sustained.

This way of seeing the problem had a number of corollaries. The purpose of Deparcieux's calculations was to reveal a substantial shortage, to legitimate the need for the project; hence the extremely low estimate of the resource, reduced to just the fountains. But, in reality, what was (or was not) counted corresponded to the objectives of the project: Deparcieux wanted to create a network of many fountains, and it was therefore consistent not to include alternative distribution methods (the water carriers), which he generally intended to replace. Deparcieux also needed to reveal a substantial shortage because he was proposing to divert the *entire* Yvette, to bring an estimated twenty-four thousand cubic meters of water to Paris, at that time considered a very large quantity. This river volume in fact exceeded the water shortage that he had estimated, but Deparcieux added a few public uses such as street cleaning and firefighting, which enabled him to match needs to the quantity of water diverted.

This way of formulating the water problem in Paris, in terms of global need that justified the diversion of an entire river, proved influential and powerful, convincing the elite and the court, despite what would soon appear to be a staggering cost (essentially due to the lining of the canal). Competitors quickly grasped that the Yvette proposal threatened to ruin them, for in calculating and meeting the needs of the entire city, Deparcieux was proposing global management of water in Paris by a single actor. All the serious competitors therefore appropriated Deparcieux's rhetoric and in turn framed water supply to Paris as a global, citywide issue, although they generally proposed pumping water from the Seine as a solution. While the issue of quantity was on everyone's lips, pumping enterprises and diversion enterprises expressed it in different terms. The former generally did not attempt to quantify needs, as they intended to respond to actual demand and install as many pumps as required,[11] whereas the second had to justify a priori the quantity they intended to divert, because it would be virtually impossible to increase volume once the canal was built. The idea of a quantified need was therefore linked to both the concept of global, a priori water management and the fairly rigid technical aspects of the canal, which made later expansion unlikely. Diversion projects thus tended to consider needs as remaining stable over time: the city was relatively static in terms of population and individual consumption.

Diversions therefore presented a specific problem of reasoning. Most authors would appropriate Deparcieux's reasoning but adapt it to some degree. The Ponts-et-Chaussées engineers who discussed the Ourcq diversion project at the dawn of the nineteenth century disagreed not only on the relevant quantity but on the river as well. Some would reduce individual need from nineteen to seven liters and the population estimate from eight hundred thousand to four hundred thousand,[12] revealing a much smaller need and thus discrediting the Ourcq, which would be too large, compared to a smaller river, the Beuvronne. The Beuvronne diversion project, submitted in 1801 by the engineer Bruyère as the reasonable alternative, was defended on technical grounds (the river was much closer to Paris and therefore less difficult and less expensive to divert) but also by matching Paris's needs very precisely to this river's flow. The Beuvronne's defenders condemned the Ourcq proponents' estimates, which they deemed to be "arbitrary." Indeed, the other approach to this estimate was not only to inflate requirements by increasing individual needs and the population of Paris but by including a number of public uses—street cleaning, firefighting, and, above all, decorative fountains—that the engineers wanted to multiply endlessly: they often declared that, as such uses were innumerable, there could never be too much water. But what is remarkable is that these Ponts-et-Chaussées engineers, whether they planned to divert the Ourcq or the Beuvronne, intended to divert *the entire river*: whether they calculated needs very precisely or saw them as infinite, almost all proposed a complete river diversion. This choice was sometimes justified by economics: such an enterprise is very expensive, and it therefore makes sense to take full advantage of it by diverting as much water as possible. But most often, apparently to avoid being accused of being arbitrary (why that quantity instead of another?), the engineers made the city's needs correspond exactly to the flow of the river selected. In these projects, the city as a whole was matched against a river in its entirety.

COMPARING QUALITY

The years 1760 to 1780 were a period of intense struggle between proponents of pumping enterprises (particularly the Perier brothers and the Vachette brothers) and supporters of diversions (the Yvette and, beginning in the 1780s, the Ourcq and the Beuvronne, proposed by a number of entrepreneurs). As all these people now intended to provide global distribution, what distinguished these enterprises was their economic viability and the quality of the product they could provide. On the latter issue, diversion started out with a handicap: it was to bring distant and therefore unknown water to Paris, while Parisians had always consumed the water from the Seine. One could therefore speculate on the respective qualities of the diverted water and that of the Seine. In a history of water quality and potability, the Yvette canal was a seminal moment: while most earlier projects only assigned marginal importance to the question, quality became a major issue beginning with Deparcieux's project, precisely because he intended to have Parisians drink new, externally sourced water.[13] Once importing foreign water was proposed, a comparison of city and country water became unavoidable.

In the case of the Yvette, we see two parallel strategies. First, there was reliance on scientists, with each side recruiting its own. First Deparcieux, and then his successors, called in doctors and chemists, who proceeded to perform various analyses that were generally the same as those used for mineral waters: the reagent method, still a highly uncertain way of identifying components but one that would make substantial progress at the end of the eighteenth century in the area of potability; the specific weight method, which consisted of weighing water to deduce its composition, a technique developed in particular by Lavoisier and finally abandoned toward the end of the century; the evaporation method, which consisted of evaporating the water and evaluating quality by weighing the residue, the most effective method even though it yielded fairly similar results for most river water; and finally, pragmatic methods that relied on the appearance, odor, and taste of the water, or on operations like cooking dry vegetables, soap dissolution, and so forth. The full range of existing methods could be found in the Yvette dispute. This scientific work was disseminated by publications and claimed to establish definitively the water quality of the Yvette, but the Seine's defenders soon retorted by defending the superiority of the Seine's water and calling in the experts in their turn. The main scientific defender of the pumping projects was Parmentier, who, in addition to chemical analyses, advanced a theory of the superiority of water from large rivers over small rivers due to mixing and decomposition of waste and air and water exchanges, which echoed classical theories on the importance of movement for water quality and purification:

the Seine would be better because it flowed faster and was wider and consequently mixed better.

This face-off of scientific opinion proved incapable of deciding the debate, and the various parties would resort to public strategies, publishing
pamphlets describing the other water as repugnant or using the testimonies of
members of the court, getting them to taste the water. In the 1780s, this public confrontation escalated sharply when two large ventures squared off: that
of the Perier brothers, who began distributing water from the Seine in 1782,
and that of De Fer de la Nouerre, who proposed building a new version of the
Yvette canal and would finally be authorized to do so in 1787. The two sides
then hired well-known writers, Beaumarchais and Mirabeau, to defend publicly their causes. None of this proved decisive in establishing the superiority
of one water over the other, but a number of terms emerged from this debate,
in particular the insistence on flow velocity and river size.[14] After these debates, diverting spring water would not be proposed again until the second
half of the nineteenth century: the rivers carried the day, theirs was the water
already being consumed that people liked and believed to be healthy. But not
everyone was sold on the Seine: the other major consequence of the debate
was the creation of a deep divide between the proponents of the Seine water
and those who saw it as impure, polluted by sewage and human activity, and
who wished to replace it with other water, also from a river, also fast flowing,
but from outside the city and therefore presumably less polluted.

As the purity of distant rivers was difficult to establish in town—most
of the diversion projects involved small, little-known, and therefore somewhat suspect rivers, and even some rivers with industrial activities—a majority of the diversion projects would pay particular attention to purification
processes.[15] The quality of the water at the point of diversion finally became
less important than the transformation of this water on its journey from the
river to the city. In addition to movement, certain soils, particularly sand and
gravel, were also recognized to have purifying qualities. The distance of the
water from the city was therefore not simply a disadvantage in these debates;
it could become an argument for quality, as the journey to the city could
become a source of improvement if the canal was lined with stone or had a
gravel bed.

THE LOSERS OF DIVERSION

Diverting a river inevitably poses problems, as it takes water from one area,
where there are inhabitants who use it, and gives it to the city. Consequently,
as soon as they became somewhat concrete, diversion projects provoked resistance, more or less visible and long lasting, from riparian residents.

In the case of the Ourcq, although the archives bear few traces of it, there was indeed opposition, as evidenced by a navigation council held in the *sous-préfecture* of Meaux in January 1803, where millers, boatmen, merchants, farmers, and landowners cried foul.[16] The ravaged properties and destroyed mills all evoked little sympathy from state engineers and the capital: the benefits that the capital would enjoy from the Ourcq canal were sufficiently important and generous to overrule private interests. The destruction was not really given full attention until the interests of the city were threatened: the water diversion eliminated a navigation way (the Ourcq River), which was important for supplying Paris with timber; it was therefore considered advisable to either retain this navigation (by leaving sufficient water in the Ourcq River) or recreate it on the new canal.[17]

Local resistance emerged much more clearly during the construction of the Yvette canal, in the version that De Fer began building in 1787, a case that we shall examine in somewhat more detail. In the 1780s, Nicolas de Fer de la Nouerre, a former artillery captain who became an engineer in Berry and later in Bresse, offered to execute the Yvette project.[18] In the 1770s, after Deparcieux died, Ponts-et-Chaussées engineers Perronet and Chézy were retained to study this project and prepare a detailed estimate. These engineers made some changes to the original project—in particular, they wished to also divert the Bièvre River, because they found that the Yvette alone had too small a volume—but their estimate came to the colossal sum of 7.8 million pounds, and the project was not executed. Shortly thereafter, in 1777, the king authorized the Perier brothers' pumping enterprise, which for a while appeared to sideline the diversion projects: in 1782, a first pump began distributing water to a number of Parisian quarters, and the company's shares soared but then crashed, victim to both speculation and the economic conditions under which the company was obliged to operate.[19] At the same time, as early as 1780, De Fer was in Paris, particularly at the Académie des Sciences, promoting his solution to the diversion of the Yvette (with the Bièvre) for under a million pounds—savings that he achieved by doing away with the canal lining. In 1786, De Fer managed to have a request in this regard presented to the king's council, which appointed a committee of councilors of state (*conseillers d'Etat*) and academicians to study the project. On November 3, 1787, in the midst of the speculation surrounding the Perier brothers' stock, the king's council issued a ruling authorizing De Fer to form a corporation to execute the diversion (under certain conditions).[20]

One of the main tasks of the committee in 1786 was to ensure that the canal would not hamper field irrigation or destroy mills, particularly those that supplied Paris. The issue of prejudice was therefore present from the outset, but this consideration was in fact very limited. Indeed, in 1787, the report of the committee, largely dominated by academicians, concluded that

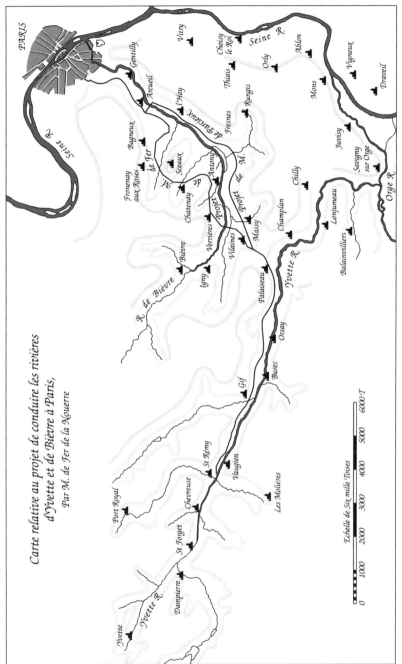

FIGURE 10.1. Rivers and canals of Paris. Adapted from "Carte relative au projet de conduire les Rivières d'Yvette et de Bièvre à l'Estrapade à moins d'un million de dépense . . . , par M. de Fer de la Nouerre," engraved by Bariolles. Archives Nationales (Paris), F14-683A.

the project would "in no way" harm field irrigation. As for the mills' down-time, the experts recognized this as "inevitable" but "impossible to assess for the moment" due to the high irregularity of the river flow. The commission-ers noted, however, that even eliminating these mills would in no way affect Paris's provisions, "to which they contribute such a modest amount that they do not even merit consideration."[21] The mills could disappear because they were not indispensable to the city: the inhabitants protested in vain, pointing out the importance of the mills at the local level.[22] In any event, the actual ex-tent to which the mills would be idle would only be clear once the canal had diverted the water. Here, the commissioners adopted the same try it and see approach—leave De Fer to it and see what happens—that in the end they ap-plied to every aspect of the project.

In fact, the committee raised serious doubts on De Fer's competence and his ability to complete successfully such a large undertaking: the project elements were recognized as "very flawed," the work was clearly underestimated, and the details of the workings were completely absent; as for compensation, it "appeared to have been evaluated as lightly as all the rest." The commission-ers also noted the uncertainty surrounding the water quality of the Yvette and the Bièvre, as well as the volume of water that could be expected. But, despite all these reservations, they did not reject the project. On the contrary, they proposed a pragmatic solution: they asked that the king order De Fer to begin by diverting just the Bièvre, which would constitute "by and large a test of an enterprise that has long been desired." The diversion of the Bièvre would be a kind of *experiment*: it would allow "identification of the appropri-ate uses for its water and of its potential flow" and determination of whether De Fer was truly capable of carrying out this project, all while controlling the risks. De Fer did not make a counterproposal, as he had intended to start with the Bièvre anyway, counting on the success of this first canal to entice the capitalists and finance the Yvette canal itself. From the outset, then, it was a question of building the Bièvre canal, but in all the prospectuses, memo-randa, and reports it was referred to as the Yvette canal, for obvious strategic reasons. The commissioners in fact wished this initial limitation to the project to remain confidential, because "the public and the capitalists would fear . . . seeing [the enterprise] limited to the Bièvre." There would have been many inconveniences associated with announcing just a diversion of the Bièvre. The presumed volume of the Bièvre, relatively small (nine thousand to ten thou-sand cubic meters per day at the low-water level), could in no way be consid-ered as meeting the stated objective of supplying very abundant, cheap water so as to compete with the Perier brothers. But, above all, in the debate that set the diversion project against the latter company in terms of quality, while the Yvette was a distant river, largely unknown to Parisians—which in a publicized debate could also be an advantage—the Bièvre entered into Paris, into Faubourg Saint-Marcel, where it was polluted by a large number of tanneries, butchers, and dyeworks.[23] Most of these establishments had been transferred onto the Bièvre in the seventeenth century to remove them from the center of Paris, thus contributing to the river's industrial vocation: Faubourg Saint-Marcel, at the city's edge, became one of the most industrial, working-class quarters in the eighteenth century. While there was a whole series of police measures governing the handling of waste from these artisanal and industrial activities, which must not end up in the river, Parisians considered the water of the Bièvre in Paris to be very polluted. A diversion of the Bièvre would have sounded much less attractive than a diversion of the Yvette.

The 1787 ruling authorizing De Fer to build the Yvette canal reiterated the commissioners' conclusions and ordered the entrepreneur to limit the project initially to the Bièvre. It was this Bièvre canal that would quickly give rise to many protests from riparian residents, owners, and beneficiaries, who would note the play on the rivers' names and would point to the diversion of the Bièvre in the name of Yvette as proof that what was being said was completely different from what was actually being done.[24]

COMPENSATION: A MEASURE OF THE PROBLEM

Opposition to public works projects was a fairly common phenomenon, particularly under the Old Regime, where the method of expropriation could easily turn to the owner's disadvantage: up until the beginning of the nineteenth century, it was not uncommon for property evaluation to take place after work had begun and for compensation never to be paid.[25] The 1787 ruling, like other similar rulings, required that the entrepreneur put an amount on deposit to ensure that he was indeed able to compensate owners and begin paying compensation before starting work. But De Fer went ahead without bothering with this. Among other things, as a kind of advertisement for his project, he started by diverting a small stream that he passed off as the Yvette.

Opposition to the project was first sounded by riverside owners, who saw their vines torn out and their fields dug up, and who were indignant that an evaluation would be done later on a devalued asset. Their attempts to impede De Fer's workers ended badly, as the latter, sure that they were in the right, did not hesitate to intimidate the inhabitants, levy fines, and even resort to insults and blows whenever they encountered opposition.[26] The residents appealed repeatedly to the authorities, particularly Bertier, the intendant of Paris, who was in charge of complaints regarding the canal.[27] But he barely heeded their protests, deeming that the "vague" cries could not make an impression on "educated people," and that inhabitants' claims were exaggerated and only aimed at driving up property prices.[28] The residents took advantage of competing jurisdictions, a feature of the Old Regime, to bypass Bertier and obtained several favorable rulings from the Paris parliament prohibiting De Fer from continuing work and throwing his foreman, earthwork contractor Antoine Armand, into prison.[29] In February 1789, De Fer in turn appealed to the king's council and succeeded in having these decisions annulled.[30] Having become a matter of some importance in the public sphere, the canal was finally halted by a council ruling in April 1789.[31] The official explanation was that the king had been informed of the many protests from owners, riverside residents, and inhabitants, and he wanted to make sure that the project would not cause anyone inconvenience, particularly the industries of Faubourg Saint-Marcel, which the ruling acknowledged had barely been considered earlier. Despite his efforts to revive the project and have it bought back by the government or city of Paris, it became evident that De Fer had lost government support: from then on, the inhabitants became bolder, filling in many sections of the canal and cutting down the seven thousand trees that De Fer had had planted along the route.[32]

While the compensation issue was certainly at the root of early protests, the way the issue was understood by the various actors during the proceedings also conveys the extent of the damage. In his initial *mémoire*, De Fer estimated the cost of both compensation and diversion work for the Bièvre at two hundred and fifty thousand pounds. The commissioners appointed in 1786, noting that De Fer had not provided the information needed to assess compensation, required that the security deposit for the Bièvre project alone be increased to four hundred thousand pounds. Despite this, the commissioners assigned a very narrow scope for compensation: it was limited to expropriations, mill downtime, and irrigation water shortages. Quarries, which were numerous in the area, were mentioned as a security risk (the canal water should not drain into them), but the commissioners did not see them as a production space that could be damaged by infiltration, which the on-site operators feared. The commissioners made no particular mention of the benefits of local use of the river or its feeder streams that were to be diverted, for which no compensation had been provided—except at Bourg-la-Reine and Fontenay-aux-Roses, where inhabitants succeeded in obtaining a guaranty that the local stream would be replaced by water from the canal. There were many launderers along the stream and retting of hemp was also common, although legally prohibited since the seventeenth century. The river also served as a watering hole, particularly in Pont-d'Antony, where there was a concentration of innkeepers, blacksmiths, saddlemakers, and wheelwrights who served the wagoners, all activities that would disappear along with the river.[33] The commissioners made no mention of the possible impact of the new canal on the surrounding spaces either, although nearby residents feared that the mist would be catastrophic for the vines and fruit trees, the roots and shade of the poplars planted alongside the canal would damage crops, and the small number of bridges would hamper traffic and require farmers to make long detours to get to their fields.[34]

Finally, and most important, the commissioners did not for a moment consider the factories whose operations could be disrupted. The Jouy canvas factory, far upstream from the Bièvre, was often accused of coloring the river with waste from the dye works; the issue of this initial pollution was never mentioned either by De Fer or the commissioners, and it is difficult to imagine how this water could be proposed as a source for Paris without eliminating the discharges altogether. But mostly there were many factories downstream, in Faubourg Saint-Marcel, that neither De Fer nor the commissioners considered to be threatened by the diversion. It must be said that, initially, the artisans and manufacturers of the faubourg, possibly led astray by the misleading name of the canal, appeared barely interested in the Yvette project and the faraway expropriations that it had entailed. Bertier indeed pointed out that the interested parties "awoke from their stupor" fairly late and decided that their claims were excessive.[35] As of the early months of 1788, however, they would become increasingly concerned over the threat of destruction of their establishments (which could not function without water). Compensation figures therefore rose to a level far beyond anything considered by the commissioners: manufacturers and artisans of the faubourg evaluated their establishments at anywhere from fifteen to twenty million pounds.[36] This was another order of magnitude that would render the enterprise totally impossible, particularly given that, as many inhabitants noted, it was not only the industrial establishments that faced possible ruin but also homeowners and inhabitants of the faubourg, "who would be obliged to leave once no work or resources remained."[37] Opponents, while for the most part prosperous enough, claimed to be concerned about the injustice done to workers, the thirty thousand people fed by the establishments and therefore the river, who risked being thrown into abject misery. The argument was not completely ungrounded, given the bustling, working-class nature of Faubourg Saint-Marcel, and one might wonder whether it was just the concerns of local industry or also the impact on the population that finally motivated the government's decision to halt work in April 1789.[38] Bertier's order of April 12, 1789, prohibiting De Fer from continuing work was thus posted in the faubourg to "calm concerns and prevent any subsequent protest movements in the quarter."[39]

If the commissioners failed to foresee the scope of the damages and changes that the canal could cause, it was at least in part due to ignorance of the local situation. While the ruling that formed this committee in 1786 explicitly called upon it to "transport itself to the site" to study the various issues and to consult Parisian officials, it is not clear, in light of their work, that the commissioners ever went anywhere. Opponents did not fail to condemn this sloppiness of expertise and sought to show that most of the commissioners were content to sign without ever having seen the Yvette or the Bièvre.[40] The inhabitants' reproach was soon more general: not only had the commissioners not visited the site, they had not consulted anyone—apart from the Parisian officials who had approved the project. Opponents therefore demanded that the matter be studied in the field,[41] and they even demanded that a *de commodo et incommodo*[42] inquiry be ordered, an investigation procedure often held prior to the registration of letters patent or authorization of certain polluting establishments.[43] For opponents, the absence of consultation and information, and the ignorance of the sites and usage, indicated that the canal was more about financial speculation than the public good.

Such speculation involved not only water but land as well. The 1787 ruling allowed De Fer to acquire a fairly wide strip of land, at least 25 meters, that owners were obliged to sell him, in theory to enable him to build berm ditches to prevent runoff water from flowing into the canal. Yet owners and riverside residents noted that the riverbed rarely exceeded 4.5 meters, and generally even 2.4 meters, and that De Fer was therefore in the process of acquiring, cheaply and in the name of the public good, a property ten times wider than the river, depriving the owners of a huge field in the process.[44]

WATER OWNERSHIP OR APPORTIONED USE

De Fer and the commissioners were not overly concerned with compensation because they claimed that the canal would not overly disrupt the various uses of the river. De Fer repeatedly asserted that his intention had never been to remove all the water, only some of it, which would only affect the operation of the mills during periods of drought—to an extent that could only be determined a posteriori. In reality, his position was far more ambiguous: he affirmed that "very far from taking water away from the Factories of Saint-Marceau, this very project will necessarily provide them with a larger quantity, and undoubtedly cleaner and better," implying that the mills would later be able to buy water from his company, for a fee. Besides, De Fer left little doubt as to his intention of cleaning up the Faubourg Saint-Marcel: for instance, he made reference to Buffon, who, when contacted by the manufacturers of the faubourg, replied that, far from supporting them, he would like to expel them and transform this "cesspool" into "the most joyful, populated" district.[45] The commissioners were no less ambiguous: they asserted that sufficient water would remain in the river for the various uses, while at the same time underscoring that De Fer's promises to bring Paris ten thousand cubic meters of water from the Bièvre (i.e., slightly more than the low-water flow) were only credible if he included all the tributary streams and did not give too large a quantity to the locals. To succeed with his Bièvre project, which was the test for the Yvette canal, De Fer had to produce as much water as possible, a fact fully grasped by the project's opponents:

> In vain he strives to imply that he will only take some of the water, but nothing is less sure than what he is proposing in this regard; in any case, the slightest decrease in the volume of this water would render the dyers, tanners, tawers and starch-makers absolutely unable to operate their factories, and Sieur De Fer himself would not have the means of meeting the supply levels to which he has committed, because as abundant and prone to overflowing as the Bièvre is in winter and in stormy, rainy weather, it is dry in summer and in the slightest drought, and it is only with the greatest care, the most precise vigilance in preventing the locals from diverting water . . . that the syndics of the parties interested in preserving the waters of this river are able to get a small supply.[46]

The Bièvre was indeed a river managed by a group of artisans and manufacturers from Faubourg Saint-Marcel, who were the *intéressés*, the parties interested in preserving the waters of the Bièvre River. After setting themselves up on the banks of the Bièvre in the seventeenth century, these artisans and manufacturers had, through a series of council rulings and letters patent, secured a certain "enjoyment of the river."[47] They elected three managing syndics (from the tanners, dyers, and tawers guilds) and employed two guard sergeants, which enabled them to "keep constant watch" on the river, preventing anyone without clear title from taking or using water or changing the river flow in any way and carried out various maintenance operations (most notably dredging) to maintain good flow.[48] Under these regulations, the entire river, particularly the upstream section outside the city, was controlled by the intéressés of Faubourg Saint-Marcel, who ensured that the water flowed to them in sufficient quantity for their activities. For these intéressés, there was no question of removing a single drop of water from the Bièvre without threatening both the functioning of the river and a legal situation that guaranteed them exclusive use.

This was all the more important because, by sustaining the ambiguity regarding the quantity that he would take, De Fer could well have eventually acquired the entire river: indeed, provided that he compensate the owners, the 1787 ruling authorizing him to build the canal gave him "full ownership, not only of said canal and its freeboards and other accessories, but also of the water that it will convey."[49] De Fer would thus become the owner of as much water as he could divert, water that up until then had only been governed by its usage.

While most Old Regime jurists considered running water to be essentially public—navigable rivers had been under the sovereignty of the king since the 1660s, and the unnavigable rivers had generally remained under the high justice of the seigneurs[50]—the status of the Bièvre was complex: while unnavigable, the Bièvre was under the jurisdiction of Eaux et Forêts, the water and forest authorities, but its use was regulated by council rulings in favor of the intéressés of the faubourg. The latter did not own the water: in fact, as under Roman law, one could not as a general rule own running water, except in specific cases (with restrictions), for nonperennial water, springwater, rainwater, and groundwater. The intéressés only controlled the use of the water, but as De Fer obtained ownership of the water from the council, it became essential for them to try to establish that they indeed owned the water: De Fer could not be authorized to take the water, because it did not belong to him. To achieve this, they pointed to history to show that "the Bièvre River in its present state is primarily their creation": "they have in some sense acquired ownership" because they made the river, because they invested substantially to convey springs and streams and maintain the flow; "they have indeed been granted [such ownership] or at least full and complete enjoyment" by the rulings and letters patent of the seventeenth century. They would never have moved to the river without the firm assurance that their activities would be protected there. Initially timid on the subject, the intéressés ended up declaring themselves "inalienable owners": "the intéressés, the Faubourg Saint-Marcel, are undisputably the owners of the water of the Bièvre over its entire course," and before diverting that water, one had first to consider acquiring it; but this was in fact impossible, as this property was not private, it was "so much theirs that they cannot sell it, it belongs to the public, the Citizens, the entire faubourg, all the owners, the owners of the mills, the owners of the fields. The State, once having made arrangements to their benefit, can no longer backtrack, override a concession by which it is so irrevocably bound, and that it must hold to all the more, as the public interest requires it."[51] The ownership argument would prove decisive when De Fer attempted, under the revolution, to have work resume: the plaintiffs appealed to Article 17 of the Declaration of the Rights of Man and of the Citizen, to the sacred, inviolable nature of property (particularly the Gobelins section in 1791), and the authorities agreed that this settled the matter.[52]

IN PROPOSING TO MOVE large quantities of water from the country to the city, diversion projects introduced new issues: they reconfigured the way that the city viewed the water it consumed, in terms of needs and quality, and they gave rise to conflicts over this urban appropriation of water.

In a city that essentially consumed the water from its wells and river, the idea of bringing a new river to Paris was not just any proposal. The diversion canal, a relatively inflexible facility in the sense that the volume of water conveyed was hardly likely to be increased later, required that an a priori choice be made with regard to volume. Deparcieux and his successors reversed what might be seen as a structural disadvantage by proposing a new perspective on water: they redefined the city as an isotropic space that could be managed a priori and as a whole by calculating the total needs of the population and by matching this urban need to a river that was to be redistributed "throughout." Both the river and the city were considered in their entirety, so as to prevent the needs assessment from being deemed arbitrary. Deparcieux thus helped give birth to an organicist vision of the city, entirely and precisely fed by the new river, and thus able to turn its back (for potable water) on the river that flowed through its center.

Indeed, the diversion projects helped set up opposition between the defenders of river water and those of the new water, opposition that would be particularly structured around the issue of water quality. This issue was not completely new, but it crystallized above all in the form of police management that regulated what could not be thrown into the water and where water should be drawn to be good.[53] Defining what constituted good quality water was not of great importance in the absence of an alternative. But by introducing new water, foreign water, diversion projects caused the theme of water quality, and the question of its analysis and eventual purification, to emerge as central. The sometimes long distances between Paris and the river to be diverted were in this case somewhat of an inconvenience—the water was far away, unknown, and therefore suspect—but could become an advantage: in a context that valued above all movement and the soil as the criteria of purification, the route to Paris could be considered an opportunity for improvement.

Finally, the diversions proposed to take water from many riparian residents and users and give it to the city, which did not go unresisted. This appropriation of a distant river was done in the name of the public interest, which here became confused with the city's interests, with the protests of riverside residents rejected as private interests: all sacrifices were warranted for the capital city because of its centrality, political importance, and size. These projects were not seriously threatened until they opposed the interests of the city. Because they drew from a hydrographic system that was, in the end, fairly close by, these projects indirectly affected the city, particularly its supply, either by closing a navigation way or eroding (and even wiping out) milling activities. Some attempt could then be made to recreate what would be destroyed: transfer the driving force of the mills to Paris, along with the water, or reestablishing navigation on the diversion canal. Local destruction was thus com-

pensated for by re-creations that essentially benefited the city. The case of the
De Fer project was fairly original, to the extent that one of the rivers to be diverted was a Parisian river. The rural upstream portion of the Bièvre was already controlled by Faubourg Saint-Marcel manufacturers—ensuring them
optimal flow for their many activities at the expense of riparian residents.
When it became evident that diversion might deprive the faubourg of its precious resource, the manufacturers formed an alliance with rural residents to
oppose the project—an urban protest that appears to have spelled the end for
the project. Ultimately, diversion did not just call into question how the river
was managed from a technical and police standpoint (mostly to the benefit of
Faubourg Saint-Marcel), it mainly posed the question of whether the water
itself could be privately owned.

11

FLUID GEOGRAPHIES

Urbanizing River Basins

CRAIG E. COLTEN

URBAN BASINS

HICAGO, BY NATURE, is not upstream from St. Louis. But beginning in 1900, it began sending its effluent by gravity via the Illinois River to the Mississippi River. The somewhat clandestine and deliberately premature opening of a canal linking the two basins fundamentally reconfigured the hydrology of the country's interior and repositioned Chicago hydrologically upstream from St. Louis rather than Lake Michigan.[1] This engineering feat inverted both its downstream and upstream relationships to protect the city's public health and enable larger scale waterborne commerce. During an extended drought a century after Chicago's hydraulic imperialism, a seriously parched Atlanta attempted to reconfigure its "legal," if not natural, watershed by staking a claim for water in the tantalizingly proximate Tennessee River basin. Its unsuccessful grasp extended across a state boundary and a basin divide where a more abundant supply of potable water flowed out of the southern Appalachians. Contrasting priorities between upstream urban consumers and downstream riparian users have prompted interstate water conflicts.

These two examples illustrate the complex relationship of cities to their respective watersheds. Several factors frame the relationships of cities to adjacent waterways and by consequence their urban-hydrological metabolism. Scale, the river's characteristics, and the city's location on the waterway all play critical roles. Both the size of the city (and its needs for water and effluent removal) and the volume and seasonality of the river's discharge influence the underlying relationships as well. The position of the city in the drainage basin—near the headwater, downstream from other cities, or near the mouth—shapes the political, legal, economic, and technical challenges a city faces when seeking to use the essential fluid resource. And of course, the prevailing technological, political, and legal capabilities to deal with water resource issues directly influence choices urban leaders make. Furthermore, larger climatic and meteorologic events can provide powerful impetus to compel manipulations of waterways.

Scholarly attention to rivers has seen numerous high stages. Richard White introduced the widely adopted term "organic machine" in his discussion of the Columbia River, and it emphasized the physical reconfiguration of a stream's hydrology to benefit the needs of an urban and industrial society.[2] The organic machine approach focuses primarily on the river channel and its ecology while advancing the notion that society and the environment are thoroughly intertwined. Joel Tarr introduced the concept of the "search for the ultimate sink," which proposes that society discharges undesirable wastes into water bodies until that sink is overwhelmed.[3] After passing the point of toleration, society may turn to another waste disposal sink or modify the means of effluent release to reduce its objectionable qualities. Another option is to seek a purer source of water—either from an untainted supply or by treating the polluted water so that it is acceptable. Ted Steinberg and Christine Rosen have directed their attention toward the legal role in river management. While their conclusions differ, their analyses place water into a container as a commodity.[4] The search for the ultimate sink and the water-as-commodity approaches step back from the riverbanks and examine the larger social context, sacrificing some of the direct concern with the waterways themselves.

Tarr also has borrowed the notion of urban metabolism from the sanitary engineer Abel Wolman. He states that "cities consume their environments and cannot survive unless they reach a point of equilibrium with their sites and their hinterlands in regard to the consumption of air, water, and land resources."[5] Other scholars have adopted the urban metabolism metaphor but see the relationship as more than the bio-physical-hydrologic flows of energy and related resources, and they place greater emphasis on socio-physical networks. That is, they argue "nature and society are . . . combined to form an urban political ecology, a hybrid, an urban cyborg that combines the powers of nature with those of class, gender, and ethnic relations."[6] Their perspective emphasizes the social production of urban space that takes scholarship beyond the organic machine, the search for the ultimate sink, and urban metabolism. They seek to understand the expanding influence of cities, the urbanization of rural spaces or the creation of an urban nature that is thoroughly intertwined with natural process but that is no longer apart from nature.[7] Despite claims to the contrary, these authors deemphasize the physical properties of rivers and their basins while highlighting the political economy of riparian spaces.

My goal here is to add to these theoretically distinct but topically related treatments. I seek to move beyond the narrow confines of human influences on the river channel and offer a broader geographic perspective in order to situate the major urban centers within their respective river basins. All the while, I hope to acknowledge the important role of both the energy flows and the socio-natural networks. Social production of urban space and the city's hydrology are critical, yet a basin's physical geography (the channel, floodplain, and weather and climate) can play important roles in the urbanization of rivers. It is not only the social priorities that drive change, but oftentimes natural processes that are larger than an urban system instigate varied human responses. I want to keep these aspects on equal footing with the political economy.

This chapter blends concerns with locational, environmental, and social influences on urbanized rivers. To highlight a wide range of influential forces, I consider three river basins: the Illinois, the Potomac, and the Chattahoochee. Each had a major metropolis that came to dominate water management issues, but the position of the dominant city along the river, the chronology of urban growth, the particular river modifications, the uses of the waterway, and environmental factors are distinct within each basin. By considering three basins, this chapter encompasses a wider range of factors that drove manipulations of their respective hydrologic regimes. This, I hope, will introduce a more complete range of influences and expose more of the complexities of urbanized rivers and the power of cities to dominate a basin as much as the waterway that formed it. It is important to note that river management decisions arise from complex social political processes that involve urban, state, and national policies. So although concern with the principal city has come to dominate policy decisions in these three basins, the influence of a single city in other basins may not be as prominent.

THE ILLINOIS RIVER AND NATURE'S METROPOLIS

The Illinois River (figure 11.1) owes its selection here as an urbanized waterway to Chicago, a city that in the nineteenth century was hydrologically separate from the Illinois basin. There were numerous smaller cities along the river's course that had a direct impact, but Chicago became the regionally dominant metropolis and hence the overwhelming influence. Its initial connection to the Illinois River, through the Illinois and Michigan Canal, sought to redirect the previously downstream movement of agricultural commodities back upstream into the city on Lake Michigan. Completion of the canal in 1848 enabled farmers to ship grain and other produce loaded on steamboats up the river and via canal boats across the natural drainage divide. The canal greatly enlarged Chicago's effective hinterland and diverted some com-

FIGURE 11.1. Illinois River basin. Cartography by Clifford Dupelchin.

merce that had formerly flowed down the Mississippi toward New Orleans. Railroads expanded the reach of Chicago still further across the upper Midwest during the later half of the nineteenth century. As William Cronon has shown, Chicago's economic reach transformed the prairies into cornfields and delivered livestock to its packing plants for processing and transshipment to

eastern markets. What the waterways began, the railroads accelerated and expanded, and as Cronon put it, "transportation broke free from the limitations
of geography."[8] Both the canals and the railroads enabled the efficient movement of goods in a direction that reversed nature's hydrology. This enlarged
and reshaped the hinterland of Chicago, expanding its metabolic base.

The economic and population booms that accompanied the packing industry produced huge increases in biological sewage—both domestic and industrial. Initial efforts to contend with burgeoning volumes of effluent led
Chicago to begin construction of a sewer system in 1855 that included a series of sewer lines to drain the city's developed area and "recommended that
the Chicago River be committed to the life of an open sewer."[9] Of course,
this decision also assigned a dual role to Lake Michigan with potentially serious adverse consequences—that of sewage sink and potable water supply.
As the city gradually expanded the sewerage system over the ensuing years,
the effluent of over one hundred thousand people and thousands of slaugh-
tered livestock mingled with Lake Michigan water and became a threat to
public health. The initial resolution to this situation was to extend the water
intake two miles out from the shoreline where water was uncontaminated.
Construction of a more remote water collection crib began in 1863 and was
the first in a series of efforts to extract water farther from the Chicago River's mouth and the foul waters it carried.[10] Chicago defied nature again and
reached "downstream" for its potable water, further enlarging its hydrologic
territory.

By the 1870s, continued extension of the water intakes farther into the
lake failed to keep pace with public health threats produced by the dual use of
the lake, and the city installed pumps to transport the sewage sediment over
the drainage divide and into the Illinois River via the Illinois and Michigan
Canal that followed a stepped course up and over the low summit separating
the Mississippi River and Great Lakes drainage basins. The pumping system
was a tenuous apparatus that operated with limited benefit depending on the
wind direction. While it reversed the flow of the river under favorable conditions, it was not a consistently effective system. Meteorologic and hydrologic
conditions forced sewage to flow into the lake for thirty consecutive days
in the summer of 1879. Shortly thereafter, in August 1885, runoff produced
by a summer thunderstorm flushed urban effluent to the distant intakes that
returned the tainted water to households throughout the city. Typhoid and
cholera outbreaks followed and killed over 10 percent of the city's population.
This event made it all too apparent that the existing sewerage and water systems were inadequate to protect Chicago's residents.[11]

The Illinois State Board of Health had been monitoring the impact of
sewage diverted down the Illinois River from the Illinois and Michigan

Canal and remained vigilant as Chicago began discussions about building a larger drainage canal that would flush its effluent directly into the nearby waterway. While the state expressed concern about the large share of flow that would be sewage during a dry period in the 1880s, it concluded that additional flow from Lake Michigan would help dilute any pollution.[12] The state firmly embraced the notions of dilution and self-purification.[13]

After extensive deliberations and engineering studies, the city opted to excavate a larger canal system that would connect both the Chicago and the Calumet Rivers with the Illinois and Mississippi systems to the west. It rushed to complete the Sanitary and Ship Canal in 1899 and dynamited the final link between the canal segments ahead of schedule in order to preclude a court injunction to halt excavation. Nonetheless, Illinois ended up in a legal battle with Missouri on behalf of St. Louis, which objected to the delivery of Chicago's bacteria to its water intakes. Ultimately the U.S. Supreme Court authorized Chicago's diversion that permanently enlarged the Illinois' drainage basin. To paraphrase Cronon, connecting the Great Lakes to the Mississippi River allowed the region's hydrology to break free from the limits of geography.[14]

State investigators optimistically proclaimed "that no nuisance will result from sewage at Joliet and below, and that the potability of the water in the Illinois River at Peoria will not be in the least affected from that source."[15] With greater dilution than was offered by the Illinois and Michigan Canal, the Sanitary and Ship Canal's diluting effect led observers to conclude that it "unquestionably sustains the theory of self-purification of running streams."[16] With a fairly constant flow of Lake Michigan water, the downstream diluting capacity of the river varied from season to season. During flood stage, sewage constituted less than 10 percent of the total discharge, but during dry periods sewage represented upwards of 70 percent of the total flow.[17] Canal supporters argued the canal mitigated low-flow conditions. Lyman Cooley, an engineer for the Chicago drainage authority, observed that drought often had harmed the commercial fisheries in the Illinois River. After 1900, however, he noted: "Since the opening of the Drainage Canal the fisheries have become an important and reliable industry, the catch having risen to 400,000 pounds."[18]

Biologists, however, offered a different perspective. The State Board of Fish Commissioners lamented that "the beautiful cold, clear rivers of the State are fast becoming only common sewers, and cannot help being a menace to life and health. . . . Water foul enough to kill fish should be a hint to localities that serious consequences would follow in other directions." They recommended proper sewage treatment to abate the damages they witnessed.[19] Following a brief spike in fish populations in the Illinois brought on by an increased food supply that fed on the sewage, water quality deteriorated and commercial fishing declined precipitously. In 1900 fisherman reported taking eleven million pounds of fish from the Illinois River. This increased to over twenty-three million pounds in 1908—due in part to rising demand in Chicago and more fishermen working the waterway. By 1912, the catch had dropped to less than seven million pounds—far below the prediversion levels. Investigators noted that the upper river was heavily polluted by 1911 and deteriorated conditions moved downstream over the next decade.[20] One study reported that the Illinois was transporting the "population equivalent" of 6.2 million people by 1922.[21] The impact on the fisheries was profound but reflected more than just declining water quality. Related bio-physical impacts included the drainage of floodplain wetlands and lakes that served as nursery areas for the fish populations.[22] Drought conditions during the 1911 and 1922 investigations also made adverse conditions more extreme and obvious. Thus, the timing of observations during low-flow conditions directly impacted conclusions.

Wetland drainage followed the opening of the drainage canal and illustrates the prominence of a series of human actions on the Illinois River. Increased rail access to the urban market and refrigerated boxcars made residents in the regional metropolis consumers of the abundant aquatic resources of the river, thus propelling increased fishing. Technology and market forces also combined to make wetland drainage an economically viable option. High market prices for corn, heightened flood risk resulting from the increased flow down the river, and improved dredging technology enabled floodplain landowners to form levee and drainage districts. Erecting levees prevented spring floods while pumps enabled efficient drainage of former wetlands.[23] Destruction of the local fishing and mussel-gathering economies were inconsequential to political leaders who sided with Chicago's sewage transport and navigation proponents. Even though biologists noted the decline in aquatic life, there was little protection for the fisheries. A first set of lock and dams constructed by 1907, which was succeeded by larger replacements by mid-century, further diminished aquatic life, all in the service of the city on Lake Michigan.[24]

The long-term metabolic impact on the Illinois River basin was that it became Chicago's ultimate sink. While the Illinois transported Chicago's sewage, it did not assimilate this liquid waste. Indeed, over the long run biological observations refuted the theory of natural purification. In fact, they demonstrated quite convincingly that urban effluent could overwhelm a waterway. In 1937, a national assessment of river basins reported that the Illinois and its basin had been "the subject of an extraordinary amount of human manipulation which has completely changed the character of the flow conditions of the basin." It went on to point out that "the outstanding problem is the deplorable degree of pollution" produced by nearly 5 million residents of the basin and a volume of sewage that equaled that of another 1.5 million people from industry.[25] These were staggering totals that were only exacerbated by a court-ordered reduction in the diversion of Lake Michigan water in 1938 that reduced dilution capabilities.[26]

Responding to this pollution burden, and with federal support, cities and industries gradually increased the capacity of their sewage treatment works. By 1950, municipal treatment works were handling some 97 percent of urban domestic wastes.[27] There was no comparable expansion in industrial waste treatment. During the early 1950s, industrial effluent constituted the population equivalent of 1.9 million people and represented twice the volume of municipal discharges.[28] In 1951, a U. S. Public Health Service (PHS) survey of river basin pollution indicated that within the natural basin of the Illinois just under 1 million people and thirty-seven industries sent sewage down the waterway. The Illinois may have been able to handle this volume, but Chicago continued to alter the magnitude of the pollution load. It sent the sewage of an additional 4.3 million residents and fifteen (reporting) industries seaward through the Illinois. According to the PHS, most of the municipal and industrial wastes received treatment. But, of the seventy municipal treatment works, nearly half (thirty-two) performed unsatisfactorily, as did twelve of the fifteen industrial waste sources.[29] Consequently, water quality in the Illinois remained seriously polluted into the mid-1960s.[30] Chicago's waste load prevailed over both natural purification and technological treatment and created long-standing damages. Obviously demographic and economic conditions contributed to the need and justification for river modifications, but nineteenth-century storms provided the extreme conditions that compelled the initial and largely irreversible human response.

POLLUTING THE NATION'S RIVER

The situation of the Potomac River is almost the inverse that of the Illinois. The major urban center, water consumer, and source of pollution occupies a site near the river's mouth. While there are numerous smaller cities and industries upstream, they never constituted the pollution threat posed by Washington, D.C. Nevertheless, they were upstream and therefore presented either a real or imagined threat to the drinking water supply of the nation's capital (figure 11.2). As the seat of government, Washington and its political power brokers exerted a considerable influence over the Potomac's watershed but never with the transformative capabilities to link two previously separated basins. While steps to make the Potomac into an "organic machine" were

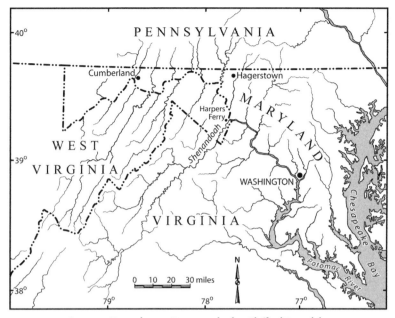

FIGURE 11.2. Potomac River basin. Cartography by Clifford Dupelchin.

modest by measures taken elsewhere, the needs of the dominant metropolis were the major influence in altering its water quality.

Initial concern with the Potomac centered on urban public health, specifically the delivery of typhoid-carrying water to consumers in the nation's capital. Situated near the lower river estuary, Washington was downstream from numerous small towns and industries. Typhoid outbreaks plagued the city regularly before 1900 and prompted the construction of a water filtration system in 1905, and it began cleansing Potomac River water for distribution to residents.[31] On the eve of the plant's opening, the U.S. Geological Survey (USGS) reported to Congress that it must assume that Washington's water supply would be polluted given upstream development. M. O. Leighton, the report's author, declared that the "Potomac River is grossly abused."[32] Nonetheless, he noted with optimism that Washington's new water filtration plant would "absolutely protect the District from serious consequences in the use of this water for domestic purposes."[33] Leighton had modest hopes for the long-term viability of this new technology and concluded that with rapid population growth and continued industrial development in the basin, pollution would overwhelm the water treatment system. He recommended that "wise and considerate prohibitory measures are necessary and should be enforced as soon as possible."[34] There was no comparable attention paid to effluent from the District of Columbia and its downstream impacts.

Despite Leighton's call for pollution abatement regulations, political bodies did not enact controls and the consequences became all too obvious. Typhoid outbreaks continued with great frequency and the PHS conducted a series of studies to determine the disease's origins. Noting that most sewage sources were more than 175 miles upstream, typhoid outbreaks were seasonal, and they seldom occurred throughout the city, the PHS investigators discounted the public health threat posed by the filtered city water.[35] In 1912, the PHS sent a team to survey pollution sources in the Potomac watershed, and they concluded that "at no point above Washington is the water of the Potomac safe to use as a public water supply without reasonable treatment."[36] As the USGS study had reported, the PHS investigation declared that increasing population growth would inevitably overtax the river. Unlike the earlier report of 1905, however, these authors called for sewage treatment rather than regulation.[37] Modifications to the river's hydrology, other than dams on tributaries, were minor and the installation of water treatment, rather than sewage treatment, systems was typical for the time.[38]

Pollution from the numerous, relatively small upstream sources and their threat to the major metropolis of the basin remained the focus in subsequent investigations. They consistently indicated that concern was warranted. By the early 1930s, numerous upstream communities had abandoned land sinks for their domestic sewage and had installed sewerage systems. These public works of course moved untreated household wastes more efficiently to the river. Industrial wastes also continued to flow into the river without treatment. Yet, observers reported that the upstream sources were sufficiently distant and that natural purification eliminated the threat they posed to Washington's potable water supply, even during low flow.[39]

In a position to receive exceptional scrutiny from Congress and federal agencies, the Potomac became the object of ever more attention. By the time the National Resources Committee addressed river basins nationwide in 1937, pollution figured as a primary concern. To address the interstate character of pollution, Congress enacted legislation that enabled Maryland, Virginia, West Virginia, Pennsylvania, and the District of Columbia to enter into a compact that would facilitate pollution abatement.[40] Sewage treatment was the desired remedy for both municipalities and industries, but provision of these services was far from complete. Washington had just completed its treatment plant in 1937, but it was not in operation at the time. Keeping pace with population growth proved to be a losing proposition. By 1943, sewage treatment reduced the population equivalent sewage load from 1.1 million residents to about 781,000. Yet by the late 1950s the Potomac carried a 36 percent greater sewage load than it did in 1932.[41]

Plans for grand hydrologic structures appeared during the 1930s, and they all centered on the needs of Washington.[42] The nation's capital placed the greatest demands on the river, consuming water from upstream and releasing its effluent downstream. And among its residents were powerful legislators who expected clean water. The creation of the interstate compact reflects the measures politicians could take to overcome political fragmentation inherent in a multistate river basin and to blend water resource management with nature's geography. While Chicago was able to break free of its hydrologic endowment, Washington struggled to bring policy in line with the fragmented political overlay on the Potomac's basin. Nonetheless, metropolitan hegemony over a river basin was a feature shared by the two cities.

Washington's rapid population growth during the 1940s provided the impetus for additional inquiries into the Potomac's water quality. A report in 1950 by the president's Water Resources Policy Commission expressed frustration with the inability of municipal sewage treatment facilities in the D.C. area to keep pace with spiraling demographics. Plants designed and installed before the Second World War had become hopelessly undersized. Over two-thirds of the basin's municipal sewage received primary treatment, but less than one-fifth received more advanced treatment. Treatment offered to industrial waste lagged well behind that provided to municipalities.[43] A key reason for waste treatment inadequacies was an ineffective regulatory apparatus according to the commission.[44] The burden for providing clean, potable water remained with Washington, D.C. Despite the problems it faced cleansing its water supply, the metropolitan area neglected to treat its own sewage before release into the Chesapeake Bay.[45] The predictions of the early 1900s remained valid—population growth continued to overtax the river's carrying capacity.

Although human agency did not invert the river's hydrologic flow, by the late 1950s public agencies reversed their concern with stream pollution. A combination of upstream pollution treatment and downstream filtration of drinking water supplies provided an acceptable technological fix for Washington. Meanwhile, population growth was most dramatic in the lower river metropolitan area, and consequently the pollution load was greatest downstream. Concern with water quality on that stretch emerged by midcentury. Some 1.7 million tons of sediment delivered to the lower river, below Washington, were impacting oyster beds and fisheries. Other than a few headwater sections, the river sections that received a "lower grade" water quality characterization in 1950 were the lower Anacostia and the Potomac below Washington.[46] In 1954, the Interstate Commission on the Potomac River concluded that water arrived in the D.C. area relatively clean, but below Washington low dissolved oxygen levels threatened aquatic life and unsightly and malodorous conditions prevailed. Subsequent openings of new treatment facilities in the Washington area addressed the most obvious aspects of urban sewage.[47]

Yet pollution persisted, and it was a clear case of interstate pollution since the urban population sprawled across two states and the district. Since the Interstate Compact was largely a public relations organization, the downstream users of the Potomac had to turn to the federal government to abate pollution. A pair of interstate conferences on water pollution in the 1950s and 1960s put pressure on the states to implement remedial measures, but pollution from the metropolitan area continued to create an overwhelming problem. Indeed by the mid-1960s the district had not achieved water quality targets agreed upon in the late 1950s.[48]

As communities made improvements to their treatment facilities, planning was also under way for a major overhaul of the basin's hydrology. Under the auspices of the U.S. Army Corps of Engineers, a team addressed a pair of related issues: flood control and a more consistent water supply. With urbanization along the riverbanks, flood damages had increased as a result of a series of floods in the 1940s and 1950s. Hurricanes traveling across the basin produced particularly heavy precipitation and subsequent flooding in 1952, 1954, and 1955. Drought in the mid-1960s accentuated concern with the wide variations in flow.[49] Furthermore, the same population increases produced greater demands for potable water. With a notoriously inconsistent discharge, according to the U.S. Army Corps of Engineers, the Potomac obviously needed dams and reservoirs to collect and store peak flow and prevent its waste. Public testimony at hearings on the corps' plans offered contrasting viewpoints. Environmental groups countered that by providing adequate treatment to sewage and ensuring a clean water supply, the river could easily meet water quantity demands without major in-stream dams and impoundments.[50] The erratic nature of the river presented troublesome challenges for communities expanding along its banks and using its water. Infrequent meteorologic events, in the form of tropical disturbances moving over the basin, served as the basis for arguments to begin the basin makeover. Yet, with two reservoirs to serve the D.C. area and a pair of dams in the upper basin, the main stem of the Potomac remained largely unimpeded into the 1970s.[51]

With a major metropolitan area near the mouth of the river, water managers did far less to manipulate the hydrology of the Potomac than the Illinois as the era of dam building came to an end. While concerns shifted from upstream pollution to downstream impacts, attention remained focused on the basin's major city. The same held true for flooding. Expanding population in the D.C. area prompted plans for flood control. And although the river did

not undergo the complete reconfiguration suggested by the U.S. Army Corps
of Engineers, the urban focus drove the planning process.

COTTON FIELDS, SKYSCRAPERS, AND THE CHATTAHOOCHEE RIVER

The Chattahoochee River traverses nearly the entire north-south length of
Georgia, flowing from the southern Appalachians, forming a portion of the
state's western border with Alabama, and then merging with the Flint to form
the Apalachicola that passes through the Florida panhandle on its way to the
Gulf of Mexico (figure 11.3). Like the Potomac, it was interstate by nature.
At the time of the Water Resources Commission study of 1937, the drainage

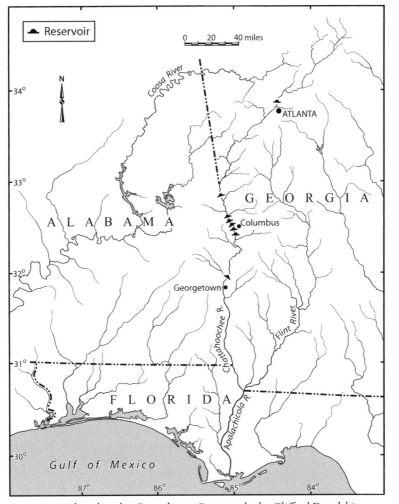

FIGURE 11.3. Chattahoochee River basin. Cartography by Clifford Dupelchin.

basin was largely rural, and agriculture and forest products provided the local economic base. There was an emerging textile industry along the Alabama border near Columbus that manipulated flow with small dams to tap water power. Hydrologic concerns, as might be expected, aligned with the prevailing land uses in the basin and were relatively modest. Local interests had not yet fully reworked the Chattahoochee into an urbanized river, although that would change.

In 1937 the Water Resources Committee (WRC) reported that malaria control was its key concern in the basin.[52] Wetlands, particularly along the lower river, provided a habitat for disease-bearing mosquitoes. Erosion on piedmont and coastal plain farms was prevalent and contributed to sedimentation and wetland creation in the lower basin. The WRC promoted soil conservation as means to eliminate a public health menace.[53] The health of nonurban residents provided one impetus for New Deal–era drainage works.

Navigation on the lower river, to serve the forest products and agriculture-related industries, became a second driving force to transform the waterway. Responding to local advocacy for navigational improvements, the U.S. Army Corps of Engineers' report to Congress in 1939 recommended additional work. To accommodate projected commercial traffic, the Mobile District proposed dredging a nine-foot channel to Columbus, which would require several locks and dams (plus dredging and maintaining a seven-foot channel on the Flint, which combined with the Chattahoochee to form the Apalachicola). The corps also recommended installation of hydroelectric power facilities at strategic dams and concluded that demand would rise to meet capacity after the navigation improvements stimulated commerce. Both upper branches of the Apalachicola would need several upstream water storage facilities to maintain the desired discharge and associated channel depths during the dry season. Thus, manipulation of the lower river to serve anticipated economic demands called for upriver alterations—although these actions had to wait. Buoyed by federal backing of large-scale public works, the corps slowly advanced both navigation and power projects.

At the time of the proposed hydraulic transformation, there was virtually no mention of water needs for the upper river urban area. Indeed, in its cost-benefit analysis of future water storage facilities, the corps casually observed that "The city of Atlanta obtains its supply for domestic and industrial use from the Chattahoochee at the present time. With the rapid growth of population and industry in this area the storage capacity of a larger reservoir might be of benefit for an assured continuous water supply. This potential asset is given no monetary value in this report."[54] It allocated much greater recreational value to the proposed water storage reservoirs. The humid Southeast and a river issuing from one of the wettest areas of the country, even in the

wake of the droughts in 1931, 1933, and 1934, seemed immune to water shortages. Atlanta had not reached the size to drive basin-wide decisions.

In 1945 Congress approved the Lanier Reservoir on the upper Chattahoochee for hydroelectric power and to maintain low-water flow for downstream navigation. No mention of public water supply appeared in the project
summary of 1948. Channel modifications on the Chattahoochee, including
several locks and dams and hydroelectric plants to serve economic interests
on the lower river, eventually set the stage for the ensuing water wars among
Georgia, Alabama, and Florida. Yet these early efforts clearly focused on the
lower river. Despite reporting that there had been practically no waterborne
traffic to the head of navigation on the lower Chattahoochee for twenty years,
the corps projected that commercial activity would follow channel modifications.[55] By the late 1950s, the corps was nearing completion of a series of four
dams on the Chattahoochee—three included navigational locks on the lower
river, and the forth provided water storage to ensure adequate water levels on
the navigable segment.[56]

Conflict eventually emerged over the water impounded in this upper
river reservoir. Between 1950 and 1990, metropolitan Atlanta experienced the
most rapid growth of any metropolitan area in the country. Its population
rose from 726,000 to over 2.9 million. During that same time, the U.S. Army
Corps of Engineers completed the Buford Dam that impounded Lake Lanier
on the upper river. This reservoir, designed to provide low-water flow for
navigation on the lower Chattahoochee, had no specific allocation for public water supply. Nonetheless, its convenience to Atlanta, and congressional
acquiescence to the city's growing demand, allowed the city to tap it as its
principal municipal potable water supply.[57] As of 2004, Lake Lanier supplied
72 percent of the city's municipal and industrial needs. With normal precipitation, there was adequate supply to satisfy all demands. Following a series
of droughts in the 1980s that lowered the reservoir levels, the corps and the
City of Atlanta announced plans to withdraw more water from the upriver
reservoir to meet the burgeoning water supply needs of the basin's largest
metropolis. The same droughts impacted neighboring downstream states by
threatening Alabama's access to hydroelectric power and navigation and damaging Florida's oyster production near the river's mouth and threatening endangered species as well. To protect their access to established flows, Alabama
and Florida filed suit to block the proposed diversion to Atlanta households.[58]
Thus, the major city became the center of water management deliberations,
although traditional legal priorities tended to prioritize navigation on interstate waters.[59] Environmental issues that were not in place when the corps
designed the Apalachicola-Chattahoochee system now counterbalanced the
diminished status of navigation on the lower river. Protection of the Florida

oyster industry and also endangered species that depend on a minimum flow into the Apalachicola and its bay emerged as important legal considerations. Further complicating the situation has been the growing demand for irrigation water by large-scale riparian farmers. Seeking to ensure dependable water delivery to crops, they have placed a new demand on the limited water supply, mostly along the Flint River.[60]

Ultimately the three states opted to remove the court case from the active docket, and they created an Interstate Basin Compact in 1997 to forge a mutually agreeable water allocation. Unable to achieve their goal by the compact's 2003 deadline, the compact automatically dissolved. Shortly thereafter, the nationally publicized drought of 2007 exacerbated an already challenging situation.[61]

With access to the Chattahoochee's water tied up in litigation, Atlanta turned its sights elsewhere. City leaders sought to transfer water from the Coosa River in north Georgia, but Alabama rebuffed this effort.[62] Subsequently, Atlanta looked further afield to the even more abundant Tennessee River. A legal memorandum offering a potential solution to the water supply needs recommended interbasin and interstate transfer—that is, diverting a portion of the water impounded by a Tennessee Valley Authority dam in Tennessee to serve Atlanta's growing water supply needs.[63] Tennessee had declined requests for interbasin transfers previously, but in 2008 Georgia sought to establish a riparian claim by deploying a historic boundary dispute that would have shifted its northern border to intersect the Tennessee River.[64] Essentially, Georgia claimed that a surveying error in 1808 placed a bend in the Tennessee River in Tennessee, instead of in Georgia. Georgia merely sought to restore control over territory, and a small segment of the Tennessee River, that was "rightfully" its own. This assertion over disputed territory brought still another state into the complex maneuvering for water to slake Atlanta's thirst, although this question has taken a secondary position to the legal wranglings over water in the Chattahoochee.

A federal judge issued a decision on the long-standing court case over municipal allocations from Lake Lanier in July 2009. It declared the corps had no authority to reallocate water originally impounded for navigation to municipal water consumption, noting that this authority resides with Congress.[65] This decision will shift the debate to Congress that ultimately will decide if Atlanta's consumers take priority over lower river navigation, power, and natural resource demands.

Early river modifications focused on developing navigation to serve rural populations, resource-dependant industry, and agriculture. The growth of Atlanta in the upper basin has altered the fundamental water resource demands, but existing legal structures did not provide a simple means to reallocate the Chattahoochee's water. Increasing demand for agricultural irrigation water and new environmental concerns driven by the Endangered Species Act have further complicated the management of the Chattahoochee. As a consequence, legal battles, attempted compromises, and searches for additional water extended and expanded the multistate conflict. Legal scholars suggest that the traditional priority given to navigation may be at stake and that Alabama and Florida may face a difficult battle as the courts weigh the harm they anticipate compared to the benefits of allocating additional water to Georgia.[66] Urban growth focused in one section of the basin has completely altered historical priorities and water management issues. At the most critical stages of this interstate encounter, drought propelled human adjustments, which in turn instigated conflict. The organic machine of the Chattahoochee could not escape the influences of climate, but Atlanta, unlike Chicago, has been unable to break free of its geography. Drought has accentuated water conflicts, but post-1960s environmental regulations have complicated Atlanta's desire to satisfy its growing water demands. And the recent court decision imperils its access to impounded water.

THESE THREE URBANIZED rivers offer a panorama of the relationships that cities have had with their river basins over the past century. In each case we can see efforts to create an organic machine, the search for the ultimate sink, the creation of an instrumental view of water, and the struggles to balance urban metabolism with a river's hydrologic regime. The interconnectedness of humans and their environment was obvious as well. In each river basin, the principal city came to dominate water issues but in different ways, shaped, in part, by the position of the city within the watershed. Chicago manipulated nature's geography to make the Illinois serve as its sewage sluice and unleashed long-term ecological harm downstream. Concern over Washington's water supply drove upstream pollution control efforts and water treatment installations in the nation's capital. Atlanta's late emergence as a major metropolis inverted water management strategies and produced interstate water wars.

As each city attempted to synchronize a river to match its metabolism, extreme events—droughts or floods—tested that synchronization. In the wake of disruptions, public officials were able to gain support for costly public works projects to further align waterways with the city's needs. Floods in Chicago produced devastating cholera outbreaks and prompted construction of the Sanitary and Ship Canal. The "flashy" regime of the Potomac, accentuated by hurricane-induced floods and intermittent droughts, prodded the U.S. Army Corps of Engineers to prepare plans for an extensive infrastructure overhaul of the waterway. The timing of the planning occurred *after* the era of dam building, and the river and communities along its banks remain susceptible to erratic discharge. The corps completed a series of dams along the Chattahoochee on the eve of major environmental legislation and the emergence of Atlanta as the dominant regional metropolis. Within the basin, economic and water priorities have shifted to the upper basin, yet traditional navigational priorities and relatively recent environmental regulations protect the lower river. The investments in infrastructure no longer fit the basin's metabolic needs, and conflicts over water are the order of the day.

Across the riparian landscapes I have discussed, the principal decisions about how to manipulate waterways arose from political and economic leaders. The fishermen of the Illinois and the Chesapeake have suffered from pollution. Small farmers on the Georgia piedmont experienced little benefit from the federal investments in locks and dams along the Chattahoochee. In that sense proponents of the "urban cyborg" are correct that manipulations of urban nature are deployed to the benefit of the powerful. Nonetheless, I would hope that we continue to factor in the impact of erratic extreme events, such as drought and flood, that enable those in power to push through proposed plans. Yet, as we saw on the Potomac, even the corps was not able to synchronize that river with its designs. Ultimately, urbanized rivers are more than human constructs and natural systems, and it is appropriate to think of their basins as urban territories as much as fluvial forms.

A single city may not figure as prominently in the management of larger basins such as the Mississippi, St. Lawrence, or Rhine. Additionally, international rivers present even more complex river management concerns. Competition among numerous large cities and political entities can complicate the relationships among riparian urban centers and rivers. Analyses of larger scale urbanized rivers offer rewarding prospects that can build on this comparative investigation.

～ 12

TO HARMONIZE HUMAN ACTIVITY
WITH THE LAWS OF NATURE

Applying the Watershed Concept in
Manitoba, Canada

SHANNON STUNDEN BOWER

I N MAY 1958, THE Manitoba provincial government, as part of its effort to promote watershed management, published an educational pamphlet designed
to explain this new idea.[1] Watershed management was described as a method
that could be implemented to redeem lands degraded through intensive agriculture, thereby harmonizing human activity with the laws of nature.[2] The
description was both an explanation of what was for many an unfamiliar idea
and an argument in favor of a watershed-based approach to environmental
management. This chapter examines the scientific investigation and public
promotion of the watershed concept in the province of Manitoba, Canada.
It focuses on the provincial government's role in both endeavors, examining
what the government did and did not do to improve environmental management in degraded areas of the province through incorporation of the watershed idea. It situates the provincial government's actions in relation to local
environmental and human conditions on the one hand and the division of
powers between the province, the involved rural municipalities, and the Canadian federal government on the other. Each of these factors helped define
the possibilities for, as the provincial government portrayed it in the late
1950s, bringing humanity and nature into harmony.

In Manitoba the watershed idea was controversial in large measure because it overlaid the geography of privately owned farms established through
federal government efforts to guide the settlement of the Canadian prairies by
newcomers. The Dominion Land Survey, a massive undertaking conceived
in 1869 as a means of dividing the lands about to be acquired from the Hudson's Bay Company, split the northwest into large squares known as town-

ships. Each township was divided into sections of 259 hectares, which were then divided into quarter-sections of 64.7 hectares. It was quarter-sections that would be made available to newcomers as homesteads.[3] As communities developed in the new province, municipalities grew up around them, with boundaries that reflected the underlying settlement grid. Municipal government emerged as an important means of managing local affairs and expressing local sensibilities.

The federal government's system of land division was brilliant, if the ultimate goal was the rapid peopling of an enormous landscape. If the goal, however, was the long-term prosperity of the agricultural civilization thereby established, the matter is less clear. Under the perfectly regular geography of the township survey, property lines and municipal boundaries trumped the irregular whorl of environmental patterns and processes. Over decades, problems arose that were attributable in part to the tension between a private property landscape and a variety of natural forces that created an ecological commons. Across the Canadian Prairies and the North American Great Plains, weed control is perhaps the best and most documented example of such a problem.[4] In Manitoba, the management of surface water was another important issue. Flood waters spread across privately owned farms and between independently managed municipalities, with the result that property lines and municipal boundaries complicated attempts to improve the situation. In the area of Manitoba considered in this chapter, it was particularly significant that control of upper watersheds and lower watersheds fell to different parties, with the result that one area's solution might be another area's problem.

In Manitoba as in other Canadian provinces, the provincial government, along with municipal authorities where established, had responsibility for local infrastructure. Though the issue of flooding was complicated by the mismatch between the federal government's grid-based settlement landscape and underlying waterflow patterns, it was the responsibility of the province to undertake the drainage works intended to protect farms from floods. This chapter examines efforts by the provincial government, with some participation by federal authorities, to produce another sort of landscape, one in which environmentally attuned boundaries would assume significance through efforts to coordinate environmental management within a watershed. Scholars have examined attempts to modify management practices through the adoption of watershed-based approaches.[5] In diverse landscapes, managers have sought to change the size and shape of relevant administrative units, with significant consequences for people and landscape. In the terminology employed by the geographer Karl Zimmerer, these attempts amount to a rescaling of environmental management. This chapter examines the rescaling process in

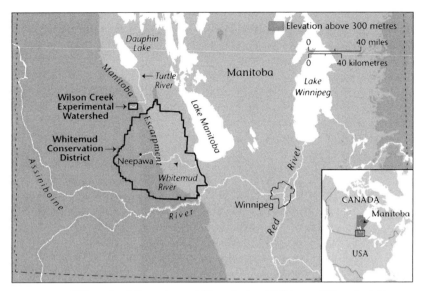

FIGURE 12.1. Wilson Creek Experimental Watershed and Whitemud Watershed Conservation District. Adapted from William Carlyle, "The Management of Environmental Problems on the Manitoba Escarpment," *Canadian Geographer* 24, no. 3 (Fall 1980): 260.

mid-twentieth-century Manitoba in the context of persistent surface water management problems. It considers the production of scientific knowledge in support of watershed management and the process through which the watershed approach gained local approval in an area vulnerable to flooding and erosion.

During the years considered in this chapter (roughly 1958 to 1976), there were six provincial elections and three changes in administration, with all the attendant upheaval and realignments in government priorities. However, across this period and in relation to surface water management, the provincial government goal seems to have remained relatively consistent: to move from a blinkered focus on the square grid to a broader view that included the irregular watershed defined in relation to local environmental conditions. This chapter focuses on the Wilson Creek Experimental Watershed and the Whitemud Watershed Conservation District (figure 12.1). Both were situated in western Manitoba in proximity to each other. Both emerged in response to the same local trends in surface water management: an increasing awareness of past mistakes and present ignorance and a resulting eagerness to gain better knowledge and avoid further missteps. Each reflects an aspect of the provincial government's attempt to rescale environmental management during the period in question.

THE WILSON CREEK EXPERIMENTAL WATERSHED

The Manitoba escarpment angles across southwestern Manitoba in a south-east to northwest direction. A notable landscape feature in a relatively flat province, the elevation change between the escarpment and the lowlands to its east varies from about three hundred meters in some places to over six hundred meters in others. The highest elevations are recognized as distinct landforms: the Riding, Duck, and Porcupine Mountains. The escarpment is composed of sedimentary shale deposited in the preglacial era. While a re-sistant silica-based upper layer preserved it from scouring during glaciation, the escarpment is now subject to significant erosion. Creeks flowing from the height of the escarpment have carved deep channels, with incisions of up to sixty meters.[6] Along the escarpment, the higher areas receive more precipita-tion than the surrounding lands. Above the six-hundred-meter contour line, the annual average is about 750 milimeters. Much of this precipitation arrives in heavy storms that occur in the period between May and July.[7] Runoff from these storms contributes to the formation of large low-angle alluvial fans in areas where small waterways hit flatter lands and decrease the speed of flow, thus depositing material eroded from higher up.[8]

These patterns are evident in the Wilson Creek area. The Wilson Creek watershed was an unsettled area located in Township 20, Range 16 W, some 241 kilometers north and west of Manitoba's capital city of Winnipeg.[9] The creek's upper catchment area is a relatively flat plateau at an elevation of about 732 meters above sea level in the upper reaches of the Manitoba escarpment. This plateau is drained by Packhorse and Bald Hill Creeks, the two tributar-ies that eventually come together to form Wilson Creek. From this height the land drops 396 meters in 6.4 kilometers, with water flowing through deeply incised channels. At 335 meters about sea level, with a rapid decrease in slope and thus flow rate, an extensive alluvial fan has formed (figure 12.2).[10] Finally, Wilson Creek flows east through 11.3 kilometers of artificial drainage before finding its way to Turtle River.[11] The north-flowing Turtle River eventually dumps into Dauphin Lake at about 259 meters above sea level.

The local topography and precipitation patterns contributed to problems with excess surface water. Farmers below the escarpment in the Wilson Creek area had a lot of experience with crop losses related to flooding. As early as 1921, a Manitoba provincial government report documented that land use changes on the highlands had affected conditions in the lowlands.[12] In Mc-Creary, the rural municipality situated directly to the east of the Wilson Creek Experimental Watershed, the severity of flooding is documented in agricultural losses. Between 1943 and 1947, for instance, 264 farmers reported crop damage estimated at a total value of $209,736. This amounted to an aver-

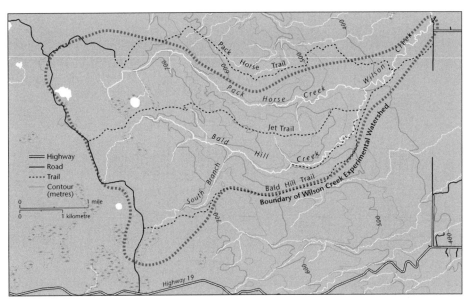

FIGURE 12.2. Wilson Creek Experimental Watershed. Adapted from Library and Archives of Canada, RG 124, File 740/86024, Wilson Creek Watershed, Vol. Supp., 1972–1974, Wilson Creek Experimental Watershed—Joint Effort of Canada and Manitoba.

age loss per farmer per year of $158 in crop value, though the irregular nature of the hydroclimate meant that in some years the losses would be nonexistent, while in others they would be intolerably high.[13] Agricultural flooding was due not only to excess water but also to infilling of drains, as deposition of eroded material clogged the natural and artificial channels that might otherwise have carried away the floodwaters.[14] As infilling continued, the flood risks worsened. Clearly, improvements to water management were needed if agriculture was to succeed in the area.

In the late 1940s, the Manitoba provincial government argued the cost of improving environmental management in the region should be shared between the provincial and federal governments. M. A. Lyons, an engineer sometimes employed with the provincial government, drafted a letter to the Manitoba Minister of Public Works Errick Willis in which this case was made. Lyons pointed out that at the time this region was settled in the late nineteenth century the lands of the area and so control over settlement fell to the federal government. Despite surveyors' reports indicating the land was not suitable, the federal government continued to promote agricultural settlement. By 1948, Lyons reported, the provincial government had already spent seven hundred and fifty thousand dollars on projects intended to improve the agricultural situation on the eastern slopes of Riding Mountain.[15] These were

largely drainage projects in the lower watershed, and they had failed to resolve the environmental problems in this area. Indeed, they had only made
clear that a far greater commitment of resources would be necessary to adequately address the situation.

The pressure for the federal government to take some responsibility was
even greater in the Wilson Creek area, where the headlands formed part of a
national park. Riding Mountain National Park was created in 1929. Twenty-
six square kilometers of Wilson Creek's headwaters lay within the park.[16] Additionally, by the mid-twentieth century, organizations such as the Prairie
Farm Rehabilitation Administration, a federal entity that supported agricultural development across the prairies, and programs such as federal government contributions to flood control in the Rocky Mountain headwaters
of the Saskatchewan River together had paved the way for the federal government to become involved in projects that once would have been the sole
responsibility of the provinces.[17] Ultimately, provincial and federal governments recognized that grid-based settlement had not been successful in the
region. Local prosperity was stymied by flooding, erosion, and siltation, and
both governments recognized the need to address the situation.

The Northwest Escarpment Agreement of 1949 represented an attempt by
both governments to cooperate on assistance for suffering farmers and strategies to improve the situation. By this time, various approaches had been attempted in areas along the escarpment, including dyking to protect against
flooding and damming to retain the headwaters. But in the absence of concrete information about environmental processes in the region, it was difficult
to assess the success or failure of any undertaking. As the geographer William Carlyle made clear in his article on environmental management in the
escarpment region, at this stage "there were no meteorological data, records
of runoff, or measurements of the amounts of erosion and deposition for the
northwest escarpment area."[18] Government officials had recognized the need
to address a gap in knowledge if water management was to be prosecuted
effectively. The Committee on Headwater, Flood, and Erosion Control was
established in 1957 in part to support efforts to generate the necessary information.[19] For William Carlyle, the committee's formation amounted to "a
crucial turning point in government policy."[20] Finally, the federal and provincial governments had recognized the need to attain good environmental
information as the basis for sound management policy.

Wilson Creek, as a waterway typical of the over sixty streams that began
on the escarpment, was selected as the object of study. Due to "the immediacy and seriousness of the problems" in the area, the committee was also
expected "to experiment with programs aimed at improving the situation."[21]
Over the next twenty-five years, Wilson Creek became the focus of much

activity. While the area certainly had environmental problems of its own, Wilson Creek was studied not for its unique elements but for those characteristics it shared with other similar landscapes. The Dominion Land Survey was an extensive project, reaching across the Canadian prairies over a period of decades. In contrast, Wilson Creek was an intensive undertaking, a focused effort to understand a relatively small watershed in the hope that this would illuminate processes at work in similar regions.

If the Wilson Creek watershed was to be examined, it had to be made accessible. In order to allow for the transport of heavy machinery used by scientists, the governments built roads. Bald Hill and Packhorse Trails, both graveled, ran along the watershed boundaries. Jet Trail, which seems to have remained more rustic, ran up the middle of the watershed. There were at least thirty-eight kilometers of gravel road and trail as well as a further four kilometers of rough trail.[22] From October 1957 to March 31, 1975, 26.2 percent of total project funds were spent on the roads, providing an unparalleled opportunity to observe hydrological processes in a relatively remote region.[23] And it was not only government and scientific eyes that were viewing the area. The National Park Service used the watershed for part of its interpretative program operating out of the nearby Riding Mountain National Park, conducting tours for an interested public on a biweekly basis throughout the tourist season.[24] From April 1973 to March 1974, for instance, there were fifteen tours for a total of 347 visitors.[25] Because of its identification as an experimental watershed, the area was opened up to human scrutiny in a way it otherwise would not have been. And because Wilson Creek was taken as representative of other escarpmental landscapes, visiting this one watershed meant gaining awareness of regional environmental processes.

What came of the Wilson Creek project? An important outcome was improved understanding of the specific environmental processes implicated in flood events. Detailed records of meteorological and hydrological events in the Wilson Creek area were maintained from 1958, allowing for numerous important studies that contributed to a more detailed understanding of the relations between variables such as amount of rainfall, timing of rainfall, and rate of siltation. These illustrated the importance of seasonal patterns in contributing to flood events. A heavy rainfall in a dry season is unlikely to cause problems; a more minor storm in a wetter season may have far more serious consequences.[26] For a twenty-five-milimeter rainstorm, for instance, the runoff varied from 0.3 percent for dry conditions to 50 percent for wet conditions. Specific findings such as these provided some basis from which to make predictions about the severity of flooding in a particular year, allowing farmers and managers to prepare for what was to come.

Beyond improved understanding of local environmental processes, there were also some physical improvements to the experimental watershed. Because Wilson Creek was used as a study area, works were undertaken that otherwise may not have been attempted. For instance, headwater retention structures were built in the upper watershed without consideration of whether the value of the flood protection they provided would justify the cost of construction.[27] The benefit to the small watershed may not have been sufficient justification in itself, but the project was made worthwhile by the potential to gain knowledge applicable to all comparable watersheds.[28] At this stage, authorities were more concerned with exploring what could be done rather than with determining what should be done. As the hope was that Wilson Creek watershed would provide insight into the workings of a larger geographical area, the needs of the larger geographical area justified the transformation of the Wilson Creek watershed.

Perhaps the most significant outcome of the Wilson Creek Experimental Watershed project was the confirmation of headwater control as an efficient and effective means of managing flooding and sedimentation. Authorities recognized that flood control along the escarpment had long focused on drainage projects in the lower portions of the watersheds. These projects were both very expensive and relatively ineffective, in large measure due to infilling by material eroded from higher up the escarpment.[29] Many experiments conducted at Wilson Creek were part of efforts by the Committee on Headwater, Flood, and Erosion Control to redirect attention from the lower to the upper watershed. According to the terms of reference provided to the committee, investigations were to determine how much of the flood problem originates in the headwaters, to identify the causes of any deterioration of headwater conditions that may contribute to local environmental problems, and to find ways that action in the headwaters might improve problems in the watershed.[30] In a summary report of 1983, R. W. Newbury made clear that, on the basis of work in the watershed, it was established definitively that much floodwater originates in the upper watershed.[31] The shift in perspective justified and demanded by the experimental watershed project illustrated the importance of a watershed perspective for environmental management, in Wilson Creek and elsewhere.

Even as the Wilson Creek project demonstrated the importance of the watershed perspective, so did it illustrate some of the limitations of this approach to environmental management. While scientists wished to study certain natural processes under way in the area, the watershed could not be abstracted from the larger environment in which it was embedded. Stream structures had to be guarded with heavy spikes to discourage interference with their operations, as local bears were fond of scratching their stomachs on the equipment.[32] In the experimental watershed, care had to be taken to manage the relation between the watershed dynamics under study and the other natural processes (such as the roaming patterns of animals) that could come into play, sometimes inconveniently. While there were good reasons to expect that land management by watershed might be more successful than land management by quarter section, the watershed remained a bounded area in a natural world that was animated in part by processes that transcended the boundary.[33]

The Wilson Creek Experimental Watershed was a project undertaken by governments working together across their distinct jurisdictions in order to gather information about a problematic landscape. While the provincial and federal governments were only too familiar with the flood problem, they recognized that the processes and relationships at play in areas like Wilson Creek were poorly understood. A history of failed attempts at flood protection through lower watershed activities meant the Wilson Creek project was oriented to assessing the potential of upper watershed flood protection. The project amounted to an attempt to gain greater understanding of the environmental processes at work in the region and also to assess the utility of refocusing attention from downstream to upstream. Through the project, environmental processes were revealed, scientists and students were assisted in their work, and new environmental management techniques were developed. Discussed in theses and articles, Wilson Creek became a landscape of significance for scientists, even those working elsewhere, concerned with environmental questions similar to those explored in this experimental watershed. While the importance of larger environmental processes could not be dismissed, the Wilson Creek Experimental Watershed illustrated the utility of the watershed approach. The provincial and federal governments worked together to flesh out understanding of environmental processes that transcended the gridded landscape of privately worked farms that federal government settlement legislation had helped to create.

THE WHITEMUD WATERSHED CONSERVATION DISTRICT

The Whitemud River watershed lies to the west of Lake Manitoba, slightly to the south of the Wilson Creek Experimental Watershed. The watershed reaches from 721 meters above sea level in the Riding Mountains down to 345 meters above sea level at the eastern end, where the Whitemud River dumps into Lake Manitoba. Elevation decreases sharply on descending from the Riding Mountain area and then more gradually eastward through the watershed (figure 12.3).[34] In selecting sites for settlement within the Whitemud region, newcomers to the lower areas favored areas offering good drainage in what was otherwise a somewhat marshy area. Newcomers to the higher areas chose flatter land near streams.[35] By the mid-twentieth century, many who settled in the area had much experience with flooding.

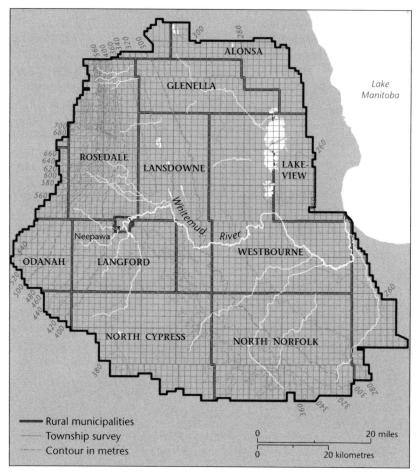

FIGURE 12.3. Whitemud Watershed Conservation District. Adapted from Manitoba, Department of Mines, Resources, and Environmental Management, *Whitemud River Watershed Resource Study* (Winnipeg: Whitemud River Watershed Board, 1974), 13.

The explanation for flooding in the Whitemud area was quite similar to that for flooding in the Wilson Creek watershed. The upper watershed received comparatively heavy precipitation, with a significant portion arriving in the form of spring and summer storms. Coming all at once and in significant quantity, the runoff from these storms caused major problems. The cost of flood damage in the Whitemud watershed averaged about $40,000, but there were occasional peaks as in 1960 ($236,000), 1969 ($138,000), and 1970 ($454,000).[36] In 1975, the engineer William Newton explained in a presentation to the Engineering Institute of Canada how in lowland areas of the Whitemud watershed flooding made farming "more of a gamble than it logically should be."[37] After years of losses, government administrators and local residents alike wondered what could be done to tip the odds in favor of farmers.

Though the height of the escarpment in the Riding Mountain district made the problem especially acute in the Whitemud area, many agricultural regions in Manitoba were subject to agricultural flooding. Primarily in the Manitoba lowlands to the east of the escarpment, excess surface water had often interfered with farming. Flat land and clay-based soils created a landscape in which spring melt, runoff from higher areas, and precipitation were slow to drain away. The Land Drainage Act was passed by the provincial legislature in 1895, providing formal mechanisms through which drainage districts could be created throughout the province. A number of districts were created in the lowlands, with the cost of drain construction levied on district residents. As drainage districts did not possess independent administrative infrastructure, each rural municipality was responsible for collecting the levies from the drainage district residents living within the municipal boundaries and forwarding the money to the province. The provincial government coordinated drainage work in each drainage district. Through this particular arrangement involving the provincial government, rural municipalities, and drainage districts, artificial drainage projects were undertaken in the Whitemud area by the mid-1910s.[38] These undertakings certainly improved the situation for some. However, in the Whitemud area as in others, many surface water problems went unresolved. Some affected Manitobans were convinced the provincial government had either worsened the situation or not done enough to help it.

Particularly incensed were downstream Manitobans, those who lived in the lowlands alongside the Red River and Lake Manitoba. They believed that runoff from higher upstream areas placed an unfair burden on their drainage systems. From when the matter first came to a head in the 1910s, upstream residents resisted any suggestion they should contribute to the costs of downstream drainage.[39] The situation eventually began to change toward the mid-twentieth century, when those who lived on higher lands on or near the escarpment became increasingly aware of damage to their own lands. Uncontrolled surface water was sweeping away valuable topsoil and threatening slope stability along the escarpment. In his presentation in 1975, engineer William Newton referred to mid-twentieth-century conditions in the highlands. He described how in the upper watershed there were areas "where erosion has progressed to such an extent that in some places what were once farmlands are now fields of gray-white shale with little or no economic value."[40] Newton explained that by 1950 there were already two million acres of scarp land subject to erosion.[41] Opposition between downstream farmers who wanted action on flooding and upstream farmers who feared any action would come at their expense was replaced with consensus that something had to be done to address these increasingly severe environmental management problems.

In fall 1956, reeves of the affected rural municipalities formed the Riding Mountain-Whitemud River Watershed Committee. "The major purpose and objectives," the new committee's constitution read, "are to promote and assist in developing over-all policies to facilitate co-operation, co-ordination and action on soil and water conservation and flood prevention."[42] This constitution reflected a remarkable process of effacing old divisions of interest and creating new ones. Residents were being encouraged to identify not with those who experienced environmental problems similar to their own but with all people who lived within the watershed. Individuals interested in taking action were divided into committees based on the needs of a functional watershed-based environmental management entity: education and publicity, legislation, finance, and reforestation.[43] So rather than voicing the complaints of those who lived along streams and so were subject to certain sorts of flooding, for instance, streamside residents might work with those who lived in higher areas to develop the sort of legislation that would benefit the entire watershed. The implication was that whatever environmental problems beset an individual were ultimately related to the problems experienced by others in the watershed, even if the connections were not immediately apparent.

Provincial government officials attended many of the meetings that led to the creation of the watershed committee, even on occasion making presentations on the idea of watershed management.[44] The Manitoba Minister of Agriculture C. L. Shuttleworth indicated that his purpose in attending a meeting on November 9, 1956, was to gauge the local interest in watershed management.[45] Indeed, government officials had real reasons to want watershed management to emerge from local impetus. Generally, the public consensus was that Manitoba's artificial drainage system had never worked particularly well. The provincial government did not want to impose watershed management and so risk further dissatisfaction among those who were already distrustful of government undertakings.[46] An electoral system in which rural voters still held a disproportionate amount of power only increased provincial government reticence.[47] Yet as research along Wilson Creek was confirming, the way forward for the region seemed to lie in watershed management. The province was convinced of the need for watershed management but reluctant to take responsibility for any problems that may ensue. The way to get around this was to promote the watershed idea, even while leaving the specific task of watershed district formation in the hands of local movers.

How did the province promote watershed management? A few techniques merit consideration. First, the provincial government addressed the concrete ways watershed management might change life in the Whitemud region through focus on actual conditions in the local watershed. In early August 1956, for instance, a gully stabilization field day was held in the Whitemud area. The aims were to increase understanding of local environmental challenges and to demonstrate techniques through which new agricultural machinery could assist in stabilizing gullies. These very practical lessons were paired with a discussion of how watershed management might support the efforts at progressive environmental management that individual farmers were making. Approximately 125 people attended, mostly farmers.[48] Government agents were promoting watershed management by meeting farmers in their fields and addressing challenges they faced every day in a manner that related these challenges to watershed-wide issues and approaches.

The province sought out and shared information about the successes of watershed management in other locales. Projects under way in the United States and in Ontario attracted the government's attention. Indeed, provincial officials went so far as to go on tours of the relevant areas.[49] The province made efforts to share this experience with local residents. For instance, at the meeting at which the Riding Mountain-Whitemud Watershed Committee was created, a film was shown detailing water and land management. Produced in 1952 at the University of Nebraska, *Valley of Still Waters* provided a twenty-two-minute introduction to the watershed concept as applied in the Salt-Wahoo watershed, an area stricken with problems of flooding and erosion.[50] Insofar as exposure to projects under way elsewhere increased local understanding of and comfort with the watershed idea, the Riding Mountain-Whitemud River Watershed Conservation District, a local land unit, depended on the formation of other watershed-based land units located in far away areas.

The province also tried to explain watershed management as an abstract concept. Provincial officials often deployed comparisons or analogies in effort to make matters clear for their audiences. On April 10, 1963, the *Neepawa Herald* published what was called a "Special Water Edition," which amounted to an eight-page insert focused on various water issues in Manitoba. A section titled "What is a Watershed?" included a comparison between a watershed and various examples designed to make the watershed seem straightforward and familiar. A watershed, the document explained, was comparable to "the drainboard that carries rinse water into your kitchen sink" or the area of your childhood yard that drained into your "favourite mud puddle in which you liked to play."[51] An undated pamphlet explaining watershed management compared it to an insurance policy, as it offered some security "against the destruction of the resource base."[52] If the drainboard and backyard comparisons emphasized the simplicity of the watershed idea, the insurance policy comparison underlined its importance. Described in the abstract, the watershed seemed an ideal solution to the real-world environmental problems with which district residents were all too familiar.

Over the late 1950s and 1960s, the provincial government sought to put conditions in place to favor the adoption of watershed management. The Watershed and Soil Conservation Authorities Act of 1958 was quickly replaced by the Watershed Conservation Districts Act of 1959, in an effort to address what were perceived as the deficiencies of the first. In 1961, the federal government introduced the Agricultural Rehabilitation and Development Act (which was later retitled the Agricultural and Rural Development Act, ARDA), as a means of disseminating funds to support projects in four key areas: alternative use of land, soil and water conservation, rural development, and research.[53] In particularly needy areas, ARDA districts could be formed, and these would become the focus of significant effort and resources. In 1963, word got out that the Whitemud watershed was being considered as Manitoba's second ARDA district because of the watershed management issue.[54] This proved an impetus to further legislative changes, as the province sought to ensure any watershed district would be positioned to benefit from federal funding.

But despite initial local enthusiasm and continued provincial government efforts, no watershed districts were formed in this period. This was due in large measure to changes under way across the rural prairies as much as in the Whitemud region. Total watershed population dropped from 25,460 in 1941 to 21,571 in 1971 (a drop of 15 percent). Rural population in the watershed declined from 23,168 to 15,662 (a drop of 32 percent) over the same period.[55] As Manitoba urban centers like Winnipeg and Brandon expanded and even the local town of Neepawa developed, the rural experience was transformed. Farmers worked increasingly large farms through increasingly mechanized means, in a landscape that was becoming less populated than previously. Lower population meant fewer people to bear the burden of local taxation. Particularly in light of concerns about impending school district consolidation and resulting tax increases, some residents were reluctant to create another local authority with the power to tax.[56] Some people feared the creation of another administrative entity would diminish both the power of their municipal leadership and the sense of community they shared with their fellow municipal residents. All of these factors amounted to a significant barrier to the formation of a watershed-based conservation district.

In 1970, the provincial government passed the Resource Conservation Districts Act. Under this legislation, districts would be defined along municipal lines rather than watershed boundaries.[57] This represented an attempt to woo reluctant municipalities by further accommodating their fears about the loss of local autonomy and destruction of municipal community. Still, there was little immediate response. From a historical perspective, this extended lull in the move toward watershed management is perhaps the best illustration of the role the provincial government was playing. Despite the apparent failure of the province's promotional strategy, there was no attempt to impose watershed management. The matter simply fell into abeyance. In the absence of local support, there would be no watershed management districts.

The Whitemud Watershed Conservation District was eventually incorporated on March 22, 1972.[58] The district encompassed 6,216 square kilometers of land, including four towns and fourteen municipalities, in whole or part.[59] In 1973, W. R. Newton, director of operations for Manitoba Water Resources, explained that a rise of environmental consciousness among locals had changed the context for discussion of watershed management, leading to the formation of the district.[60] According to Len Evans, the acting minister of Mines, Resources, and Environmental Management, watershed residents had come to recognize "the problems of divided jurisdiction" and so had "taken the initiative in doing something to solve the problem."[61] Government rhetoric on the creation of the district suggests that a tipping point had been reached: sufficient numbers of residents were concerned enough about environmental management to support the district's creation. This interpretation is borne out by how the Whitemud Watershed Conservation District was incorporated under the more environmentally attuned Watershed Conservation Districts Act of 1959, despite the availability of the recently passed Resource Conservation Districts Act.

By the mid-twentieth century, the Manitoba provincial government was convinced that watershed management offered the best opportunity to tackle the land and water problems that had long bedeviled the area west of Lake Manitoba. In part because of a history of failed projects, the government was unwilling to impose management by watershed district. Instead the provincial government adopted a promotional strategy, working to educate the population and so generate support for watershed management. Various means were tried, from meetings to publications and from seminars to films. At the same time, the government tinkered with its legislation, seeking to take advantage of federal government programs and to appeal to reluctant segments of the population. Despite lengthy delays, the government maintained that districts would be formed only with the support of the affected area. The province was willing to sacrifice the watershed idea if it failed to find public approval and even put legislation in place that would allow districts to form with boundaries that were not watershed based. Eventually, due largely to greater public understanding of the situation, the Whitemud Watershed Conservation District was formed.

IT IS PERHAPS IMPORTANT that watershed management was taken seriously in Manitoba only at a relatively late date in the province's history of surface water management. A series of unsuccessful attempts at environmental management, in which agricultural areas were flooded and valuable land was eroded despite government and public efforts, underlay the government's choices. Officials were all too aware of their own inability to plan successful undertakings and predict environmental outcomes. The province had already been humbled. The Wilson Creek Experimental Watershed was an attempt to gain insight into the workings of an escarpmental watershed, in hopes that examination of this one area would translate into more effective management throughout environmentally similar regions of the province. The Wilson Creek project provided opportunities for scientific research, much of which confirmed that conditions downstream depended in large measure on events upstream. From an environmental management perspective, it became abundantly clear that the watershed was a concept of significant importance.

If the province had been humbled, officials also felt they had been chastised, subject to significant public anger because of projects perceived as less than successful. Reluctant to risk further public dissatisfaction, the provincial government was willing to go only so far with watershed management. The government worked to reeducate the population, offering ways of thinking about land and water management that encompassed a region larger than the individual farm. Ultimately, officials limited their efforts to the promotion of watershed management. If watershed management was to be adopted, it would be at the pleasure of the local municipal leaders. It is important to recognize that governments did not always act so diffidently in the management of the Manitoba landscape. For example, the historian John Sandlos has examined the eviction in 1936 of the Keeseekowenin Ojibway from a small reserve within Riding Mountain National Park. Tourists visiting the Wilson Creek Experimental Watershed may well have travelled over land from which the Keeseekowenin had been removed.[62] The behavior of the province in relation to reluctant municipal officials reflects the extent to which rural municipalities occupied a position of relative power in the province. In contrast with comparatively powerless aboriginal people, rural municipalities merited respect and serious consideration from higher levels of government, at least in relation to issues of land and water management.

It is likely also important that the Whitemud watershed was not closely connected hydrologically to Winnipeg, Manitoba's most populated city, and that the towns within the watershed such as Neepawa were relatively small.

In his chapter in this edited volume, the historical geographer Craig Colten demonstrates how watersheds containing large cities should be considered urban territories as much as fluvial forms. The prominence of rural Manitoba voices in relation to watershed management may suggest that fluvial forms can also serve to curtail the urban influence, sparing areas outside the urban watershed from the effects of policy tailored to the needs of the city. Even in the absence of a major urban influence, however, all parcels of land within the Whitemud watershed were of interest to multiple parties, from landowners through the rural municipality to the provincial government. Members of each group envisioned how best to use the land in relation to their own geographical scale of interest, in the context of a broad array of economic and social circumstances. Many landowners in the Whitemud area, for instance, worried not only about the state of their land but also about the financing of watershed management, particularly in light of changes in the human geography of rural areas. Even a common focus on the watershed could not eliminate the differences of opinion derived from distinctions of scale and perspective.

The provincial and federal governments worked together to support scientific inquiry into watershed processes in the province, and the provincial government sought to translate scientific insights about the value of watershed management into terms Manitobans were likely to understand. In addition to important insights into natural processes, science also provided a justification for watershed management that skirted the stark reality that the adoption of this new strategy was in part an attempt to correct the grid-based system employed by the governments that had managed settlement. As advocates for the scientific approach to environmental management, contemporary governments could be promoting a new idea rather than correcting their own mistakes. The geographer Erik Swyngedouw documents how the adoption of watershed-based management was in Spain an attempt by advocates to assume a position of power through the modernization process.[63] In Manitoba, the investigation and promotion of watershed management was related as much to avoiding past errors as to planning future triumphs.

The Whitemud Watershed Conservation District did not begin a rush to extend watershed management across the province. The acts of 1959 and 1970 were consolidated in the Conservation Districts Act of 1976, which allowed districts to be created according to either watershed or municipal boundaries or a mix of the two. By the early twenty-first century, there were eighteen districts in operation, covering approximately 85 percent of municipal Manitoba.[64] The vast majority of these districts, however, defined their areas of concern according to municipal rather than watershed boundaries.[65] A recent report by the International Institute for Sustainable Development has argued that for this reason, Manitoba's conservation districts "have merely created an additional layer of administration" without dealing progressively or even effectively "with the challenge of surface water management."[66] From this perspective, conservation districts have not only failed to reconcile productive agriculture and environmental conditions throughout the province but also have further complicated an already complex jurisdictional situation. In many parts of Manitoba, from a watershed management perspective at least, human activity and the laws of nature remain in discord.

CONCLUSION

STÉPHANE CASTONGUAY AND
MATTHEW EVENDEN

URBAN RIVERS OPENED with the river Irwell flowing through Manchester, pungent and polluted. The river served as a metaphor for a broader process; we claimed that the Irwell might be conceived as the epitome of the urban-industrial river. Many of the changes evident in an extreme form on this river could, in different measures, be witnessed in other cases elsewhere. Now, in the comparative light of the contributions to this book, we would like to make the opposite point as well. The river Irwell suggests also particularity. Read alongside the case of Edinburgh and the Firth of Forth, or Vienna and the Danube, Montreal and the St. Lawrence, or Brussels and the Senne, we see the Irwell's features expressing both general and unique patterns. The same point can be made about any of the city-river cases in this book. Having examined in depth their particular features, it now remains to elaborate some broader themes and arguments.

Despite the many cases examined, one unifying line of interpretation in *Urban Rivers* is that the industrial and urban revolutions of the Western world changed how urban societies used rivers. Traditional modes of energy generation, transportation, and river fishing faced pressures from increased population levels, economic demands, and newly developed socio-technical systems. Although Chloe Deligne importantly reminds us that not all riverine changes were driven by industrialization and urban growth, one can identify in the nineteenth century a scale shift in urban demands for water supply as well as sewage and industrial waste removal, which also coincided with emerging ideas of hygiene, purity, and order in the liberal city. This occurred in cities ranging from Paris to Christiania (Oslo) to Montreal. As ideas about the proper treatment and distribution of water and waste evolved, rivers were also reconstructed as infrastructure for transportation through channelization projects and dredging and as energy systems, driving mill wheels, filling reservoirs, and ultimately powering hydroelectric facilities. These reconstructions ultimately changed the nature of rivers in terms of their chemistry, aquatic ecology, fluvial geomorphology, and flow.

Rivers, however, were not simply acted upon; they entered into the process of urbanization. At a broad structural level, the locations of cities on rivers of different sizes and discharges shaped urban possibilities and perils. As cities interacted with rivers and became inseparably bound up with them in terms of waste removal, water supply, and industrial drive, rivers could not be easily disentangled from urban infrastructure, operations, and morphology. Urban linkages extending beyond the city proper often travelled along rivers or drew resources from rivers at a distance. Urbanization remade rivers, to be sure, but rivers also limited the possibilities, shaped urban form and functions, and with a predictable unpredictability challenged the foundations of urban life with hazards of several kinds.

A second and related line of interpretation in *Urban Rivers* is that the changes provoked by new industrial and urban demands on rivers set the stage for social conflict. New demands on rivers not only challenged previous uses, they also frequently worked at cross-purposes. Industrialists running mills on the Akerselva, for example, worried that withdrawls of potable water by the municipal corporation would undermine their operations. On the Lea, the use of the river as a navigation channel decreased over time owing in part to the slow accretion of industrial pollution and waste on its bed. On the Senne, the Illinois, and the rivers feeding the Firth of Forth, sewage and pollution damaged fisheries. In broad terms, evolving socio-technical systems ran into conflict with one another and past river uses. These conflicts occurred among urban interests but also provoked disputes between places and beyond the city.

As industrialization and urbanization increased sewage loads and raised water demands, cities impacted their hinterlands to a greater degree. Sabine Barles argues that Paris externalized its metabolism in the nineteenth and twentieth century, creating new dependencies for the inflow of waters and the outflow of wastes. This process, as Frederic Graber suggests, was already well under way in the late eighteenth century in Paris, though large-scale diversion projects generally occurred later elsewhere, more typically in the mid-nineteenth century. In the United States, where one central city existed in a large river basin, Craig Colten argues that its needs tended to dominate others in river basin planning, though the particular circumstances of scale, location, and river discharge proved to be important contributing factors to how such influence was exerted and realized. This is not to say that urban imperialism either went uncontested (protests against water diversion in Paris date to the late eighteenth century) or always shaped rural experience. Shannon Stunden Bower reminds us that in rural Manitoba, in areas beyond Winnipeg's effective reach, water planning operated in a nexus linking rural municipalities, water districts, and the provincial government all grappling with the basic conflicts between surface water management and the property lines of the settlement grid.

Social conflict also resulted from the transformation of rivers as ecological and physical systems. Established interests depended on rivers of a particular kind. The increased sewage burden changed aquatic ecosystems, channelization and levee construction altered existing and potential riverbed and flood conditions, and dams affected river flows and their ability to remove wastes. On the Rivières de Prairies, a hydroelectric dam built in 1930 challenged the existing use of the channel as a sewage receptacle, heightening fears of contamination, at the same time as popular use of the river for swimming increased because of the controlled flow and lake-like conditions of the reservoir. On the Firth of Forth, the combined long-term effects of pollution and dams in surrounding watersheds undermined fisheries, while environmental regulations in the 1970s helped to eliminate habitat for birds and other fauna that thrived in a hybrid industrial ecology. In many cases, the environmental consequences of large-scale riverine change went uncontested or were so transformational that minor interests were simply swept away. When Chicago diverted sewage into the Illinois River, fish populations spiked with the new nutrient supply and then over a period of years declined precipitously, along with the commercial fishery.

Social conflict partly turned on the idea of the river as a finite resource, partly on the nature of environmental change, and partly on the unpredictable but unsettling potential of rivers to break the bounds of expected behavior. Frontier cities in the U.S. Midwest, built on floodplains, instilled a path of vulnerability for urban development that lasted generations. City building always contained an element of reconstruction as bridges were rebuilt, sewer lines mended, and water supplies restored. In larger, established cities with longer relationships with rivers, floods and droughts could still challenge basic assumptions. The flood that struck Paris in 1910 provoked basic administrative changes in the management of the Seine and elevated Paris's control in the process. Although experts made claims about rivers and public health, the ideology of self-purification and the slow acceptance of the germ theory meant that waterborne diseases also delivered a recurring threat and hazard to urban populations. As Craig Colten argues, and the book illustrates as a whole, not only social priorities drove change.

The social conflicts that accompanied new uses of rivers led to attempts at resolution. The word "resolution" suggests a calm, orderly process, but conflict whether channeled through a legal process, the state system, or a more unwieldy public sphere, could be brutal and unfair. The combined might of Christiania industrialists fought legal war with the municipal corporation and courted (unsuccessfully) the favor of the established plank nobility. Brussels took a hundred years punctuated by disputes and rival systems to develop amicable water distribution arrangements with its surrounding faubourgs; while Paris characteristically imposed its needs on surrounding areas, annexing them or removing their resources at the pleasure of the state. Chicago moved ahead with its sewage canal, sending its problems to a new downstream catchment, rushing construction to avoid legal obstructions. Dynamite sticks were another aggressive form of resolution.

Social conflicts of these sorts were partly mediated by a new class of experts emerging in the nineteenth century to interpret the environment, adjudicate disputes, and create administrative order over dynamic social and natural processes. In some cases, prominent authorities played a role in disputes well before the rise of expertise as a cultural category. Thus in late eighteenth-century France, contending voices argued for the proper definition of water purity. In other places, commissions of experts gained power in the wake of crises such as floods or droughts, as did Alfred Picard and the Commission des inondations in 1910 following the one-hundred-year flood on the Seine. In some cases, experts hardly mediated situations but rather drove debate, as they did over the question of channelization and flood control in Vienna. Such expertise elevated individuals with specific knowledge of rivers but also corresponded to the emerging administrative structures of the city, region, and the state. By the mid-twentieth century, such scientific-administrative structures were ubiquitous. Experts not only responded to river disputes, they also helped to set the very language by which rivers were known, including the watershed idea in Manitoba. In other cases, they led the state to introduce new environmental measures, with or without public pressure; in the case of Scotland the balance of evidence suggests without.

These new experts assumed administrative positions within dynamic and evolving systems of governance. There was no one way to govern rivers, to distribute state powers over them, and to integrate these with existing levels of jurisdiction. In some cases, urban authority extended over vast areas and dependent regions were annexed, as in the case of Paris; in others, like Brussels, long-term conflict between the central city and surrounding communities produced asymmetries in the provision of environmental services. In federal states, like the United States, urban attempts to control river basin planning had to work also within the limits of the Constitution and through federal and state bodies with river planning powers, such as the federal U.S.

Army Corps of Engineers. In others, like Canada, legal provisions asserting the primacy of navigability under federal authority had to contend with the rising social values attached to hydroelectric power development under provincial jurisdiction. Whatever the case, the particular circumstances of urban aspirations, contending demands, and the division of authority within the state set the boundaries of the contest.

A third line of interpretation suggests that the changing urban-riverine relationship also unfolded in new urban spaces, extending from the city center to distant hinterlands. This perspective emerges first from the observation that the new metabolic demands of cities caused distant supply areas to be enrolled for urban purposes. As a material process, urbanization extended over distance. Paris's Ourcq canal was one example; Glasgow's capture of the Forth's headwaters another. In the other direction, the material outflows of the city, its wastes, flowed over distance, entering distant water courses and changing their aquatic ecologies in the Firth of Forth, the lower Potomac, and the Illinois River. These flows suggest the long supply and connection lines between the city center and surrounding regions and play havoc with the idea of the city boundary proper. Rivers, rather, facilitated the integration of outlying areas and in some cases their wholesale annexation.

The material flows, as we have already suggested, were complicated by social claims and conflicts. Building administrative systems, expertise, and authority to govern a flow resource over distance meant that urban power was also extended. Different authors in this edited volume have expressed the idea somewhat differently. Chloe Deligne refers to a "silent territory" to suggest the linkages between places produced by underlying biophysical boundaries. Craig Colten argues that river basins in the United States became urban territories as much as fluvial forms. By contrast, Shannon Stunden Bower argues that watersheds were also ideas, not fixed physical forms that determined connections. Just as space is socially produced, so too was the very idea of nature, in this case the watershed or the river basin.

The idea of the city's new urban spaces also relates to the internal division of the city, its morphology. The grounds of the city were remade in conjunction with riverine transformations. In many cities, the threat of diseases such as cholera, as well as emerging bourgeois ideals of urban order and space, which ran parallel to and were folded into hygienic discourses, produced a wave of river-burying exercises, as smaller streams were turned into plumbing under city streets. The Senne in Brussels fundamentally changed its relationship when buried between 1867 and 1871, shifting from a dynamic element of urban space to a component of urban infrastructure, removed from sight and the other senses. In Vienna, the long-term project of channelization and flood control on the Danube changed the zone of vulnerability in the city and opened up new areas for settlement. In the process, the city was more sharply defined against the river, and the river became a primary element of urban transportation infrastructure. In Montreal, located on an island in the St. Lawrence, the importance of the city in continental transportation drew the emerging industrial port toward the river, its settlements defined as an inverted "T," with the river serving as the defining feature. As new forms of environmental regulation and urban planning deindustrialized urban rivers in the late twentieth century, parks were established, green spaces emerged, as well as meeting grounds for sociability, and large scale events like Montreal's celebrated Expo '67.

This is the common idea of the urban river today, a place of connection between city and nature, a site of harmony, recreation, green space, and fresh water. The restoration ideal has its merits, but this historical analysis of urban rivers—rivers that either ran through the city or were folded into the urban-ization process at a distance—suggests that the very aims of the "urban river" ideal are a product of the processes we have analyzed. The new urban river is, in this sense, running down a previously cut channel.

NOTES

INTRODUCTION

1. On the commission, see James Winter, *Secure from Rash Assault: Sustaining the Victorian Environment* (Berkeley: University of California Press, 1999), 118.

2. Neil Smith, *Uneven Development: Nature, Capital, and the Production of Space* (Athens: University of Georgia Press, 1984).

3. Richard White, *The Organic Machine: The Remaking of the Columbia River* (New York: Hill and Wang, 1995).

4. Paul Stanton Kibel, ed., *Rivertown: Rethinking Urban Rivers* (Cambridge: MIT Press, 2007); Mark Cioc, *The Rhine: An Eco-Biography* (Seattle: University of Washington Press, 2002), 173–230; Timothy M. Collins, Edward K. Muller, and Joel A. Tarr, "Pittsburgh's Three Rivers: From Industrial Infrastructure to Environmental Asset," in *Rivers in History: Perspectives on Waterways in Europe and North America*, ed. Christoph Mauch and Thomas Zeller (Pittsburgh: University of Pittsburgh Press, 2008), 41–62.

5. Anne Chin, "Urban Transformation of River Landscapes in a Global Context," *Geomorphology* 79, no. 3–4 (September 2006): 460–87; Michael J. Paul and Judy L. Meyer, "Streams in the Urban Landscape," *Annual Review of Ecology and Systematics* 32 (2001): 333–65.

6. Martin Melosi, *The Sanitary City: Urban Infrastructure in America from Colonial Times to the Present* (Baltimore: Johns Hopkins University Press, 2000); Jean-Pierre Goubert, *La conquête de l'eau: L'avènement de la santé à l'âge industriel* (Paris: Hachette, 1986); Christopher Hamlin, *A Science of Impurity: Water Analysis in Nineteenth-Century Britain* (Berkeley: University of California Press, 1990); Matthew Gandy, *Concrete and Clay: Reworking Nature in New York City* (Cambridge, Mass.: MIT Press, 2002); Erik Swyngedouw, *Social Power and the Urbanization of Water: Flows of Power* (New York: Oxford University Press, 2004); Maria Kaika, *City of Flows: Modernity, Nature, and the City* (New York: Routledge 2005).

7. Harold L. Platt, *Shock Cities: The Environmental Transformation and Reform of Manchester and Chicago* (Chicago: University of Chicago Press, 2005); Craig Colten, *Unnatural Metropolis. Wresting New Orleans from Nature* (Baton Rouge: Louisiana State University Press, 2005); Arn Keeling, "Urban Waste Sinks as a Natural Resource: The Case of the Fraser River," *Urban History Review / Revue d'histoire urbaine* 34 (2005): 58–70; Matthew Kingle, *The Emerald City. An Environmental History*

of Seattle (New Haven: Yale University Press, 2007); Sarah S. Elkind, *Bay Cities and Water Politics: The Battle for Resources in Boston and Oakland* (Lawrence: University of Kansas Press, 1998); Sabine Barles and Laurence Lestel, "The Nitrogen Question: Urbanization, Industrialization, and River Quality in Paris, 1830–1939," *Journal of Urban History* 33, no. 5 (2007): 794–812; Jamie Benidickson, *The Culture of Flushing: A Social and Legal History of Flushing* (Vancouver: UBC Press, 2007); Stéphane Castonguay and Dany Fougères, "Les rapports riverains de la ville: Sherbrooke et ses usages des rivières Magog et Saint-François au 19e-20e siècle," *Urban History Review / Revue d'histoire urbaine* 36 (2007): 3–15.

8. Goubert, *La conquête de l'eau*; Georges Vigarello, *Le sain et le malsain: Santé et mieux-être depuis le Moyen Âge* (Paris: Éditions du Seuil, 1993); Michèle Dagenais, "At the Source of a New Urbanity: Water Networks and Power Relations in Montreal in the Second Half of the Nineteenth Century," in *Metropolitan Natures: Urban Environmental Histories of Montreal,* ed. Stéphane Castonguay and Michèle Dagenais (Pittsburgh: University of Pittsburgh Press, 2011), 101–14; Patrick Joyce, *The Rule of Freedom: Liberalism and the Modern City* (London: Verso, 2003).

9. William Cronon, *Nature's Metropolis: Chicago and the Great West* (New York: Norton, 1991); Steven Stoll, *Fruits of Natural Advantage: Making the Industrial Countryside in California* (Berkeley: University of California Press 1998); Joel Tarr and Clay McShane, "Urban Horses and Changing City-Hinterland Relationships in the United States," in *Resources of the City: Contributions to an Environmental History of Modern Europe,* ed. Dieter Schot, Bill Luckin, and Geneviève Massard-Guilbaud (Aldershot: Ashgate, 2005), 48–62.

10. Franz-Josef Brüggemeier, "A Nature Fit for Industry: The Environmental History of the Ruhr Basin, 1840–1990," *Environmental History Review* 18, no. 1 (1994): 35–54; Fridolin Kraussmann, "The Process of Industrialization from the Perspective of Energetic Metabolism: Socioeconomic Energy Flows in Austria, 1830–1995," *Ecological Economics* 41, no. 2 (2002): 177–201; Jérome Buridant, "Flottage des bois et gestion forestière: L'exemple du bassin parisien, du XVIe au XIXe siècle," *Revue Forestière Française* 58, no. 4 (2006): 389–98; Dieter Schott, "Remodeling 'Father Rhine': The Case of Mannheim, 1825–1914," in *Water, Culture, and Politics in Germany and the American West,* ed. Susan Anderson and Bruce Tabbin (New York: Peter Lang, 2001), 203–25; Sabine Barles, "Urban Metabolism and River Systems: An Historical Perspective. Paris and the Seine, 1790–1970," in "Man and River Systems: Long-Term Interactions between Societies and Nature in Regional Scale Watersheds," special issue, *Hydrology and Earth System Sciences* (2007): 1757–69.

11. Bruce Braun, "Writing a More-than-Human Urban Geography," *Progress in Human Geography* 29, no. 5 (2005): 635–50.

12. William Cronon, "Kennecott Journey: The Paths Out of Town," in *Under an Open Sky: Rethinking America's Western Past,* ed. William Cronon, George Miles, and Jay Gitlin (New York: Norton, 1992).

13. Jacques Bethemont, *Les grands fleuves: Entre nature et société* (Paris: Armand Colin, coll. U Géographie, 2002).

14. Ari Kelman, *A River and Its City: The Nature of Landscape in New Orleans* (Berke-

ley: University of California Press, 2003); Stéphane Castonguay, "The Construction of Flood as Natural Catastrophe: Extreme Events and the Construction of Vulnerability in the Drainage Basin of the Saint-François River (Quebec), Mid-nineteenth to Mid-twentieth Century, " *Environmental History* 12, no. 4 (2007): 816–40; Christopher Armstrong, Matthew Evenden, and H. V. Nelles, *The River Returns: An Environmental History of the Bow* (Montreal-Kingston: McGill-Queens University Press, 2009); David Blackbourn, *The Conquest of Nature: Water, Landscape, and the Making of Modern Germany* (New York: Norton, 2006); Stuart Oliver, "The Thames Embankment and the Disciplining of Nature in Modernity," *Geographical Journal* 166, no. 3 (2000): 227–38.

15. Jacques Bethemont, *Les grands fleuves*, 214–15; Frédéric Molle, "River-basin Planning and Management: The Social Life of a Concept," *Geoforum* 40, no. 3 (2009): 484–94; Shannon Stunden-Bower, "Natural and Unnatural Complexities: Flood Control along Manitoba's Assiniboine River," *Journal of Historical Geography* 36, no. 1 (January 2010): 57–67.

16. Isabelle Backouche, *La trace du fleuve: La Seine et Paris (1750-1850)* (Paris: Éditions de l'ÉHESS, 2000); Chloé Deligne, *Bruxelles et sa rivière: Genèse d'un territoire urbain (12e-18e siècle)* (Turnhout: Brepols, 2003).

17. Estelle Baret-Bourgoin, *La ville industrielle et ses poisons: Les mutations de sensibilités aux nuisances et pollutions industrielles à Grenoble 1810–1914* (Grenoble: Presses de l'Université de Grenoble, 2005); Bill Luckin, *Pollution and Control: A Social History of the Thames in the Nineteenth Century* (Bristol and Boston: Adam Hilger, 1986); Andrew Hurley, *Environmental Inequalities: Class, Race, and Industrial Pollution in Gary, Indiana, 1945–1980* (Chapel Hill: University of North Carolina Press, 1995).

18. Theodore Steinberg, *Nature Incorporated: Industrialization and the Waters of New England* (Amherst: University of Massachusetts Press, 1991); Christopher G. Boone, "Language Politics and Flood Control in Ninenteenth-Century Montreal," *Environmental History* 1, no. 3 (1996): 70–78.

19. Matthew Gandy, "Vicissitudes of Urban Nature: Transitions and Transformations at a Global Scale," *Radical History Review* 107 (2010): 178–84.

20. Richard C. Hoffmann, "Elemental Resources and Aquatic Ecosystems: Medieval Europeans and Their Rivers," in *Rivers and Society: From the Birth of Agriculture to Modern Times, A History of Water*, ed. Terje Tvedt, Terje Østigård, and Richard Cooper, series 2, vol. 2 (London: I. B. Tauris, 2010), 163–200; André Guillerme, *Les Temps de l'eau* (Seyssels: Champs Vallon, 1993).

I. BRUSSELS AND ITS RIVERS, 1770-1880

1. F. Daelemans, "La démographie aux XIXe et XXe siècles," in *La Région de Bruxelles, des villages d'autrefois à la ville d'aujourd'hui*, ed. J. Stengers and A. Smolar-Meynart (Brussels: Ed. Crédit Communal, 1989); and R. Mols, *Bruxelles et les Bruxellois* (Brussels: Éditions de la Société d'études morales, sociales et juridiques, 1961): 212–17.

2. M. Fincoeur, M. Silvestre, and I. Wanson, *Bruxelles et le voûtement de la Senne* (Brussels: Bibliothèque royale de Belgique, Catalogue d'exposition, 2000); Y. Le-

blicq, *Avant, pendant et après le voûtement de la Senne: Images d'un Bruxelles en mutation* (Brussels: Bibliothèque royale de Belgique, 2000); T. Demey, *Bruxelles: Chronique d'une capitale en chantier* (Brussels: Paul Legrain and C. F. C. Editions, 1990), 39–93.

3. J. Guyaux, "L'assainissement de la vallée du Maelbeek," *Bulletin du crédit communal de Belgique* 22, no. 85 (1968): 154–63.

4. On the subject of nineteenth-century "inventions" to "construct" the territory, see Benedikte Zitouni's *Agglomérer: Une anatomie de l'extension bruxelloise (1828-1915)* (Brussels: VUB Press, 2010).

5. On the medieval development and anthropization of the Senne basin and the importance of the Senne in urban development, see C. Deligne, *Bruxelles et sa rivière: Génèse d'un territoire urbain* (Turnhout: Brepols, Studies in European Urban History, 2003).

6. These branches were likely created and routed by man over the course of the eleventh and twelfth centuries. See C. Deligne, *Bruxelles et sa rivière*, 59–80.

7. The importance of fish in economic relations and trade, and in the transformation of environments and landscapes over the long term, has been the subject of recent research as passionate as it is abundant. A good example is the work of Richard Hoffmann, primarily relating to the medieval period, as well as the recent collective work of L. Sicking and D. Abreu-Fereira, ed., *Beyond the Catch: Fisheries of the North Atlantic Sea and the Baltic, 900–1850* (Leiden-Boston: Brill, 2009).

8. Some mills were owned by several individuals, sometimes grouped into virtual ante litteram shareholder systems.

9. Among the many works devoted to these subjects, see: T. Soens, "Het waterschap en de mythe van de democratie in het Ancien Régime: Het voorbeeld van de Vlaamse Kustvlakte in de Late Middeleeuwen," *Jaarboek voor Ecologische Geschiedenis* 6 (2001): 39–56; M. Van Mielhof and P. J. E. M van Dam, *Waterstaat in Stedenland: Het hoogheemraadschap van Rijnland voor 1857* (Utrecht: Stichting Matrijs, 2006); H. Van der Linden, "De Nederlandse waterhuishouding en waterstaatorganisatie tot aan de moderne tijd," *Bijdragen en mededelingen betreffende de Geschiedenis der Nederlanden*, 4, no. 103 (2004): 534–53.

10. As an indicative bibliography, I cite a few recent contributions on this subject from northwestern Europe: I. Backouche, *La trace du fleuve: La Seine et Paris, 1750–1850* (Paris: Ed. de l'École des hautes études en sciences sociales, 2000); D. Schott, "Stadt und Fluss: Flüsse als städtische Umwelte im 19. und 20. Jahrhundert," in *Beiträge zum Göttinger Umwelthistorischen Kolloquium, 2004–2006*, ed. B. Hermann (Göttingen: Universitätsverlag Göttingen, 2007): 141–62. See the contributions of I. Backouche and C. Closmann in *Rivers in History: Perspectives on Waterways in Europe and North America*, ed. C. Mauch and T. Zeller (Pittsburgh: University of Pittsburgh Press, 2008). For Belgian cities, see more particularly L. Honnoré, *Mons au fil de l'eau. Des crises aux remèdes. Préoccupations sanitaires et politiques communales d'hygiène publique (1830–1914)* (Mons: Cercle archéologique de Mons, 2005); I. Parmentier, *Histoire de l'environnement en pays de Charleroi (1730–1830): Pollutions et nuisances dans un paysage en voie d'industrialisation* (Brussels: Mémoires de l'Académie royale de Belgique, Classe des Lettres et des Sciences et des Beaux Arts, 2008).

11. A number of urban planning and architecture projects aim to effect this "return" of water to the city. On this subject, see Valérie Mahaut, "La ville et l'eau. Les temps de la réconciliation. Jardins d'orage et nouvelles rivières urbaines," (PhD thesis, Université catholique de Louvain, 2009).

12. The Austrian Low Countries were incorporated into the French Republic in 1792. The suppression of religious orders was proclaimed in 1796 under the Executive Directory.

13. In France, much more than in the Austrian Low Countries soon to be integrated into the French Republic (1792–1815), the disappearance of the ponds is linked to a veritable policy of draining the wet zones, considered unhealthy and hazardous as of the second half of the eighteenth century. There are a number of historical works devoted to the effects of this policy on a regional scale (work by Corinne Marache on the Double, Yannick Le Marec on the Brière, Jean-Michel Derex on the Brie, and Michel Cassan on the Limousin, which appeared in the publications of the Groupe d'Histoire des Zones humides). See also R. Abad, *La conjuration contre les carpes: Enquête sur les origines du décret de dessèchement des étangs du 14 frimaire an II* (Paris: Fayard, 2006).

14. J. Garnier, G. Billen, and C. Billen, *Modélisation des modifications du paysage écologique, application à la Senne* (Brussels: Rapport de l'Université Libre de Bruxelles, 1992).

15. Ministère des travaux publics, Administration des ponts et chaussées, *Inondations de la vallée de la Senne aux abords de Bruxelles. Travail de la commission spéciale instituée le 7 mars 1839 et propositions du conseil des Ponts et Chaussées du 2 octobre 1839*; À Messieurs les représentants du peuple belge au Palais de la Nation à Bruxelles (Brussels: H. Ve Remy, imprimeur du roi, 1840); *Inondations de la Senne aux abords de Bruxelles. Requête des communes riveraines de la Senne en amont de Bruxelles au conseil provincial de Brabant, précédé de quelques considérations sur l'état de la question des eaux après l'inondation du 16 janvier 1841* (Brussels: Imprimerie F. Parent 1841); and so on.

16. M.-R. Thielemans, "Le démarrage industriel dans l'agglomération bruxelloise avant 1830," *Bulletin trimestriel du crédit communal de Belgique* 149 (1984): 151–83; M.-R. Thielemans, "La localisation des industries aux alentours de 1830," in *La Région de Bruxelles, des villages d'autrefois à la ville d'aujourd'hui* (Brussels: Ed. Crédit Communal, 1989), 246–61; J. Puissant and M. De Beule, "La première région industrielle belge," in *La Région de Bruxelles, des villages d'autrefois à la ville d'aujourd'hui* (Brussels: Ed. Crédit Communal, 1989), 262–91; M. De Beule, "Bruxelles. Une ville industrielle méconnue: Impact urbanistique de l'industrialisation," *Les dossiers de La Fonderie* 1 (1994): 24–35.

17. G. Billen, J. Garnier, C. Deligne, and C. Billen, "Estimates of Early Industrial Inputs of Nutrients to River Systems: Implication for Coastal Eutrophication," *Science of Total Environment* 243–44 (December 1999): 43–52, accessible online at http://www.sciencedirect.com/science/article/pii/S0048969799003277.

18. See, for example, conflict in 1791 between a paper mill owner named Van Ypen and the nearby Abbaye de Forest south of Brussels regarding the "infection by the colors and other refuse from Van Ypen's mill" See L. Verniers, *Histoire de Fo-*

rest-lez-Bruxelles (Brussels: Maison d'édition A. De Boeck, 1949), 103; and a file kept in the State Archives in Anderlecht (Brussels-Capital Region), Ecclesiastical fonds, 7082.

19. Fr. Onclincx, "Le textile et l'eau à Anderlecht, Forest et Uccle entre 1830 et 1870," *Les Cahiers de la Fonderie* 16 (1994): 41–48. The author qualifies this figure somewhat, noting that the activities of these establishments could be irregular or seasonal in nature.

20. L. Viré, "Quelques aspects de la distribution publique d'eau à Bruxelles, 1830–1870," *Contributions à l'histoire économique et sociale* 4 (1966–1967): 113–54; L. Viré, *La distribution d'eau à Bruxelles, 1830–1870* (Bruxelles: Pro Civitate, Crédit Communal de Belgique, 1973), 33; L. Viré, "Innovation technologique et hygiène publique: La distribution d'eau à Bruxelles au 19e siècle," in *L'innovation technologique, facteur de changement (19e-20e siècle)* (Brussels: Éditions de l'Université de Bruxelles, 1986) 93–111; C. Deligne, M. Dagenais, and C. Poitras, "Gérer l'eau en milieu urbain 1870–1970: Bruxelles-Montréal, regards croisés," in *Vivre en ville: Bruxelles-Montréal XIXe-XXe siècle*, eds. S. Jaumain and P. Linteau (Bruxelles: P.I.E. Peter Lang, 2006), 169–202.

21. P. Cornut, "La circulation de l'eau potable en Belgique: Enjeux sociaux de la gestion d'une ressource naturelle" (PhD thesis, Université Libre de Bruxelles, 1999).

22. E. Putzeys, *Les eaux de Bruxelles en 1902* (Brussels: Typographie et Lithographie E. Guyot,1902).

23. This information comes from a request from the communal council of Virginal (a commune about thirty kilometers south of Brussels) to the Permanent Deputation of the Province of Brabant (the intermediate executive body between the communes and the State) in 1839.

24. L. Viré, *La distribution d'eau à Bruxelles*, 84.

25. Up until the beginning of the twentieth century, over 60 percent of the quantities of water drawn from the extra-urban intakes were used for street maintenance, public spaces, sewers, filling of certain city park lakes, and firefighting. A. Deblon, "Les eaux alimentaires de l'agglomération bruxelloise en 1903," *Annales des Travaux publics* 8, no. 4, series 2 (August 1903): 677–790.

26. T. Verstraeten, *La guerre de l'eau de l'agglomération bruxelloise et la campagne contre les eaux de roches calcaires* (Brussels: Imprimerie des Travaux Publics, 1903).

27. P. Cornut, "La circulation de l'eau potable en Belgique"; C. Deligne, "Bruxelles et le bassin de la Senne: Gestion hydraulique et dynamiques urbaines (Moyen Age-XIXe siècle)" (PhD thesis, Université Libre de Bruxelles, 2001), 391–99. See also the following works of L. Viré, "Quelques aspects de la distribution publique d'eau à Bruxelles, 1830–1870"; *La distribution d'eau à Bruxelles, 1830–1870*; and "Innovation technologique et hygiène publique."

2. THE RIVER LEA IN WEST HAM

1. Dale H. Porter, *The Thames Embankment: Environment, Technology, and Society in Victorian London* (Akron: University of Akron Press, 1998).

2. There are two spellings for the river Lea. Government documents and agencies spell it "Lee," while the more common spelling is "Lea." This chapter uses the more

common spelling except when referring to the Lee Navigation or the Lee Conservancy Board.

3. Craig E. Colten, "Environmental Development in the East St. Louis Region, 1890–1970," *Environmental History Review* 14, no. 1 (Spring–Summer 1990): 93–114; A. Hurley, "Creating Ecological Wastelands: Oil Pollution in New York City, 1870–1900," *Journal of Urban History* 20, no. 3 (1994): 340; Craig E. Colten, "Chicago's Waste Lands: Refuse Disposal and Urban Growth, 1840–1990," *Journal of Historical Geography* 20, no. 2 (April 1994): 124–42.

4. The LCC replaced the MBW in 1889.

5. The Lea's mouth is six kilometers as a bird flies. It would be significantly longer if you travelled by boat, as the Thames bends around the Isle of Dogs.

6. See Craig E. Colten's chapter in this edited volume.

7. W. R. Powell, ed., "West Ham: Industries," in *A History of the County of Essex*, vol. 6, Victoria Country History (London: British History Online, Institute of Historical Research, University of London, 1973), 79–89, http://www.british-history.ac.uk/report.aspx?compid=42755#n121.

8. There are a number of very good sources on the industrial history of West Ham. John Marriott, "West Ham: London's Industrial Centre and Gateway to the World I: Industrialization, 1840–1910," *London Journal* 13, no. 2 (1987): 121–42; John Marriott, "West Ham: London's Industrial Centre and Gateway to the World II: Stabilization and Decline 1910–1939," *London Journal* 14, no. 1 (1989): 43–58; Edward Goldie Howarth and Mona Wilson, *West Ham: A Study in Social and Industrial Problems: Being the Report of the Outer London Inquiry Committee* (London: J. M. Dent and Company, 1907); Powell, "West Ham: Industries"; John Marriott, "Smokestack: The Industrial History of the Thames Gateway," in *London's Turning: Thames Gateway-Prospects and Legacy*, ed. Philip Cohen and Michael J. Rustin (London: Ashgate Publishing, Ltd., 2008), 17–30.

9. A similar pattern of industrial development took place on Long Island and in New Jersey, beyond the jurisdiction of New York City, in the late nineteenth century. See Hurley, "Creating Ecological Wastelands."

10. Gareth Stedman Jones, *Outcast London: A Study in the Relationship Between Classes in Victorian Society* (Harmondsworth: Penguin, 1976), 152–55; Marriott, "Smokestack," 17–18.

11. Jim Clifford, "The Urban Periphery and the Rural Fringe: West Ham's Hybrid Landscape," *Left History* 13, no. 1 (2008): 129–42.

12. Ian Gregory and Paul S. Ell, *Historical GIS* (Cambridge: Cambridge University Press, 2007).

13. The following are the maps consulted for the GIS database produced in this chapter: "Area immediately east of River Lea, now covered by West Ham, Canning Town and Royal Victoria Docks," *Church Commissioners Parish Survey Map* (West Ham, circa 1850), Closed Access Map Case 263, Guildhall Library; Alan Godfrey Maps, "London Sheet 42: Stratford 1867," *Old Ordnance Survey Maps* (Gateshead: Alan Godfrey, 1983); Alan Godfrey Maps, "London Sheet 42: Stratford 1893," *Old Ordnance Survey Maps* (Gateshead: Alan Godfrey, 1983); Alan Godfrey Maps, "Lon-

don Sheet 42: Stratford 1914," *Old Ordnance Survey Maps* (Gateshead: Alan Godfrey, 1983); Alan Godfrey Maps, "London Sheet 43: Forest Gate 1894," *Old Ordnance Survey Maps* (Gateshead: Alan Godfrey, 1983); Alan Godfrey Maps, "London Sheet 43: Upton, Plashet & Forest Gate 1867," *Old Ordnance Survey Maps* (Gateshead: Alan Godfrey, 1983); Alan Godfrey Maps, "London Sheet 44: East Ham & Barking 1894," "London Sheet 44: East Ham & Barking 1915," *Old Ordnance Survey Maps* (Gateshead: Alan Godfrey, 1990); Alan Godfrey Maps, "London Sheet 44: East Ham & Barking 1915," *Old Ordnance Survey Maps* (Gateshead: Alan Godfrey, 1999); Alan Godfrey Maps, "London Sheet 53: Bow, Bromley & West Ham 1867," *Old Ordnance Survey Maps* (Gateshead: Alan Godfrey, 1983); Alan Godfrey Maps, "London Sheet 53: Bow, Bromley & West Ham 1893," *Old Ordnance Survey Maps* (Gateshead: Alan Godfrey, 1990); Alan Godfrey Maps, "London Sheet 53: Bow, Bromley & West Ham 1914," *Old Ordnance Survey Maps* (Gateshead: Alan Godfrey, 1990); Alan Godfrey Maps, "London Sheet 54: Plaistow 1867," *Old Ordnance Survey Maps* (Gateshead: Alan Godfrey, 1983); Alan Godfrey Maps, "London Sheet 54: Plaistow 1894," *Old Ordnance Survey Maps* (Gateshead: Alan Godfrey, 1986); Alan Godfrey Maps, "London Sheet 65: Poplar & Canning Town 1867," *Old Ordnance Survey Maps* (Gateshead: Alan Godfrey, 1983); Alan Godfrey Maps, "London Sheet 65: Poplar 1894," *Old Ordnance Survey Maps* (Gateshead: Alan Godfrey, 1983); Alan Godfrey Maps, "London Sheet 65: Poplar 1914," *Old Ordnance Survey Maps* (Gateshead: Alan Godfrey, 1990); Alan Godfrey Maps, "London Sheet 66: Custom House & Plaistow Marsh 1867," *Old Ordnance Survey Maps* (Gateshead: Alan Godfrey, 1983); Alan Godfrey Maps, "London Sheet 66: Canning Town & Custom House 1894," *Old Ordnance Survey Maps* (Gateshead: Alan Godfrey, 1986); Alan Godfrey Maps, "London Sheet 66: Canning Town & Custom House 1914," *Old Ordnance Survey Maps* (Gateshead: Alan Godfrey, 1992); Alan Godfrey Maps, "London Sheet 67: Beckton 1894," *Old Ordnance Survey Maps* (Gateshead: Alan Godfrey, 1986); Alan Godfrey Maps, "London Sheet 67: Beckton 1914," *Old Ordnance Survey Maps* (Gateshead: Alan Godfrey, 2000); Alan Godfrey Maps, "London Sheet 79: West India Docks & Greenwich Marshes 1894," *Old Ordnance Survey Maps* (Gateshead: Alan Godfrey, 1983); Alan Godfrey Maps, "London Sheet 79: West India Docks 1867," *Old Ordnance Survey Maps* (Gateshead: Alan Godfrey, 1991); Alan Godfrey Maps, "London Sheet 79: West India Docks 1914," *Old Ordnance Survey Maps* (Gateshead: Alan Godfrey, 1991); Alan Godfrey Maps, "London Sheet 80: Silvertown 1867," *Old Ordnance Survey Maps* (Gateshead: Alan Godfrey, 1983); Alan Godfrey Maps, "London Sheet 80: Silvertown 1893," *Old Ordnance Survey Maps* (Gateshead: Alan Godfrey, 1986); Alan Godfrey Maps, "London Sheet 81: North Woolwich 1869," *Old Ordnance Survey Maps* (Gateshead: Alan Godfrey, 1985); Alan Godfrey Maps, "London Sheet 81: North Woolwich 1894," *Old Ordnance Survey Maps* (Gateshead: Alan Godfrey, 1988); "Map of the River Lee Navigation from the River Thames at Limehouse to Lee Bridge also of the River Lee with its Tributary Streams from the River Thames at Bow Creek to Lee Bridge in four parts," 1852, ACC/2423/X/, London Metropolitan Archive; Alfred Dickens, "Map Published in the Report to the General Board of Health on a Preliminary Inquiry into the Sewerage, Drainage and Supply of Water and the Sanitary Condition

of the Inhabitants of the Parish of West Ham, in the County of Essex," Public Health
Act 11 and 12 Vict. (London: General Board of Health, Great Britain, 1855), Brit-
ish Library; "Navigation and Proposed Improvements: Parliamentary Plans," Lee
Conservancy Board Engineer's Office Plans, 1849, ACC/2423/X/007, London Met-
ropolitan Archive; "Ordnance Survey of London and Its Environs" (Southampton:
Ordnance Survey Office, 1893), British Library; "Ordnance Survey of London and
Its Environs: Surveyed 1862–70" (Southampton: Ordnance Survey Office, 1869),
British Library; Edward Stanford, "Outer London," *Stanford's London Atlas of Univer-
sal Geography Exhibiting the Physical and Political Divisions of the Various Countries of the
World* (London: Edward Stanford, Geographer to Her Majesty, 1901), David Rum-
sey Historical Map Collection, online at http://www.davidrumsey.com/luna/serv-
let/detail/RUMSEY~8~1~34248~1171163; Edward Stanford, "Stanford's Library
Plan of London and Its Suburbs: 24 Sheets" (Lympne Castle: Harry Margary, 1980);
H. Waters, "The Environs of London, 1832," *Maps of the Society for the Diffusion of Useful Knowledge* (London: Chapman and Hail, 1844), David Rumsey Historical Map
Collection, online at http://www.davidrumsey.com/luna/servlet/detail/RUM-
SEY~8~1~20931~530115; G. W. Colton, "The Environs of London, 1856," *Colton's
Atlas of the World, Illustrating Physical and Political Geography* (New York: J. H. Colton
and Co., 1856), David Rumsey Historical Map Collection, online at http://www.da-
vidrumsey.com/luna/servlet/detail/RUMSEY~8~1~1584~130073; Thomas Milne
and London Topographical Society, "Thomas Milne's Land Use Map of London &
Environs" (London: London Topographical Society, 1975); *Ordnance Survey of London
and Its Environs, Surveyed 1862–70*, New Series, Five Feet to One Mile (Southampton:
Ordnance Survey Office, 1869); *Ordnance Survey of London and Its Environs*, Second
Series. Revised and Extended Survey, Five Feet to One Mile (Southampton: Ordnance Survey Office, 1893).

14. See "Havering Level Commission of Sewers Rate Survey," 1851, Newham
Local Studies Library and Archive; "Havering Level Commission of Sewers Rate
Survey," 1881, Newham Local Studies Library and Archive; "Kelly's Stratford, West
Ham, Forest Gate and Plaistow Directory" (Kelly's Directories, 1887), Newham
Local Studies Library and Archive; "Kelly's Stratford, West Ham, Forest Gate and
Plaistow Directory" (Kelly's Directories, 1888), Newham Local Studies Library and
Archive; "Kelly's Stratford, West Ham, Forest Gate and Plaistow Directory" (Kel-
ly's Directories, 1889), Newham Local Studies Library and Archive; "Kelly's Strat-
ford, West Ham, Forest Gate and Plaistow Directory" (Kelly's Directories, 1893),
Newham Local Studies Library and Archive; Powell, "West Ham: Industries";
Howarth and Wilson, *West Ham*, 137–84.

15. The first act of parliament concerning the navigation of the Lea passed in
1424, but the construction of locks and canal beds continued through to the twenti-
eth century. See the "Minutes of Evidence" in the Hugh MacClamont Cairns, First
Earl of Cairns, "Report from the Select Committee on Rivers Pollution (River
Lee); Together with the Proceedings of the Committee, Minutes of Evidence, and
Appendix," *House of Commons Papers*; Reports of Committees (London, 1886), 1–4,
House of Commons Parliamentary Papers Online, http://gateway.proquest.com

.ezproxy.library.yorku.ca/openurl?url_ver=Z39.88-2004&res_dat=xri:hcpp
-us&rft_dat=xri:hcpp:rec:1886-062337 (requires access to ProQuest database); Frederic Johnson, *Weldon's Guide to the River Lea, from London to Hertford* (London: Weldon
and Co., 1880), 6—7.

16. There is a legend that King Alfred the Great of Wessex diverted the Lea in
the ninth century to trap the Viking fleet and created the multiple streams either in
the Lower Lea or perhaps in the Upper Lea. There is no indication that this legend is
true, but it does demonstrate a long historical consciousness of the Lea changing its
course. W. R. Powell, ed., "West Ham: Rivers, Bridges, Wharfs and Docks," in *A
History of the County of Essex*, vol. 6, Victoria Country History (London: British History Online, Institute of Historical Research, University of London, 1973), 57—61,
http://www.british-history.ac.uk/report.aspx?compid=42755#n121.

17. W. R. Powell, ed., "West Ham: Ancient Mills," in *A History of the County of
Essex*, vol. 6, Victoria Country History (London: British History Online, Institute
of Historical Research, University of London, 1973), 89—93, http://www.british-
history.ac.uk/report.aspx?compid=42755#n121.

18. Powell, "West Ham: Ancient Mills."

19. The conflicts between millers and upstream communities discussed below
confirm there were conflicts over the limited energy resources on the Lower Lea.

20. Powell, "West Ham: Industries."

21. Ibid.

22. W. R. Powell, ed., "West Ham: Introduction," in *A History of the County of Essex*, vol. 6, Victoria Country History (London: British History Online, Institute of
Historical Research, University of London, 1973), 43—50, http://www.british-history
.ac.uk/report.aspx?compid=42755#n121.

23. Mary J. Dobson, *Contours of Death and Disease in Early Modern England* (Cambridge: Cambridge University Press, 2003), 71.

24. W. R. Powell, ed., "West Ham: Agriculture," in *A History of the County of Essex*,
vol. 6, Victoria Country History (London: British History Online, Institute of Historical Research, University of London, 1973), 74—76, http://www.british-history
.ac.uk/report.aspx?compid=42755#n121.

25. This increase somewhat exaggerates the amount of land reclaimed, as it includes uplands brought under the control of the court to improve drainage of
the whole area. Nonetheless, it shows that thousands of acres of land were slowly
drained in the centuries before industrial development began in West Ham, creating the land on which many of the factories and homes were later built. See W. R.
Powell, ed., "West Ham: Markets and Fairs, Marshes and Forest," in *A History of the
County of Essex*, vol. 6, Victoria Country History (London: British History Online,
Institute of Historical Research, University of London, 1973), 93—96, http://www
.british-history.ac.uk/report.aspx?compid=42755#n121.

26. Dickens, "Board of Health Inquiry West Ham," 44—46 and the GIS database
shows the close correlation between ditches and the later street pattern.

27. The calico grounds on this map were found on 1850 maps of the river at the
end of the cloth printing industry in this area. See "Map of the River Lee Naviga-

tion from the River Thames at Limehouse to Lee Bridge also of the River Lee with its Tributary Streams from the River Thames at Bow Creek to Lee Bridge in four parts"; and "Navigation and Proposed Improvements: Parliamentary Plans."

28. Powell, "West Ham: Industries."

29. Committee of the Floods of the Lea, *A Brief Statement of a Case, Involving Not Only the Rights, Privileges, and Property of the City of London, but the Due Administration of Justice* (London: Maurice and Co, 1830), British Library; Committee of the Floods of the Lea and George Hart, *Second Report of the Committee of the Floods of the Lea* (London: Robson, Brooks, and Co., 1825), British Library; Committee of the Floods of the Lea and George Hart, *New Tumbling Bay Statement of the Case of the King Versus the Commissioners of Sewers* (London, 1824), British Library.

30. The Old Lea often remained in place to drain water and sewage as the canals were embanked above the surrounding landscape. See P. M. Crosthwaite, "River Lee and Stort Flooding" (Local Government Board, June 30, 1919), 5–6, Social Science, British Library.

31. Committee of the Floods of the Lea, *Brief Statement of a Case*, 4.

32. Committee of the Floods of the Lea and Hart, *New Tumbling Bay*, appendix 1.

33. Committee of the Floods of the Lea, *Brief Statement of a Case*; Committee of the Floods of the Lea and Hart, *New Tumbling Bay*; Committee of the Floods of the Lea and Hart, *Second Report*.

34. Charles Tween, *Lee Conservancy Board Engineer Report 1908* (London: Lee Conservancy Board's Engineer's Office, October 2, 1908), ACC/2423/011, London Metropolitan Archive.

35. Charles Mackay, *The Thames and Its Tributaries* (London: R. Bentley, 1840), 164.

36. James Thorne, *Rambles By Rivers* (London: Charles Knight and Co., 1844), 199.

37. James Winter, *Secure from Rash Assault* (Berkeley: University of California Press, 2002), 8–9, 143–45.

38. W. A. Parks, "The Development of the Heavy Chemical Industry of West Ham and District" (master's thesis, University of London, 1949), 18.

39. Howarth and Wilson, *West Ham*, 185–87; Marriott, "West Ham: Industrialization," 129–30.

40. Marriott, "West Ham: Industrialization"; Marriott, "Smokestack," 22.

41. Archer Philip Crouch, *Silvertown and Neighbourhood (Including East and West Ham)* (London: T. Burleigh, 1900), 64.

42. Ibid., 64–65.

43. Crouch, *Silvertown*, 64; Marriott, "West Ham: Industrialization," 130–33; Marriott, "Smokestack," 22.

44. Quoted in Marriott, "Smokestack," 17, originally from J. L. Hammond, "The Industrial Revolution and Discontent," *New Statesman* 21 (March 1925).

45. Raphael Samuel, "Workshop of the World: Steam Power and Hand Technology in Mid-Victorian Britain," *History Workshop Journal* 3 (1977): 6–72.

46. Marriott, "Smokestack," 17–22; Marriott, "West Ham: Industrialization," 123, 136–40.

47. Marriott, "West Ham: Industrialization," 130–33, 137–38.

48. This means the 1867 GIS map below is more complete than the first two industry GIS maps as the layer was created directly from these two maps.

49. Howarth and Wilson, *West Ham*, 145–47.

50. Hurley, "Creating Ecological Wastelands"; Craig E. Colten, "Industrial Wastes in Southeast Chicago: Production and Disposal, 1870–1970," *Environmental Review* 10, no. 2 (Summer 1986): 93–105; Colten, "Environmental Development in the East St. Louis Region, 1890–1970"; Andrew Hurley, *Environmental Inequalities: Class, Race, and Industrial Pollution Gary, Indiana, 1945–1980* (Chapel Hill: University of North Carolina Press, 1995).

51. Marriott, "West Ham: Industrialization," 124–26.

52. Christopher Otter discusses the movement of unpleasant industries to Greenwich, directly across the Thames from the Lea's mouth but within London boundaries. See Christopher Otter, "Cleansing and Clarifying: Technology and Perception in Nineteenth-Century London," *Journal of British Studies* 43, no. 1 (January 1, 2004): 40–64.

53. Powell, "West Ham: Industries."

54. Parks, "Development of the Heavy Chemical Industry," 18.

55. Environment Agency, "Fact Sheet. Newham Borough: Environmental summary" (Environmental Agency, 2009), http://www.environment-agency.gov.uk/static/documents/Research/NEWHAM_factsheet.pdf.

56. J. J. Terrett, *"Municipal Socialism in West Ham: A Reply to "The Times," and Others* (London: Twentieth Century Press, Ltd., 1902), 4–5.

57. Marriott, "West Ham: Industrialization," 130–37.

58. Howarth and Wilson, *West Ham*, 29–60.

59. Ibid.

60. The 1914–1916 Ordnance Survey maps show many new allotment gardens and a major recreation ground built by the Thames Ironworks company. See Alan Godfrey Maps, "London Sheet 42: Stratford 1914"; Alan Godfrey Maps, "London Sheet 53: Bow, Bromley & West Ham 1914"; Alan Godfrey Maps, "London Sheet 65: Poplar 1914"; and Alan Godfrey Maps, "London Sheet 66: Canning Town & Custom House 1914."

61. J. Andorn (pseud.) and A. W. Barnett, *Industrial Explorings in and around London* (London: J. Clarke and Co, 1895), 136.

62. Stirling Everard, *The History of the Gas Light and Coke Company, 1812–1949* (London: Benn, 1949), 237, 246, 253–54, 289.

63. Everard, *History of the Gas Light and Coke Company*, 247.

64. Ibid., 254, 289, 316.

65. Ibid., 287, 301.

66. Marriott, "Smokestack," 29.

67. Tween, *Lee Conservancy Board Engineer Report 1908* (January 10, 1908; February 7, 1908; April 24, 1908; and October 26, 1908); *Lee Conservancy Board Minute Book 1908*

(Lee Conservancy Board, 1908), January 24; October 30, 260; November 27 288–89; RAIL 845, British National Archive; "The Channelsea Nuisance" *Herald*, September 17, 1898. First Earl of Cairns, "Report from the Select Committee," 21, 60–62.

68. B. B. Marston, "Letters to the Editor: State of the River Lea Below Tottenham," *Times*, August 1, 1884; "The Channelsea Nuisance," *West Ham Herald*, September 17, 1898.

69. Editorial, *West Ham Guardian*, January 14, 1899.

70. West Ham Corporation, "Public Health Committee Minutes," (June 7, July 5, September 6, and September 19, 1899), 1236, 857, 998, 1167, 1236.

71. Environment Agency, "Fact Sheet"; Leo Hickman, "Journey along the River Lee," *Guardian*, October 9, 2009, http://www.guardian.co.uk/environment/2009/oct/09/river-lee-polluted-source; Environment Agency, "Case study—Water quality in the Lower Lee catchment," (Environment Agency, 2010), http://www.environment-agency.gov.uk/research/library/publications/116038.aspx.

72. *Lee Conservancy Board Minute Book 1908* (February 7, 1908), 29.

73. Tween, *Lee Conservancy Board Engineer Report 1908* (January 27, 1908).

74. "The Channelsea Nuisance," *Herald*, September 17, 1898.

75. Tween, *Lee Conservancy Board Engineer Report 1908* (February 7, 1908).

76. *Lee Conservancy Board Minute Book 1908* (October 30, 1908), 260; (November 27, 1908), 288–89.

77. The 1914 Ordnance Survey maps show limited development of this marshland, but a large amount of undeveloped marsh remained on those maps as well. Alan Godfrey Maps, "London Sheet 66: Canning Town & Custom House 1914"; Alan Godfrey Maps, "London Sheet 53: Bow, Bromley & West Ham 1914."

78. Marriott, "West Ham: Stabilization and Decline," 43–57; Marriott, "Smokestack," 23.

3. AN URBAN INDUSTRIAL RIVER

This chapter springs out of research conducted in conjunction with an exhibition in 2000 on the industrial history of the Akerselva at the Norwegian Museum for Science and Technology, Oslo, where the author then worked as curator. A draft manuscript was presented at the Water History Conference in Bergen, Norway, in 2001. Many points here have also been covered by the historian Tor Are Johansen in his broad work on the water and renovation history of Oslo, *Under byens gate: Oslos vann- og avløpshistorie* (Oslo: Municipality of Oslo, 2002). This chapter is greatly indebted to Johansen's work.

1. The concept of waterpower systems in the preelectric era is based on Loius C Hunter, *A History of Industrial Power in the United States, 1780–1830,* vol. 1: *Waterpower* (Charlottesville: University of Virginia Press, 1979), 52–53.

2. Denmark, having sided with the French in the Napoleonic Wars, had to relinquish the province of Norway in 1814. After a few months of independence Norway entered a union with Sweden that lasted until 1905.

3. Jan Eivind Myhre, *Oslo Bys historie. Bind 3: Hovedstaden Christiania* (Oslo: Cappelen, 1990), 33.

4. Myhre, *Oslo Bys historie*, 60–61.

5. The Danish economist and writer C. H. Pram (1756–1821) cited in Kari Hoel Malmstrøm, *Fabrikk og bolig ved Akerselva* (Oslo: Norwegian Museum for Science and Technology, 1982), 18.

6. Johansen, *Under byens gater*, 13.

7. Martin Nord, "Om fabrikvirksomheden ved Akerselven," *Skillingsmagazin*, February 1856. Republished in P. R. Sollied, ed., *Industrielle anlegg i Aker. Særtrykk av Aker 1837–1937. Bind V* (Oslo: Grøndahl and Søns Boktrykkreri, 1947).

8. Kristine Bruland, *British Technology and European Industrialization: The Norwegian Textile Industry in the Mid-Nineteenth Century* (Cambridge: Cambridge University Press, 1989).

9. Myhre, *Oslo Bys historie*, 275; and Lars Thue, "Framveksten av et industriborgerskap i Kristiania 1840–1875" (MA thesis, University of Oslo, 1977)

10. Kari Hoel Malmstrøm, *Fabrikk og bolig ved Akerselva* (Oslo: Norwegian Museum for Science and Technology, 1982), 119–20.

11. Malmstrøm, *Fabrikk og bolig ved Akerselva*, 21.

12. Additions to the watercourse after 1900 are omitted here.

13. Tallak Moland, *Nordmarkas historie* (Oslo: Christiania Forlag, 2006), 15.

14. Ståle Dyrvik and Ole Feldbæk, *Aschehougs Norgeshistorie. Bind 7* (Oslo: Aschehoug, 1996), 188–91.

15. The story is found in complete anthologies of the fairy tales collected by Asbjørnsen and Jørgen Moe, e.g., Peder C. Asbjørnsen and Jørgen Moe, *Samlede eventyr Bd 1–2* (Oslo: Gyldendal, 2000).

16. Ola Teige, "Byfiskere—fiskerne i Christiania i tidlig nytid," *Norsk Sjøfartsmuseums årbok* (Yearbook of the Norwegian Maritime Museum, 2008).

17. Myhre, *Oslo Bys historie*, 197–98.

18. Tone Rasch, "Gurkemeie og anilin violet—Om overgangen fra naturlige til syntetiske fargestoffer ved Hjula Veveri," *Volund* (Yearbook of the Norwegian Museum for Science and Technology, 2001).

19. Jan Eivind Myhre, *Sagene-en arbeiderforstad befolkes* (Oslo: Universitetsforlaget, 1978), chaps. 4–6, p. 40. Not all of Sagene was included in the 1859 enlargement, this being the case in 1878.

20. Hans Bull, *Akerselvens Brukseierforening gjennem femti aar 1867–1917* (Christiania: Akerselvens Brukseierforening, 1918), 240.

21. See the Harald Jensen archive, 2553, in an unpublished manuscript on Myren's history by J. Berggrav, p. 13, at the Norwegian Museum for Science and Technology, Oslo.

22. Kari Hoel Malmstrøm, *Fabrikk og bolig ved Akerselva* (Oslo: Norwegian Museum for Science and Technology, 1982), 185.

23. Malmstrøm, *Fabrikk og bolig ved Akerselva*, 188.

24. Knut Kjelstadli, *Oslo bys historie. Bind 4: Den delte byen* (Oslo: Cappelen, 1990), 8.

25. Myhre, *Oslo Bys historie*, 39.

26. Myhre, *Sagene-en arbeiderforstad befolkes*, 37.

27. Ibid., 38.

28. Gunnar Jerman, *Akerselva. Fra sagatid til opera* (Oslo: Schibsted, 2004), 95.

29. Jerman, *Akerselva,* 95.

30. Anne Marit Noraker, "Koke, skrubbe, bære vann," in *Tobias: Tidsskrift for Oslo Byarkiv* (Journal of the Oslo City Archives, Oslo), 2–3 (2007).

31. This section is based on Johansen, *Under byens gater,* chaps. 1–3.

32. Johansen, *Under byens gater,* 37.

33. Hans Bull, *Akerselvens Brukseierforening gjennem femti aar 1867–1917,* 23. The reserve water pipe at Nydalen was opened for the first time in 1874 to augment the water supply.

34. Johansen, *Under byens gater,* 39.

35. "Love for Akerselvens Brugseierforening 1867–1880," D1, Akerselvens Brukseierforening archive, Oslo City Archives.

36. Bull, *Akerselvens Brukseierforening gjennem femti aar 1867–1917,* 80.

37. Myhre, *Oslo Bys historie,* 341.

38. Finn Erhard Johannessen, *I støtet. Oslo Energi gjennom 100 år 1892–1992* (Oslo: Ad Notam Gyldendal, 1992), 15, 36.

39. Johannessen, *I støtet,* 36.

40. For a discussion of the varying degrees of technical control of rivers, see Eva Jakobsson, *Industrialisering av älvar. Studier kring svensk vattenkraftutbyggnad 1900–1918* (Gotheburg: Historiska Institutionen, University of Gothenburg, 1996), 20–28. According to Jakobsson the crucial factor in deciding if a river is part of a technological system (in the Thomas Hughes sense) is whether its stream flow is under human control.

41. A1: Forhandlingsprotokoll 1867–1885, 30.11.1869, Akerselvens Brukseierforening archive, Oslo byarkiv.

42. Henry Heyerdahl, "Hvormeget den nytbare Vandføring i Akers-Elven er forøget ved de i Vasdraget foretagne Opdæmningsarbeider," *Foredrag i Den Polytekniske Forening* 17, no. 1 (Christiania, 1882).

43. A1: Forhandlingsprotokoll 1867–1885, 1.7.1874, Akerselvens Brukseierforening archive, Oslo byarkiv.

44. Heyerdahl, "Hvormeget den nytbare Vandføring i Akers-Elven er forøget ved de i Vasdraget foretagne Opdæmningsarbeider."

45. Ibid.

46. Bull, *Akerselvens Brukseierforening gjennem femti aar 1867–1917,* 110.

47. After refunding the individual companies for outlays with 40 percent interest, the ABF established a fund of two hundred thousand kroner to be used for expansion of the watercourse (Bull, *Akerselvens Brukseierforening gjennem femti aar 1867–1917,* 116).

48. X3: Akerselven 1889, printed report by P. Steenstrup, Akerselvens Brukseierforening archive, Oslo City Archives.

49. Bull, *Akerselvens Brukseierforening gjennem femti aar 1867–1917,* 234–38.

50. List of delivered turbines 1867–1919, box 2592: drawing ledger, catalogues 1.1–1.3, box 2600, Myren archives, Norwegian Museum for Science and Technology.

51. Bull, *Akerselvens Brukseierforening gjennem femti aar 1867–1917,* 235.

52. The year 1899 had the lowest rainfall since measurements were commenced in 1877. The management decided on November 30, 1899, to reduce the discharge period to 96 hours, from Tuesday at 6 AM to Saturday at 6 AM. This was carried out against the protest of the chairman G. Martinsen. A3: Forhandlingsprotokoll 1891–1929. 30.11.1899, Akerselvens Brukseierforening archive, Oslo byarkiv.

53. Thomas Hughes, "The Evolution of Large Technological Systems," in *The Social Construction of Technological Systems: New Directions in the Sociology and History of Technology*, ed. W. Bijker, T. Hughes, and T. Pinch (Cambridge: MIT Press, 1987).

4. THE RIVIÈRE DES PRAIRIES

The research underlying this chapter was carried out with the financial support of the Social Sciences and Humanities Research Council (SSHRC). I would like to thank Stéphane Castonguay, Matthew Evenden, and Claire Poitras for their comments on an earlier version of this chapter.

Epigraph: Pierre Dagenais, "Le milieu physique," in *Montréal économique: étude préparée à l'occasion du troisième centenaire de la ville*, ed. Esdras Minville (Montreal: Fides, 1943), 91–92. The original French reads as follows: "Un horizon nouveau s'ouvre vers l'est et vers l'ouest, de chaque côté de l'obstacle du Mont-Royal. . . . Comme deux têtes d'armée en marche, ces deux poussées se rapprochent de plus en plus au nord du paisible et verdoyant Mont-Royal et achèvent leur manœuvre d'encerclement. . . . L'évolution n'est pas terminée . . . entre la montagne et la rivière des Prairies notamment, puis ensuite dans les petites municipalités voisines. Ainsi, Montréal peut encore largement s'étendre sans sortir de son île."

1. Raoul Blanchard, *L'ouest du Canada français: Montréal et sa région* (Montreal, Beauchemin, 1953), 339 and after. See also Bryan Demchinsky and Elaine Kalman Naves, *Montreal in the Literary Imagination. Storied Streets* (Toronto: Macfarlane, Walter and Ross, 2000), 186–94.

2. The term "sociotechnical system" is used in the sense given by Eva Jakobsson in her work on the industrialization of rivers: "Industrialization of Rivers: A Water System Approach to Hydropower Development," *Knowledge, Technology, and Policy* 14, no. 4 (Winter 2002): 41–56.

3. Historically, the riverbanks and riverbed were the property of riparian landowners, while navigable rivers had always been public in nature. On this question studied in the context of the development of hydroelectricity, see Claude Bellavance, "L'État, la 'houille blanche' et le grand capital. L'aliénation des ressources hydrauliques du domaine public québécois au début du XXe siècle," *Revue d'histoire de l'Amérique française* 51, no. 4 (1998), particularly 8–9.

4. Michèle Dagenais and Caroline Durand, "Cleansing, Draining and Sanitizing the City: Conceptions and Uses of Water in the Montreal Region," *Canadian Historical Review* 87, no. 4 (December 2006): 621–51.

5. Mémoire du chef du Service hydraulique, Arthur Amos, à Jules Allard, ministre des Terres et Forêts, September 30, 1918, p. 3, *Ministère des Terres et des Forêts*, Département des ressources hydrauliques, rivière des Prairies—correspondance gé-

nérale (now Fonds E20), dossier no 20119/1918, vol. 1, S93, SS7, Fonds E20, Bibliothèque et Archives Nationales du Québec (hereafter BANQ),

6. Denis Vézina, *Le Site des Moulins: parc-nature de l'Île-de-la-Visitation: Guide d'interprétation* (Montreal: Cité Historia, Communauté urbaine de Montréal, 1998).

7. Michèle Benoît and Roger Gratton, *Pignon sur rue: Les quartiers de Montréal* (Montreal: Guérin, 1992), 280.

8. Hugh Quilan, vice-président de la Sault-au-Récollet Land and Power Company au ministre des Terres et Forêts, July 6, 1918, dossier no 20119/1918, vol. 1, Fonds E20, BANQ.

9. Severin Létourneau, avocat pour la ville de Montréal-Nord, à Jules Allard, ministre des Terres et Forêts, August 28, 1918, dossier no 20119/1918, vol. 1, Fonds E20, BANQ.

10. Bureau des avocats de la Ville de Montréal au ministre des Terres et Forêts, September 27, 1918, dossier no 20119/1918, vol. 1, Fonds E20, BANQ.

11. Dagenais and Durand, "Cleansing, Draining, and Sanitizing the City," 641–44.

12. Pétition de la municipalité de Saint-Vincent de Paul, October 9, 1918, dossier no 20119/1918, vol. 1, Fonds E20, BANQ.

13. The Back River Company, owner of the Île de la Visitation industrial facilities, was the first to present the project, but on September 27, 1923, the lease was transferred to Montreal Island Power, which thus became the prime contractor. See Notes de l'ingénieur J.-R. Latreille du service hydraulique, December 15, 1926, dossier no 20119/1918, vol. 2, Fonds E20, BANQ.

14. Rapport technique de T. Pringle & Sons Limited—Industrial Engineers and Architects, July 6, 1922, #20119/1918, vol. 2, Fonds E20, BANQ.

15. Rapport, "Rivière des Prairies—concernant la demande de la 'Back River Power Company Inc.'," September 2, 1922, #20119/1918, vol. 2, Fonds E20, BANQ.

16. Rapport, "Rivière des Prairies—concernant la demande de la 'Back River Power Company Inc.'," September 2, 1922, #20119/1918, vol. 2, Fonds E20, BANQ.

17. Rapport de l'ingénieur sanitaire Théo J. Lafrenière aux présidents et membres du Conseil supérieur d'hygiène de la province de Québec, January 23, 1919, #20119/1918, vol. 2, BANQ. In that era, engineers developed the concept of a river's "assimilation capacity" to measure its dilution power and adopted calculation methods aimed at managing water pollution. See Arn Keeling, "Urban Waste Sinks as a Natural Resource: The Case of the Fraser River," *Urban History Review/Revue d'histoire urbaine* 34, no. 1 (Fall 2005): 58–70.

18. Rapports de Elzéar Pelletier, secrétaire-directeur du Conseil provincial d'hygiène, March 23, 1920, May 31, 1920, June 15, 1992, *Conseil d'hygiène de la Province de Québec, Rapports d'inspection, 1887–1922*, Fonds E88, BANQ.

19. Rapport de Arthur Lessard, secrétaire Conseil provincial d'hygiène, December 15, 1922, #20119/1918, vol. 2, Fonds E20, BANQ.

20. Expression from a letter from a riverside resident, Émile Martineau, addressed to the director of the water department, February 8, 1932, #20119/1918, vol. 3, Fonds E20, BANQ.

21. "Copie du Rapport d'un Comité de l'Honorable Conseil exécutif en date du 27 nov. 1922, approuvé par le Lieutenant-Gouverneur, le 29 novembre 1922," #20119/1918, vol. 2, Fonds E20, BANQ.

22. Vézina, *Le Site des Moulins*, 18. By diverting the water toward the power station, this dam would deprive Île de la Visitation mills of waterpower. To compensate, MIP signed an agreement with the mill owners in which it undertook to "supply sufficient water power to produce 500 horsepower."

23. Projet d'amendement du contrat "concerning the request of the Montreal Island Power [. . .]," Ministry of Lands and Forest, 1929, #20119/1918, vol. 2, Fonds E20, BANQ.

24. On this question, see Jakobsson, "Industrialization of Rivers," 44; as well as Ted Steinberg, *Nature Incorporated: Industrialization and the Waters of New England* (Cambridge: Cambridge University Press, 1991).

25. "City Authorizes Power Dam Plan," *Gazette*, July 8, 1923, #20119/1918, vol. 2, Fonds E20, BANQ.

26. S. Paquin, Pont-Viau à ministre des Terres et Forêts, April 7, 1926, #20119/1918, vol. 2, Fonds E20, BANQ.

27. Various circumstances delayed work. Claude Bellavance's study on Shawinigan Water and Power covers it briefly; see Bellavance, *Shawinigan Water and Power, 1898–1963: Formation et déclin d'un groupe industriel au Québec* (Montreal: Boréal, 1994), 107–9, 216.

28. De Honoré Mercier, ministre des Terres et Forêts, à Joseph Filion, député du comté de Laval, February 4, 1932, #20119/1918, vol. 3, Fonds E20, BANQ.

29. Hormisdas Guilbault, Pont-Viau, à Honoré Mercier, ministre des Terres et Forêts, February 25, 1929, #20119/1918, vol. 2, Fonds E20, BANQ.

30. Lettre à Hormisdas Guilbault, March 8, 1929, #20119/1918, vol. 2, Fonds E20, ANQ.

31. Blanchard, *L'ouest du Canada français*, 339 and after.

32. Marcel Samson, *La résidence secondaire et la région métropolitaine de Montréal* (PhD diss., Université de droit, d'économie et des sciences d'Aix-Marseille, 1988), 78–79.

33. Paul Dauphinais, Luc Dauphinais, and Daniel Marien, *De la seigneurie à la banlieue: L'histoire de Laval-des-Rapides des origines à la fusion (1636–1965)* (Montreal, 1984), 86.

34. De Harold E. Walker, avocat, à Arthur Amos, directeur du Service hydraulique, October 16, 1931, p. 6, #20119/1918, vol. 3, Fonds E20, BANQ.

35. De Honoré Mercier, ministre des Terres et Forêts, à Joseph Filion, député du comté de Laval, February 4, 1932, #20119/1918, vol. 3, Fonds E20, BANQ.

36. De J. Alfred Ouimet, propriétaire à l'Abbord-à-Plouffe, à Arthur Amos, November 21, 1932, #20119/1918, vol. 3, Fonds E20, BANQ; Raymond Perrier, "Historique des inondations au Québec, " in *L'eau, une industrie: Actes du congrès conjoint de l'AQTE–FACE* (1974), 22–25.

37. "L'inondation envahit trois municipalités, " *La Presse*, December 13, 1932, 1–2; "Une embâcle de glace sur la rivière des Prairies cause maintes inondations, " *La Patrie*, December 13, 1932, 3 and 13.

38. Rapport interne de Arthur Amos, December 21, 1932, p. 3, #20119/1918, vol. 3, Fonds E20, BANQ.

39. Rapport interne de Arthur Amos, December 21, 1932, p. 4, #20119/1918, vol. 3, Fonds E20, BANQ.

40. On the various ways that environmental transformations are experienced, see Tina Loo, "Disturbing the Peace: Environmental Change and the Scales of Justice on a Northern River," *Environmental History* 12, no. 4 (October 2007): 895–919.

41. Lettre adressée au ministre des Terres et Forêts, Honoré Mercier, August 11, 1933, #20119/1918, vol. 3, Fonds E20, BANQ.

42. Rapport interne de Arthur Amos, December 21–22, 1932, p. 4, #20119/1918, vol. 3, Fonds E20, BANQ.

43. "Bref d'assignation, " p. 4, #20119/1918, vol. 3, Fonds E20, BANQ.

44. The writ of summons mentions this agreement, also mentioned in a petition by members of the Abbord-à-Plouffe town council sent to Montreal Island and Power on May 17, 1943, see Hydro-Québec Archives, series F9/3462.

45. Attempts were made early in the twentieth century to regulate the water in the Ottawa River hydrographic basin. This question became central after 1945.

46. Usine d'épuration des eaux, *Cinquième ordonnance de la Commission des services publics du Québec*, March 10, 1930, P30, S31, D3, Archives de la Ville de Montréal (hereafter AVM).

47. August 21, 1916, dossier no. 2615, 3e série, AVM.

48. Du Dr Le Cavalier, propriétaire, à J. A. A. Brodeur, président du Comité exécutif, August 21, 1922, dossier no. 2615, 3e série, AVM.

49. Secrétariat de la province—Service provincial d'hygiène, décisions du directeur (hereafter Fonds E4), vol. XXXVII, February 22, 1928, Fonds E4, BANQ.

50. *Sixième ordonnance des services publics du Québec*, December 22, 1930, dossier no. 50607, 3e série, AVM.

51. The public's demands likely contributed to the commission's alacrity: "Une délégation d'Ahuntsic. On demande de hâter la construction d'une usine d'épuration et de filtration dans le nord," October 20, 1933, dossiers de presse, pollution des eaux, bobine 134, AVM.

52. De Alphonse Lessard, directeur du Service provincial d'hygiène, à Jos. Étienne Gauthier, greffier de la Ville de Montréal, September 14, 1933, dossier no. 50607, 3e série, AVM.

53. "Pour contrôler les bains publics," July 13, 1933, dossier no. 50607, 3e série, AVM.

54. Dossier de presse "Pollution des eaux," no. D720.5, bobine 134, AVM; "Aux baigneurs. Endroits défendus," *Le Devoir*, July 3, 1939.

55. Blanchard, *L'ouest du Canada français*, 371.

56. The hygiene authorities set their sights on these cabins, organizing multiple enquiries into them in the 1930s and 1940s. See Rapport d'enquête de l'assistant-ingénieur sanitaire E. Langevin, July 4, 1933, Fonds E4, vol. XXXXII, BANQ.

57. November 2, 1937, dossier no. 50607, 3e série, AVM; "Une usine d'épuration réclamée à grands cris," *La Patrie*, December 11, 1937.

58. The Île Saint-Hélène beach opened in 1937 and quickly became a choice spot for Montreal swimmers. See November 30, 1937, dossier no. 50607, 3e série, AVM: Dossier de presse, bobine 134, AVM; "Beach is badly needed," *Montreal Gazette*, August 8, 1935; "La plage de l'Île Sainte-Hélène ouverte," *La Presse*, July 12, 1937.

5. THE SEINE AND PARISIAN METABOLISM

1. See, for instance, André Guillerme, "Le testament de la Seine," *Revue de géographie de Lyon* 65, no. 4 (1990): 240–50; Isabelle Bakouche, *La trace du fleuve, la Seine et Paris (1750–1850)* (Paris: Édition de l'ÉHESS, 2000).

2. See, for instance, Marie-Hélène Bourquin-Simonin, *L'approvisionnement de Paris en bois de la Régence à la Révolution (1715–1789)* (Clamecy: Confrérie Saint-Nicolas de Clamecy, 2006).

3. For the French case, see Jean-Pierre Goubert, *La conquête de l'eau* (Paris: Flammarion, 1986).

4. On this project and the debates that it sparked, see Frédéric Graber, *Paris a besoin d'eau. Projet, dispute et délibération technique dans la France napoléonienne* (Paris: Édition du CNRS, 2009).

5. Henry-Charles Emmery, "Statistique des eaux de la ville de Paris," *Annales des ponts et chaussées,* 1st sem. (1840): 145–270.

6. Emmery, "Statistique des eaux de la ville de Paris."

7. Julia Csergo, "L'eau à Paris au XIXe siècle: approvisionnement et consommation domestique," in *Paris et ses réseaux: Naissance d'un mode de vie urbain, XIXe–XXe siècles* (Paris: Bibliothèque historique de la ville de Paris, 1990), 137.

8. Eugène Belgrand, *Recherches statistiques sur les sources du bassin de la Seine* (Paris: Vinchon, 1854), 28.

9. Haussmann took credit for the paternity of this idea in his memoires (Baron Haussmann, *Mémoires*, ed. Françoise Choay, [Paris: Seuil, 2000], 946).

10. Belgrand, *Recherches,* 75.

11. Haussmann, *Mémoires,* 1016.

12. Edmond Badois, "Note sur l'alimentation d'eau de Paris et de la banlieue et sur l'assainissement de la Seine," *Mémoire de la société des ingénieurs civils* 59, no.1 (1893): 525.

13. On all this, see Sabine Barles, *L'invention des déchets urbains, France 1790–1970* (Seyssel: Champ Vallon, 2005).

14. Jules Arnould, *Nouveaux éléments d'hygiène*, 2nd ed. (Paris: J.-B. Baillière et fils, 1889), 780.

15. Adolphe-Auguste Mille, *Rapport sur le mode d'assainissement des villes en Angleterre et en Écosse* (Paris: Vinchon, 1854), 12.

16. Mille and Alfred Durand-Claye, *Compte rendu des essais d'utilisation et d'épuration* (Paris, 1869), 10.

17. *Annuaire statistique de la ville de Paris, année 1880* (Paris: Imprimerie municipale, 1881).

18. Hippolythe Marié-Davy, *Épuration des eaux d'égouts par le sol de Gennevilliers* (Paris: A. Delahaye et Lecrosnier, 1880), 6 and 3–4.

19. See Sabine Barles, "Experts contre experts: Les champs d'épandage de la ville de Paris dans les années 1870," *Histoire urbaine* 14 (December 2005): 65–80.

20. Gérard Jacquemet, "Urbanisme parisien: La bataille du tout à l'égout à la fin du XIXe siècle," *Revue d'histoire moderne et contemporaine* 26 (1979): 505–48.

21. Pierre Paul Dehérain, *Traité de chimie agricole: Développement des végétaux, terres arables, amendements et engrais* (Paris: G. Masson, 1892), 645.

22. "Le projet d'Achères ne peut donc être qu'un début: Prenez garde à vous!" as read in *Journal de Versailles et de Seine-et-Oise*, December 2, 1888.

23. Nitrogen was one of the main targets of nineteenth-century sanitation and valorization techniques.

24. Sabine Barles, "Feeding the City: Food Consumption and Circulation of Nitrogen, Paris, 1801–1914," *Science of the Total Environment* 375 (2007): 48–58.

25. The association of Paris's impermeabilization and underground channeling to sewage farms leads to an externalization of evapotranspiration and infiltration (and therefore part of the water cycle) that moved out to periurban spaces. See Sabine Barles, "L'invention des eaux usées: L'assainissement de Paris, de la fin de l'Ancien Régime à la seconde guerre mondiale, " in *The Modern Demon: Pollution in Urban and Industrial European Societies,* ed. Christoph Bernhardt and Geneviève Massard-Guilbaud (Clermont- Ferrand, Presses de l'Université Blaise Pascal, 2002), 129–56.

26. Annie Fourcaut, *La banlieue en morceaux: La crise des lotissements défectueux en France dans l'entre-deux-guerres* (Grâne: Créaphis, 2000).

27. Jean-Pierre Lecoin, ed., "L'occupation du sol en région d'Île-de-France, " *Cahiers de l'IAURIF* 48–49 (1977).

28. Georges Lemarchand, Louis Puech, and Auguste Marin, *Rapport général au nom de la commission départementale des eaux, de l'assainissement, des ordures ménagères et des fumées, sur l'assainissement général du département de la Seine* (Paris: Imprimerie municipale, 1929), 5.

29. Adrien Gastinel, *Les égouts de Paris: Étude d'hygiène urbaine* (Paris: Henri Jouve, 1894), 14.

30. Paul Vincey, *L'assainissement de la Seine et les champs d'épandage de la ville de Paris* (Paris: P. Renouard, 1910), 6.

31. Vincey, *L'assainissement de la Seine.*

32. Ibid., 9–14.

33. "Problème de la prévention des inondations dans le bassin de la Seine," *Journal officiel de la République française: Avis et rapports du Conseil économique* 1 (1956): 7.

34. Commission des inondations (Ministère de l'Intérieur et des Cultes), *Rapports et documents divers* (Paris: Imprimerie nationale, 1910).

35. Commission des inondations, *Rapports et documents divers,* 86.

36. Ibid., 92.

37. See Allan Mitchell, *Rêves parisiens: L'échec de projets de transports publics en France au XIXe siècle* (Paris: Presses de l'ENPC, 2005), 47–63.

38. François Sentenac, "Service technique des eaux et de l'assainissement," *Science et industrie*, hors série (1928): 56.

39. Joël Kerboriou, *L'extension du réseau d'assainissement de l'agglomération parisienne de 1919 à 1940* (DEA thesis, CNAM, 2001), 30.

40. H. Gilbert, "La direction technique du port de Paris," *Travaux*, hors série (1958): 239.

41. Gilbert, "La direction technique du port de Paris," 239.

42. Sentenac, "Service technique des eaux et de l'assainissement," *Science et industrie*, hors série (1934): 96–100; *Annuaire statistique de la ville de Paris et du département de la Seine, années 1942–1947* (Paris: Préfecture de la Seine, 1952).

43. Pierre Koch, "Direction technique des eaux et de l'assainissement," *Travaux,* 180 bis, hors série (1949): 152–54.

44. Paul Benoit, Karine Berthier, Philippe Boët, and Charles Reze, "Les aménagements hydrauliques liés au flottage du bois, leur impact sur le milieu fluvial XVIe–XVIIIe siècles," in *Programme PIREN-Seine, rapport d'activité 2002,* Paris, UMR CNRS 7619 Sisyphe, March 7, 2003, http://www.sisyphe.upmc.fr/piren/book/713.

45. Guillaume Ritter, "Alimentation de la ville de Paris en eau, force et lumière électrique au moyen d'une dérivation des eaux des lacs du Jura suisse, " in *Mémoires de la société des ingénieurs civils* (Paris: Chaix, 1888), 19, 27.

46. Ritter, "Alimentation de la ville de Paris en eau," 36.

47. Edmond Badois and Paul Duvillard, *Les eaux françaises du lac Léman à Paris et dans la banlieue. Projet P. Duvillard. Memorandum présenté à la commission technique des eaux de Paris* (Paris: Société d'études pour l'adduction des eaux françaises du lac Léman à Paris et dans sa banlieue, 1898), 1.

48. Badois and Duvillard, *Les eaux françaises du lac Léman à Paris et dans la banlieue,* 1.

49. Gilles-Antoine Langlois, "Henri Chabal et l'aménagement du bassin de la Seine," *Centraliens* 562 (May 2005): 41.

50. Gilles-Antoine Langlois, *Pannecière* (Paris: Somogy/IIBRBS, 2003), 24.

51. From *Annuaires statistiques de la ville de Paris et des communes suburbaines de la Seine* (Paris: Imprimerie municipale / Préfecture de la Seine, 1881–1972).

52. Georges Bechmann, *Salubrité urbaine: Distribution d'eau et assainissement*, 2nd ed. rev. and expanded., vol. 2 (Paris: Baudry, 1899), 254–55. He nevertheless declares that he is in favor of associating irrigation with soil filtration to provide for the purification of any surplus.

53. Paul Vincey, "L'assainissement de la Seine par les champs d'épandage et les lits bactériens artificiels," *Mémoires de la société des ingénieurs civils* 88, no. 1 (1907): 752.

54. A. Guiselin, "Utilisation rationnelle des déchets organiques en agriculture," *Chimie et industrie,* special edition published on the occasion of the *3e congrès de chimie industrielle de Paris,* 1923 (1924): 729.

55. Bernard Védry, *Contribution à l'histoire des procédés d'épuration biologique des eaux résiduaires* (DEA thesis, Universités de Paris IV et de Paris VIII, CNAM, EHESS, 1992), 87.

56. Védry, *Contribution à l'histoire des procédés d'épuration biologique des eaux résiduaires*, 88.

57. Sentenac, "Service technique des eaux et de l'assainissement," (1928): 63–64.

58. Pierre Koch, *L'évacuation de l'effluent urbain*, in *L'assainissement des agglomérations* (Paris: Léon Eyrolles, 1935), 2: 174.

59. Koch, *L'évacuation de l'effluent urbain,* 177. See also, François Sentenac, *L'épuration agricole des eaux d'égout* (Paris: Léon Eyrolles, 1927).

60. Koch, *L'évacuation de l'effluent urbain,* 177.

61. Jules Courmont, C. Lesieur, and A. Rochaix, *Précis d'hygiène*, 4th ed. rev. and corr. by Paul Courmont and A. Rochaix (Paris: Masson, 1932), 387.

62. Lemarchand, Puech, and Marin, *Rapport général au nom de la commission départementale des eaux*, 6–14.

63. Jean Olivesi, "Les services d'assainissement," *Travaux* (March 1966): 3.

64. Conseil général de la Seine, *Rapports et documents du conseil général du département de la Seine* 16 (1926), 7–8.

65. Sentenac, "Service technique des eaux et de l'assainissement," (1931): 100.

66. Feuillade, "L'assainissement de la Seine," *Travaux* (March 1966): 32.

67. Lemarchand, Puech and Marin, *Rapport général au nom de la commission départementale des eaux*, 55.

68. Koch, "Direction technique des eaux et de l'assainissement" (1949): 130.

69. Feuillade, "L'assainissement de la Seine," 27.

70. C. Véron, "L'épuration des eaux usées de Paris et de l'agglomération parisienne, " *Travaux* (Jan. 1983): 44.

71. Pierre Koch, "Direction technique des eaux et de l'assainissement," *Travaux* (1958): 171–72; Feuillade, "L'assainissement de la Seine," 36. The two texts are similar; the reiteration is not neutral.

72. Koch, *L'assainissement des agglomérations*.

73. Ibid., 1: 16.

74. We should add that 100 percent of the water treated did not mean 100 percent treated, as the efficiency of the purification facilities was less than one.

75. Koch, "Direction technique des eaux et de l'assainissement" (1958): 182.

76. "Problème de la prévention des inondations dans le bassin de la Seine," 7.

77. Ibid., 9.

78. *Proposition tendant à inviter l'administration à pousser ses études en cours sur les questions d'approvisionnement en eau et de protection contre les inondations* (Paris, 1925), 7.

79. "Problème de la prévention des inondations dans le bassin de la Seine," 9.

80. Langlois, *Pannecière*, 24.

81. Ibid., 37–40.

82. "Problème de la prévention des inondations dans le bassin de la Seine," 9.

83. Ibid., 15.

84. Gilbert, "La direction technique du port de Paris," 240.

85. "Problème de la prévention des inondations dans le bassin de la Seine," 13.

86. Ibid., 12.

87. Service des barrages-réservoirs (Préfecture de la Seine), *Notice sur le réservoir "Seine,"* 2nd ed. (Paris: Imprimerie municipale, 1963), 3.

88. See Gilles-Antoine Langlois, *Le lac d'Orient* (Paris, Somogy/IIBRBS, 2004).

89. "Problème de la prévention des inondations dans le bassin de la Seine," 14.

90. In 1989, the average potential summer inflow was eighty cubic meters per second (see figure 5.1), but this is outside the scope of our study period.

91. Lemarchand, Puech and Marin, *Rapport général au nom de la commission départementale des eaux,* 55–56.

92. On the national level, it was not until June 10, 1976, that it was finally taken into account in a health ministry circular on sewage systems in the agglomerations and the protection of the receiving environment.

93. See work by PIREN-Seine. For a synthetic approach, see Gilles Billen, ed. *Le bassin de la Seine* (Nanterre: Agence de l'eau Seine-Normandie, 2009), 40–41, http://www.sisyphe.upmc.fr/piren/book/974.

94. "Problème de la prévention des inondations dans le bassin de la Seine," 13.

95. Today they are managed by the Institution interdépartementale des barrages réservoirs du bassin de la Seine (IIBRBS), created by the four departments that make up the central part of the Parisian built-up area.

96. Sabine Barles and Laurence Lestel, "The Nitrogen Question: Urbanization, Industrialization, and River Quality in Paris, 1830–1939," *Journal of Urban History* 33, no. 5 (July 2007): 794–812.

6. THE CHANNELIZATION OF THE DANUBE AND URBAN SPATIAL DEVELOPMENT IN VIENNA IN THE NINETEENTH AND EARLY TWENTIETH CENTURIES

1. This chapter is only a first step in analyzing the relation between the city of Vienna and the Danube riverine landscape. Further research will be done within an interdisciplinary research project on the environmental history of the Viennese Danube, titled "The Environmental History of the Viennese Danube, 1500–1890," that is being funded by the Austrian Science Fund (no. P 22265 G18, project leader Verena Winiwarter).

2. John S. Bridge, "The interaction between channel geometry, water flow, sediment transport and deposition in braided rivers," in *Braided Rivers*, ed. J. L. Best and C. S. Bristow (London: Geological Society, 1993), 13–71.

3. Werner Kresser, "Die Hochwässer der Donau," *Schriftenreihe des Österreichischen Wasserwirtschaftsverbands* 32/33 (1957): 10–93.

4. Severin Hohensinner, "Sobald der Strom einen anderen Lauf nimmt: Der Wandel der Donau vom 18. zum 20. Jahrhundert," in *Umwelt Donau: Eine andere Geschichte,* ed. Verena Winiwarter and Martin Schmid, catalog for the Exhibition of the Provincial Archive of Lower Austria in Ardagger Markt, May 5, 2010–November 7, 2010 (St. Pölten: Niederösterreichisches Landesarchiv 2010), 39–56.

5. Sabine Grupe and Christine Jawecki, "Geomorphodynamik der Wiener Innenstadt: Fundort Wien," *Berichte zur Archäologie* 7 (2004): 14–30.

6. Bertrand M. Buchmann, Harald Sterk, and Rupert Schickl, *Der Donaukanal: Geschichte—Planung—Ausführung* (Vienna: Magistrat der Stadt Wien, 1984).

7. Lehrer-Arbeitsgemeinschaft des II. Bezirkes, ed., *Die Leopoldstadt: Ein Heimatbuch* (Vienna: Selbstverlag der Lehrer-Arbeitsgemeinschaft, 1937).

8. Wolfgang Schmeltzl, *Ein Lobspuch der Hochlöblichen weitberümbten khünigklichen Stat Wien in Osterreich* (Vienna: Matheus Kuppitsch, 1548).

9. See, e.g., a documentation of historical Danube channelization projects in Viktor Thiel, "Geschichte der älteren Donauregulierungsarbeiten bei Wien. I. Von den älteren Nachrichten bis zum Beginne des XVIII. Jahrhunderts," *Jahrbuch für Landeskunde von Niederösterreich* 1903 (1904): 117–65; Viktor Thiel, "Geschichte der Donauregulierungsarbeiten bei Wien. II Vom Anfange des XVIII. bis zur Mitte des XIX. Jahrhunderts und III. Von der Mitte des XIX. Jahrhunderts bis zur Gegenwart," *Jahrbuch für Landeskunde von Niederösterreich* 1905/1906 (1906): 1–102.

10. In most other Austrian areas flood protection only emerged as a state responsibility in the nineteenth century; the first flood-related law was enacted in 1830; see, e.g., Karl Zehndorfer, "Die Traisenregulierung," in *50 Jahre Traisen-Wasserverband: Wasserwirtschaft im Traisental*, ed. Bundesministerium für Land-und Forstwirtschaft (Vienna: Buchdruckerei Wilhelm Götz, 1970).

11. Lehrer-Arbeitsgemeinschaft, *Die Leopoldstadt*, 20; Felix Czeike, ed., *Historisches Lexikon Wien*, vol. 4 (Vienna: Kremayr & Scheriau, 1995), 38.

12. Christine Klusacek and Kurt Stummer, *Leopoldstadt* (Vienna: K. Mohl, 1978), 25.

13. Johann Adolf Tomaschek, *Die Rechte und Freiheiten der Stadt Wien*. Geschichtsquellen der Stadt Wien, vol. I/1 (Vienna: Alfred Hölder, 1877), 158–61.

14. Josef König, "Bezirksmuseum Leopoldstadt," *Wiener Geschichtsblätter* Suppl. 4 (2007), 36.

15. Lehrer-Arbeitsgemeinschaft, *Die Leopoldstadt*, 94.

16. Land use in the Danube section of the Machland basin was analyzed in detail based on GIS analyses of historical maps, see Gertrud Haidvogl, "Von der Flusslandschaft zum Fließgewässer: Die Entwicklung ausgewählter österreichischer Flüsse im 19. und 20. Jahrhundert mit besonderer Berücksichtigung der Kolonisierung des Überflutungsraums" (PhD diss., Vienna University, 2008).

17. This map was published in 1819 and has a scale of 1:7320. It is especially close to the Danube—a high accuracy (error around 3 percent at maximum). Until 1849 all projects for the Danube channelization were based on this map. See Peter Mohilla and Franz Michlmayr, *Donauatlas Wien* (Vienna: Österreichischer Kunst- und Kulturverlag, 1996), map. 6.5.

18. Lehrer-Arbeitsgemeinschaft, *Die Leopoldstadt*, 121.

19. Ibid., 122.

20. Ibid., 159.

21. The subsequent spatial development plans by Ludwig Förster and others are described below; Michael Garstenauer, "Marginalisierung in der 'Vorstadt': Soziökonomische Entwicklung Wiens und Madrids im 19. Jahrhundert" (MA thesis, University of Vienna, 2007).

22. *Plan eines Dammbaus entlang der Donau von Korneuburg bis zur Jedlseer Brücke, 1788*, cited in Mohilla and Michlmayr, *Donauatlas Wien*. Stephan de Csermend,

Hauptmann vom Großen Generalstab, *Neuester Grundriß der Haupt- und Residenzstadt Wien und der umliegenden Gegenden, 1789*, in Mohilla and Michlmayr, *Donauatlas Wien*.

23. *Donauregulierungsprojekt für Wien, 1869*, in Mohilla and Michlmayr, *Donauatlas Wien*, maps 7.3–7.6.

24. Donau-Regulierungskommission, *Bericht und Anträge des von der Comission für die Donauregulierung bei Wien ernannten Comités. Plenarversammlung am 27. Juli 1868* (Wien: K. K. Hof- und Staatsdruckerei, 1868), 5

25. Josef Cresseri, *Entwurf der Donau in den Gegenden Wiens, 1803*, in Mohilla and Michlmayr, *Donauatlas Wien*, map 4.13.

26. Franz Sartori, *Wien's Tage der Gefahr und die Retter aus der Noth: Eine authentische Beschreibung der unerhörten Überschwemmung Wien's*. 2 vol. (Vienna: Carl Gerold, 1830–1832).

27. Donau-Regulierungskommission, "Die Regulierung der Donau und der Bau einer stabilen Brücke über dieselbe bei Wien" *Allgemeine Bauzeitung* 15 (1850): 46–137.

28. Donauregulierungskommission, *Berichte und Anträge*, 7 and 60.

29. The experts were as follows: J. Abernethy, civil-engineer from London; G. Hagen, building director from Prussia; G. Sexauer, building council of Baden; A. Tostain, general inspector, France. Abernethy and Sexauer clearly recommended the solution of the majority of the second Danube Regulation Commission; the French expert, A. Tostain, emphasized the positive aspects from both options; and Hagen supported the minority, i.e., to maintain the existing main channel.

30. Donauregulierungskommission, *Berichte und Anträge*, 60 and 66.

31. Johann Mihalik, *Projekt zur Regulierung des Donau-Stromes von Nussdorf bis Theben, 1865*, in Mohilla and Michlmayr, *Donauatlas Wien*, map 6.17.

32. Cajetan Felder, *Plan der Donau-Regulierung bei Wien, 1874*, in Mohilla and Michlmayr, *Donauatlas Wien*, map 7.14.

33. Heinrich Grave, *Wien und Vororte mit Darstellung der Donau und ihrer Auen vor und nach der Regulierung* (Vienna: Beck'sche Universitätsbuchhandlung, 1874).

34. Paul Kortz, ed., *Wien am Anfang des 20. Jahrhunderts* (Vienna: Gerlach & Wiedling, 1905); Werner Michael Schwarz, "Arbeits- und Umweltschutz—Die Gefahren der Produktion," in *Umwelt Stadt: Geschichte des Natur- und Lebensraumes Wien*, ed. Karl Brunner and Petra Schneider (Vienna, Köln, Weimar: Böhlau, 2005), 286.

35. Walter Matznetter, "Von der Grundherrschaft zum Stadtmanagement: Zweihundert Jahre Stadtplanung in Wien," in *Umwelt Stadt: Geschichte des Natur- und Lebensraumes Wien*, ed. Karl Brunner and Petra Schneider (Vienna, Köln, Weimar: Böhlau, 2005), 68. During the large second city expansion in 1892 many communities were integrated into the urban area. However, it did not concern the former Danube islands. The only change here was the separation of the Leopoldstadt and Brigittenau into the second and twentieth districts.

36. Heinrich Goldemund, "Die Ausgestaltung der Donauregulierung bei Wien und die Idee eines neuen Donaustadtteiles am linken Ufer," *Zeitschrift des österreichischen Ingenieur- und Architektenvereins* 70 (1918): 217–19.

37. Friedrich Kaiser, "Siedlungs-, Bevölkerungs- und Industrieentwicklung der

Brigittenau seit der Donauregulierung in historisch-topographischer Hinsicht," (PhD diss., University of Vienna, 1966), 89–90.

38. Hans Smital, *Geschichte der Großgemeinde Floridsdorf umfassend die Orte Floridsdorf, Jedlesee, Donaufeld und das Jedleseer Fabriksgebiet* (Vienna: Verlag der Gemeinde Floridsdorf, 1903).

39. Wiener Gemeinderat, *Sitzungsbericht* November 11, 1904; *Amtsblatt der Reichs- und Residenzhauptstadt Wien* 91, November 11, 1904; see also Wolfgang Mayer, "Gebietsänderungen im Raum Wien 1850–1910 und die Debatten um das Entstehen eines Generalregulierungsplans von Wien" (PhD diss., University of Vienna, 1972).

40. Anton Waldvogel, "Donauregulierung und Hochwasserschutz Wiens," *Deutsches Volksblatt,* July 3–4, 1912; Anton Waldvogel, *Die Donauhochwasser bei Wien.* 2 vol. (Vienna: printed by author, 1905 and 1906).

41. Friedrich Kindermann "Vortrag zur Donauregulierung" *Zeitschrift des Österreichischen Ingenieur-und Architektenverbands* 71, no. 7 (1919): 72.

7. RIVERS AND RISK IN THE CITY

Epigraph: Frederick Simpich, "Men Against the Rivers," *National Geographic* 71 (June 1937): 794.

1. See, for example, Otfried Weintritt, "The Floods of Baghdad: Cultural and Technological Responses," in *Natural Disasters, Cultural Responses: Case Studies Toward a Global Environmental History,* ed. Christof Mauch and Christian Pfister (Lanham: Lexington Books, 2009), 165–82.

2. Eva Jakobsson, "Industrialization of Rivers: A Water System Approach to Hydropower Development," *Knowledge, Technology, and Policy* 14, no. 4 (2002): 41–56.

3. Gilbert F. White, "Human Adjustment to Floods: A Geographical Approach to the Flood Problem in the United States," Research Paper 29, Department of Geography (PhD diss., University of Chicago, 1945), 44.

4. Melanie C. Beckmann, Franz Schoell, and Christoph D. Matthaei, "Effects of increased flow in the main stem of the River Rhine on the invertebrate communities of its tributaries," *Freshwater Biology* 50 (2005): 10.

5. Joachim Adis and Wolfgang Junk, "Terrestrial invertebrates inhabiting lowland river floodplains of Central Amazonia and Central Europe: a review," *Freshwater Biology* 47, no. 4 (2002): 723.

6. Mark Cioc, *The Rhine: An Eco-Biography, 1815–2000* (Seattle: University of Washington Press, 2002), 33.

7. See, for instance, Michael Kempe and Christian Rohr, eds., "Coping with the Unexpected—Natural Disasters and Their Perception," special issue, *Environment and History* 9, no. 2 (2003); Theodore Steinberg, *Acts of God: The Unnatural History of Natural Disaster in America* (New York: Oxford University Press, 2000); Mauch and Pfister, *Natural Disasters.* The historiography of river floods, however, is, with a few exceptions, still characterized by a remarkable lack of research. Exceptions are Deborah Pickman Clifford and Nicholas R. Clifford, *"The Troubled Roar of the Waters": Vermont in Flood and Recovery, 1927–1931* (Durham: University of New Hampshire

Press, 2007); John M. Barry, *Rising Tide: The Great Mississippi Flood of 1927 and How It Changed America* (New York: Simon and Schuster, 1997).

8. Mary Douglas und Aaron Wildavsky, *Risk and Culture: An Essay on the Selection of Technological and Environmental Dangers* (Berkeley: University of California Press, 1982); Uwe Lübken and Christof Mauch, "Introduction," in "Uncertain Environments: Natural Hazards, Risk, and Insurance in Historical Perspective," ed. Uwe Lübken and Christof Mauch, special issue, *Environment and History* 17, no. 1 (2011): 1–12.

9. Donald Worster, *Rivers of Empire. Water, Aridity, and the Growth of the American West* (New York: Pantheon, 1985), 20.

10. Cioc, *The Rhine*, 16.

11. R. David Edmunds, "A German Chocolate Cake, with White Coconut Icing: Ohio and the Native American World," in *Ohio and the World, 1753–2053: Essays Toward a New History of Ohio*, ed. Geoffrey Parker, Richard Sisson, and William Russell Coil (Columbus: Ohio State University Press, 2005), 37.

12. See Richard C. Wade, *The Urban Frontier: Pioneer Life in Early Pittsburgh, Cincinnati, Lexington, Louisville, and St. Louis* (Chicago: University of Chicago Press, 1959), 1; George Knepper, *Ohio and Its People* (Kent: Kent State University Press, 1989), 29; John D. Barnhart, *Valley of Democracy: The Frontier versus the Plantation in the Ohio Valley, 1775–1818* (Bloomington: Indiana University Press, 1970), 20–33.

13. Quoted in Douglas R. Hurt, *The Ohio Frontier: Crucible of the Old Northwest, 1720–1830* (Bloomington: Indiana University Press, 1996), 55.

14. See Patrick Wolfe, "Settler Colonialism and the Elimination of the Native," *Journal of Genocide Research* 9, no. 4 (2006): 387–409; Ian Tyrrell, "Beyond the View from Euro-America: Environment, Settler Societies, and the Internationalization of American History," in *Rethinking American History*, ed. Thomas Bender (Berkeley, University of Califronia Press, 2002), 168–91; Knepper, *Ohio and Its People*, 73–81; Wade, *Urban Frontier*, 25f.

15. Johann David Schoepf, *Travels in the Confederation, 1783–1784*, ed. and trans. Alfred J. Morrison (Philadelphia: Campbell, 1911), 47.

16. Christian Schultz, *Travels on an Inland Voyage Through the States of New York, Pennsylvania, Virginia, Ohio, Kentucky and Tennessee, and through the Territories of Indiana, Louisiana, Mississippi and New Orleans; performed in the years 1807 and 1808; including a tour of nearly six thousand miles* (New York: Issac Riley, 1810), 114, entry of 9 September 1807.

17. W. Wallace Carson, "Transportation and Traffic on the Ohio and Mississippi Before the Steamboat," *Mississippi Valley Historical Review* 7, no. 1 (June 1920): 31.

18. Wade, *Urban Frontier*, 10. Half a century later, Christian Schultz remarked that "the natural advantages which this place possesses are so great, that it may justly be considered as the metropolis of the western country" (Schultz, *Travels on an Inland Voyage*, 124).

19. Quoted in Leland R. Johnson, *Men, Mountains and Rivers: An Illustrated History of the Huntington District, U. S. Army Corps of Engineers, 1754–1974* (Washington, DC, 1977), 141. See also William Smith, An historical account of the expedition against

the Ohio Indians in the year 1764 (Dublin, 1769), A3: "The fortifications had been greatly damaged by the floods."

20. Reuben Gold Thwaites, *Afloat on the Ohio: An Historical Pilgrimage of a Thousand Miles in a Skiff, from Redstone to Cairo* (New York: Doubleday and McClure, 1900), 87.

21. Thomas Wallcut, *Journal of Thomas Wallcut, in 1790*, with Notes by George Dexter (Cambridge: Cambridge University Press, 1879), 16.

22. See Wallcut, *Journal of Thomas Wallcut*, 17; George Jordan Blazier, ed., *Joseph Barker: Recollections of the First Settlement of Ohio* (Marietta: Marietta College, 1958), 21.

23. See Andrew R. L. Cayton, Paula R. Riggs, and Robert Frank Cayton, *City Into Town: The City of Marietta, Ohio, 1788–1988* (Marietta: Marietta College, 1991), 29.

24. Schultz, *Travels on an Inland Voyage*, 156.

25. Andrew Backus, "Diary Entry of 14 November, 1816," *A Genealogical Memoir of the Backus family, with the private journal of James Backus, together with his correspondence bearing on the first settlement of Ohio, at Marietta, in 1788* (Norwich: Press of the Bulletin, 1889), 6.

26. Julia Perkins Cutler, ed., *The Life and Times of Ephraim Cutler, Prepared from his Journals and Correspondence* (Cincinnati: R. Clarke and Co., 1890), 110.

27. Ohio Genealogical Society, Washington County Chapter, *History of Washington County, Ohio, 1788–1881: With Illustrations and Biographical Sketches* (Cleveland: H. Z. Williams, 1881), 423.

28. Cutler, *The Life and Times of Ephraim Cutler*, 111.

29. Ohio Genealogical Society, *History of Washington County, Ohio*, 423.

30. Quoted in Cayton, Riggs, and Cayton, *City Into Town*, 29.

31. See Wade, *Urban Frontier*, 10.

32. See ibid., 22; David Stradling, *Cincinnati: From River City to Highway Metropolis* (Charleston: Arcadia, 2003), 10–11; Knepper, *Ohio and Its People*, 66–67; Charles Theodore Greve, *Centennial History of Cincinnati and Representative Citizens* (Chicago: Biographical Pub. Co., 1904), 994; Wade, *Urban Frontier*, 23.

33. Wade, *Urban Frontier*, 23.

34. Stradling, *Cincinnati*, 11.

35. See Arthur E. Morgan and C. A. Bock, "A History of Flood Control in Ohio," *Ohio History* 34, no. 4 (October 1925): 477.

36. See Martin Melosi, "Path Dependence and Urban History: Is a Marriage Possible?" in *Resources of the City: Contributions to an Environmental History of Modern Europe*, ed. Dieter Schott, Bill Luckin, and Genevieve Massard-Guilbaud (Hampshire: Ashgate, 2005), 262–75.

37. John J. Audubon, "The Ohio," *The Museum of Foreign Literature, Science, and Art* 20, no. 117 (March 1832): 334.

38. Audubon, "The Ohio," 334.

39. Ibid.

40. See Robert L. Reid, "Reuben Gold Thwaites: Clio's Pilgrim," in *Pilgrims on*

the Ohio: The River Journey of Reuben Gold Thwaites, 1894, ed. Robert L. Reid and Dan Hughes Fuller (Indianapolis: Indiana Histroical Society, 1997), 1–16.

41. See Reuben Gold Thwaites, ed., *Early Western Travels, 1748–1846* (Cleveland: A. H. Clarke, 1904–1907).

42. Thwaites, *Afloat on the Ohio,* 7, 17, 45, 78, 183, and 221, respectively.

43. "Endless Frontier," *Time* 58 (July 30, 1951), quoted in Donald Worster, *The Wealth of Nature: Environmental History and the Ecological Imagination* (New York: Oxford University Press, 1993), 135. See also Leland R. Johnson, "Engineering the Ohio," in *Always A River: The Ohio River and the American Experience,* ed. Robert Reid (Bloomington: University of Indiana Press, 1991), 180–209; John R. McNeill, *Something New under the Sun: An Environmental History of the Twentieth-Century World* (New York: W. W. Norton, 2000), 182: "Recasting the world's rivers ranks among the signal environmental changes of the twentieth century." For the Rhine see Christoph Bernhardt, "Zeitgenössische Kontroversen über die Umweltfolgen der Oberrheinkorrektion im 19. Jahrhundert," *Zeitschrift für die Geschichte des Oberrheins* 146 (1998): 293–319; Cioc, *The Rhine*, 35.

44. "Vagaries of the Ohio," *New York Times,* 24 November 1895. See also Cioc, *The Rhine*, 16.

45. "The Ohio Floods," *New York Times,* 9 February 1884. "It is doubtful if any backward steps can be taken in this matter," the author added.

46. See David Welky, *The Thousand-Year Flood: The Ohio-Mississippi Disaster of 1937* (Chicago: University of Chicago Press, 2011). If one measures the destruction in flood damage per unit wealth, the flood of 1937 was even the most destructive flood in the twentieth century. See R. A. Pielke Jr., M. W. Downton, and J. Z. Barnard Miller, *Flood Damage in the United States, 1926–2000: A Reanalysis of National Weather Service Estimates* (Boulder: University Corp. for Atmospheric Research, 2002), 56–58.

47. American Red Cross, *The Ohio-Mississippi Valley Flood Disaster of 1937* (Washington, DC, 1938), 21.

48. United States Congress, House of Representatives, Committee on Flood Control, *Comprehensive Flood-Control Plan for Ohio and Lower Mississippi Rivers.* 75th Cong., 1st Sess., Washington, 1937, 3; Factory Mutual Fire Insurance Companies, "The Ohio Valley Flood," *Factory Mutual Record* 14 (March/April 1937): 1–16 (4).

49. See American Red Cross, *The Ohio-Mississippi Valley Flood Disaster of 1937,* 21; Committee on Flood Control, *Comprehensive Flood-Control Plan for Ohio and Lower Mississippi Rivers,* 3; Factory Mutual, "The Ohio Valley Flood," 4. On animals and natural catastrophes see Greg Bankoff, "Bodies on the Beach: Domesticates and Disasters in the Spanish Philippines 1750–1898," *Environment and History* 13 (2007): 285–306; Uwe Lübken, "'Poor Dumb Brutes' or 'Friends in Need'? Animals and River Floods in Modern Germany and the United States," in *Beastly Natures: Animals, Humans, and the Study of History,* ed. Dorothee Brantz (Charlottesville: University of Virginia Press, 2010), 246–63.

50. U. S. Congress, House of Representatives, Statement of Ernest Magaro, Assistant Maintenance Superintendent of Highways, Westmoreland County, PA, 75th Cong., 1st Sess., *Hearings Before the Committee on Flood Control on Levees and Flood Walls,*

Ohio River Basin. (H. R. 7393 and H. R. 7647), Washington, DC, 1937, 340; American Waterways Operators, Inc., *A Study in Economic Growth: Waterside Site Plant Locations and Expansions Since 1952,* 2nd ed. (Washington, DC: American Waterways Operators, 1962), 1; White, "Human Adjustment to Floods," 113.

51. "Private Fire Protection: The Effect of the Flood on Factory Mutual Plants," *Factory Mutual Record* 14 (March/April 1937): 13.

52. White, "Human Adjustment to Floods," 112–13.

53. See, for example, "High Water Disrupts Barge Traffic," *Louisville Courier-Journal,* 4 March 1997.

54. U.S. Congress, House of Representatives, *Memphis, Helena, and St. Louis Levee Railroad. An Important National Work. A Levee and a Railroad Combined on the Mississippi River.* 10th Cong., 2nd session. House Bill No. 745. Washington, DC, 1869, 9: "the road-bed . . . shall be so constructed as to serve the purpose of a levee."

55. Southern Indiana Gas and Electric Co., "Our Transportation System—An Early Flood Victim," *SIGECO News* 4 (March 1937): 274. For Cincinnati, see Cincinnati Street Railway, *Flood of January 1937* (Cincinnati: Cincinnati Street Railway, 1937).

56. "Public Water Systems in the Flood," *Factory Mutual Record* 14 (March/April 1937): 6.

57. Southern Indiana Gas and Electric Co., "Our Transportation System," 275.

58. U.S. Congress, Senate, Corps of Engineers, *Hearings Before the Committee on Flood Control (1937),* "Statement of Captain Miles Reber, Louisville District, U.S. Army," 109.

59. This is true, at least, for bridges, streets, and railways.

60. For examples of such flow obstructions on the Ohio River, see Ohio Water Commission, *The Problem: Floods in Ohio; An Interview with Miles M. Dawson, Brig. Gen. U.S.A. (Ret.), Consulting Engineer* (Based upon a study for The Ohio Water Commission) (Columbus: Ohio Water Commission, 1960), 8–10.

61. See A. Melih Yanmaz, "Flood Interaction with River Crossings: A Case Study," in *Coping with Floods,* ed. Giuseppe Rossi, Nilgun Harmancioglu, and Vujica Yevjevich (Dordrecht: NATO Advanced Study Institute, 1994), 565.

62. For bridges as "systems of risk," see Wolfgang Bonß, *Vom Risiko: Unsicherheit und Ungewißheit in der Moderne* (Hamburg: Hamburger Edition, 1995), 68.

63. See Department of the Interior, *The Ohio Valley Flood of March–April 1913 (including Comparisons with Some Earlier Floods),* by A. H. Horton and H. J. Jackson, Water-Supply Paper 334, United States Geological Survey (Washington, DC: GPO, 1913), 85. For the bridges in Hamilton, Ohio, especially for the collapse of the High Street Bridge, see ibid., illustration xxi. An illustrated history of the bridges in Hamilton in the last two centuries and their destruction by floods can be found in Carl M. Becker and Patrick B. Nolan, *Keeping the Promise* (Dayton: Landfall Press, 1988), 178–83.

64. Lewis S. Bigelow, *The 1913 Flood and How It Was Met by a Railroad* (Pittsburgh: Pennsylvania Lines, 1913), 54; Charles Wilbur Garrett (Comp.), *Pennsylvania Lines,*

West of Pittsburgh: A History of the Flood of March 1913 (Pittsburgh: Pennsylvania Lines, 1913). In 1927, after devastating floods in New England, twenty-three bridges were destroyed in Northern Vermont alone, see William E. Leuchtenburg, *Flood Control Politics: The Connecticut River Valley Problem, 1927–1950* (Cambridge: Harvard University Press, 1953), 29.

65. U.S. Congress, "Statement of Maj. Gen. Edward M. Markham, Chief of Engineers, United States Army, Accompanied by Lt. Col. David M. Coach, Corps of Engineers," *Hearings Before the Committee on Flood Control*, 39.

66. Yanmaz, "Flood Interaction with River Crossings," 565. See also Uwe Lübken, "'Der große Brückentod': Überschwemmungen als infrastrukturelle Konflikte im 19. und 20. Jahrhundert," *Saeculum: Jahrbuch für Universalgeschichte* 58, no. 1 (2007): 89–114.

67. White, "Human Adjustment to Floods," 2. See also Burrell Montz and Eve C. Gruntfest, "Changes in American urban floodplain occupancy since 1958: the experience of nine cities," *Applied Geography* 6 (1986): 325–38; Gilbert F. White et al., *Changes in Urban Occupance of Flood Plains in the United States* (Chicago: University of Chicago, Department of Geography, 1958); Raymond J. Burby et al., *Cities under Water: A Comparative Evaluation of Ten Cities' Efforts to Manage Floodplain Land Use* (Boulder: Institute of Behavioral Science, 1988); G. E. Hollis, "The Effect of Urbanization on Floods of Different Recurrence Interval," *Water Resources Research* 11 (1975): 431–34.

68. White, "Human Adjustment to Floods," 2.

69. See Lawrence J. Vale and Thomas J. Campanella, eds., *The Resilient City: How Modern Cities Recover From Disaster* (New York: Oxford University Press, 2005).

70. Cincinnati Chamber of Commerce, *The Great Flood in the Ohio* (Cincinnati: Cincinnati Chamber of Commerce, 1884), 106.

71. "Public Water Systems in the Flood," 7.

72. Ibid., 6. Thirsty Cincinnatians could even tap their own water at eighty-five taps that were even illuminated at night. See "Longest Faucet Bar," *Cincinnati Enquirer*, 2 February 1937; "Water, Not Beer Drawn at Brewery," *Cincinnati Times-Star*, 31 January 1937; White, "Human Adjustment to Floods," 87.

73. "Public Water Systems in the Flood," 6.

74. The absence of an expected flood, however, could become costly. See *Wall Street Journal*, 27 April 1901: "Worry, however, was the worst feature of the whole affair. So frightened were the manufacturers that preparations were made by the large majority for floods that had never before been reached with the result that the greatest damage was the moving of materials out of harm's way and the loss of time and expense of such moving."

8. THE ST. LAWRENCE AND MONTREAL'S SPATIAL DEVELOPMENT IN THE SEVENTEENTH THROUGH THE TWENTIETH CENTURY

This chapter is a revised version of an article published as "Le Saint-Laurent et la structuration de l'espace montréalais, XVIIe-XXe siècle," *Études canadiennes/Ca-*

nadian Studies (Journal of the Association française d'études canadiennes) 50 (June 2001): 19–32.

1. The title was changed in the 1956 edition, regularly reprinted since, see Donald G. Creighton, *The Empire of the St. Lawrence* (Toronto: Macmillan, 1956).

2. Raoul Blanchard, *L'est du Canada français: Province de Québec*, 2 vols. (Paris and Montreal: Librairie Masson and Libraire Beauchemin, 1935); *Le centre du Canada français: Province de Québec* (Montreal: Beauchemin, 1947); *L'ouest du Canada français: Montréal et sa région* (Montreal: Beauchemin, 1953); *L'ouest du Canada français: Les pays de l'Ottawa, l'Abitibi—Témiscamingue* (Montreal: Beauchemin, 1954).

3. Donald G. Creighton, "The Decline and Fall of the Empire of the St. Lawrence," Canadian Historical Association, *Historical Papers* (1969): 14–25.

4. Louis-Edmond Hamelin, "Raoul Blanchard, " in *Mélanges géographiques canadiens offerts à Raoul Blanchard,* ed. L.-E. Hamelin (Quebec: Les Presses Universitaires Laval, 1959), 13–26; "La géographie du Québec cinquante ans après Raoul Blanchard, " special issue, *Cahiers de géographie du Québec* 30, no. 80 (September 1986).

5. Raoul Blanchard, *Le Canada français: Province de Québec* (Montreal: Fayard, 1960), 47.

6. This text is based on extensive documentation; for a discussion of sources and a bibliography, see Jean-Claude Robert, *Atlas historique de Montréal* (Montreal: Libre Expression et Art Global, 1994).

7. Jean-Claude Lasserre, *Le Saint-Laurent: Grande porte de l'Amérique* (Montreal: HMH, 1980), 22–23.

8. Anthropologists refer to the indigenous people who Jacques Cartier encountered but who later disappeared mysteriously from the landscape at the end of the sixteenth century as the St. Lawrence Iroquoians. They are not to be confused with the Five Nations Iroquois. See work by Bruce Trigger, and in particular plate 33 in R. Cole Harris, ed., and G. J. Matthews, cartographer and designer, *Historical Atlas of Canada,* vol. 1, *From the Beginning to 1800* (Toronto: University of Toronto Press, 1987).

9. Gilles Havard, *La Grande Paix de Montréal de 1701: Les voies de la diplomatie franco-amérindienne* (Montreal: Recherches Amérindiennes au Québec, 1992).

10. Jean-Claude Robert, "Les Sulpiciens et l'espace montréalais," in *Les Sulpiciens de Montréal: Une histoire de pouvoir et de discrétion, 1657–2007,* ed. D. Deslandres, J. A. Dickinson, and O. Hubert (Montreal: Fides, 2007), 155–78.

11. Louise Dechêne, *Habitants et marchands de Montréal au XVIIe siècle* (Paris: Plon, 1974).

12. Reproductions of the maps can be found in Marcel Trudel, *Montréal, la formation d'une société, 1642–1663* (Montreal: Fides, 1976).

13. Despite this failure, the Royal Proclamation of 1763 marked the formal recognition of the rights of North American Indians to their ancestral land; in Canada, recent court rulings are based on this document, which thus acts as a treaty. For an analysis of the place of old New France in the British Empire, see Pierre Tousignant, "The Integration of the Province of Quebec into the British Empire, 1763–91," *Dictionary of Canadian Biography*, vol. 4 (Toronto: University of Toronto Press,

1979), xxxiv–liii; Philip Lawson, *The Imperial Challenge: Quebec and Britain in the Age of American Revolution* (Montreal: McGill-Queen's University Press, 1989).

14. These various consequences of the War of the Conquest are often overshadowed by the one American War of Independence in the historiography of the United States, but work by Fred Anderson suggests a reinterpretation. See Anderson's *The Crucible of War: The Seven Year's War and the Fate of Empire in British North America, 1754–1766* (New York: Alfred A. Knopf, 2000).

15. Pauline Desjardins, *Le Vieux-Port de Montréal* (Montreal: Éditions de l'Homme, 2007).

16. Robert Lewis, *Manufacturing Montreal: The Making of an Industrial Landscape, 1850 to 1930* (Baltimore: The Johns Hopkins University Press, 2000).

17. Paul-André Linteau, *Histoire de Montréal depuis la Confédération* (Montreal: Boréal, 1992).

18. Jean-Claude Robert, "Catholicisme et urbanisation au Canada français, XIXe–XXe siècles," in *Pour une histoire sociale des villes*, ed. Philippe Haudrère (Rennes: Presses universitaires de Rennes, 2006), 415–26.

19. Jean-Claude Marsan, *Montréal en évolution*, 3rd ed. (Montreal: Méridien, 1994), 161–306. An English translation also exists: *Montreal in Evolution* (Montreal: McGill-Queen's University Press, 1990).

20. Richard White, *The Middle Ground: Indians, Empires, and Republics in the Great Lakes Region, 1650–1815* (New York: Cambridge University Press, 1991).

9. URBANIZATION, INDUSTRIALIZATION, AND THE FIRTH OF FORTH

Thanks are especially due to Mairi Stewart, Margaret Richards, Tom Leatherland, the late William Halcrow, and Robert Morris for comments and help, also to Gavin McCrone and Robin Harper. I alone am responsible for errors. Thanks also to the Leverhulme Trust for helping to fund the research behind this chapter.

1. M. Wilkinson and C. M. Scanlon, "The attached algal flora of the estuary and Firth of Forth, Scotland," *Proceedings of the Royal Society of Edinburgh, Section B (Biological Sciences)* (hereafter *Proc. RSE: B* 93) (1987): 343–54.

2. R. J. Morris, "In search of twentieth-century Edinburgh," *Book of the Old Edinburgh Club*, n.s. 8 (2010): 13–25.

3. R. H. Campbell, *Carron Company* (Edinburgh: Oliver and Boyd, 1961).

4. *Glasgow Corporation Water Works Commemorative Volume* (Glasgow: 1877), 4–19.

5. City of Glasgow, *Municipal Glasgow: Its Evolution and Enterprises* (Glasgow: R. Gibson, 1914), 273–77. For unpublished details relating to Stirling council, I am indebted to Dr Jan Oosthoek.

6. *Report of the Scottish Fisheries Board* (1913), 258; H. M. Cadell, "Land reclamation in the Forth Valley," *Scottish Geographical Magazine* 45 (1929): 10.

7. S. Mullay, *The Edinburgh Encyclopedia* (Edinburgh: Mainstream, 1996).

8. Scottish Development Department, *A Measure of Plenty: Water Resources in Scotland; A General Survey* (Edinburgh: 1973), 47.

9. G. Robertson, *General View of the Agriculture of the County of Midlothian* (Edinburgh: HMSO, 1793), 48–49.

10. M. W. Flinn, ed., *Scottish Population History from the Seventeenth Century to the 1930s* (New York: Cambirdge University Press, 1977).

11. Mullay, *Encyclopedia*, 316; Report of the Royal Commission on River Pollution Fourth Report, *Scotland, Parliamentary Papers 1872* (hereafter *RC River Pollution* 1872), 2: 99, 123.

12. The definitive account is P. J. Smith, "The foul burns of Edinburgh," *Scottish Geographical Magazine* 91 (1975): 23–36; see also *RC River Pollution, 1872*, 1: 20–22; W. Baird, *Annals of Duddingston and Portobello* (Edinburgh: A. Eliot, 1898), 421–23.

13. N. Goddard, "'A mine of wealth,' the Victorians and the agricultural value of sewage," *Journal of Historical Geography* 22 (1996): 274–90; *British Medical Journal*, 27 September 1873.

14. *RC River Pollution*, 1872, 1: 19.

15. Ibid, 1: 20, 65; 2: 313.

16. Ibid, 1: 22–24, 44–45, 69–70, 316.

17. Ibid, 2: 313.

18. R. Shand, "The rise and fall of seaduck at Levenmouth," *Fife Bird Report 2006* (Fife: Fife Bird Club, 2007), 150–51.

19. *RC River Pollution*, 1872, 2: 312.

20. *Ibid*, 2: 112, 121.

21. *Hansard Commons Debates*, 4 June 1885.

22. Report to the Secretary for Scotland by the Inspector for Scotland under the Rivers Pollution Act of 1876, *Parliamentary Papers*, 1898.

23. Report of the Commissioners on Salmon Fisheries Part I, *Parliamentary Papers,* 1902, 41, 408–14.

24. J. Sheail, *An Environmental History of Twentieth-Century Britain* (Basingstoke: Palgrave, 2002), 48–56.

25. Cadell, "Land reclamation," 7–22, 81–99.

26. *Reports of the Scottish Fisheries Board* for the years cited.

27. P. Maitland, "The freshwater fish fauna of the Forth area," *Forth Naturalist and Historian* 4 (1979): 39–40; Scottish Environment Protection Agency (hereafter SEPA), East Region, "Water Quality in the Forth Estuary 1980–1999," *Report*, July 2000, 19.

28. W. F. Collett, "The Quality of the Forth Estuary (1)," *Proc. RSE: B* 71 (1971/2): 138–41.

29. D. S. McLusky, "Ecology of the Forth estuary," *Forth Naturalist and Historian* 3 (1978): 10–13; *SEPA View* 40 (2008): 4.

30. M. Elliott and A. H. Griffiths, "Contamination and effects of hydrocarbons on the Forth ecosystem, Scotland," *Proc. RSE: B* 93 (1987); D. S. McLusky, "The impact of petrochemical effluent on the fauna of an intertidal estuarine mudflat," *Estuarine, Coastal and Shelf Science* 14 (1982): 489–99; D. S. McLusky, "Intertidal habitats and benthic macrofauna of the Forth estuary, Scotland." *Proc. RSE: B* 71 (1987): 389–400; "Meiofauna of the industrialised estuary and Firth of Forth, Scotland," *Proc. RSE: B* 71 (1987):415–30.

31. R. W. Covill, "The quality of the Forth estuary (2)," *Proc. RSE: B* 71 (1971/2):

143–70; R. W. Covill, "Progress in pollution control in the Lothians, area, Scotland," *Journal of the Water Pollution Control Federation* 38 (1966): 1634–44.

32. Covill, "Forth estuary." Many of the papers in *Proc. RSE:B* 93 (1987) are directed to the problem, but see especially A. H. Griffiths, "Water quality of the estuary and Firth of Forth, Scotland," 303–14; "Microbial measurements in relation to sewage pollution of the Firth of Forth, Scotland," 363–76; P. Read, "The intertidal benthos and sediments of particulate shores in the Firth of Forth, Scotland, with particular reference to waste water discharges," 401–13; D. C. Moore and I. M. Davies, "Monitoring the effects of the disposal at sea of Lothian region sewage sludge," 467–78.

33. R. Forrester, I. Andrews et al., ed., *The Birds of Scotland* (2007), 1: 226, 238, 272; L. H. Campbell, "The impact of changes in sewage treatment on seaducks wintering in the Firth of Forth, Scotland," *Biological Conservation* 28 (1984): 173–86.

34. Shand, "Seaduck at Levenmouth"; William Halcrow, personal communication.

35. SEPA, *Significant Water Management Issues in the Scotland river basin districts* (Stirling: SEPA, 2007).

36. R. Levitt, *Implementing Public Policy* (London: Croom Helm, 1980); R. K. Wurzel, *Environmental Policy Making in Britain, Germany and the European Union* (Manchester: Manchester University Press, 2002). Thanks also to Tom Leatherland and William Halcrow for guidance here.

37. O. MacDonagh, *A Pattern of Government Growth, 1800–1860: Passenger Acts and Their Enforcement* (London: MacGibbon and Kee, 1961).

38. This is well dealt with in Sheail, *Environmental History*.

39. Wurzel, *Environmental Policy Making*, 212.

40. See R. J. Morris, "Externalities, the market, power structure and the urban agenda," *Urban History* 17 (1990): 99–109.

41. See R. J. Morris and R. H. Trainor, ed., *Urban Governance: Britain and Beyond since 1750* (Aldershot: Ashgate, 2000); J. Garrard, *Leadership and Power in Victorian Industrial Towns 1839–80* (Manchester: Manchester University Press, 1983)

42. R. Inglehart, *Silent Revolution* (Princeton: Princeton University Press, 1977).

43. Wurzel, *Environmental Policy Making*, 227, 245.

10. DIVERTING RIVERS FOR PARIS, 1760–1820: NEEDS, QUALITY, RESISTANCE

1. Antoine Deparcieux, "Mémoire sur la possibilité d'amener à Paris mille à douze cent pouces d'eau, belle et de bonne qualité, " *Mémoires de l'Académie Royale des Sciences, année 1762* (Paris: Imprimerie royale, 1764), 337–401.

2. L.-Ch.-F. Petit-Radel, *Notice historique comparée sur les aqueducs des anciens et la dérivation de la rivière d'Ourcq* (Paris: Langlois, 1803), 1.

3. Jean Bouchary, *L'eau à Paris à la fin du 18e siècle: La compagnie des eaux de Paris et l'entreprise de l'Yvette* (Paris: Marcel Rivière, 1946); Isabelle Backouche, *La trace du fleuve: La Seine et Paris (1750–1850)* (Paris: Éditions de l'École des Hautes Études en Sciences Sociales, 2000); Frédéric Graber, *Paris a besoin d'eau: Projet, dispute et délibération technique dans la France napoléonienne* (Paris: CNRS Éditions, 2009).

4. This was the case for the Arcueil aqueduct in Paris, which primarily fed the Luxembourg Gardens. In the case of Lorient, the water conveyance system was exclusively for the use of the Compagnie des Indes and ran through the city without feeding any public fountains. See D. Massounie, *Monuments hydrauliques urbains: Aqueducs, châteaux d'eau et fontaines dans la ville moderne, 1661–1791* (PhD thesis, Université Paris 1, 2000).

5. Frédéric Graber, "La qualité de l'eau à Paris, 1760–1820," *Entreprises et Histoire* 50 (2008): 119–33; L. Beaumont-Maillet, *L'eau à Paris* (Paris: Hazan, 1991); Daniel Roche, *Histoire des choses banales: Naissance de la consommation dans les sociétés traditionnelles, 17e–18e siècles* (Paris: Fayard, 1997).

6. Massounie, *Monuments hydrauliques urbains*, 18–87.

7. De Fer thus proclaimed the "six thousand arms released to industry and agriculture" and did not seem concerned by the potential protests of these water carriers, even though they had damaged the Perier brothers' business. N. de Fer de la Nouerre, *Mémoire sur l'Yvette lu à l'Académie royale des sciences le 10 janvier 1789* (n.p.: n.d.).

8. On the question of need and its reformulation by Deparcieux, see Frédéric Graber, "Inventing needs: Expertise and water-supply in late eighteenth- and early nineteenth-century Paris," *British Journal for the History of Science* 40, no. 3 (2007): 315–32.

9. Antoine Deparcieux, *Essai sur les probabilités de la durée de la vie humaine* (Paris, Guérin, 1746). On this subject, see Cem Behar and Yves Ducel, "L'arithmétique politique d'Antoine Deparcieux, " in *Arithmétique politique dans la France du 18e siècle,* ed. Thierry Martin (Paris: Éditions de l'INED, 2003), 147–61.

10. Alain Desrosière, *La politique des grands nombres: Histoire de la raison statistique* (Paris: La Découverte, 1993); Nicolas Lemas, "Le temps des projets: Poncet de la Grave, Delamair ou l'impensé de l'urbanisme au siècle des Lumières," *Histoire urbaine* 5, no. 1 (2002): 43–65.

11. As exemplified in the rhetoric of the Perier brothers, see *Distribution d'eau de la Seine dans tous les quartiers et toutes les maisons de Paris* (Paris: Veuve Ballard, 1777), 4.

12. It should be noted that there were no census or official calculations to which the authors of these projects, even if they were part of the administration or the scientific elite, had access: the difference in figures can be explained both by the desired result and the method used to estimate population size, such as the population multiplier. See Desrosière, *La politique des grands nombres*, 36.

13. On water quality in Paris, see Graber, "La qualité de l'eau à Paris, 1760–1820."

14. Contrary to the late eighteenth-century enterprises, where commercial competition fed public disputes and attempted to attract consumers, investors, and officials, the Ourcq canal, which was assigned to the Ponts-et-Chaussées corps in the early nineteenth century, would only give rise to debate within the corps itself. These engineers would distance themselves from the earlier debates and adopt an original position on water quality, replacing Parmentier's qualitative criteria (purification through movement) with a quantitative approach: they would attempt to evaluate the flow velocity at which water became pure, which allowed them to in-

clude velocity as a decisive construction parameter, and thus hope to decide one of the main issues that divided these engineers: reconciling navigation and potability.

15. Purification by filtration was sometimes considered in the eighteenth century, but most authors considered filters problematic, as they reduce the amount of air in the water, generally considered a criteria of quality.

16. *Letters from the receiver Prunay to the engineer Bruyère*, Nivose 13 and 17, Year 11, Manuscript 2406, Archives of the École nationale des Ponts et Chaussées (MENPC).

17. This alternative was at the heart of the Ourcq debate. See Graber, *Paris a besoin d'eau.*

18. On De Fer, see Bouchary, *L'eau à Paris à la fin du 18e siècle*, 53.

19. It could not oblige all the owners on a street to subscribe and had to allow the water carriers to remain masters of the fountains.

20. *Arrêt du conseil d'État du roi qui autorise l'exécution du projet de l'Yvette, 3 Novembre 1787* (Paris: Cailleau, 1787)

21. *Rapport de MM. De Fourqueux, Fargès, de Bacquencourt, Bertier, de Crosne et de la Millière, commissaires du Conseil, chargés par arrêt du 21 mai 1786 de l'examen des plans et projets relatifs aux rivières d'Yvette et de Bièvres et de MM. le marquis de Condorcet, le chevalier de Borda, l'abbé Bossut et Coulomb, membres de l'Académie des sciences qui leurs ont été associés*, August 21, 1787, Archives Nationales (hereafter as AN) F14–683A.

22. *Lettre de l'assemblée municipale d'Antony à l'assemblée de la commission intermédiaire du département de Créteil*, February 3, 1788, AN F14–682. De Fer responded that most of these mills were idle anyway in summer (the only time when a water shortage might be seen), see *Observation contre la requête au conseil*, no date, AN F14–682.

23. Thomas Le Roux, *Les nuisances artisanales et industrielles à Paris, 1770–1830* (PhD thesis, Université Paris 1, 2007), 92–97.

24. *Observations pour les propriétaires et intéressés à la conservation des eaux de la rivière de Bièvre, dites des Gobelins, contre le prétendu projet de l'Yvette* (Paris: Jorry, 1789), 2.

25. Jean-Louis Harouel, *Histoire de l'expropriation* (Paris: PUF, 2000).

26. See the complaint filed by Vitalis de Migneaux (Syndic for the Parish of Verrières, who emerged as a central figure in the dispute) with the Provosty of Antony, October 21, 1788, AN F14–682.

27. See, for instance, *Lettre à monseigneur l'intendant de la généralité de Paris, commissaire en cette partie*, March 19, 1788, signed by a large number of owners, AN F14–682.

28. *Lettre de Bertier à Breteuil*, May 22, 1788, AN F14–682. Bertier seems to have been overwhelmed by De Fer's fierce initiatives on several occasions and to have had trouble getting him to obey.

29. *Arrêt de la cour du parlement, du 3 décembre 1788, qui entr'autres choses, fait défenses au Sieur Defer . . .* (Paris: Jolly, 1788).

30. *Arrêt du conseil d'État du roi qui casse et annule les arrêts du parlement relatifs à l'entreprise de l'Yvette* (Paris: Cailleau, 1789).

31. *Arrêt du conseil d'État du roi concernant l'entreprise des travaux des rivières de l'Yvette et de la Bièvre par le Sieur Defer, du 11 avril 1789* (Paris: Cailleau, 1789). Like his opponents, De Fer issued a large number of publications, either to attract and reassure shareholders or to decry the entrepreneur's means and objectives.

32. *Canal de l'Yvette Rapport et avis du directoire du district du Bourg-la-Reine*, June 17, 1791, AN F14–682.

33. *Lettre de l'assemblée municipale d'Antony à l'assemblée de la commission intermédiaire du département de Créteil*, February 3, 1788, AN F14–682.

34. For the various uses and concerns related to the new canal, see *Extrait du Procès verbal fait par Messieurs les Officiers de la Maîtrise de Paris, commencé le 28 janvier dernier et jours suivants, en vertu des Arrêts du Parlement des 29 novembre, 10 décembre 1788, 4 et 7 février 1789*, (n.p.: n.d.).

35. *Lettre de Bertier à Breteuil*, May 22, 1788, AN F14–682.

36. The plaintiffs' lawyer mentioned 15 million (Parens, *Sur la requête présentée au roi étant en son conseil . . .*, AN F14–683A). Another brief from the opponents (*Notions sur le projet de l'Yvette*, AN F14–683A) proposed an inventory of the various establishments, with their construction costs (Gobelins, 6 million; Julien, 2 million; Moinery 1.5 million; etc.), thus arriving at a cost of over 20 million for the faubourg as a whole.

37. Parens, *Sur la requête présentée au roi étant en son conseil.*

38. Haim Burstin, *Le Faubourg Saint-Marcel à l'Époque Révolutionnaire: Structure économique et composition sociale* (Paris: Société des études Robespierristes, 1983). The canal held an important place in the grievance books of riverside parishes.

39. *Lettre de Villedeuil à . . .*, April 13, 1789, AN F14–683B.

40. *Lettre d'un habitant du faubourg Saint-Marcel au curé de V. sur l'affaire de l'Yvette*, (n.p.: n.d.), 10–12.

41. *Lettre de l'assemblée municipale d'Antony à l'assemblée de la commission intermédiaire du département de Créteil*, February 3, 1788, AN F14–682. Parens (*Sur la requête présentée au roi étant en son conseil . . .*) also stated that "De Fer was careful not to call upon any inhabitants or owners who would have established that such disadvantages existed."

42. *Observations pour les propriétaires et intéressés à la conservation des eaux de la rivière de Bièvre, dites des Gobelins, contre le prétendu projet de l'Yvette*, 12 and 33.

43. On *de commodo et incommodo* inquiries, see Le Roux, *Les nuisances artisanales et industrielles à Paris.*

44. *Lettre de Coiseron à Breteuil*, March 28, 1788, AN F14–682. A former Paris city councilor who lived on the Bièvre and was in favor of the canal, Coiseron reported a number of abuses, including the excessive width.

45. De Fer, *Mémoire sur l'Yvette, lu à l'Académie royale des Sciences le 10 janvier 1789*, (n.p.: n.d.), 7.

46. Parens, *Sur la requête présentée au roi étant en son conseil.*

47. Ibid.

48. *Arrest du conseil d'Estat du Roi, qui fait un règlement général de police et de conservation des eaux de la rivière de Bièvre* (Paris: Prault, 1732). Bertier was surprised that the Provost of merchants and the Lieutenant of Paris, members of the 1786 committee, seemed to be unaware of the existence of these regulations, see *Lettre de Bertier à Breteuil*, May 22, 1788, AN F14–682.

49. *Arrêt du conseil d'État du roi qui autorise l'exécution du projet de l'Yvette, 3 Novembre 1787* (Paris: Cailleau, 1787), 3. As is often the case in this type of concession, the king

reserved the right to later establish the entire canal as a fief. See Anne Conchon, "Financer la construction d'infrastructures de transport: la concession au 17e et 18e siècle," *Entreprises et histoire* 38, no. 1 (2005): 55–70.

50. See, for instance, Cl.-J. de Ferrière, *Dictionnaire de droit et de pratique* (Paris: Brunet, 1769), 539; or Guyot, *Répertoire universel et raisonné de jurisprudence* (Paris: Panckoucke, 1783), vol. 56, 572–78.

51. *Observations pour les propriétaires et intéressés à la conservation des eaux de la rivière de Bièvre, dites des Gobelins, contre le prétendu projet de l'Yvette*, 13 and 15–16.

52. *Canal de l'Yvette: Rapport et avis du directoire du district du Bourg-la-Reine*, June 17, 1791, AN F14–682.

53. See, for instance, Nicolas de La Mare, *Traité de police* (Paris: Cot, 1705), vol. 1, 557–59.

11. FLUID GEOGRAPHIES: URBANIZING RIVER BASINS

1. Louis P. Cain, *Sanitation Strategy for a Lakefront Metropolis: The Case of Chicago* (Dekalb: Northern Illinois University Press, 1978).

2. Richard White, *The Organic Machine* (New York: Hill and Wang, 1995); Mark Cioc, *The Rhine: An Eco-biography* (Seattle: University of Washington Press, 2002); and Matthew D. Evenden, *Fish versus Power: An Environmental History of the Fraser River* (New York: Cambridge University Press, 2004).

3. Joel A. Tarr, "The Search for the Ultimate Sink: Urban Air, Land, and Water Pollution," *Records of the Columbia Historical Society of Washington, D.C.* 51 (1984): 1–29. See also, Joel A. Tarr, *The Search for the Ultimate Sink: Urban Pollution in Historical Perspective* (Akron: University of Akron Press, 1996).

4. Theodore Steinberg, *Nature Incorporated: Industrialization and the Waters of New England* (Amherst: University of Massachusetts Press, 1991); and Christine Meisner Rosen, "'Knowing' Industrial Pollution: Nuisance Law and the Power of Tradition in a Time of Rapid Economic Change," *Environmental History* 8, no. 4 (2003): 565–98.

5. Joel A. Tarr, "The Metabolism of the Industrial City," *Journal of Urban History* 28 (2002): 511–45, quote on 511.

6. Erik Swyngedouw, "Metabolic Urbanization: The Making of Cyborg Cities," in *In the Nature of Cities: Urban Political Ecology and the Politics of Urban Metabolism*, ed. Nik Heynen, Maria Kaika, and Erik Swyngedouw (New York: Routledge, 2006), 21–40, quote on 37. See also Matthew Gandy, "Rethinking Urban Metabolism: Water, Space and the Modern City," *City* 8, no. 3 (2004): 363–79; and Erik Swyngedouw, *Social Power and the Urbanization of Water: Flows of Power* (New York: Oxford University Press, 2004).

7. See Matthew Gandy, *Concrete and Clay: Reworking Nature in New York City* (Cambridge: MIT Press, 2002).

8. William Cronon, *Nature's Metropolis: Chicago and the Great West* (New York: W. W. Norton, 1991), 63.

9. Cain, *Sanitation Strategy*, 28.

10. Ibid., see esp. ch. 3.

11. Ibid., 63–64.

12. Illinois State Board of Health (hereafter ISBH), *Water Supplies of Illinois and the Pollution of its Streams* (Springfield: ISBH, 1889), xvii.

13. L. E. Cooley, "The Illinois River and Its Relations to Sanitary Engineering," in *Water Supplies of Illinois*, ed. John H. Rauch (Springfield: ISBH, 1889), 1; and Jacob A. Harmon for the ISBH, "Report of a Preliminary Sanitary Survey of the Illinois River Drainage Basin," in *Report of the Sanitary investigations of the Illinois River and Tributaries* (Springfield: ISBH, 1901), 100.

14. See M. O. Leighton, "Pollution of the Illinois and Mississippi Rivers by Chicago Sewage," *U.S. Geological Survey Water-Supply and Irrigation Paper 194* (Washington, DC: U.S. Government Printing Office, 1907), and Cain, *Sanitation Strategy*. See also, *Missouri v. Illinois* 200 US 496, 1905.

15. ISBH, *Report of Sanitary Investigations of the Illinois Rivers and Its Tributaries*, xii.

16. Ibid., xxiv.

17. J. K. Hoskins, C. C. Ruchhoft, and L. G. Williams for the U.S. Public Health Service, "A Study of the Pollution and Natural Purification of the Illinois River," *Public Health Bulletin* 171 (Washington, DC: U.S. Government Printing Office, 1927), 196.

18. L. E. Cooley, *The Diversion of the Waters of the Great Lakes* (Chicago: Sanitary District of Chicago, 1913), 144. Subsequent reports show the fish catch was much greater for the entire basin. It is unclear what segment of the river Cooley is referring to.

19. Illinois State Board of Fish Commissioners, *Report of State Board of Fish Commissioners, 1902–1904*, Illinois State Journal (Springfield: Illinois State Board of Fish Commissioners, 1905), 32.

20. Stephen A. Forbes and R. E. Richardson, "Studies on the Biology of the Upper Illinois River," *Illinois State Laboratory of Natural History Bulletin* 9, no. 10 (1913): 481–574; and W. C. Purdy for the U.S. Public Health Service, "A Study of the Pollution and Natural Purification of the Illinois River," *Public Health Bulletin* 198 (Washington, DC: U.S. Government Printing Office, 1930).

21. Hoskins, Ruchhoft, and Williams, *A Study of Pollution*, 25.

22. J. W. Alford and C. B. Burdick for the Illinois Rivers and Lakes Commission, *Report of the Rivers and Lakes Commission on the Illinois Rivers and Its Bottom Lands* (Springfield, 1915).

23. Daniel Schneider, "Enclosing the Floodplain: Resource Conflict on the Illinois River, 1880–1920," *Environmental History* 1. 2 (1996): 70–96; and John Thompson, *Wetlands Drainage, River Modification, and Sectoral Conflict in the Lower Illinois River Valley, 1890–1930* (Carbondale: Southern Illinois University, 2002).

24. Hoskins, Ruchhoft, and Williams, "A Study of Pollution."

25. Drainage Basin Committees (hereafter DBC), *DBC Reports for the Upper Mississippi Basins* 60 (Washington, DC: U.S. Government Printing Office, 1937), 37.

26. DBC, *DBC Reports for the Upper Mississippi Basins*, 38.

27. Illinois River Pollution Commission, *Report to the 67th Illinois General Assembly* (Springfield: Illinois River Pollution Commission, 1951), 10.

28. See Craig E. Colten, "Illinois River Pollution Control, 1900–1970," in *The American Environment: Interpretations of Past Geographies*, ed. Lary M. Dilsaver and Craig E. Colten (Lanham: Rowman and Littlefield, 1992), 193–216.

29. U.S. Public Health Service, *Upper Mississippi Drainage Basin: Summary Report on Water Pollution* (Washington, D.C.: U.S. Government Printing Office, 1951), 60–71.

30. H. B. Mills, W. C. Starrett, and F. C. Bellrose, "Man's Effect on the Fish and Wildlife of the Illinois River," *Illinois Natural History Survey Biological Notes* 57 (1966): 12

31. M. O. Leighton, U. S. Congress, Senate, *Pollution of Potomac River*, 58th Cong., 3rd sess., 1905, Doc. 181; and President's Water Resources Policy Commission, "The Potomac," in *Ten Rivers in America's Future: The Report of the President's Water Resources Commission*, vol. 2 (Washington, DC: U.S. Government Printing Office, 1950), 594.

32. Leighton, *Pollution of Potomac River*, 2.

33. Ibid., 7.

34. Ibid., 9.

35. M. J. Rosenau, L. L. Lumsden, and J. H. Kastle for the U.S. Public Health and Marine-Hospital Service, "Report on the Origin and Prevalence of Typhoid Fever in the District of Columbia, " *Hygienic Laboratory Bulletin* 35 (1907); and L. L. Lumsden and J. F. Anderson for the U.S. Public Health and Marine-Hospital Service, "Report No. 4 on the Origin and Prevalence of Typhoid Fever in the District of Columbia (1909–1910)," *Hygienic Laboratory Bulletin* 78 (1911).

36. Hugh S. Cumming for the U.S. Public Health Service, "Investigation of the Pollution and Sanitary Conditions of the Potomac Watershed," *Hygienic Laboratory Bulletin* 104 (1916): 228.

37. Cumming, "Investigation of the Pollution and Sanitary Conditions of the Potomac Watershed," 230.

38. See for example, Tarr, "Search for the Ultimate Sink."

39. U. S. Congress, Senate, *Disposal of Sewage in the Potomac River*, 72nd Cong., 2nd sess., 1933, Document 172, 10–14.

40. U.S. National Resources Committee and Water Resources Committee (hereafter WRC), *Drainage Basin Committee Report for the Chesapeake Bay Drainage Basins* (Washington, DC: U.S. Government Printing Office, 1937), 13. The WRC prepared a series of reports for river basins nationwide. This series provides one point of intersection for the three basins considered here.

41. U. S. Congress, *Hearing before the Joint Committee on Washington Metropolitan Problems: Water Supply and Pollution Problems in Maryland, Virginia, and the Washington Metropolitan Area*, 85th Cong., 2nd sess., 1958, 518.

42. U.S. National Resources Committee and WRC, *Drainage Basin Committee Report for the Chesapeake Bay Drainage Basins*, 14–16.

43. President's Water Resources Policy Commission, "The Potomac," 594–95.

44. Ibid., 596–97; and Federal Security Agency, Public Health Service, *Report on Water Pollution Control: Potomac River Basin, 1951* (New York: U.S. Government Printing Office, 1951), 34–46.

45. Federal Security Agency, Public Health Service, *Summary Report on Water Pollution: North Atlantic Drainage Basins* (Washington, DC: U.S. Government Printing Office, 1951), 126–31.

46. President's Water Resources Policy Commission, "The Potomac," 595–96. See also, John R. Wennersten, *Anacostia: Death and Life of an American River* (Washington: Chesapeake Book Company, 2008).

47. F. W. Kitrell for the Public Health Service, "A Review of Interstate Pollution of the Potomac River in the Washington Metropolitan Area," in U.S. Congress, *Hearing before the Joint Committee on Washington Metropolitan Problems: Water Supply and Pollution Problems in Maryland, Virginia, and the Washington Metropolitan Area*, 85th Cong., 2nd sess., 1958, 517 and 523.

48. U.S. Congress, *Hearing before the Joint Committee on Washington Metropolitan Problems*, 196 and 199; and U.S. Department of the Interior, Federal Water Pollution Control Administration, *Potomac River Water Quality* (Cincinnati: Federal Water Pollution Control Administration, 1969), 7.

49. U.S. Army Corps of Engineers, North Atlantic Division, *Washington Metropolitan Water Supply Study Report* (Baltimore: Dept. of Defense, Dept. of the Army, Corps of Engineers, North Atlantic Division, 1975), 9.

50. U.S. Army Corps of Engineers, North Atlantic Division, *Potomac River Basin Report* (Baltimore: Dept. of Defense, Dept. of the Army, Corps of Engineers, North Atlantic Division, 1963), 1: 15 and 3: 11–17.

51. For an overview of the plans see, U.S. Army Corps of Engineers, North Atlantic Division, *Potomac River Basin Report.*

52. National Resources Committee, *Drainage Basin Committee Report for the Southeastern Basins* (Washington, DC: U.S. Government Printing Office, 1937), 15.

53. National Resources Committee, *Drainage Basin Committee Report for the Southeastern Basins*, 16.

54. U.S. Congress. Senate, *Apalachicola, Chattahoochee, and Flint Rivers, Georgia and Florida*, 76th Cong., 1st sess., 1939, Document 342, 79–80, quote on 80.

55. U.S. Congress, House of Representatives, *Apalachicola, Chattahoochee, and Flint Rivers, Georgia and Florida*, 80th Cong., 1st sess., 1948, Document 300, 3–13.

56. D. Gregory Jeane, *A History of the Mobile District Corps of Engineers, 1815–1985* (Mobile: U.S. Army Corps of Engineers, Mobile District, 2002), 151–55. See also, Lynn Willoughby, *Flowing through Time: A History of the Lower Chattahoochee River* (Tuscaloosa: University of Alabama Press, 1999), esp. ch. 9.

57. Stephen E. Draper, "Legal Issues of Water Allocation for the Apalachicola-Chattahoochee-Flint River Basin," *Proceedings of the 1991 Georgia Water Resources Conference* (Athens: Institute of Natural Resources, University of Georgia, 1991), 148–50, esp. 148.

58. C. Hansell Watt, "Who Gets the Hooch: Georgia, Florida, and Alabama Battle for Water from the Apalachicola-Chattahoochee-Flint River Basin," *Mercer Law Review* 55 (2004): 1453–87.

59. Draper, "Legal issues of water allocation."

60. Nicole T. Carter et al., *Apalachicola-Chattahoochee-Flint Drought: Federal Water Management Issues* (Washington: Congressional Research Service, 2008).

61. As of March 2008, the legal questions remained in the hands of the Supreme Court, see Carter, *Apalachicola-Chattahoochee-Flint Drought*, 23–29.

62. Stephen Draper, "Sharing Water through Interbasin Transfer and Basin of Origin Protection in Georgia," *Georgia State University Law Review* 21 (2004): 339–72.

63. Brad Carver, "Tapping the Tennessee River at Georgia's Northwest Corner: A Solution to North Georgia's Water Supply Crisis," *Water Policy Memorandum*, February 2008, http://www.hbss.net/www/pdf/publications/TappingtheTennesseeRiver Feb08.pdf, accessed June 2009.

64. Dan Chapman, "Feds May Be Key to Tapping Tennessee Water," *Atlanta Journal-Constitution*, 27 March 2008, http://www.ajc.com/metro/content/metro/stories/2008/03/26/tenn_0327.html, accessed June 2009.

65. U.S. District Court for the Middle District of Florida, *Tri-States Water Rights Litigation*, 17 July 2009.

66. Watt, "Who Gets the Hooch," 1485.

12. TO HARMONIZE HUMAN ACTIVITY WITH THE LAWS OF NATURE

1. The term "watershed" can refer to the division between two drainage basins, a usage that is particularly important in Europe. In North America, though the term watershed is used figuratively to denote a dramatic change in a manner that would seem congruent with the European usage, it is more common to use watershed as a synonym for drainage basin. It is the watershed as synonym for drainage basin that is examined in this chapter.

2. E. A. Poyser, *Your Watershed*, Manitoba Department of Agriculture and Immigration Publication no. 298, 1958.

3. Kirk N. Lambrecht, *The Administration of Dominion Lands, 1870–1930* (Winnipeg: Hignell Printing Limited, 1991), 20. John Langton Tyman, *By Section, Township, and Range: Studies in Prairie Settlement* (Brandon: Assiniboine Historical Society, 1972), 12–13. The classic study is Chester Martin, *"Dominion Lands" Policy* (Toronto: Macmillan, 1938), note especially chapter nine, "The Free Homestead for 'Dominion Lands.'"

4. Clinton L. Evans, *The War on Weeds in the Prairie West: An Environmental History* (Calgary: University of Calgary Press, 2002); Mark Fiege, "The Weedy West: Mobile Nature, Boundaries, and Common Space in the Montana Landscape," *Western Historical Quarterly* 35, no. 1 (2005): 22–47; Mark Fiege, "Private Property and the Ecological Common in the American West," in *Everyday America: Cultural Landscape Studies after J. B. Jackson*, ed. Chris Wilson and Paul Groth (Berkeley: University of California Press, 2003), 219–31, 343–46.

5. Karl S. Zimmerer, "Rescaling Irrigation in Latin America: The Cultural Images and Political Ecology of Water Resources," *Ecumene* 7, no. 2 (2000): 150–75; François Molle, "River-basin planning and management: The social life of a concept," *Geoforum* 40 (2009): 484–94; Erik Swyngedouw, "Scaled Geographies: Nature, Place, and the Politics of Scale," in *Scale and Geographic Inquiry: Nature, Society,*

and Method, ed. Eric Sheppard and Robert B. McMaster (Malden: Blackwell Publishing, 2003), 129–53; Erik Swyngedouw, "Modernity and Hybridity: Nature, *Regeneracionismo,* and the Production of the Spanish Waterscape, 1890–1930," *Annals of the Association of American Geographers* 89 (1999): 443–65; Alice Cohen and Seanna Davidson, "The Watershed Approach: Challenges, Antecedents, and the Transition from Technical Tool to Governance Unit," *Water Alternatives* 4, no. 1 (2011): 1–14.

6. M. Timothy Corkery, "Geology and Landforms of Manitoba," in *The Geography of Manitoba: Its Land and Its People,* ed. John Welsted, John Everitt, and Christoph Stadel (Winnipeg: University of Manitoba Press, 1996), 19; William John Carlyle, "Relationship Between Settlement and the Physical Environment in Part of the West Lake Area of Manitoba from 1878 to 1963" (M.A. thesis, University of Manitoba, 1965), 17.

7. Carlyle, "The Management of Environmental Problems on the Manitoba Escarpment," *Canadian Geographer* 24, no. 3 (Fall 1980): 255–69, 255.

8. M. Timothy Corkery, "Geology and Landforms of Manitoba," 19; William John Carlyle, *Relationship Between Settlement and the Physical Environment in Part of the West Lake Area of Manitoba from 1878 to 1963,* 17.

9. G. H. MacKay and C. R. Stanton, *Wilson Creek Study Erosion and Sedimentation Control* (Winnipeg, 1964), 4.

10. MacKay and Stanton, *Wilson Creek Study Erosion and Sedimentation Control,* 4–5.

11. See the pamphlet titled *Wilson Creek Experimental Watershed,* file 740/86024 Wilson Creek Watershed, Vol. Supp., 1972–1974, Department of Regional Economic Expansion, vol. 13, RG 124, Library and Archives of Canada (hereafter LAC), 3.

12. Canada, Manitoba, *Report of the Manitoba Drainage Commission* (Winnipeg: King's Printer, 1921).

13. Letter from M. A. Lyons, Engineer, to Errick F. Willis, Minister of Public Works, May 6, 1948, file: Special Drainage Survey Conducted by M. A. Lyons, GS 0123, G 1609, G 8046, Archives of Manitoba (hereafter AM).

14. MacKay and Stanton, *Wilson Creek Study Erosion and Sedimentation Control,* 4.

15. Letter from M. A. Lyons, Engineer, to Errick F. Willis, Minister of Public Works, May 6, 1948, file: Special Drainage Survey Conducted by M. A. Lyons, GS 0123, G 1609, G 8046, AM.

16. *Wilson Creek Experimental Watershed,* file 740/86024 Wilson Creek Watershed, Vol. Supp., 1972–1974, vol. 13, RG 124, LAC, 3.

17. Letter from M. A. Lyons, Engineer, to Errick F. Willis, Minister of Public Works, May 6, 1948, file: Special Drainage Survey Conducted by M. A. Lyons, GS 0123, G 1609, G 8046, AM.

18. Carlyle, "The Management of Environmental Problems on the Manitoba Escarpment," 259.

19. Wilson Creek Watershed Program, no date, file 740/86024 Wilson Creek Watershed, vol. 1, vol. 13, RG 124, LAC, 2.

20. Carlyle, "The Management of Environmental Problems on the Manitoba Escarpment," 260.

21. Robert W. Newbury, *Summary Report of the Wilson Creek Experimental Water-*

shed Study 1957–1982 (Winnipeg: Committee on Headwater Flood and Erosion Control, 1983), 1.

22. MacKay and Stanton, *Wilson Creek Study Erosion and Sedimentation Control*, 4.

23. Manitoba, Committee on Headwater Flood and Erosion Control, *Report on Activities in Wilson Creek Watershed, April 1, 1974 to March 31, 1975* (Winnipeg: Prairie Farm Rehabilitation Administration, 1975), 1.

24. Manitoba, Committee on Headwater Flood and Erosion Control, *Report on Activities in Wilson Creek Watershed, April 1, 1972 to March 31, 1973* (Winnipeg: Prairie Farm Rehabilitation Administration, 1973), 11.

25. Manitoba, Committee on Headwater Flood and Erosion Control, *Report on Activities in Wilson Creek Watershed, April 1 1973 to March 31 1974* (Winnipeg: Prairie Farm Rehabilitation Administration, 1974), 16.

26. Newbury, *Summary Report of the Wilson Creek Experimental Watershed Study*, 4.

27. Ibid., 11.

28. Canada, Prairie Farm Rehabilitation Administration, Manitoba Region, Forsyth, G. T., *Progress Report: Northwest Escarpment and Interlake Region Agreement* (Winnipeg: Prairie Farm Rehabilitation Administration, Manitoba Regional Division, 1958), 4.

29. *Wilson Creek Experimental Watershed*, file 740/86024 Wilson Creek Watershed, Vol. Supp., 1972–1974, vol. 13, RG 124, LAC.

30. Letter of Agreement, Shuttleworth and Shortinghuis, November 6, 1957, included in Newbury, *Summary Report of the Wilson Creek Experimental Watershed Study*, 1.

31. Ibid., 11.

32. Manitoba, Committee on Headwater Flood and Erosion Control, *Report on Activities in Wilson Creek Watershed, April 1, 1962 to March 31, 1963* (Winnipeg: Prairie Farm Rehabilitation Administration, 1963), 22.

33. On debates among geographers over the utility of management by watershed, see James L. Wescoat, *Integrated Water Development: Water Use and Conservation Practice in Western Colorado*, University of Chicago Department of Geography Research Paper 20, 1984, 10–12. For a more recent view of watershed management, see Cohen and Davidson, "The Watershed Approach."

34. Agriculture and Agri-Food Canada—PFRA, *Summary of Resources and Land Use Issues Related to Riparian Areas in the Whitemud River Watershed* (Winnipeg: Prairie Farm Rehabilitation Administration, 2004), 1–14.

35. Carlyle, "Relationship Between Settlement and the Physical Environment in Part of the West Lake Area of Manitoba from 1878 to 1963," 169.

36. Manitoba, *Whitemud River Watershed Resource Study* (Winnipeg: Whitemud River Watershed Board, 1974), 9.

37. William R. Newton, "Watershed Conservation Districts in Manitoba: the Aims, Functions and Objectives," *89th Congress of the Engineering Institute of Canada* (Winnipeg, 1975), 14.

38. Carlyle, "Relationship Between Settlement and the Physical Environment in Part of the West Lake Area of Manitoba from 1878 to 1963," 169–70.

39. Shannon Stunden Bower, "Watersheds: Conceptualizing Manitoba Drained Landscape, 1895–1950," *Environmental History* 12, no. 4 (2007): 796–819; Shannon Stunden Bower, *Wet Prairie: People, Land, and Water in Agricultural Manitoba* (Vancouver: UBC Press, 2011).

40. Newton, "Watershed Conservation Districts in Manitoba," 14.

41. Ibid., 8.

42. J. C. MacPherson, *A Brief History of the Whitemud Watershed Committee* (Manitoba: Department of Mines, Resources, and Environmental Management, 1971), 7.

43. MacPherson, *A Brief History of the Whitemud Watershed Committee*, 11–12.

44. Ibid., 2–3.

45. Ibid., 6.

46. Manitoba, *Eleventh Extension Course in Municipal Administration and Public Finance* (Winnipeg, 1958), 53.

47. Chistopher Adams, *Politics in Manitoba: Parties, Leaders, and Voters* (Winnipeg: University of Manitoba Press, 2008), 144.

48. "Agricultural Notes," *Neepawa Herald*, August 16, 1956, 6.

49. MacPherson, *A Brief History of the Whitemud Watershed Committee*, 7; Manitoba, Whitemud River Watershed Conservation District #1, *Watershed Management Seminar Proceedings* (Brandon, 1972), 7.

50. H. W. Wilson, Dorothy Elizabeth Cook, Frederic A. Krahn, Josephine S. Antonini, *Educational Film Guide* (New York: H. W. Wilson Co.), 1953, http://www.archive.org/stream/11theeducationalfilmo0wilsrich/11theeducationalfilmo0wilsrich_djvu.txt. For more on the Salt-Wahoo watershed, see Otto Paul Thieman, *The Salt-Wahoo Watershed District, with Particular Emphasis on the Economic and Organizational Aspects* (PhD diss., University of Nebraska, Lincoln, 1966).

51. "What Is a Watershed?," *Neepawa Herald*, April 10, 1963, "Special Water Edition," 5.

52. Manitoba, Department of Mines, Resources, and Environmental Management, *Watershed Conservation Districts in Manitoba* (Winnipeg: Department of Mines, Resources, and Environmental Management, n.d.), 5 (but pages unnumbered).

53. Economic Council of Canada, Helen Buckley, and Eva Tihanyi, *Canadian Policies for Rural Adjustment: A Study of the Economic Impact of ARDA, PFRA, and MMRA* (Ottawa: Economic Council of Canada, 1967), 94–95.

54. "Proposed ARDA Region Would Include Neepawa," *Neepawa Herald*, April 2, 1963, 1. The interlake was Manitoba's first ARDA district.

55. Manitoba, *Whitemud River Watershed Resource Study*, 9.

56. MacPherson, *A Brief History of the Whitemud Watershed Committee*, 51; and Manitoba, *Whitemud River Watershed Resource Study*, Winnipeg, 11.

57. Lawrence N. Ogrodnik, *Water Management in the Red River Valley: A History and Policy Review* (Winkler: Lower Red River Valley Water Commission, 1984), 14.

58. Manitoba, Department of Mines, Resources, and Environmental Management, *Annual Report for the Year Ending March 31, 1973* (Winnipeg: Department of Mines, Resources, and Environmental Management, 1973), 13.

59. Manitoba, *Annual Report of Watershed Conservation District(s) of Manitoba* (Winnipeg, 1972), 12.

60. Newton, "Watershed Conservation Districts in Manitoba," 1–3.

61. Article from unnamed source headlined "Whitemud Watershed District Established," file 740/86027 Comprehensive Soil and Water Conservation Program, Vol. Supp., 1970–1978, vol. 13, RG 124, LAC.

62. John Sandlos, "Not Wanted in the Boundary: The Expulsion of the Keeseekoowenin Ojibway Band from Riding Mountain National Park," *Canadian Historical Review* 89, no. 2 (2008): 189–221.

63. Erik Swyngedouw, "Modernity and Hybridity."

64. See the Manitoba Conservation Districts Association website, http://mcda .ca/index.php?option=com_content&task=view&id=46&Itemid=44.

65. International Institute for Sustainable Development, *Designing Policies in a World of Uncertainty, Change and Surprise—Adaptive Policymaking for Agriculture and Water Resources in the Face of Climate Change* (Winnipeg: International Institute for Sustainable Development, 2006), 129.

66. International Institute for Sustainable Development, *Designing Policies in a World of Uncertainty, Change and Surprise*, 132.

CONTRIBUTORS

EYVIND BAGLE is assistant director at the Norwegian Maritime Museum in Oslo (http://www.marmuseum.no/). He holds an MA in history from the University of Oslo and has spent his career working on various aspects of the industrialization of Norway.

SABINE BARLES is professeur des Universités at the Université Paris 1 Panthéon-Sorbonne and researcher at Laboratoire Géographie-Cités. She has an interdisciplinary background in history of technology, civil engineering, and urban planning. She has published books and articles on the environmental history of Paris and the Seine, dealing with garbage disposal, sewage treatment, food supply, nutrient cycles, and material flow analysis, as well as urban infrastructures.

SHANNON STUNDEN BOWER is a Social Sciences and Humanities Research Council of Canada postdoctoral fellow in the department of history and classics at the University of Alberta. She has recently published *Wet Prairie: People, Land, and Water in Agricultural Manitoba* (University of British Columbia Press, 2011). Her work has also appeared in journals, including *Environmental History* and the *Journal of Historical Geography*.

STÉPHANE CASTONGUAY is the Canada Research Chair in Environmental History at Université du Québec à Trois-Rivières. He recently coedited, with Michèle Dagenais, *Metropolitan Natures: Environmental Histories of Montreal* (University of Pittsburgh Press, 2011). He has published articles on the pollution, the rehabilitation, and the protection against flooding of urban rivers in Quebec.

JIM CLIFFORD completed his PhD in the history department at York University in early 2011. He is interested in the social and environmental consequences of rapid urbanization in nineteenth- and twentieth-century Britain. He is also a founding editor of the website ActiveHistory.ca.

CRAIG COLTEN is the Carl O. Sauer Professor of Geography at Louisiana State University. He is the author of the award-winning *An Unnatural Metropolis: Wresting New Orleans from Nature* (Louisiana State University Press, 2005) and more recently *Perilous Place Powerful Storms: Hurricane Protection in Coastal Louisiana* (University Press of Mississippi, 2009). Currently he is the editor of the *Geographical Review*.

MICHÈLE DAGENAIS is professor of history at Université de Montréal. She has recently published *Montréal et l'eau: Une histoire environnementale* (Boréal, 2011) and coedited with Stéphane Castonguay *Metropolitan Natures: Environmental Histories of Montreal* (University of Pittsburgh Press, 2011).

CHLOÉ DELIGNE is a research associate of the Fonds National de la Recherche Scientifique in Belgium, working in the department of history, arts, and archaeology at the Université Libre de Bruxelles. As a historian, geographer, and environmentalist, she has dedicated several works to urban spatial dynamics and transformations in premodern Low Countries and modern Belgium, focusing in particular on the history of Brussels.

MATTHEW EVENDEN is an associate professor of geography at the University of British Columbia and chair of Canadian Studies. His previous books include *Fish versus Power* (Cambridge University Press, 2004) and (with Christopher Armstrong and H. V. Nelles) *The River Returns* (McGill-Queen's University Press, 2009).

FRÉDÉRIC GRABER is a researcher at the French national center for scientific research (CNRS), based at the Centre de recherches historiques (Paris, France). He is a historian of science, technology, and the environment. His main research interests are in the history of water, project making, and anticipatory knowledge. He recently published *Paris a besoin d'eau. Projet, dispute et délibération technique dans la France napoléonienne* (CNRS Editions, 2009).

GERTRUD HAIDVOGL has an MA and PhD in history from the University Vienna, Austria; she is senior scientist at the Institute of Hydrobiology and Aquatic Ecosystem Management, University of Natural Resources and Life Sciences Vienna. Gertrud Haidvogl works especially on the environmental history of Austrian rivers with a focus on the history of riverine landscapes, fish, and fisheries as well as ecological conditions.

UWE LÜBKEN is an environmental historian who focuses on the history of natural hazards, catastrophes, and climate change. He recently completed his habilitation thesis on the history of flooding on the Ohio River and is currently the project director at the Rachel Carson Center, Ludwig-Maximilians-

Universität Munich, for the collaborative research project "Disaster Migration in Historical Perspective."

JEAN-CLAUDE ROBERT is professor emeritus at the history department of Université du Québec à Montréal, where he taught from 1975 to 2007. Specializing in economic and social history of Canada, he worked on nineteenth-century urbanization of Quebec and became interested in the spatial dimension of the past. He contributed to a few historical atlases and also wrote on the history of Quebec, from 1867 to the present.

CHRIS SMOUT is professor emeritus of Scottish history at the University of St Andrews, Scotland, and historiographer royal in Scotland. Formerly a social and economic historian, he became an environmental historian around 1990 and in 1999 gave the Ford Lectures at Oxford, later published as *Nature Contested: Environmental History in Scotland and Northern England since 1600* (Edinburgh University Press, 2000). He has written extensively on woodland history and is currently engaged on a book about the Firth of Forth.

INDEX